From Brodiach to Bervie

A History of Skene and Westhill

Jim Fiddes

PRESS

Published in 2012

Copyright © Jim Fiddes

The right of Jim Fiddes to be identified as author of this book has been asserted under the Copyright, Designs and Patents Act 1988

All rights reserved. No part of this publication may be reproduced, stored in a retrieval system, or transmitted, in any form or by any means, electronic, mechanical, photocopying, recording or otherwise, without the prior permission of the copyright holder.

A catalogue record for this book is available from the British Library

ISBN 978-0-9570999-1-3

Design and typesetting by
Leopard magazine www.leopardmag.co.uk

Printed and bound in Scotland by more_Glasgow

Published by Leopard Press,
Auld Logie, Pitcaple, Inverurie, Aberdeenshire AB51 5EE

To
Mary McMurtrie
1902–2003

The publication of this book has been funded through the generous
contributions of the following individuals and organisations:
Adam Craigmile, Westhill
Margaret Glascodine
Aberdeenshire Council
Skene Heritage Society
Westhill Gala Committee
Harry Fraser Catering Services Ltd

Acknowledgements

It may seem strange that the two people I have to thank most for this book are two that I never met. G. M. Fraser was City Librarian of Aberdeen from 1899 to his death in 1938. He wrote a huge amount on Aberdeen and the North East. Much of this material is in his notebooks held in Aberdeen Central Library. He visited Skene Parish on several occasions, beginning in 1918. I had used these notebooks for short articles in the first few SKENE HERITAGE NEWSLETTERS, but the first article I wrote for LEOPARD magazine, in May 2006, was called *Following in Fraser's footsteps,* where I revisited places he had mentioned in his travels to see what they looked like today. Fraser, then, was the start.

Mary McMurtrie probably knew more about Skene than anyone, and she collected information from a variety of sources and informants; in some ways this book could be called *Following in Mary's Footsteps*. I am grateful to her daughter Elspeth Haston, and her son, John McMurtrie, for giving me this material. Mary's own memories have helped bring alive the period from 1900 until the mid-20th century.

I would also like to thank the following people. Bert Rennie helped with a lot of information on Brodiach for my original Fraser article. I spent most of the very first Skene Heritage coffee morning talking to Gordon Argo as we sold tickets at the door. I have subsequently spent many hours listening to Gordon, who has a policeman's memory for detail and knew everyone in the parish. Gordon helped me open doors to other important informants such as the late Leslie Durno, Bill Troup, etcetera.

Then we have Adam Craigmile who, as with Mary McMurtrie, has a tremendous memory, even though he is approaching his first century. As well as providing many stories, Adam has encouraged the whole endeavour. Numerous others have helped with information – Tibbie Reid for all things related to the Kirktoun; Roy Lyall and his sister Edna, whose family have been associated with Lyne of Skene for around 150 years; Alistair Ogg whose family had the shop in the Kirktoun for over 80 years; Eric Thompson and Alex Mair who provided much help on Carnie and Garlogie; Kathleen Reid who, as well as providing information on Mason Lodge, also gave Skene Heritage the unique collection of lantern slides that belonged to the Rev. Cran of Westhill Congregational Church; Lucy Macleod who early on in Skene Heritage gave us information on Westhill; Harold Munro from Rogiehill; John Milne who has provided material kept by his mother, Bunty.

I would like to thank all members of Skene Heritage Society past and present, especially our first chairman, Sandy Weir, long-serving officials, George Morrison and Caroline Hunter, Ron Black, Jack Macaulay, Bill Rose, Rona Livingstone, Gillian Thompson, John Ritchie, John Troup, Bill Leslie, and Nick Renny. Several overseas members have provided information and photographs that we would never have found over here – Glenda Gentleman from Canada, a direct descendant of Peter Jamieson of Leddach; Maureen Burr from Canada, a descendant of the Proctor Family; Charles Davidson from New Zealand, whose father had a shop in the Kirktoun in the 1920s; and Mary Mitchell from San Francisco with whom I discovered the 17th century Dunlop grave in St Machar Graveyard. To all the people of Skene who have given of their photographs to the Skene Heritage Society I would say that this book would have been far less interesting without them.

Thanks also to Dorothy Brown, an old colleague from The Robert Gordon University, who has helped check the manuscript for typing and punctuation (if I chose to ignore some of her corrections the fault is mine).

As a librarian myself I appreciate the work done by the custodians of our various archive collections. The staff of the following have all been of great help to me – Aberdeen City Archives, Aberdeen Central Library, Aberdeenshire Library Service and Aberdeen University Historic Collections.

Of course I have to especially thank Lindy Cheyne and Ian Hamilton from LEOPARD magazine, not only for the production of this book, but also for publishing my early articles and giving me the confidence to carry on writing.

Finally I thank my wife, Jenny, my daughter Kerry, and son Stephen, for encouraging me in my new life after RGU.

ACKNOWLEDGEMENTS

This is not the end of the story. I feel that there is more to come from the massive SKENE PAPERS, and from the ABERDEEN JOURNAL and the ABERDEEN FREE PRESS. However, the time was right to put my research on to paper and invite comment and criticism. Who knows, this publication may well bring forward more people with stories and photographs of byegone Skene. Ten years from now I may feel that a second edition is necessary, but in the meantime look out for the SKENE HERITAGE SOCIETY NEWSLETTER, freely available in Skene and Westhill, and on our website www.skeneheritage.org

Contents

	INTRODUCTION	1
1	**The landscape and its prehistory**	3
2	**Skene: the early history**	13
3	**Skene in troubled times**	27
4	**Skene and Easter Skene** from the Restoration until the end of the 18th century	35
5	**The break up of Easter Skene** and the condition of the parish at the end of the 18th century	43
6	**The new estates** and some of their owners	57
7	**The parish church of Skene**	89
8	**The dissenting churches**	115
9	**Education** in the parish	129
10	**Poverty and medicine** in the parish	145

11	**Aspects of rural life** in the 19th century	167
12	**Established Church versus Free Church:** Parish Politics and John Bruce of The Fornet	185
13	**Roads and transport**	203
14	**Skene House** and estate	223
15	**The Kirktoun of Skene** and other communities	245
16	**Aspects of rural life** in the first half of the 20th century	299
17	**Skene in two world wars**	315
18	**Some Skene worthies** and some perhaps not so worthy!	323
19	**The new Westhill** and the era of oil	345
	Appendix	357
	Bibliography	365
	Index	371

Introduction

"Skeyne never had the colour of its sound. It lay on the threshold of Deeside, a doormat against which hungry tourists wiped their feet, their eyes straining ever forwards towards the greater glories of the Moor of Dinnet and Lochnagar. Skeyne lay skulking eternally under this slight, its grey face lined and loured with the perpetual shadow of the Cairgorm Mountains".

– **Jessie Kesson: The White Bird Passes**

The Old Skene Road (originally just the Skene Road or the King's Highway) enters Skene parish at Brodiach, the six mile inn, and leaves at Bervie, the twelve mile inn, hence the title of this book. In many ways a parish is an artificial creation, even though natural features are often used in outlining its boundaries. The legend of Skene would have us believe that the lands of Skene were gifted to a follower of an early medieval king because he saved the king from a wolf using his sgian or dagger from whence came the name Skene. This follower was given the choice of the land covered by a deer's run or a hawk's flight and chose the latter. Conveniently the hawk flew from one natural feature, the bridge over the burn at Bervie near Dunecht, to the Brodiach Burn, the boundary with the later Freedom Lands of Aberdeen.

A history of a parish such as Skene can be seen as artificial, adjoining areas having a profound effect on it, not least the major city seven miles away. Land holdings often straddled its boundaries and wealthy citizens from Aberdeen owned land within the parish. Places at the extremeties of the parish were often linked to locations in the neighbouring parishes. Garlogie joined with Cullerlie to form a Mutual Improvement Society, for example. Even today its Women's Rural is a joint one with Cullerlie, and Garlogie School was deliberately sited away from the main settlement in Garlogie because that was felt necessary to draw it more into the parish. The Lyne of Skene area in the 19th century and into the 20th century was often listed as Lyne of Skene, Dunecht or Waterton, and people there might go to Echt or Dunecht for church or educational activities. The children at Lyne were often missing from school when it was the Echt Feein' Market. At the east of the parish, Auchinclech and Kinmundy were sometimes listed with Kingswells, Counteswells, Newhills or Kinellar, and children at Westhill School were off during the Aberdeen Feein' Market.

Skene was created a separate parish in the 17th century from an earlier chapelry that came under the larger parish of Kinkell, and we can accept that at one time most of this land had belonged to the Skene family, excepting, perhaps, some land on the northern and southern boundaries of the parish. This gave a certain unity to the area, further strengthened when it did become a full parish in its own right. Most of the inhabitants of the parish would have looked to the centrally located parish church, certainly before the establishment of dissenting churches. When local affairs – educational, medical, social, etc. – became more regulated with the establishment of parochial and school boards, they were organised on a parish basis. The parish meant something and therefore I think that a parish history is valid, all the while acknowledging the influence of events outside the parish.

Name usage

In the spelling of place names I have used the earlier versions on occasion to show how the names developed over the years, the earlier versions sometimes giving a clue as to their pronounciation and origin. This applies to the name and place Skene (Skein, Skeyn, Skeen) as much as anything. I have preferred the spelling Kirktoun of Skene rather than Kirkton or the more genteel Kirktown. I have also used Easterskene for the name of the estate created by Thomas McCombie and his son William in the early 19th century, to differentiate it from the lands of Easter Skene mortgaged to the Earl Marischal before Harlaw and subsequently coming into the possession of the town of Aberdeen through its Merchant Guild. Using the form Westhills is something done by many older inhabitants of the area; equally it annoys other people. In truth both versions have been used in the 19th and 20th centuries, even for official purposes such as by the Parish Council. Hence both might be found here.

The landscape and its prehistory

Topography

Lacking any real hills, it is the Loch of Skene that defines the physical character of the parish. A small part of it is in parish of Echt, but the greatest part is in Skene. Even within living memory the nature of the loch has changed due to the hand of man. The loch area has fluctuated over the years, notably when the water level was raised by around two feet to help power the Dunecht Hydro Electric Scheme in the 1920s. As I will mention later, the raising of the water level removed a sandy beach on which children played. Also during the 1920s an attempt was made to introduce trout and create a fish breeding centre. Fishermen from Fife tried to clear the loch of pike, removing them by the cartload. In the end, though, they were unsuccessful and the pike persist. Eels at one time were exported to London from the loch.

Mary McMurtrie remembered that in her childhood there was a grassy path that led past the sandy beach and you could walk to the Leuchar Burn. The same was true on the other side. Mary also remembered being taken on a farmer's cart along the edge of the loch, with the water coming half way up the wheels as the horse splashed on ahead. To Mary it was an exciting adventure; to the farmer it was "*a gey roch hurl*". Dense forestry planting removed all this. Artificial islands were created for duck shooting, the largest island also having the so-called 'temple' on it. The islands did not interfere with sea planes landing on the loch, a common sight before World War II. Lord Semple of Craigievar, as well as the Cowdrays, landed planes on the loch. Today the loch attracts large amounts of bird life, including being an

Loch of Skene from Taposheetie

important roost for Icelandic Greylag Geese and Icelandic Whooper Swan. It is also used by the Aberdeen and Stonehaven Yacht Club.

Most of the higher ground in the parish is in a line to the north, with the Hill of Kinmundy, Souterhill, Berryhill, Hill of Keir, Hill of Auchronie and

THE LANDSCAPE AND ITS PREHISTORY

on to the Fornet. Hill of Keir at 728 feet (222 metres) is the highest point in the parish. Hill of Auchronie is just slightly lower and is divided between Skene and Kinnellar parishes.

Because of the location of the high ground, most of the water drainage in the parish is to the south and the River Dee. The Brodiach Burn on the eastern boundary of the parish becomes the Ord Burn after the Mill of Ord. It eventually flows into the Dee by way of the Culter Burn. The Brodiach forms the boundary with the Freedom Lands of Aberdeen and the parish of Newhills. As the Ord it continues to be the boundary with neighbouring parishes. The Soddie Burn drains from Hill of Westhill, and runs through the industrial estate where you can walk alongside it. It later joins the Brodiach south of Damhead. Further west the Kirktoun Burn runs down from Rogiehill and through Easterskene. It joins the burn draining the Hill of Keir which goes through Kilnhillock, Burnland and down below Whitestone Farm and then west past Burnhaugh and together they go into the Loch of Skene.

Lyne of Skene stands on the watershed of the Dee and the Don. North of Broomhill drains to the Don, while south goes to the Dee by way of the Loch of Skene. The Corskie Burn enters the parish from the west where it was also known as the Kinnernie Burn. The Bogentory Burn drains the Letters, Lauchentilly, Corskie Brae and the Moss. It connects with the Corskie Burn at Bervie and flows to the loch.

Of course many of these burns, as we see them today, are the result of the drainage improvements carried on in the 18th and 19th Centuries. The Loch of Skene itself drains south via the Leuchar Burn, which then runs into the Culter Burn and thereby to the Dee. So the vast majority of Skene water ends up in the River Dee. Beyond the hills mentioned, a small part of the parish drains north into the River Don.

Prehistory

The first Statistical Account, written in 1790 by the parish minister James Hogg, describes various remains which give evidence of settlement from the Neolithic era, through the Bronze age to the Iron Age: – *"Besides two druidical temples* (stone circles), *pretty entire, and a number of barrows or tumuli, there are, on a moor covered with barrows, about an English mile south of the church, evident traces of an encampment near which is a very large collection of stones or a cairn. About ¾ of a mile North East of the church, on top of a hill, are the remains of a wall, which appears to have been formerly resorted to as a place of strength."*

5

The two stone circles mentioned here can probably be identified as those at South Fornet and at Gask or Springhill. Dating from the late Neolithic or early Bronze Age, they can no longer be described as 'pretty entire'. Both circles conform to the majority type of stone circles in the North East by being in an elevated position. The one at Gask gave its name to a nearby farm called Standing Stones, of which no trace now remains. It is marked as "*The Temple Lands – an old place of worship*" on a plan of 1832. A description of the circle in 1914 records that there were only two stones remaining; respectively 6.5 feet (2 m.) and 6.2 feet (1.9 m.) high, one of the stones having several cup marks on its southern side. More recently a third stone has appeared and the others are not the same height as originally recorded. It is known that one of the stones was moved by a farmer a few years ago and he may have erected the third stone. Whether or not the latter was originally part of the circle it is difficult to say, but it seems unlikely that all three are in their original positions.

A plan of the Skene House estate from 1863 records only two stones at Fornet (though this may refer just to the upright ones). In 1902 the stone circle is described as having a pair of flanking stones with space for a recumbent between them, a layout unique to the North East. In addition there were five fallen stones from the circle still visible. Today the flankers remain, but there are only two of the latter stones. Presumably the recumbent and some of the others were broken up over the years and re-used in building work. In fact, there is evidence of attempts to break up the flankers and broken pieces lying nearby.

The remains of a further stone circle are shown on the first and second Ordnance Survey (OS) maps south-east of Auchinclech, and north-east of Newton of Auchinclech. The 1864 OS name book says that only one stone remains and that the then owner had removed some of the stones. It was still there in 1961, but the Royal Commission say that it was not there in 2005. Others are of a different opinion and possible photographs of it appear on a website. To the south east of Newton of Auchinclech there is a single standing stone not marked on early OS maps, so this may be a cattle rubbing stone erected later, perhaps even a stone removed from the circle. Elsewhere in the parish there are more individual stones, some of which may be remains of circles or they may be individual standing stones. Others, especially those not shown on the first or second OS maps, have been re-classified as cattle rubbing stones put up in the early 20th century, such as the one at Newton near Lyne of Skene.

THE LANDSCAPE AND ITS PREHISTORY

Stone circle at Fornet

The minister's moor, covered with barrows a mile to the south of the church, refers to the large concentration of hut circles and cairns in what is now Garlogie Wood. This really is a significant site, though it is difficult for the untrained eye to make out the remains because of later farming, tree planting and vegetation growth. It was evidently easier to view the remains in Mr Hogg's day. The area has been surveyed, but not fully excavated; therefore it is difficult to be exact about the structures. A survey of Garlogie Wood in 1994 recorded 36 sites including hut circles, enclosures and possible cairns. This does seem to represent settlement over a long period. Mr Hogg's other barrows and tumuli may refer to several barrows or cairns found in the Woods of Carnie to the south of the main Echt road (not to be confused with the Carnie Woods recreation area near

In 1902 the stone circle is described as having a pair of flanking stones with space for a recumbent between them. In addition there were five fallen stones from the circle still visible.

Mason Lodge). Other possible cairns are sited at Hillhead of Carnie and on Souterhill, and there are two dozen in the woods at Wester Ord.

Mr Hogg's place of strength to the north-east of the church refers, of course, to the supposed hill fort on the Hill of Keir. This would appear to be a smallish Iron Age fort that gave the name to the hill – Keir being from the same Celtic word as *Caer* in Wales and *Cahir* in Ireland, meaning round stone circle or stone fort. There are entrances in the walls of the enclosure, but the site is small. It has been suggested that it is a signal station, situated between the larger hill forts at the Barmekin of Echt to the south, and the Mither Tap of Bennachie to the north. The fort has not been excavated, although a pygmy urn was found there, much earlier than the fort. Inside was an ammonite, and a flint arrowhead was also found nearby. These objects are in the University of Aberdeen Museum.

Burial sites and other finds have also turned up in the parish, often as a result of agricultural improvement or ploughing. The subsequent location of some of these early finds is not always clear. As early as 1821, during drainage improvements, an earthen urn containing what was thought to be human bones was dug up at Whitestone Farm near Mason Lodge. According to the report, this was the third such find on Whitestone, with one of the urns being almost complete.

A further find in Skene parish is recorded in a newspaper of November 1821. It describes the find as a small vessel of ancient pottery enclosed in a stone coffin 2ft x 1ft 6ins which was 10 or 12 inches under the surface and surrounded by a cairn. It does not say where exactly the find was made, but does comment that numerous similar cairns had been found on the property during recent improvements.

In 1832 a burial was found between Gask Hill and West Gask. It contained what were called vases (urns), charcoal and calcined bones (burned to ashes or powder). At Leucharbraes, in 1914, a Late Bronze Age cremation burial was found. A beaker in Aberdeen Art Gallery and Museum is supposed to have been found at Kinmundy, though there are no details as to exactly where. Two cists were found in 1853 during land drainage at a wooded knoll just north of Westhill House. In 1905 a significant short cist was unearthed during ploughing, again at Whitestone Farm. The finds from this burial, including a male skeleton, two beakers, flint scrapers and charcoal, are still in the University of Aberdeen Museum.

The ABERDEEN JOURNAL carried the following account of the discovery:

Exciting episodes at Skene: the finding of the coffin and urns

The quiet Parish of Skene was thrown into an abnormal state of excitement last Friday morning by the announcement that grave and human remains had been discovered within a stones throw of the village of Mason Lodge. It almost seemed as if the wireless telegraphy had been in active operation for by 10 o'clock, about an hour after the discovery, the locality was all alive with people. Mr Johnstone, butcher, Lochview Villa, kindly took charge of the two urns found and his house was thronged the whole Friday and Saturday with visitors who wished to see the interesting relics. Various conjectures were made as to what the urns had been used for. Some had it that they had heard or read that one

Burial cist at Whitestone Farm photographed in 1905

Beakers from Whitestone cist photographed in 1905

was for the heart and the other for the liver. Others declared that one urn was for corn and the other for wine. How long is it since the grave was erected? This was another question keenly discussed. Some said it was 50 years and some put its age at 250 years. But alas these conjectures got a severe blow on Saturday afternoon when up came a motor car which halted at the local post office. Three gentlemen stepped out and asked for the old grave. The crowd were all agog with excitement, newspaper folk, was the rumour, but it turned out later that the new arrivals were professors from Marischal College, Aberdeen. And now bakers, tailors, postmen, ploughmen and carters left their work and followed the professors to the interesting spot. After minutely inspecting the urns the visitors closely examined the grave. One of the bystanders asked the men of learning how old he thought the grave was. In all probability 2,000 or 3,000 years old was the reply. Some took the statement with a good deal more than the proverbial gram of salt. They shook their heads and winked slyly to each other as much as to say – the toon billies are awful leears.

The professors were greatly helped in their work of exploration by Mr Geo. Mitchell, MA, headmaster of Skene Central School, Mr Geo. Rae, postmaster, Mr Robert Allan, Whitestone, tenant of the field, Mr Wm. Bannerman, Governor of Proctor's Orphanage and Mr A.F. Murdoch, Mason Lodge.

The skull found was in a good state of preservation and so were the leg and arm bones. The deceased had not been a very big man. Four or five different photographs were taken of the grave and urns by one of the professional party. One of the urns was a very uncommon specimen, the professor declared. By this time the field was almost surrounded by sightseers, boys on the tops of trees, women with babies perched on the tops of dykes, ploughmen and horsemen from the adjoining fields, all wondering what the men from the city were after. No arrowheads were found, just one pergler (flint). The remains were all carefully wrapped in cotton wool and packed into a box and were taken away in the motor car, one of the natives declaring they had now seen a motor funeral. Picture it for yourself, Mr Editor, what the deceased would have thought if he had suddenly returned to life again and found himself going dashing down Union Street in a horseless carriage. Mr Allan, Whitestone, has now the urns but if the factor of the estate has no objection Marischal College will get them, as they have secured the skull and bones.

Several stone axes have also been found in the parish. These include one donated to Inverurie Museum by the late Mr Alexander of Brodiach in 1960. His son-in-law, Bert Rennie, has a further stone axe found by Mr Alexander, though he is not sure where the axe was found as his father-in-law was known to have gone digging for archaeological finds on nearby Brimmond Hill.

A polished felstone axe from Skene was purchased for the Museum of the Society of Antiquaries of Scotland in 1892. It is now in the Royal Scottish Museum. Another stone axe was found at Millbuie in 1887 and was exhibited at the Scottish Exhibition of Natural History, Art and Industry in Glasgow in 1911. It is now in the Hunterian Museum at Glasgow University. A further axe found in Skene was exhibited at the same exhibition, but its whereabouts are not known; perhaps it was the one found in the 1890s at Southbank.

George Sim, naturalist and antiquary visited Skene House in 1890 and recorded that "*Mr Hamilton showed me a stone axe 12 inches long, which was found in the wall of an old house while being taken down, also another 9 inches long, found on the south-east side of the loch, also on his property. They appear to be both of greenstone. The larger one is fairly well polished, the smaller one although very good, has a weathered appearance. Mr Hamilton had also a box filled with flint knives, which were found in the Letter Moss, some 10 or 12 feet from the surface, and another box of flint chippings found in the Gask Moss.*" The whereabouts of these finds is not known.

At Elrick a carved stone ball was found, of granite with six cut projecting knobs. Because of the patterns used on these balls they are thought to be Neolithic, but their use and style of decoration may have continued into the Bronze Age. Their purpose is unclear; it may have been ceremonial, a sign of leadership or authority.

All of these objects and remains help us paint a picture of the development of civilization through the Neolithic and Bronze ages. Here were settled people gradually developing agriculture and building communities, communities that were able and willing to invest the huge time and effort involved in building stone circles. They were also willing to bury family members, perhaps leaders, in graves containing objects that would have been very precious and valuable to their communities. Although later agriculture has damaged many of the remains, we should nevertheless be thankful that in our north-east corner the rural nature of much of the area has meant that a lot of evidence of earlier societies has survived.

Skene:
the early history

There is very little evidence of people and events in the Skene area during the 5,000 years of the Christian era. A find of a spear, javelin and sword, found in the moss on the Kirkville estate, was attributed at the time to the Romans. Modern archaeologists are of the opinion that they were more likely Bronze Age. The weapons have long since disappeared, so we cannot be sure. Similarly, the so-called Roman road, marked on old maps of the area, is dismissed today. The Romans, though, would probably have crossed through the parish on their route from Normandykes camp near Culter, to their next camp at Kintore. Did the native people watch them from their small fort on the Hill of Keir, or had they already fled to Bennachie, perhaps to do battle with them at the Battle of Mons Graupus? We will never know.

There are no known Pictish stones in the parish, nor any Pit-names, and we do not know if the Hill of Keir fort was still used in the Christian era. Skene only starts to appear in the historical record in the mid 13th century.

Skene: the myth and the Gaelic pun

Most informed writers would agree with William M. Alexander when he said that "*the popular derivation (of Skene) is, of course, a mere invention*". The origin of the place name and family of Skene are obscure and may never be known for certain. William Forbes Skene, Historiographer for Scotland, in the *Memorials of the Family of Skene of Skene*, published in 1887, records that Alexander Skene, in 1678, recounted the legendary origin of the family. This tale tells how they

The Skene sgian!

were descended from a Struan Robertson of Atholl, who in turn was descended from McDonalds, and that they were given Easter and Wester Skene as reward for saving the king from "*a devouring wolfe*" in the forest, near the Freedom Lands of Aberdeen. The family coat of arms therefore had three wolves' heads impaled upon three skeens or sgeins, hence the name. The very dagger is said to have been in the Skene charter chest as recently as the 19th century.

Alexander Skene also records that there was a charter in Skene House recording a restoration from forfeiture granted by King William the Lion (1143–1214). Before the end of the 17th century the story had been embellished, with the king now named as Malcolm III, known as Canmore (1031–1093), returning south after defeating the Danes at Mortlich.

The Skene ancestor is said to have been a second son of Donald of the Isles who thrust his arm, wrapped in his plaid, into the wolf's mouth, and dispatched it with his sgein. A further document adds to the story and pushes the king still further back in time to Malcolm II and gives the date 1014. The author of this version of the story names John de Skene joining Donald Bane's rebellion against the sons of Canmore, forfeiting his land and then subsequently having them restored by Alexander I (c.1078–1124) for services to that king. In 1796 George Skene's epic poem *Donald Bane* mistakenly changed the wolf into a boar, two statues of which are still at Skene House. These two boars were not added to Skene House until 1849, by which time the Skene of Skene line was extinct and Skene House had passed to the Duff Family.

W.F. Skene in the *Memorials* makes no mention

of that part of the legend whereby the Skene ancestor is given the choice of the land covered by a hawk's flight or a deer's run and this may be a much later addition to the story. In this addition the Skene ancestor chooses the hawk which flies from the bridge at Bervie, and conveniently alights at the bridge over the Brodiach Burn, the natural boundary of the Freedom Lands of Aberdeen. Of course neither the Freedom Lands nor the bridge would have existed at the time of the legendary land grant, the Freedom Lands being granted to Aberdeen by Robert the Bruce. The story of the grant of land for saving a king and being given land covered by an animal's flight is not unique to the Skene family, appearing in other Scottish clans. Nor is the killing of a dangerous animal unique – the originator of the Forbes Family allegedly killed a bear on the Braes of Forbes and the muzzled bear appears on their coats of arms.

Despite his love of all things Celtic and Highland, it is clear that W.F. Skene is dismissive of the legendary origins of his own family. Conveniently the charters of restoration from forfeiture were already missing when Alexander Skene gave his account of the legend in 1678, though he says he is sure that they were there recently. In any case the fabrication of ancestry was common among families and dynasties in medieval times. They were also not above creating false charters, and even objects, in the same way as religious establishments created false relics for financial gain.

There was great prestige and status to be obtained by having a lengthy genealogy. Early kings of Scotland even traced their ancestry back to Troy. One of the manuscripts used as a source by W.F. Skene records the Laird of Skene, at the end of the 17th century, being introduced to the Countess of Dundonald, by Sir John Cowpar of Gogar. Cowpar told the countess that Skene could show 31 generations of his family from documents in his charter chest.

Skene was the countess's clan chief and she summoned her husband who was so impressed by the Skene ancestry that he ushered Skene into an adjoining room to be introduced to a gathering of nobles. Skene had arrived, but had his charters been real then his ancestry would have been carried back to the 11th century. Pure invention I am sure.

This process of altering the original meaning or sound of a word to become something more familiar used to be known as folk etymology. Today, Professor Bill Nicolaisen of the University of Aberdeen would prefer "*secondary re-interpretation*". (SEE THE APPENDIX FOR SOME SUGGESTED MEANINGS OF SKENE).

Skene: the history

The various arguments for the real origin of the family name and the land they possessed are laid out in the *Memorials*. In response to that, and immediately after it was published, Andrew Philip Skene, then chief of the Skene family, wrote several lengthy articles countering W.F. Skene's opinions and arguing for alternative interpretations of the evidence. Both men, it should be said, had their own agendas. W.F. Skene sometimes seems to play down anything which is detrimental to his family and, eminent historian though he was, his work does show signs of being too hurried, accepting family stories rather than checking historical sources. A.P. Skene seems intent on showing how near the Skene family was to the throne at certain times in its history.

The first authentic mention of Skene comes from the *Registrum Episcopatus Aberdonensus* which records that, between the years 1247 and 1257, Alan Durward granted to Peter, Bishop of Aberdeen, an annual rent of 22 shillings sterling from *"terra sua de Schene"* – *"his lands of Skene,"* in exchange for the second tithes of Onele. Durward was hostarius or justiciar of Scotland and an important and powerful figure at the time. His father had a claim to the ancient Earldom of Mar and, around 1228, in return for giving up this claim, was given the lands in the east of the earldom which became the Barony of Onele. Centred on the Peel of Lumphanan, this barony seems to have included Skene. If there was a Skene family at this time, then they presumably held their land from Alan. Alan Durward died in 1275 leaving three daughters and neither they nor their husbands inherited his lands. It is impossible to establish if the Skene family was related to the Durwards, and the lands of Skene may have reverted to the Crown from which the Skene family subsequently held them.

The next mention of Skene was from 1296 when *"Johan de Skene del counte de Edneburh,"* and *"Johan De Skene, Patrick de Skene del counte de Aberdene,"* did homage to Edward I and attached their seals to the so-called 'Ragman Roll'. The two Johns had the same seal, the head of John the Baptist on a charger or bowl with a hand above possibly giving the sacerdotal benediction. Most commentators say that this means they are the same person, holding land in Edinburgh and Aberdeenshre, though Andrew Skene suggests they could have been father and son. Patrick de Skene is described on his seal as Cl'ici or clericus, with the seal having a shield on which are three daggers facing down. (No wolves' heads though!)

W.F. Skene suggests that it is probable that John de Skene did homage for the lands of Skene with the tower, and that Patrick de Skene held the lands of Easter Skene with the Kirktoun, and that he was the vicar of Skene. He goes on to say that the name is plainly territorial and that as these church lands always formed part of the subsequent barony, we may infer that, like other families, the Skenes were hereditary possessors of the vicarage of Skene and took their name from it. It does not seem to have occurred to him, as it did to Andrew Skene, that it is odd that the clericus has weapons and a shield on his seal, while the layman has a saint on his. Andrew also suggests that Patrick may have been a clerk not a cleric and therefore not vicar of Skene, though, of course, in the 13th century a clerk would still have belonged to the clergy as they were the only educated class. Andrew goes on to suggest, less plausibly, that the daggers on his seal may have been shamrocks, the symbol of St Patrick. The seals are only 0.8 inches (2 cms) across, so it is ultimately very difficult to say.

I think W.F. Skene is projecting a later division of the lands back to the 13th century. I am not convinced that there was an Easter and Wester Skene at that time. The division is not mentioned in the subsequent charter from Robert the Bruce and I think it came later. Moreover, Easter Skene seems to have been the larger part, certainly at the time it was mortgaged to the Earl Marischal in 1410. *(see Skene and the Keiths)*. My own view in part agrees with W.F. Skene; that the family name was territorial, derived from the place name. The place name may come from the loch which may have a water derivation, possibly from a word such as easc or esc (water), and the loch is the most significant feature in the area. It may come from some other physical feature from which the loch got its name, and we really need linguistic experts to study other occurrences of the name Skene elsewhere in Britain and Ireland, including suggested variations such as Scone. Many other names in the parish have a Celtic origin — Affloch, Auchinclech, Craigiedarg, Brodiach, Kinmundy, etc.. We can assume that Skene is the same, whether Gaelic or Pictish. Johan de Skene was just that, John of Skene, who held land in Aberdeen and Edinburgh.

Was the Skene family a native one? If there ever was any evidence of the antiquity of the family it has long since disappeared. A Gilian de Skene is mentioned in 1358 and this is a Gaelic name, its derivation from servant of St John perhaps suggests a descent from John de Skene who had John the Baptist on his seal in 1296. There is no indication that the Skenes were Anglo-Norman *inabootcomers*. The Earldom of Mar itself was of Gaelic origin and, as

Arms of Alexander Skene and Giles Adie, dated 1692, from Skene House

Richard Oram, says, "*the absence of families of recognizably Anglo-Norman descent within Mar remained a characteristic of the earldom down to the late 14th century.*"

Whatever its derivation, the name was local,

though that does not necessarily mean that the family was. Later Skenes were happy to accept a highland origin myth with a crest derived from the Robertsons.

An armorial panel from Skene House, dated 1692, contains two highlanders with one of the earliest representations of the short kilt. This does not make the Skenes a highland clan, but it does show they were willing to accept a highland ancestry at a time when that did not have the romantic nature it would later acquire. So the family may well have been as old as the hills!

Skene and Bruce

A further mention of Skene comes in the early 14th century, when Partick of Skene was one of those witnessing a charter from Robert Bruce of land at Longforgan in the Carse of Gowrie. Presumably this is the same Patrick who had done homage to Edward. The charter was in favour of Alexander Keith whose family would later become so involved with the Skenes and the lands of Skene. According to Geoffrey Barrow, this charter dates from between 1304 and 1306 and indicates that Skene was part of Bruce's retinue at this early date. In 1317, shortly after the Battle of Bannockburn, we have the loyal Skene being given a charter by Bruce confirming his holding of the lands of Skene. Fortunately copies of this charter do survive, although it does not define the boundary of the lands.

Carnie

From then on the story of most of the western part of the parish is tied up with the family of Skene of Skene until the demise of the family in 1827. For the eastern part of the parish the story is a more troubled one. However, even as early as 1323 it is clear that the entire parish did not belong to the house of Skene. In that year a charter was granted to Alexander Burnard (Burnett) granting him land in compensation for giving up the title to the Forest of Drum to William of Irwyn (Irvine). The lands granted to Burnard included "*the six merk lands of Easter and Wester Cardney*". This division of Carnie into two parts survives to this day. The description of the lands at Carnie are as follows: "*from the Thornbush east of Wester Cardeny down to the Stainlethe, and thence to the high road of Cardeny, and down the burn to the water of Locher, and up to Badyennach, and thence to the bog of Gask, and thence to the burn of Frifady, and thence to the road through the midst of Skene of Wester Cardeny, and back up by a cart road to the said Thornbush.*"

Some of these places can still be traced today – Carnie, of course, but also the Leuchar Burn and Gask. Wester Carnie, at least, seems to have become part of the Barony of Leys and to have been annexed to the Sheriffdom of Kincardine. It is referred to as such in a charter of 1628. Two years later this annexation was dissolved and it is became part of the Sheriffdom of Aberdeen. Carnie as a placename has a surviving reference to it as early as that for Skene in that, for, in October 1247, King Alexander I granted to Robert, son of Alan Walchope, various lands including Culter and Ardboik to the Burn of Cardany, and along to the wolves' den (!) towards the lands of the Bishop of Aberdeen.

Skene, the Keiths and Harlaw

In 1411 Adam of Skene joined the army of Alexander Stewart, Earl of Mar, opposing the claim of Donald, Lord of the Isles, to the Earldom of Ross. Adam was married to Janet Keith, daughter of the hereditary Marischal of Scotland, William Keith. The latter family, originally from Keith in East Lothian, had been staunch supporters of Bruce, and Robert de Keith received lands in the North-East following his role in the defeat of the Comyns in the North-East. Robert was made Great Marischal of Scotland and was also given the royal hunting lodge at Hallforest, later building the stone castle there. The Keiths moved up to the North-East and, later in the 14th century, added lands in Kincardine through marriage. They built Dunnottar Castle and it became their principal seat. Around 1458 William Keith was given the title Earl Marischal. A powerful family indeed, and one that was to have a profound influence on the lands and family of Skene.

Adam borrowed 300 merks from his father-in-law to finance his retinue going off to do battle at Harlaw. In exchange, the Earl Marischal was a given a wadset or mortgage on the lands of Easter Skene, presumably redeemable on repayment of the money. Incidentally, this may help date the death of William Keith, sometimes given as around 1408. He would have been alive to make the loan to his son-in-law, which surely would not have been much before Christmas 1410, when the Earl of Mar met with his supporters in the North-East to plan the campaign.

Adam died at Harlaw leaving a young son, James. It was to be 35 years later, in 1446, before James could try to recover the mortgaged lands; possibly it took him that long to raise the money to redeem the loan. The Skenes seem to have lost the original documents, however, and a series of courts was held to look into the case, with the first one at St Machar Cathedral in September 1446. Skene had to rely on the memory of witnesses who had either seen the relevant documents at some point, or had been present at the agreement some 35 years earlier. One such was William Norvelle who was present in the Marischal's house in Aberdeen before the battle. William de Keith was establishing two chaplaincies at the cathedral at an annual cost of 20 merks from the lands of Easter Skene, but his wife, Lady Margaret, declared that he had no right to these lands. Keith went into a rage and declared that "*he would not found a single chaplainrie for their souls*" but was persuaded to do so out of the lands of Easter Skene or from his lands of Kintore if Easter Skene should fail. Another witness testified that he had seen the document with the seals of Adam Skene and the Bishop of Aberdeen.

Despite this evidence this first hearing seems to have led to nothing and another was held in the parish church of Kincardine, 10 years later, in November 1456. On this occasion "*a discreet man*" (i.e. honest), John Yoill, testified that eight days before his death, Sir John Yoill, vicar of Peterculter, who at an earlier hearing said that he had read the relevant document, was interrogated by the then Lord Marischal's late mother, Lady Keith. Yoill stated on oath that the lands of Easter Skene were held by the Earl Marischal "*in formalyn*". Here the lands of Easter Skene are defined for the first time as including "*the Ledache of Skeyn, the Kyrktoune of Skeyn, Moylboy and Garlogy, with the myln of that ilke, with the pertinents lyand in the Barony of Skeyne wythin the Shiradom of Aberdene.*"

Despite a further hearing in 1457 at which the jury found for Skene, the Keiths took the case to Parliament. James Skene seems to have died in 1461, but the case was apparently resolved in favour of his son, Alexander, according to the Memorials.

Note: Easter Skene here, and up to the end of the 18th century, should not be confused with the later, and much smaller, estate of Easterskene.

Relations with the Keith family seemed resolved for the time being with Alexander's half-brother, Alan Kinnaird, even marrying one of the protagonists, Janet Keith. The normal picture painted is that the matter was in abeyance until a staggering 160 years later when the Earl Marischal brought it up again in 1629. Contrary to William Forbes Skene's view, however, it is clear that the Earl Marischal continued to possess the lands of

Easter Skene as well as other holdings in Skene parish, the evidence being as follows:
- In 1506 the Register of the Great Seal records Robert Keith and Elizabeth Douglas having possession of the lands of Leddacht and Mulboy in the parish of Skene
- In 1525, in the Register of the Great Seal, William Keith confirms his son Robert as heir to his lands including Kirktoun of Skene, Easter Cardney, Garlogie, Fornet, Leddach, Milbuy, etc..
- In 1531 the Register of the Great Seal records William, Earl Marischal, in possession of the lands *of Kirktoun of Skene, the villis de Garlogy et Ord in baronia sua de Skene*
- By a charter at the Castle of Kintore, on 12th December 1539, the Earl Marischal granted Alexander Galloway, rector of Kinkell, a croft next to the church of Skene on which to erect a manse for the vicar of the church.
- A few years later, in 1549, he is recorded as being taxed for his baronies of "*Kyntour and Skein*".
- Similarly in the *Taxt Roll of the County of Aberdeen* from 1554, the Earl Marischal is taxed £21.10/- for his lands in Skene and Kintore compared with the Laird of Skene's £10 for his lands in Skene
- Aberdeen City Archives has a charter dated 1554, as part of its holdings of the lands of Easter Skene, by which William, Earl Marischal, grants to William Keith, his eldest son and heir, and Elizabeth Hay, his spouse, daughter of George, Earl of Errol, the lands of "*Auchquhyrtin, Strathry, Milboy, Kirktoun of Skene with the smith's croft and brewhouse thereof, the lands of Leyddacht with the crofts of the Shepherd, Edward, and Mylfuird, the lands of Cardne, Ord, Hill of Kynmondy, and the lands of Wardries, lying in the baronies of Skeyne and Kyntour in fulfillment of a contract entered into between the saids earls by which the said Earl Marischal was bound to infest his said son and his spouse in lands of the yearly value of £200 Scots.*"
- There is a back letter or bond dated May 1591 by William Fraser and Katherine Bennet, his spouse, acknowledging that the lands of Ord and Fiddy lying in the Barony of Skene, had been disponed (made over) to them by George, Earl Marischal, only in security of the sum of £1,000 Scots.
- The records of the Aberdeen Presbytery record that in July 1600 Mathew Stenchin, kirk officer of Skene, made repentance for procuring from the Earl Marischal an "*assedatioun*" or lease on "*Johnn Quhyt's*" (John White's)

croft, despite the fact that White had three years of his tack (tenancy) to run. Stenchin also lied and slandered Alexander Youngson, minister of Skene, telling the earl that Mr Youngson had sold his rights to the croft. He was ordered to pay five pounds penalty to the collector of Skene, and sit three Sundays on the stool of repentance. If he ever pursued the croft again he would be "*excommunicant ipso facto*".
- There are various charters, precepts of sasine, and registered tacks from 1619 to 1624, relating to the lands of Fiddy and Ord, which show that the Earl Marischal, William Keith, was the superior of these lands.

Conclusion

The Earl Marischal possessed the Earldom of Kintore which he gave to his son. Kinkell was the mother church of the earldom, with Skene as one of its chapels. It seems likely that the lands of Skene were at some time also part of the earldom after the demise of the Durwards. We would therefore expect the earl to have a major influence over the church of Skene, possibly appointing the minister.

These examples also show that he went further than this and seems to have exercised, or to have claimed, rights over land in Easter Skene and to act in judgement over disputes in those lands despite Skene of Skene having his own barony court. Was this because he was acting as an overbearing neighbour and simply using his might to claim the barony of Easter Skene, or was he acting this way because Skene had not paid the 300 merks (a merk is two-thirds of a pound) to redeem the land? It seems certain that the Earl Marischal, contrary to the traditional view, continued to be the actual possessor of the lands of Easter Skene and was so when the matter came up before the Lords of Council and Session much later in 1629.

The Drumstone

The Drumstone is a large granite boulder within a circular stone enclosure standing on Auchronie Hill in the parish of Skene. It is situated just beside the road which is signposted off the Skene to Lyne of Skene road. Legend has it that Alexander Irvine, Laird of Drum, stopped there on his way to do battle at 'Reid Harlaw' in 1411. From this elevated position he could see back to his home at Drum Castle and on to the battlefield beyond Inverurie. At the stone he had a premonition of what lay ahead, or maybe he was just being prudent, because he sat down and made his will and put his affairs in order.

At Harlaw Red Hector, Chief of the Macleans, recognised the Laird of Drum's rank by his armorial bearings on his shield, and engaged him in single combat. An epic fight ended with both men dead. The older version of the ballad records:

Gude Sir Alexander Irvine
The much renounit Laird of Drum
None in his dais wer better sene
Quhen thai wer semblit all and som
To paris him we sud not be dumm
For valour, wit, and worthiness
To end his dais he ther did cum
Quhois ransom is remedyles

In 1835 William McCombie, laird of Easterskene, had an inscription carved on the stone – simply Harlaw and the date, 1411. By the terms of McCombie's will, his successor had a wall built round the stone in 1892. The neighbouring farm also takes it name from the stone.

Fornet

These curious figures were until recently built into the roof of the Grade C listed farmhouse at Nether Terryvale. Local tradition asserts that they originally came from the old house or 'castle' of Fornet and the legend tells that the man is the farmer carrying the woman's head for non-payment of her rent. The man is sometimes called 'The Executioner'. Another story is that a former Laird of Skene gave each of his three sons a farm, and there was a figure on each farmhouse. There is very little documentary evidence of an old house of Fornet, and no physical evidence. It was at one time, however, a place of some importance.

Fornet is one of only a handful of places in the parish marked on Robert Gordon's map published in Blaeu's atlas of Scotland 1654, testifying to its importance at that time. As late as 1827 sasines were still referring to the Manor Place of Fornet, though this is legal language and any manor place would have been long gone by this time.

Once again the Earl Marischal is involved in the story of Fornet. In the first half of the 16th century it belonged to him and is mentioned in various documents, along with his other lands in Skene. As noted above, the Register of the Great Seal records in 1506 that Robert Keith and Elizabeth Douglas

SKENE: THE EARLY HISTORY

had possession of the lands of Leddacht and Mulboy in the parish of Skene, but they also had Fornocht, Auchincloich, Auchquorsk in the Barony of Kintore. Presumably Fornet and Auchinclech were still in Skene Parish despite being in a different barony, though it is possible they were not. In the late 16th century Fornet was in the possession of the Irvine Family. In 1552 Alexander Irvine of Drum was married to Elizabeth Keith, second daughter of the Earl Marischal. Their second son, Robert, became Irvine of Fornet and Moncoffer.

The coat of arms is from Skene House and is also said to have come from Fornet. It shows the

Figures reputedly from the House of Fornet

Coat of arms from Skene House

arms of the Irvine's below (holly leaves), with the initials of Robert Irvine, and with the arms of the Earl Marischal above. Although Fornet was never part of the disputed lands of Easter Skene and it was on Skene of Skene's doorstep, it may never have been part of the original Skene lands. Evidence of this is that its farms were thirled to the mill at Garlogie, rather than the much closer mills at Skene House and at Craigiedarg which belonged to Skene of Skene. It was also on the boundary of Skene parish and adjacent to lands held by the Keiths as part of the Earldom of Kintore. Possibly the Earl gave it to the Irvines as part of Elizabeth's marriage settlement.

In any case the Irvines of Fornet did not last long, the line being extinct by around 1688. Their last mention in the book of the Irvines of Drum refers to a receipt of money paid to Robert Irvine, younger, of Fornet by Alexander Irvine of Murthill on 8th July 1688. Before that the estate had been sold to Cumming of Culter, and then to the Earl of Kintore who was the owner in the late 1670s according to the Kirk Session records. Alexander Livingstone, Dean of Guild, is described as being *of Fornet* in 1730, his son also Alexander, becoming Provost of Aberdeen in 1750. Subsequent to that it did eventually come into the possession of Skene of Skene.

Skene in troubled times

The Skene family was never a major one in the history of Scotland, or even within the North-East. However, they were involved in the conflicts which engulfed Scotland in the 16th and 17th centuries. We have already seen that a Skene was killed at Harlaw and James Skene, brother of Alexander Skene of Skene, died at the Battle of Pinkie in 1537. The various wars of the 16th and 17th centuries were also to affect Skene and its folk. In September 1574 James Skene, heir apparent of Alexander Skene, was one of numerous lairds who tendered allegiance to King James VI at Aberdeen. In the 1590s Alexander Skene of Skene had to stand surety of £500 each for James Skene of Baldodill, Gilbert Skene, Patrick Skene and Alexander Skene, his sons, so that they would not harm Thomas Buk, burgess of Aberdeen.

In the North-East the various battles that took place in the post-Reformation period were partly political and partly religious, but also partly clan related.

The Gordons, under the Earl of Huntly, stayed loyal to the old religion and hoped that the accession of the Catholic Queen Mary would create the conditions for a bid to restore Catholicism. Mary disappointed them by accepting the reformed religion, but the Gordons went ahead with their rebellion anyway, leading to the Battle of Corrichie, followed later by Tillyangus, the burning of Corgarff Castle, and the Battle at the Crab Stane at the top of the Hardgate in Aberdeen. The families traditionally opposed to the Gordons, led by the Forbeses, took the Government/Protestant side, and were their enemies in these battles. The Skenes took the side of their near neighbours, the Forbeses.

Skenes and Forbeses

As well as being neighbours, there was considerable intermarriage between the Skenes and Forbeses, from as early as the late 15th/early 16th century when Alexander Skene of Skene married a daughter of Lord Forbes. Thereafter marriage to Forbeses was common for both male and female members of the Skene family. For most of the 16th century the Laird of Skene was Alexander, known as *"the little laird"* because he had reputedly been dropped by his nurse when climbing up the ladder entrance to Skene House and was, as a result, hunch-backed. He also married a Forbes, Margaret, daughter of the laird of neighbouring Corsenday (Corsindae). One of his sons and two of his daughters also married Forbeses, as did two of his granddaughters. Margaret Skene, a great-granddaughter, married two Forbeses, Duncan Forbes in Letter and John Forbes of Leslie. In between, the unlucky Margaret married Robert Irving of Moncoffer (see previous chapter). An entry in the Register of the Privy Council records that, despite his handicap, the 'little laird' was one of the supporters of the Forbeses in a warring feud with the Gordons, though it is unclear as to whether or not he took an active part in the battles mentioned above. Marriages between the Skenes and the Forbeses continued into the 17th and 18th centuries, notably James Skene of Skene marrying Elizabeth, daughter of Arthur, Lord Forbes, in 1637, just prior to the start of the Civil War. These marriages would no doubt have cemented the place of the Skenes on the side of the Forbeses. In the 15th century Alexander Skene acted as witness to a number of Forbes charters. In 1563 Alexander Skene is referred to, with others, in a Forbes document as *"thair speciall belowit freindis"*.

Two violent incidents in the Kirktoun

Robert Irvine was involved in two incidents which show that these were violent times, even in a small place like Kirktoun of Skene. In December 1605, John Johnston of Auchronnie and James, John and Patrick Forbes of Millbuie, were charged with murdering a Robert Irvine, presumably a kinsman of Robert Irvine of Fornet and Montcoffer. The previous February Irvine had been with a party of friends having a banquet in a house in the Kirktoun. The accused were part of a band of up to 10 men who went to the Kirktoun, well armed with a colourful array of weapons and armour – with *"jakis"* (jacks – a type of leather jerkin reinforced with metal plates), *"secreitis"* (a coat of mail hidden under their clothes), steel bonnets, spears, lances, swords, *"quingeris"* (a short stabbing sword), *"gantillettis"* (gauntlets), *"hagbuttis"* (a type of firearm), and pistols, all weapons supposedly banned by act of Parliament. At 10 o'clock at night the alleged murderers are said to have entered the house, shot Irvine, and stabbed him with their swords. The jury, however, led by Robert Watson of Auchinclech, found the men innocent and they were freed.

Also in December, Robert Irvine of Fornet and Moncoffer, together with David Gray from the Lyne of Skene and two others, was charged with slaughter and 'hamesucken' (attacking someone in their own house), on 10th February, shortly after the earlier incident and presumably in revenge for it. It was alleged that they came to John Hall's house at the Kirktoun of Skene and broke the door down. They then stabbed John Forbes of Millbuie in the belly, wounds from which he died. Once again the accused were unanimously found not guilty.

In 1606 Arthur, Master of Forbes, had to provide security of £1,000 to ensure he did not communicate with *"John Forbes, brother of the Goodman of Corsindae, William Forbes in Tullivail, Robert Skene, tutor of that ilk, Patrick Forbes, Walter Wode in the Kirktoun of Skene and Gilbert Johnestoun, son natural of the late William Johnestoun of Standinstanes, while they remain at the horn* (i.e. made outlaws) *to which they have been put for the slaughter of Robert Irving in Baidis."* Many of the same characters were involved with the following actions.

'The Societie of the Boyis'

A further entry in the Register of the Privy Council for 1609 records the activities of a colourfully named band of ruffians headed by members of the Forbes family, with Skene associates. They were called 'The Society of the Boyis' or the 'Knychts of the Mortar'. A Commission of Justiciary was called against John Forbes of Logie and others of this society. Among the others were William Forbes of 'Mylbuy' (Millbuie), Patrick Forbes, his brother, John Mortimer, called 'The Baron', Robert Johnstoun, called 'Ding the Devil', Walter Wod at the Kirktoun of Skene, Robert Skene, called 'The Tutor', all described as *"fugitives from the law for divers crimes, bonded together in a most rebellious societie with oaths and promises of mutual support, passing through the countrie armed with hagbuts and pistols for slaughters, robberies and oppressions"*. George, Earl of Enzie, was commissioned to capture them, but eventually Arthur, Lord Forbes, undertook to answer for the future conduct of his kinsman, John Forbes of Logie.

'The Tutor' was Robert Skene of Tilliebirloch, tutor or guardian to his nephew Alexander Skene of that ilk.

We can see, then, that the Skenes and Forbeses were closely involved with each other and that Forbeses held land in parts of Skene and Skenes held land near Forbes territory. Bandodill, for example, is near Forbes holdings in Echt and Midmar.

The lands of Easter Skene

In 1629 the issue of the ownership of the lands of Easter Skene was raised once more with the Lords of Council and Session. We have already seen that the Earl Marischal seems to have had actual possession of the lands and there are also several instances of these lands of Easter Skene being referred to as the Barony of Kintore and Easter Skene. The action in 1629 seems to have been raised by Alexander Skene of that ilk, and I would suggest that it was a case of Skene trying to get back the lands rather than the other way round. Moreover if it had been the case that Skene had suddenly, in 1629, lost the lands he had possessed since the 1460s, then surely he would have tried to recover them when the Marischal fell foul of Cromwell's Government and ended up in the Tower of London. Similarly, when the Marischal's debts eventually lost him most of his lands, including Easter Skene, after the Restoration, Skene of Skene still made no attempt to regain his former lands.

The arbitration judgement handed down by the Lords is quoted in Skene's Memorials – "*the said Alexander Skene to resign in favour of the Earl Marischal, all claim to the lands of Kirktown of Skene, Ledach, Mylnebowie, and Garlogie, with the pertinents, to be bruiket* (enjoy possession of) *be the said Earl in his own proper lands in all time coming.*"

I would suggest that, in all the years since Harlaw, the Skenes never redeemed these lands by paying back the 300 merks and that the Earl *ipso facto* had actual possession for all that time. By the 1680s the Kirk Session records refer to Skene of Skene's lands as the Barony of Wester Skene, as opposed to the Barony of Easter Skene, though this title does not seem to appear in any official records.

The Earl Marischal exercises his power

The Register of the Privy Council records that, in 1635, James Seaton, a burgess of Aberdeen, with Sir Thomas Hope of Craighall, King's Advocate, brought a case to the Privy Council against the Earl Marischal. Seaton had been given a five year tack (lease) on the lands of Leddach of Skene after they had lain waste for four years. John Keith and Patrick Forbes, then chamberlain to the Earl Marischal, along with several others, including more Keiths, came to Seaton's house well armed "*at the special instigation of the said Earl, by way of hamesucken*". They carried Seaton off to the Tolbooth in Aberdeen where he was forced to renounce the tack. Thereafter Robert Keith, John's brother and general chamberlain to the Earl, augmented his tack duty and it was renewed under new conditions.

This still was not enough for the Earl Marischal and John Keith came to Seaton's house again and "*brake up the doors thereof, rugged doun the rooffe of the house, barnis and chalmers, so as ten bollis of meale being in his chaumer, and ane stacke of corn conteaning sixteen bollis aitts, being in his cornyard, were all lost*". Robert Keith came from Staniehyve (Stonehaven) and wounded Seaton. Then with John Keith in Auquhorsk, Alexander Forbes in Rodgerhill, William Strachane in Kirktoun of Skene, Alexander Norie in Liddach of Skene, Robert Forbes in Milbowie, and John Thomsone in Kirktoun of Skene he "*demolished and kuist doune the wallis of the saids houses and raised the same to the ground*". All these men were charged; incidentally, this also shows that the Earl Marischal's supporters were occupying many of the main farms in Easter Skene.

All the defendants appeared in Edinburgh, except John Keith and Alexander Forbes for whom Robert Keith produced two certificates, under the hand of the minister of Kinellar and of the elders of the Kirk of Skene, stating their inability to travel in regard of their age and the present storm. The Lords acquitted all the defendants who admitted taking the pursuer and demolishing his houses, but said that they had a warrant for his arrest.

The matter rumbled on and the following year Dame Mary Erskine, Countess Marischal, brought a complaint against James Seaton of "*Liddoke of Skene*" accusing him of summoning 30 of her tenants before the Justice, "*on some frivolous cause,*" the previous June. This latter being "*the meane tyme of the sawing of thair bear said* (the common time for sowing their barley seed), *and before the terme quhairat they have thair fermes and dewties to pay*". The countess alleged that this prosecution was done out of simple malice to cause them expense and "*oblige them to compone with him*" (come to a settlement). This issue was referred to Alexander Jaffray, Provost of Aberdeen, and Irvine of Drum or Seaton of Pitmedden to arbitrate.

The Privy Council Register further records, in November 1636, that James Seaton again accused the group of taking him under arms to Dunnotar

Castle, imprisoning him for a day, and coming to his barnyard and stealing his oats and beir. The Lords found for the Countess, reserving Seaton the right to take a civil action. Among those accused on this occasion were "*James Arthbuthnet' sometime in Kinmundie; Alexander Forbes in Rogershall; Robert Forbes, sometime in Redshill; Alexander Thomsoune in Cottoun; Robert Hall, younger, in Kirktoun of Skene; John Keith, officer, sometime in Aquhorsk; James Cowper in Kilmundie* (Kinmundie); *William Ronaldstoune in Whytestone; Alexander Norie in Riddoch* (Leddoch)."

Skene and the Civil War

W.F. Skene's Memorials includes an unreferenced quote saying "*James of Skene was a great loyalist, and suffered many hardships on account of his attachment to the interest of the Royal Family*". The quote goes on to say that although Skene had subscribed to the Covenant, along with James Graham, Marquis of Montrose, at Aberdeen, he later became a "*close companion*" of Montrose and that the latter, once he had changed over to the Royalist side, protected Skene's estates. This could hardly be further from the truth. As we have already seen, James Skene was married to Elizabeth Forbes, daughter of Arthur, Lord Forbes, and the Forbeses were leading Covenanters. Spalding in his *Memorials of the Troubles* says that Echt, Skene and Monymusk were all great Covenanters. As early as 1639 the Laird of Skene is mentioned in a gathering of Covenanters headed by the Earl Marischal and numerous Forbeses. The Earl Marischal's tenants in Easter Skene were also involved in the muster. In fact it is recorded that so many men from Skene and Kintore were called up that there were scarcely enough men left to "*call the plough*". The Marischal's men from Skene and Kintore are recorded plundering around Inverurie, especially on the lands of Thomas Crombie of Kemnay.

At the skirmish known as the Trot of Turriff, in May 1639, the lairds of Skene and Echt were actually taken prisoner by the Gordons. Once the Civil War really got going Sir Alexander Irvine of Drum, in 1644, was charged with capturing John Gordon, Lord Haddo. Among those with Irvine were Skene, Echt, Fedderate, Monymusk, Udny and Pittodrie. James Skene also seems to have been present on the Covenanting side at the momentous Battle of Aberdeen (or Justice Mills) in September 1644. Unfortunately his actions at the battle are not recorded.

In 1645 Montrose camped near Skene, perhaps near the loch. Several houses in the area were plundered including that of the parish minister,

William Chalmers. Two local men were killed by Montrose's Irish troops.

In March 1649 an Act of Probation was passed and granted in favour of the Master of Forbes, Lord Fraser, James Skene of Skene, and various Forbeses including Echt, Monymusk and Leslie, for the setting fire and burning of the house of Pitcaple. "*The Estates approved and allowed the burning of the house and any act of hostility to it.*" Presumably this was because John Leslie, 7th Baron of Pitcaple, was a Royalist, who was later wounded at the Battle of Worcester in 1651, subsequently dying from his wounds.

The Skene family and their neighbours in the Earl Marischal's lands of Easter Skene were certainly involved in the events of the Civil War period on the side of the Covenanters. James Skene would have been accompanied by some of his tenants and family members in the actions in which he took part. We have already seen that the tenants of the Earl Marischal in Easter Skene were also involved. Unfortunately we do not have the names of any Skene men who were casualties in this time of troubles.

Skene and Easter Skene from the Restoration until the end of the 18th century

Skene of Skene

Despite being on the Covenanting side, the Skene family did not really suffer any loss of land at the Restoration in 1660. James Skene had died in 1656 and his son, John, inherited. In 1678 King Charles II issued John a charter under the Great Seal, ratifying his title to the Barony of Skene and other lands in neighbouring parishes. In polite language the charter refers to *"the good, true and faithfull service done to his highness and his progenitors, in time past, by John Skene of that ilk and his predecessors"*.

James Skene: The Martyr

Skene The Martyr was the second son of the James Skene who was active during the Civil War. His brother, John, inherited the Skene lands, but James's path was to be a completely different one from his brother's. With the restoration of King Charles II in 1660, and the re-establishment of Episcopalian religion in Scotland, there was a growing persecution of the Presbyterian Covenanters, particularly in the South-West of Scotland. In 1680 James Skene was arrested for his beliefs, rather than for any act of actual insurrection, and he was held at the Tolbooth in Edinburgh where he was interrogated. From there he wrote to his brother, the Laird of Skene. This letter, as well as Skene's last speech and testimony as he stood at the scaffold, are printed in *A Cloud of Witnesses*, published in 1714.

His speech begins: "*Dear people I am come here this day to lay down my life for owning Jesus Christ's despised interest, and for asserting that He is a King, and for averring that He is head of His own Church, and has not delegated or deputed any, either Pope, King, or Council, to be his viceregents on earth*". James Skene was hanged on 1st December 1680. Sir John Lauder of Fountainhall spoke to Skene in his cell the day before his execution and describes his state of mind and attitude at the time. He goes on to say, "*Skeen being all cloathed in white linen, to his very shues and stockings, in affectation of puritie and innocence, and I wish it might be a praelibation and type of white robe to be given him in Heaven; however the singularity was unnecessary, if not vain*".

The Earl Marischal and Easter Skene

The Earl Marischal was not as fortunate as the Skene family in the Civil War and its aftermath. Although a Covenanter, William Keith was not a fanatic. Despite his actions on the side of the Covenant, he was a friend of the Marquis of Montrose and he entertained Charles II at Dunnotar in 1650. As a result he was subsequently captured by Cromwell and imprisoned in the Tower of London until the Restoration. Although restored to possession of his lands, the war had left him in some considerable debt and he was forced to sell off much of his lands almost immediately. William died in 1671.

The *Register of the Great Seal* records that in 1665, George, 4th Earl of Wintoun, received vast amounts of the Earl Marischal's lands in the North-East, including those in Kintore and Easter Skene, for debts owed. Wintoun was related to the Marischal, William Keith, having married Elizabeth Seaton, daughter of the 3rd Earl of Wintoun. The Easter Skene lands at this time are described as Fornet (Fuirdtoun), Auchinclech, Auchreine, Birshakmilne (or Berlackmilne), Garlogie, the mill thereof, Mulbie (Millbuie), Kirktoune of Skene, Edwardscroft, Smithscroft, Hill of Keir, Leddauch, Shipperscroft (Shepherdscroft), Milnfuird, Douncansons of Hilcarnie, Feddie, Kinmundie and Hill of Auchronie.

Part of the Marischal's debt was to Alexander Burnett of Craigmyle, the debt being over £16,000 Scots, and Burnett was given some of Keith's lands in payment, including Easter Skene. As early as 1653 the Keepers of the

Great Seal granted to Alexander Burnett of Counteswells, merchant burgess of Aberdeen, various lands including Fornet, Auchinclech, Eister and Wester Kimudies, Blackhills, Lyddoch of Skeyne, Cairnie, Kirktoune of Skeyne, Kinrodger, Hyllialbrux, and Garlogie. This may have been rescinded later, as detailed in the previous paragraph, but the lands did end up with Burnett.

Burnett was succeeded by his son, also Alexander, in 1677, and in 1682 the latter was knighted by King Charles. Sir Alexander Burnett was issued with a charter under the Great Seal, dated July 1678, erecting Easter Skene "*of new*" into a barony. Interestingly the principal messuage (dwelling house) of the barony is declared to be the manor place of Garlogie. This suggests that at one time there was a laird's house somewhere at Garlogie, but I have not found any other reference to it.

The Kirktoun market and fair

Sir Alexander Burnett must have taken a close interest in his newly acquired lands as, in September 1681, he obtained from the Parliament in Edinburgh a warrant enabling him to establish a fair and market at the Kirktoun of Skene. The warrant says that the Kirktoun "*is a convenient place for fairs and for a weekly market, for selling and vending of butcher-meat, fish and other victuals and goods necessary to his majesty's lieges in that place of the country, there being no fairs or weekly markets kept within a considerable distance of the same*". Two fairs would be held annually, one on the first Tuesday of June and the other on the first Tuesday of October. The markets would be held weekly. It was not entirely an altruistic move on Burnett's part, of course, as he would be empowered to collect tolls, customs and duties at the fairs and markets. How long the markets lasted I cannot say; they may not have lasted long as they do not seem to be mentioned anywhere in any records I have seen. Much later a market was held at the Broadstraik Inn.

The lands and barony of Easter Skene

As we have seen, from the 15th century the lands of Easter Skene were defined as Millbuie, Garlogie, Kirktoun of Skene and Leddach. Leddach was larger than the later estate and seems to have included Blackhills, and Easter and Wester Kinmundy. At various times Fiddy, Ord, and Easter and Wester Carnie were also included in the barony, and this was certainly true by the end of the 17th century when they belonged to the Burnetts of Craigmyle. In physical size, then, a look at the map of the parish would show that Easter

Skene comprised roughly two-thirds of the parish. This is confirmed in valuation by the 1696 Poll Tax record which shows the following for the parish of Skene:
- The Earl of Kintore (son of the Earl Marischal) had lands valued at £170 for Auchinclech and £290 for Fornet
- The Laird of Skene had lands valued at £700
- The Burnetts of Craigmyle (Easter Skene) £1400.

Likewise in the 1715 Jacobite Cess Roll, by which time Easter Skene belonged to the Merchant Guild of Aberdeen, the valued rents are as follows:
- Fornet £260
- Concraig £200
- Ye Town of Aberdeen £1,340
- The Laird of Skene £700

We can see that in the original dispute the land loss suffered by the Skene family to the Earl Marischal was huge, i.e. comparing the lands held by the Burnetts and Skene (the Earl of Kintore's lands at Fornet and Auchinclech were probably not part of the original deal between Skene and the Keiths). The Skenes did manage to buy, acquire through marriage, and inherit land in some of the neighbouring parishes, but the Easter Skene loss was significant and also meant that the eastern half of the parish developed in a different way from the Skene lands.

Sir Alexander Burnett married Nicholas Young of Auldbar in Angus, and by her had three daughters, Isobel, Ann and Margaret. Burnett family histories record that on his death in 1694, because there were no male heirs, considerable litigation followed, mainly by James Burnett of Monboddo, whose line was descended from an earlier Burnett of Craigmyle. Also involved was Thomas Burnett of Kemnay, claiming to be the nearest male heir and cousin german to the deceased Sir Alexander. However, the daughters were declared heirs portioners in 1696, and so the land was divided between them. The Burnett ladies were well connected, with Margaret married first to Sir Charles Maitland of Pittrichie, then Thomas Erskine of Pittodrie. Isobel was married to John Farquharson of Invercauld. No doubt their husbands looked after their interests in the various Craigmyle lands, including Easter Skene. Ann Burnett died shortly after inheriting, in 1697, and her share seems to have been divided between her two sisters.

The Youngs may have claimed a say over the Craigmyle lands as well, because we find that by 1701 Robert Young of Auldbar is receiving from Isobel her half of Easter Skene. Two years later, in 1703, the Sheriff of Aberdeen issued a decree of division saying that the east half of the lands belonged to Margaret and her husband, Sir Charles Maitland, and the west half belonged to Robert Young of Auldbar. Interestingly, under feudal tenure, the current Earl Marischal was still at this stage recognized as feudal superior of the land and feu duty was paid to him. The Earl Marischal was to join the Jacobite Rebellion in 1715 and end his life abroad with his remaining lands forfeited.

Skene Parish in 1696

The List of Pollable Persons within the Shire of Aberdeen 1696 is one of the few poll tax lists to survive in Scotland. It listed everyone except those under 16 and those living on charity, and allows us to see the names, occupations, etc., of each household in the parish in that year. People were liable for six shillings tax each, plus an extra six shillings if they had a trade, plus a fortieth of their rental value. In addition to the tenants, sub-tenants and farm workers listed under each fermtoun there were also the following:

- Thirteen weavers in the parish – three in the Kirktoun, two at Leddach, and one each at Birsack, Blackhills, Wester Carnie, Garlogie, Easter Kinmundy, Easter Carnie, Ord and Millbuie.
- There were five cordiners (shoemakers) – one each at Auchinclech, Birsack, Kirktoun, Easter Carnie and Millbuie.
- There were six tailors – one each at Birsack and Leddach, two at Terryvale and two at Kirktoun
- One skinner at Brodiach
- A sivvright at Millbuie (a wright who makes sieves)
- A wright at Easter Carnie
- Two smiths – one at Hattoun of Skene and one at Terryvale

Only two corn millers are mentioned, with Alexander Reid being the miller at Garlogie and James Mitchell at Birsack. However, we know from the Kirk Session records that there was also a corn mill at Ord in the 17th century.

As well as there being a corn mill at Garlogie, Robert Walker was described as *"walker at the Milne of Garlogie"*. This would be the waulk or fulling mill at Garlogie, which later became the woollen mill.

The two smiths mentioned as being in the parish were both on Skene of Skene's lands. James Lyon was at Hattoun of Skene, and James Gillespie at Terryvale. We do know from the Parish Session Book, however, that there was also a smith in the Kirktoun in the 1680s. In the 1690s they were still using the old wooden plough pulled by a team of oxen. There was also very little wheeled transport in the parish because the roads were not suitable for it. By the end of the 18th and into the 19th century the use of metal ploughs and horses, which needed shoes, meant that the demand for smiths grew considerably. There would also have been more carts, carriages and coach transport as the turnpike roads opened up early in the 19th century. Possibly a more specialized wheelwright might have seen to them, though normal blacksmiths may also have been involved.

Most of the communities mentioned in the Poll Tax record were 'fermtouns' (in old documents sometimes referred to as touns or tounships) rather than villages, with one or more main tenants and sub-tenants, cottars, herds and grassmen/grasswives/gresswomen. The latter were near the bottom of the social scale, having no land but only right of pasturage for what was probably a solitary milk cow. One reason for this organization into fermtouns was that the ox teams were so big that tenants needed to join together their animals and labour at ploughing time. A typical ox team could be from eight up to 12 – the 'twal owsen ploo'. We read in the Kirk Session records in the 17th century, for example, that every two ploughs (i.e. teams of ploughs) should join together to transport material for repairing the church.

No inn-keepers are recorded in the parish, though we do know that there were taverns, in the Kirktoun at least. Possibly the other inns later recorded on the King's Highway/Skene Road at Brodiach, Broadstraik, Lochee and Bervie were not in existence at this time. It may be that traffic on the road from Aberdeen was not sufficient to sustain inns.

Dean of Guild

The Burnetts' and Youngs' ownership of Easter Skene did not last long since, from 1710 onwards, they gradually sold it off to the Dean of Guild in Aberdeen. David Young of Auldbar, successor to his father Robert, sold the west half of the lands of Easter Skene to the Guild in 1711 for the sum of £37,966.13.4d Scots and 50 guineas (£52/10/-) of gold for a gown for Lady Auldbar. With the lands came the seats in the parish church belonging to those lands, as well as the duties of a heritor. The Merchant Guild also bought land to the west of Garlogie, in the parish of Echt, from George Skene of Rubislaw. As we shall see later, this purchase seems to have been shared with the Aberdeen Kirk Session and part of the land bought was to help fund the Guild Wine Fund, i.e., rents from the lands would go into the wine fund. The Guild kept these lands for most of the 18th century, except for a few years from 1726–1733 when they were disponed in trust to George Fordyce, late Provost of Aberdeen (perhaps in exchange for a loan).

The break up of Easter Skene and the condition of the parish at the end of the 18th century

Statistical Account

As mentioned in a previous chapter, the first STATISTICAL ACCOUNT for Skene was written by the parish minister, James Hogg. This provides a picture of the condition of agricultural land in the parish at that time. Most of the land was still unenclosed and unimproved, especially in the lands of Easter Skene owned by the Dean of Guild. The land was still mainly tilled by the inefficient infield and outfield system, with shared ploughing. The minister does say that the number of farms was diminishing due to improvements carried out by one heritor (presumably the Laird of Skene) and by the feuing out of the Dean of Guild lands. The latter has reduced the number of ploughs from 31 to 14. He gives the parish acreage as over 8,000 acres with 2,300 infield, 3,056 outfield, 1,640 pasture, 534 moss and 520 moor, and says that some land is fertile but other bits barren. He mentions great quantities of waste land in the parish, suitable only for tree planting, but that the latter has not been done. The nature of the soil, predominantly gravel, means that it used up a lot of manure. The land was difficult to improve because of the amount of stones on it and much of it was wet and spongy.

James Anderson's comments on the whole county of Aberdeen in 1794 would certainly apply to Skene parish at the time. He wrote: "*the appearance of the county is rather bleak and unininviting on account of the general want of wood around the hamlets, the imperfect culture of the fields, and the too frequent marshy appearance of the low grounds*".

Peat moss

Peat was vital as a source of fuel before the widespread mining and transport of coal. Although each moss belonged to a landowner, all inhabitants of the parish, including tradesmen, the minister and the dominie, had their section of the moss where they were allowed to cast peats. Once the moss was exhausted it reverted to the landowner. Charters, sasines, land dispositions, etc., all stipulated the rights people had to the peat moss. In the documents relating to the division of the Dean of Guild's lands, much of this is detailed for the purchasers of each lot and their tenants, including the area of hard ground next to the moss to dry their peat, e.g.,"*marked off by props on the ground with liberty and privilege to the possessors of each lott to row and dry their peats on the hard ground within the said several lotts, to the extent of sixty yards, next to their several mosses, they noways doing any damage to grass or corn.*" The landowners had the right to use the moss for pasture but only at certain times of the year – "*no beastial whatever shall be allowed to pasture on any of the lotts of said mosses where peats are cast and drying, from the first of May to the first of October yearly, under the penalty of one shilling sterling for each beast, besides paying damages.*"

The moss was also one of the areas where turf could be dug and this is also detailed in the documents. Turf was important in the pre-improvement age because houses might be built from turf, or a combination of turf and stone; roofs might be made of turf, and temporary enclosures for keeping animals had fail (turf) dykes.

Much of the peat moss was in the southern part of the parish – Garlogie, Carnie, Leddach and what is now Arnhall, the latter sometimes called the Moss of Blackhills. The best peat, however, came from the Lyne of Skene moss which was not part of the Dean of Guild lands. The peat moss was often divided into sections and stone boundary markers erected; this was certainly the case at Garlogie. Two stones close together, with numbers on them, on the track through Garlogie Wood to Gask, may be moss boundary markers rather than the usual boundary stones.

The Skene estate rentals for 1785/86 shows that there was a moss grieve

THE BREAK UP OF EASTER SKENE

at Lyne of Skene at that time, and he was receiving a salary. This continued up to the 1950s. His role was important to make sure that all tenants had an appropriate section of the moss for casting peat and that there was no encroachment. It was not unkown for boundary markers to be moved. The later section on roads will also mention how moss roads were important to give access to the moss and had to be kept open for everyone.

In common with several parishes near to Aberdeen, much of the peat moss in Skene was used to supply Aberdeen. In fact the minister said that, until the recent feuing of the Dean of Guild lands, the tenants on those lands spent a great part of their time digging and driving peat to Aberdeen, with little reward. It may be that part of the rent on these lands was paid in peat for the fires of Guild members in Aberdeen.

The roup and feuing of Easter Skene

In 1787 the Merchant Guild decided to sell off their holdings in Easter Skene. The Guild at that time was to a great extent synonymous with the Town Council. Hence a great number of sasines, charters and other documents relating to Easter Skene survive in the City Archives, dating from the Earl Marischal in the 16th century onwards. The sale documents for these lands tell us a huge amount about the eastern two-thirds of the parish at the end of the 18th century, and show that this part of the parish had a different development from the Skene estate lands. Numerous new landowners moved into the rouped lands, built country houses, and set about improving their estates and the parish generally.

The Dean of Guild and the Aberdeen Kirk Session

The lands were held jointly with the Kirk Session in Aberdeen and included the lands of Mill of Air and Easter Echt in Echt Parish, adjoining their lands in Garlogie. The first thing that had to be done before Easter Skene could be sold was to divide up the relevant lands between the Kirk Session and the Dean of Guild. The lands were to be divided two-thirds to the Dean of Guild and one third to the Kirk Session, and an arbitration panel was established to draw up three equal lots. Boundary stones were set up showing the three lots, or at least they were supposed to be, but in one document describing the lots it says that the stones are not yet put up.

As we shall see later, boundary stones from this time do survive in Skene, although these may relate to the subsequent lots when the Guild actually sold off their land. Some boundary stones were probably used for both purposes, where the two overlapped, and some of the first group may have been removed when the sale lots were created.

Lot one comprised Over, Nether and Wester Millbuie, Rogershill, Hill of Keir, part of the Kirktoun (the western part) and crofts near the Kirktoun called Bents, Dykenook and Lochhead. In describing the areas of this lot it mentions other crofts near the Kirktoun, one called the Doctor's croft and one called Meggy Reid's croft, the location of both now lost to us, unfortunately. The description of the lot refers to common loanings and common water near the loch; these would both be lost to the community at the enclosure of the lands into new estates. All the lands were to be "*disjoined from thirlage or astriction to the Mill of Garlogie*". This refers to the imposition, which had existed from medieval times, whereby tenants were bound to take their grain to a specific mill for grinding.

Lot two comprised the remaining parts of the Kirktoun, along with Leddach, and Wester Carnie, reaching the lands of Margaret Udny Duff of Culter to the south. Leddach at this time also included "*Whitestain*", Blackhills, Wester and Easter Kinmundy "*comprehending the pendicle called Broadiach,*" and Easter Carnie.

Lot three comprised Easter Echt, Mill of Air and Garlogie.

The lots were drawn and the Kirk Session drew lot three which they subsequently sold in its entirety to George Skene of Skene; the Guild drew the two lots wholly in the parish of Skene.

All the lots were allocated access and use of land in the peat moss. All the moss areas were measured, as was their depth and solid contents. Each lot's share of the moss was marked by numbered or 'cutt' march stones, similar to the boundary stones for the land division. Lot one was allocated a portion of the moss of Wester Carnie bounded on the west by the minister's part of the moss. Lot two was to the east of lot one and also had the middle division of the "*great moss of Air*" next door in the parish of Echt. Lot three had that part of the moss of Wester Carnie lying west of the minister of Skene's portion, and also the westernmost parts of the moss of Air and the moss of Garvock. Each of the three lots had equal rights of fishing on the Loch of Skene.

Lot one had to pay stipend to the minister of Skene, and also a sum of £2 sterling to the College of St Andrews, £1 13s 4d (£1.67) to the Hospital of Old Aberdeen, and £1 to the schoolmaster of Skene. Lot two had a similar payment but with £1 13s 4d to the schoolmaster. The stipend for lot three was split between the ministers of Skene and Echt, but also had a payment to the college and a payment for the salary of the schoolmaster of Echt.

The description of the land in roup documents

The Dean of Guild lands were divided up into lots to be sold off to the highest bidder. The description of each lot is very detailed and tells us much about the area in 1788. The boundaries of many of the lots can still be traced today, some of the boundary stones still being in place. In addition, many of the placenames still exist, but there are some which cannot be found. This is sometimes because they were descriptive and improvements have changed the land. In addition, as we have seen above, those referring to properties of specific people are difficult to place even if the croft house still exists, and most do not.

The minister reported on the poor state of land at the time, particularly the many wet, boggy bits. This is reflected in the descriptions of the lots, with a wide variety of Scots words used to describe poor, wet ground. One of the documents describes the marches (boundary) between the Dean of Guild lands and those of George Skene. They began north of Millbuie farm near a piece of green swampy ground called the Latch of Millbuie. There was also a Latch of Carnie; the gable wall of a house there still survives. Latch refers to a bog or a small stream flowing through a bog, mire having the same meaning. The boundary then goes westward to a mossy hollow called the Bouden. Then it seems to go to another 'laigh' (low) mossy ground, also called the Bouden. The name bowden or boldin is an old Scots word which seems to mean swollen; in this case it would be swollen with water.

Further east at Leddach the boundary ran through some "*faugh moorish*" ground (fallow moorland) called Craigyhill, somewhere between Souterhill and the Old Skene Road. It also ran through some more fallow ground called the Knab Faughs (possibly meaning the fallow ground covered in boulders) on the north side of that part of the Moss of Arnhall called the Moss of Leddach. This reminds us that the very significant Arnhall Moss did run in a belt to Leddach, the remains being seen beside the Westdyke Lesiure Centre. In fact the turnpike road, opened in 1803, ran in a curve south to go round this moss. It was only straightened in the mid-20th century and part of the line of the original road can still be seen behind the Shepherd's Rest Inn.

To the south of the road at Elrick was the large Carnie Moss, remains of which can be seen in the Carnie Woods, particularly at the south end, and between the woods and the Fox Lane Garden Centre. The trees in the Carnie Woods are more recent. Other terms used in the Leddach description are "*reesky faugh ground*" and "*reesky stony moor*" near Mackie's Steps, reesky here referring to coarse grass or rushes. Towards the south-east corner of the Leddach property, at the boundary with some land belonging to Easter Carnie, was the quaintly named Dogdirtfold. A fold was a pen or enclosed piece of ground – an early dog walking area, perhaps! A further heathery moor on the Leddach property was the Ballmoor, somewhere between the houses of Leddach and Whitestone farm, probably around where Mason Lodge was later built.

The boundary descriptions confirm, for Easter Skene at any rate, what the minister said about the nature of the parish, and they do it in a colourful Scots way. There were also large areas of moss to the south-east of the Easter Skene lands where the inhabitants of the Kirktoun had their peat-cutting rights. This latter has variously been known as the Carnie Moss, the Gask Moss and, more recently, the Garlogie Moss. Much of it is still moss or woodland today. In other areas, particularly on the hilly areas such as Rogiehill and Hill of Keir, the land was equally rough, this time covered in heather, whin and stone. Much of this would, have changed by the time the next minister was writing the Second Statistical Account.

The 'lotts' of Easter Skene and who bought them

On 5th August 1788 the ABERDEEN JOURNAL carried an advertisement relating to lands in Skene and Kinellar owned by the Dean of Guild to be feued. The various touns and lands were briefly mentioned, with full details of the roup to be announced.

On 18th August the Kirk Session also advertised for sale the toun and lands of Burelley, Garlogie and Mill of Garlogie, as well as their lands of Easter Echt in the neighbouring parish. The Kirk Session lands were to be in three lots and, as noted earlier, they were subsequently bought by George Skene of Skene. For the Guild lands of Easter Skene the following lots were created and would be the basis of the future estates in the area:

Lott first: Easter Kinmundy, including the east parts of Wester Kinmundy and the croft of Brodiach and some small crofts on both sides of the King's Highway

Lott second: Wester Kinmundy

Lott third: Blackhills, including the farmhouses of Blackhills and the croft of Knabs

Lott fourth: Leddach, including the farms of Leddach and Hill of Keir,

THE BREAK UP OF EASTER SKENE

Broadstraik (i.e. Broadstraik on the Old Skene Road) and the moss of Easter Carnie

Lott fifth: Easter Kirktoun, including the east part of the Kirktoun, the greater parts of Whitestone, the farmhouses of Rogiehill, some of the west parts of Leddach and Hill of Keir, and some of the north parts of Wester Carnie

Lott sixth: Wester Kirktoun, including a considerable share of the west side of the Kirktoun, the croft of Bents, some of the west parts of Rogiehill and north parts of Wester Carnie

Lott seventh: Dykenook, containing the houses presently occupied by James Orchardtown or Orcherton

Lott eighth: Millbouie, including Wester, Over and Nether Millbuie, and some ground acquired in the straightening of the marches between the lands of Auquhorsk, Fornet and Terryvale

Lott ninth: Loch Head

Lott tenth: Lochside, including the south and west parts of the Kirktoun and the croft lying between the King's Highway and the Loch of Skene

Lott eleventh: Wester Carnie, including nearly the whole of the farm of Wester Carnie and some parts of the south-west parts of Whitestone and the houses of Picktillam

Lott twelfth: Easter Carnie

Lott thirteenth: Fiddie, including Fiddie and Milltoun of Ord

Lott fourteenth: Ord, including the farm and Mill of Ord, and Millcroft

Lots fifteen and sixteen were Auchronie and Rotten in Kinnellar parish.

The divisions must have been in some way based on the historical areas from which they took their names, perhaps based on ancient land holdings. The two Carnies, Ord and Fiddie, were in the south-east corner of the parish and were old land holdings. Most of the others seem to have been almost sliced through the parish in a north south way. This gave each potential estate some high ground to the north, often poor ground covered in whin and heather. They also had some ground that may have been reasonable quality in their middle section. Then they had poor areas of marsh and bog to the south. The King's Highway ran through all these central ones, an important point, even though the quality of the road was not great. The same would more or less apply when the turnpike road was built a few years later.

There seems to have been no attempt to make the lots equal in size as the following table of acreages shows:

	Intown	**Outfield**	**Pasture**	**Moss**	**Total**
E Kinmundy	76	182	145	18	**421**
W Kinmundy	25	31	40	10	**106**
Blackhills	31	73	87	15	**206**
Leddach	58	210	100	17	**385**
E Kirktoun	86	185	50	9	**420**
W Kirktoun	37	141	60	9	**247**
Dykenook	2	20	-	-	**22**
Millbuie	85	189	125	9	**408**
Lochhead	10	75	-	-	**85**
Lochside	5	58	-	-	**63**
W Carnie	52	300	300	60	**712**
E Carnie	62	260	131	22	**475**
Fiddy	18	92	67	7	**184**
Ord	26	107	91	22	**246**
Mr Allan's Croft	3	7	-	-	**10**

From this we can see that the two Carnies were big lots, but that the great majority of the land there was poorer quality outfield, pasture and moss. The lots nearer the Kirktoun had both infield and outfield, but much less pasture and practically no moss. Millbuie also had a lot of outfield and pasture. This is reflected in the rental values, with the two Kirktouns being worth £83, Millbuie and Wester Carnie £80. Dykenook and Mr Allan's Croft were obviously not lots in the same sense as the other lots. Dykenook was also used as reference point in the descriptions of some of the lots. Roads are described as running from it to Kintore, and south to the Moss of Wester Carnie and Garlogie. It is marked on Taylor & Skinner's map of the Skene Road from 1776 and, although the name no longer exists, we can position it to about where Skene School stands. At this time we can see from the lot descriptions that it was occupied by James Orchardtown and his barn was specifically used as a reference point.

Orchardtown must have been a musician of some kind since an account for entertainment exists in his name in the Skene House papers. He was also a wright as an account also exists, from 1790, for making an axle for a cart, for mending a horse cart, and making a new box for a cart, for which he was paid 11s / 9d (58p). Mr Allan was the long-serving schoolmaster and his croft was probably adjacent to the then school, about half way along the current road (the 'Half-Milie') from Kirktoun of Skene to Skene School. Neither croft was added to larger lots at this time. This is understandable for the school croft which would have to be preserved, but why Dykenook was not incorporated I don't know. Even if Orchardtown had several years of his tenancy left, that would have applied to other tenants and their tenancy was simply transferred to the new purchaser of the estate. In time these two small holding would be incorporated into the Easterskene estate of the well known McCombie family of improvers. The name Dykenook survived as the name of the field of East Dykenook on Easterskene Estate until the 1950s.

The lots, then, were put up for sale to the highest bidder. Most of the buyers were men from Aberdeen, often merchants or similar, and as such they would have been members of the guild which was selling the lands (insider trading perhaps). They went on to make great changes on their new estates, their aim being to make money from the estates, and that required enclosure, land improvement, changes in tenancy and higher rents. The initial buyers were:

Lot one. Easter Kinmundy was bought by James Davidson, an existing tenant from Skene. He must have had difficulty making the land pay since, some 10 years later, he petitioned the Town Council to become a tenant again and be remunerated for the improvements he had made. The failure of the harvest of 1799 had made it difficult for him to pay his feu duty. Those still tenants on what remained of the the Town lands also petitioned the Council at this time "*for liberty to defer payments of their victual rents*". They were all turned down by the Council.

Lots two and three. Alexander Fiddes, a weaver in Aberdeen, bought the second lot, Wester Kinmundy, though he later said that he had made the offer on behalf of Alexander Smith, a merchant in Silverburn of Counteswells. Smith also bought, in his own name, the third lot, Blackhills. Some 70 years later these two lots would become Westhill.

Lot four. Alexander Crombie, described as a writer in Aberdeen, bought the fourth lot, Leddach. Crombie would go on to become President of the Society of Advocates in Aberdeen, and a very wealthy man as we shall see later.

Lot five. William Knowles, a wright in Aberdeen, bought the fifth lot, Easter Kirktoun, which would become Kirkville.

Lot thirteen. George Moir, a vintner from Aberdeen, bought the estate of Fiddy.

Lot fourteen. John Smith, from the Hole Mill of Culter, bought Ord, presumably to run the mill there.

The other lots attracted no bidders at this time, though shortly afterwards George Skene bought the tenth lot, Lochside, which adjoined his own lands. Some of them did eventually sell, though it took several years, and some were never sold. Easter Carnie continued to be owned by the Dean of Guild and then the City of Aberdeen until well into the 20th century. By then it comprised the farms of Burnside, Eastside, Sunnybrae, Mackie Steps, Northside, Westside and Woolhillock. The City of Aberdeen still owns Carnie Woods.

The boundary stones

There are two stones quite near each other on the Old Skene Road, between the ATC Hut and Prospect Cottage. One has a number seven and one with a number eight carved on their face and, like many other people, I had walked past these many times without realizing what they were. When Alastair Ogg, owner of the shop at the Kirktoun of Skene for many years, bought a house just beside them, he noticed a stone with a number six on it in some rough grass just beyond his garden, beside the telephone exchange. Alastair asked me if I knew what it was. At that time I didn't, but shortly after I started researching the old charter and sasine documents held by the City Archives on the lands formerly owned by the Guild in Aberdeen.

It quickly became obvious that these were boundary stones relating to one of the lots of the lands of Easter Skene and that they can be dated to 1788. In fact these three relate to Wester Kinmundy (half of the future Westhill). The relevant document defines the lot of Wester Kinmundy as beginning at a *"cutt march stone marked 1 placed at the march dyke twixt the farms of Kinmundy and Auchinclech near the east end of the Galleymoss"*. The boundary went south from there across the hill to stones two and three, four, five, and downhill to number six, *"placed on the north side of the King's Highway*" (what is now known as The Old Skene Road). *Then across the highway to number seven, then westward along the roadside to number eight placed at the north-east point of the road which runs from the Kings Highway to Fiddy."* (This road is now the path leading from Prospect Cottage to Berriedale Funeral Home).

And so the boundary description goes on. As we have seen stones six, seven and eight survive in their original locations and I subsequently found

THE BREAK UP OF EASTER SKENE

number three beside a path going north from Hillside Road near Craigston Gardens. Numbers one and two may also survive in the fields to the north, though four and five are probably buried under modern houses. It is unusual for several stones to survive in sequence like this, especially in an area of modern housing development.

In the days before accurate OS maps, boundary stones were very important to define estate boundaries. Larger estates did sometimes employ surveyors to draw up an accurate estate plan outlining boundaries, especially once fields became enclosed and common land taken into estate ownership. But even large landowners could have boundary disputes. In 1743 George Skene received a letter from the Earl of Kintore *"agreeing that gentlemen should meet often and keep their marches clear"*. The Earl said that he was going to come to Skene and *"sight our marches"*. These boundaries would be among the first to have boundary dykes built. In 1811 Skene had a stone dyke built between his lands and the Earl's – 3 feet wide at the bottom, 18 inches at the top, and 4 feet high.

The City of Aberdeen had its boundary stones, both for the inner boundaries of the burgh and for the outer Freedom Lands, many of them still in existence. The stones were important and had to be checked regularly to prevent people encroaching onto burgh-owned land – hence the Riding of the Marches. In the case of Easter Skene, the stones were set up at a fixed date (1788) and for a specific purpose. The stones had to be made and erected by a stonemason. Prior to the division of the Easter Skene lands into lots using newly-erected boundary stones, the marches between the lands owned by the Laird of Skene and the Dean of Guild had to be fixed. Recorded in the Skene Estate accounts is a payment in 1788 to Charles Winchester (he signs himself Winster) for squaring and dressing march stones.

March or boundary stones used numbers and letters in sequence, and sometimes a combination of both. One at the east edge of Westhill has a B (Brodiach) on one side and K (Kinmundy) on the other. One beside Garlogie Mill is three-sided – with the numbers one, two, three on different sides, possibly the meeting place of three estates. On the former Leddach Estate, Ann Morrison from Mason Lodge showed me two stones to the south of Mason Lodge. One has a nicely-shaped L on one side and a K on the other. The other stone has a V on it, this latter being one beside the roadside that I had walked past many times without ever seeing! It was recently moved and then re-positioned as that section of road was straightened.

Leddach/Kirkton boundary stone

"... a cutt March Stone placed on the opposite side of the road having L denoteing Leddach cutt on the Eastside"

Again the 1788 documents include in the boundary of the Leddach lot the description *"to a cutt March Stone marked with a letter V placed in some green faughs in the south side of the road from Broadstraik to Garlogie and Echt – and from thence crossing said road to a cutt March Stone placed on the opposite side of the road having L denoteing Leddach cutt on the Eastside and K denoteing Kirktown on the Westside."* These surviving stones, as well as helping plot the boundary of the Leddach Estate, also help us position the line of the old pre-turnpike road, part of which survives as a track here. Another Leddach boundary stone with an S survives at the east entrance to the Carnie Woods. Following the line from that stone west along a boundary dyke we come to a massive stone called the Earlick stone. So here we see a natural stone being used as boundary marker, whilst another one in the Leddach lot is described as an earthfast stone. The boundary dyke was built later than the boundary stones, but it incorporated the Earlick stone.

At Kirktounbridge, just south-east of the Loch of Skene, the 1901 OS map shows a stone at the south-east corner of the bridge. The 1788 boundary for West Kirktoun describes this stone as having a number nine on the top face, a K (Kirtkoun) on the east face, and a G (Garlogie) on the west face. As yet I have not been able to find this stone, but the document then says that going directly south from this stone there should be two more. Trusting to the accuracy of the old time surveyors I took my compass and walked through the Garlogie woods in a due south direction. Thankfully much of this area has now been felled, though it was still rough and boggy. Eventually I did find the number seven stone with a G and K on the other faces as described, and the document says that this stone was *"placed near the northwest of the Causeway of the Gask which is the line of the road from Garlogie to Broadstraik."* This old road can also be traced as we shall see in the chapter on roads and transport.

All the various lots of the Dean of Guild's lands had boundary stones, erected in 1788 to define their boundaries, and these are listed in the land dispositions. Using the old documents, I have been able to find a number of stones and the search goes on. The information they, and the related documents, can tell us about the area is considerable.

The new estates and some of their owners

By the time of the second STATISTICAL ACCOUNT in 1843 the parish minister, George Mackenzie, was able to report that the number of heritors was now 14. For most of the previous 200 years it had only been around three. He said that there had been a considerable improvement in the condition of the land in the parish, being favourably impressed by the amount of plantation (tree planting) which almost every heritor had undertaken. Agricultural land had seen a great improvement, with furrow-draining and enclosing of fields with dry-stone dykes, especially on the estate of Easterskene. Waste land had been brought into cultivation (above 1,000 acres) particularly on the lands of Ord, Fiddie, the Carnies, Easterskene, Leddach, Blackhills, Kinmundy, Concraig, Newton and Auchinclech. No mention, though, of the Skene of Skene lands which by this time would be in the possession of the Earl of Fife.

Knowles of Kirkville is singled out for praise, having added two new farms to his property through improved drainage. As noted earlier, many of these new landowners were merchants. Some, especially from the 1830s onwards, had made their money in India and the East. These included men who had worked for the East India Company or in the army in India. They and their tenants all revolutionised agriculture in the parish and left a legacy in the landscape that we can still see today.

William Paul described it thus: "*Now are to be seen the barren land cleared of stones and cultivated; the mosses drained, reclaimed, and covered, in the season, with waving crops of yellow corn or other produce; the ground surrounding the beautiful loch fringed with wood or cultivated to the very edge; proprietors' seats erected, and the policies about them tastefully laid out; and no lack of wood in the parish, both profitable and ornamental*".

Kirkville/Kirkton: the Knowles family

As we have seen this estate was begun in the late 18th century when William Knowles, a wright in Aberdeen, feued the lands of East Kirktoun. William was also a merchant of some kind in Aberdeen, with premises in Virginia Street. He actually tried to sell the lands again as early as 1801, and again in 1802 and 1803. Even by then he was advertising the improvements done on the estate – with improved ground, substantial stone dykes, subdivided into 30 enclosures, and a few acres of planting of trees. The estate didn't sell, perhaps because he was in the middle of a dispute with the turnpike authorities over compensation for the road through his land. William must have become a hands-on laird as he is said to have been farming at Rogiehill on the estate at the time of his death in 1818. He had four sons; one was a pianoforte manufacturer in Aberdeen, another a physician and one "*stayed at home*". It was the fourth son, James Knowles, who inherited the fledgling estate from his father. He was to be a significant figure in the history of manufacturing in Aberdeen, as well as a man who transformed the re-named Kirkville Estate.

James was also a merchant, and a draper and haberdasher, with premises in Marischal Street from where, in 1802, he was one of the witnesses at a supposed riot where the Ross and Cromarty Rangers shot and killed several people, leading to a court case. James also had a property in Adelphi Court in Aberdeen, traded with Rotterdam, and the Aberdeen street directories of 1824/25 and 1825/26 describe him variously as Danish Consul and Vice Consul for Russia, Prussia, Sweden and Norway.

In 1798 he had leased the Cothal Mill on the Don near Dyce for woollen manufacture. James was not a manufacturer, however, and he needed to find one to operate his mill. Shortly after taking the lease he met John Crombie, whose father was probably a handloom weaver and, by 1805, the partnership of Crombie, Knowles & Co. was established, the beginning of the famous Crombie Mills.

The same year that James inherited his father's estate at Skene (1819) he married Isabella Pitcairn, daughter of a Dundee wine merchant and, at 19 years of age, much younger than James. Incidentally 1819 is also the date on the walled garden at Kirkville, so I presume that at that time there was an earlier house on the estate, possibly where his father had lived, and the

THE NEW ESTATES AND SOME OF THEIR OWNERS

wedding is commemorated by the garden. In 1825 his growing wealth enabled James to hire Aberdeen's leading architect, City Architect John Smith, to build Kirkville House on his estate.

This is commemorated with a stone set into the wall beside the door with JK 1825 IP. Kirkville/Kirkton House is a lovely classic villa with Doric portico. It was added to in 1848 by John Smith working with his son William; they also added the south-east gatehouse at that time. Subsequent alterations were done in the early 20th century when Lord Cowdray bought the estate, and when the nursing home took it over in 1986. Unfortunately for James, the young Isabella died shortly after the building of the house, either in 1827 or 1828, so she didn't spend much in her new home.

Initials of James Knowles and Isabella Pitcairn from Kirkville

James went on to increase the size of the estate by buying land at Wester Carnie (sometimes called Hillcarnie) where much of the land was poor. He greatly improved it, as he did with the estate generally. As we have already seen, the second STATISTICAL ACCOUNT of 1843 records some of his improvements: "the late proprietor of Kirkville added (by draining) two new farms, with farm-steadings, where farm had never been before, on the haughs (rather bogs) of the Leucher Burn, on his lands of Hillcairnie. This he effected by straightening, cutting, and deepening the burn at considerable expense, part of which, of course, was borne by the heritor on the opposite side of the Leuchar."

This was down by the Leucharbrae area, one of the lowest parts of the parish, and where the Leuchar Burn would have made the area quite boggy. A plan of 1832 records that, in 1827, Knowles employed George Bisset, contractor, to deepen the Leuchar Burn. In 1830 he planted three plantations of trees in the area, just to the east of the burn and, in 1832, he made a new road past Tillybreck and on to Leucharbrae. The various surviving plans of the estate allow us to date the changes made by Knowles. A plan of 1827 shows unenclosed land with small infields, outfields, folds, and pasture, and cottar crofts also marked. By 1832 the landscape has changed dramatically, with enclosed fields, plantations, new farms, etcetera.

Although the mill in Aberdeen had been successful, by the 1820s the textile industry was in a depression. After his wife's death James tried to resign from the business, but the depression made this difficult as the business had considerable debts. Knowles juggled the debts, paying off some; he even put his house and lands on the market in August 1828, for an upset price of £17,000. He managed to avoid the sale, but various lawsuits arose from the break-up of the company and Knowles moved to Edinburgh, perhaps to get over his wife's death and perhaps better to fight the lawsuit. He again put the estate up for sale in 1830 but eventually had to settle for renting it out.

At the time of the 1828 proposed sale the description of Kirkville House is as follows:

> "The house is delightfully situated in the middle of the ground, on a gentle eminence, having a southern aspect; is only 8 miles from Aberdeen, by an excellent Turnpike Road; commands a grand and extensive view, terminating from the front with the Grampians, from the west with Morven, Lochnagar, and other mountains, while a beautiful lake, of nearly 300 acres, and a great extent of young planting (both of which it overlooks within a mile), render the near prospect highly interesting. The ground is of superior quality, and comprehends about 8 acres in wood, disposed in belts and clumps, for shelter and ornament. The garden is surrounded with high walls, and is most productive.
>
> The House and Coach House are quite new – the former having been painted and completed only last year. The principal floor is entered under a handsome portico (by 5 steps and platform of dressed granite), and by a vestibule, 14 feet by 10, and lobby 36 by 9, lighted by a cupola – both laid with polished Turin stone; and contains dining and drawing rooms, with large folding doors between; breakfast parlour; 6 bed rooms, in one of which is a slipper and shower bath, arranged so as to form dressing rooms to each other; water closet and butler's pantry, both abundantly supplied with water.
>
> In the basement are kitchen, wash and brew houses, all supplied with water by lead pipes introduced directly to the boilers; 2 good bedrooms, 2 apartments for servants, milk house, cooks' pantry, store room, shoe room, wine, beer and wood cellars."

One building it does not mention is the small chapel to the east of the walled garden. The walls of this chapel still survive, of fairly rough hewn stone, but the date of the building is unknown.

At St Bernard's Crescent, Edinburgh, on 31st October, 1833, James Knowles died suddenly of cholera. The ABERDEEN JOURNAL of 6th November reports that he was "*attacked by cholera on Wednesday and died the following morning, only 7 hours from the commencement of the attack. His death will be deeply deplored by his family and sincerely regretted by a wide circle of friends.*"

Crombie & Co. survived and eventually moved to Grandholm where they went on to prosper.

According to the book CROMBIE OF GRANDHOLM, James's estate at the time of his death was considerable – including his share in the firm of Knowles & Smith in Rotterdam, which was worth £9,100. Rent from Kirkville and Wester Carnie or Hillcarnie was worth £1,170 a year. In his will he directed his trustees to educate his children "*above rather than below their station*". He was succeeded by his son, William, who, in 1844, married a Miss Smith of Rotterdam, who may have been the daughter of his father's partner, in which case she was William's first cousin once removed.

The ABERDEEN JOURNAL for August 1840 records celebrations at Kirkville at his coming of age. It says that he was at present on a visit to this country, suggesting he spent most of his time abroad. He was entertained to a dinner at Carnie and the chair was taken by Captain Grant. Described as Army Half Pay in the 1841 Census, Grant was then the tenant of Kirkville House and the man supposed to be responsible for the unfinished Skene Reform Bill Monument near Braelea farmhouse.

Among others attending were McCombie of Easterskene, McCombie of Jellybrands, Dr Ewing of Tartowie and William's brother, James. The Journal goes on:

> "A number of other toasts followed after which the party was joined by the bonny lasses of the estate and the days proceedings were concluded with a ball which was kept up with great spirit until an early hour in the morning. While the necessary preparations were making for the ball the company was entertained by a brilliant display of fireworks from an adjoining eminence and a huge bonfire blazed in front of Kirkville. The evening being fine the fireworks were seen to a great advantage. The dinner was highly creditable to Mr Troup, Carnie, by whom it was furnished, and the mountain dew distributed from a bushel measure was of first rate quality. In the course of the evening Mr John McDonald, tenant in Hatton (of Carnie), presented Mr Knowles with a Roman spear, javelin and sword, which were discovered a few years ago in the course of improvements to the estate, embedded in moss".

A similar celebration was held at the time of his marriage, with 70 tenants and neighbouring proprietors attending a dinner and ball. The ball being kept up with the "*spirit stirring strains of Drumnagarrow*," which seems to have been a favourite tune of McCombie of Easterskene. To further mark the occasion Knowles later ordered a sum of money to be spent on clothes for the poor on his estate. It does not seem likely that William ever lived at Kirkville House and he eventually sold it to Captain Thomas Shepherd in 1845.

From William's time onwards the family adopted the hyphenated name Pitcairn-Knowles, after his late mother. Pitcairn Lodge is also the name of a nursing home on the same site as the present Kirkton House Nursing Home. William, like his father, was a woollen merchant in Rotterdam and deacon of the Scots College in Rotterdam. He was also well known as a collector of Dutch 17th century art. His brother, James, died in Bombay in 1857 while serving in the 5th Regiment Bombay Native Infantry. William's son, James Pitcairn-Knowles, although little known now, became an influential artist involved with the Nabis group in Paris, which included artists such as Vuillard, Lacombe, Bonnard and Maillol. Pitcairn-Knowles mainly made woodcuts, but very little of his work has survived. He particularly influenced the Hungarian artist Joseph Rippl-Ronai who painted a portrait of his Scottish friend. William's other son, Andrew, was also artistic. He became a pioneer in photo-journalism, particularly in the area of leisure, customs and sport, founding an early sports magazine in Germany. His descendants still live in England and his grandson has written a book about his photographic career.

Kirkville: the Skene Reform Bill Monument

The Skene Reform Bill Monument has largely been forgotten, even by those living beside it. When I enquired about it at Braelea I was told by a lady who had lived there since the early 1950s that "there's nae monument here". Having shown her the map and where it should be, she kindly directed me in that direction through her parks, still insisting that there was nothing there. A note in SCOTTISH NOTES AND QUERIES for October 1923 records that even the local minister and schoolmaster didn't know of its existence, despite its being marked on OS maps. That note also mentions that other monuments to commemorate the 1832 Reform Act were erected elsewhere in the North-East. Tradition ascribes its creation to Captain Grant who was the tenant of Kirkville House in the late 1830s, and early 1840s. The Reform Act (Scotland having a separate one from England, but at about the same time) made considerable changes to the voting system in the country and is seen as the first step on the way to universal suffrage. There was also a local tradition that the monument was actually built to commemorate the REPEAL OF THE CORN LAWS. The Corn Laws dealt with import duty and free trade and were somewhat later than the Reform Act. However, it is shown as the Reform Cairn and dated 1832 on the plan of the estate at that date. This suggests that perhaps a cairn was set up at the time of the Reform Act and maybe Captain Grant tried to erect a more substantial monument when he became tenant of Kirkville a few years later.

Money or enthusiasm ran out before the monument was finished (or perhaps Captain Grant had given up his tenancy). It had a flight of steps at one time, and these were to have led to a tower, never built. G.M. Fraser visited it in the early 1920s and says that it was then on the farm of Burnside. It is in the form of a semi-circle set against a stone dyke. Fraser says, *"six courses of hammer-blocked masonry have been built all around the semi-circle, to a height of six feet, and a central foundation had been constructed as a base for the monument proper. Great numbers of gathered stones are piled on this general foundation."* Fraser gives the monument as measuring 25 yards (22.86 metres) on the dyke side and 50 yards around the semi-circle. He drew a sketch of it in his unpublished notebooks. The farmer at the time, Mr Low, told him that many years before there had been a flag on the monument, but he had taken it down because people trampled his crops going up to it.

At the time it was built the monument was on Knowles's Hillcarnie or Wester Carnie Estate. In 1923 the estate was bought by Lord Cowdray and Dunecht Estates who, as far as I know, still own it. Unfortunately it has been used as a dump for unwanted stones and is piled high with them, so you get no impression of it ever having been an enclosure. The entrance appears to have been filled in, but in a deliberate manner with shaped stones.

Kirkville / Kirkton: subsequent owners

In the middle of the 19th century the estate of Kirkville comprised the following areas in the eastern half of Kirktoun of Skene:
- The Home Farm which was located in the buildings on the left of the drive as you enter Kirkton House from the village.
- Whitestone Farm
- Rogiehill Farm
- Roadside Farm

- East Kirktoun Farm (later renamed Claylands, though a sale document in 1830 lists these as two separate farms at that time).
- Various crofts, houses and the smithy in the Kirktoun

Wester Carnie is dealt with below in the section on Carnie.

Captain Thomas Shepherd, Honourable East India Company, (H.E.I.C.S.) came from Daviot, where his father was the minister, and while in the service of the East India Company he commanded one of their ships. On retiring and returning to the North-East he rented Straloch House in Newmachar in 1841. Shepherd was related to Mary Ramsay of Barra and Straloch. He supported the Free Church at the disruption and helped build one at Straloch. He bought Kirkville in 1844, having initially been a tenant, and farmed the Home Farm himself. He continued to support the Free Church and, as well as being an elder, for several years he was also Commissioner to the Free General Assembly. His eldest daughter, Christian Susan, married the Reverend Robert H. Ireland, the Free Church minister at Skene, the marriage taking place at Kirkville. Captain Shepherd was a supporter of evangelical religion and spoke at evangelical meetings. He was also a strong supporter of the temperance movement.

Shepherd involved himself in local government and in charitable causes, being a JP, a Commissioner of Supply for the County, and sitting on the board of the County Local Authority. His charitable work included being a member of Aberdeen Medical Mission, the County Prisons Board, and the board of the Industrial and Reformatory School Association. He died in 1875 and is buried in Skene Kirkyard, as is his wife Helen. His gravestone also commemorates his son Alexander who served as a major in the 4th Punjab Infantry and died in India aged 39. The Kirkville Estate was bought in 1879 by James Proctor, whose story is told in the section on Proctor's Orphanage.

Lord Cowdray bought the estate for £11,500 at auction in 1927. The same year the Home Farm buildings were converted – a steading becoming the laundry for Kirkville House and other buildings becoming homes for the estate workers.

McCombie of Easterskene

The name McCombie was well known in Aberdeenshire in the 19th century and three William McCombies, all cousins, were particularly notable.

THE NEW ESTATES AND SOME OF THEIR OWNERS

Kirkville c.1905 with Mrs Proctor

William McCombie of Tillyfour was a celebrated breeder of the Aberdeen Angus, the statue of the Aberdeen Angus bull just outside Alford is a place of pilgrimage for cattle breeders the world over and commemorates the work he and others did in developing the breed. This William was also Liberal MP for West Aberdeenshire, the first tenant farmer to sit in the House of Commons. William McCombie number two farmed at Cairnballoch, Alford, and subsequently became best known as owner and first editor of the ABERDEEN FREE PRESS, one of the forerunners of the PRESS & JOURNAL.

The third member of the family was William

The Kirkville Estate was bought in 1879 by James Proctor, whose story is told in the section on Proctor's Orphanage.

McCombie of Easterskene and Lynturk, less well known than the other two, but in his time equally renowned as an agricultural improver and breeder of the Aberdeen Angus. All three of these men, as with most of the McCombies from West Aberdeenshire, were large men, over six foot tall, testimony to their descent from the 'McComie Mor'! (for more on the legendary McComie More and the origins of the McCombies, see an expanded version of this in an article in LEOPARD magazine April 2010). McCombie of Easterskene is described as being 6ft 2in and very muscular, his brother James being of a similar build.

The McCombies were a branch of Clan McIntosh, reputedly descended from the seventh chief of that clan, and they came to Aberdeenshire from Glenisla. There they had been known as McThomas and the names McThomas and McIntosh were used interchangeably at least until one line of the family moved to Aberdeenshire. Gradually McThomas became corrupted into McThomie, McHomie, McOmie and finally McComie, generally anglicized versions of Gaelic names. Weakened by disputes with other clans, they moved to Aberdeenshire at the end of the 17th century and settled in the Alford area.

William McCombie of Easterskene

Despite one or two of the family flirting with Jacobitism, the McComies settled to a life of farming and prospered in the Alford area, leading to William McCombie, grandfather of our three Williams, being farmer at Lynturk in the second half of the 18th century. He had seven sons, the fifth of whom, Thomas, father of McCombie of Easterskene, was a tobacco and snuff manufacturer in Aberdeen, also owning a snuff mill at Peterculter. Another member of the family also had a snuff and tobacco business in the Castlegate "on the north-east corner of the Plainstones".

THE NEW ESTATES AND SOME OF THEIR OWNERS

Thomas was a baillie and served on the Council at various times in the early 1800s, but refused the Provostship. Thomas's premises were at 51 Netherkirkgate, where Marks & Spencers side entrance is now. His house was at 52 Netherkirkgate, just opposite. Hence when Archibald Simpson came to build on Union Street in 1814, a court running through to Netherkirkgate was named McCombie's Court, one of the few remaining courts in Aberdeen. William, his eldest son, was born in 1802, and was made an infant burgess, normal practice at the time. He attended the Grammar School before graduating from Marischal College in 1820. Thomas's success in business led to him buying various country estates – Jellybrands at Newtonhill, Asleid in Monquhitter. In 1816, he bought lot six (Wester Kirktoun) of the Guild lands, this lot having remained unsold since 1788.

Easterskene House

In 1832 he employed Aberdeen's City Architect, John Smith, to build him a new house at Easterskene. This lovely house, with its walled garden, has views across to the Loch of Skene and Hill of Fare.

67

Shortly afterwards he also bought Millbuie, Lochhead, Dykenook and the Schoolcroft, except for the schoolhouse and the schoolgreen. William fell heir to the snuff mill at Culter and also to Easterskene, as they renamed it, on the death of his father in 1824, a year after William was himself admitted as a full Burgess of Guild of the City. It was at Easterskene that William was to make his mark.

Easterskene comprised the farms of Lochhead, Southbank, Howemoss, Millbuie, and Northbank, as well as the Homefarm and most of the village of Kirktoun of Skene. In a letter dated 1951 his great-nephew, Colonel William Duguid McCombie, wrote, *"when my grand-uncle succeeded to the estate much of the low ground was an unreclaimed marsh, while most of the higher ground was a bare heather moor."* William's work improving the estate included tree planting on a massive scale, enclosing fields, drainage and laying out of roads. In later life William recalled that he had laid out 30 miles of stone dykes. In 1832 he employed Aberdeen's City Architect, John Smith, to build him a new house at Easterskene. This lovely house, with its walled garden, has views across to the Loch of Skene and Hill of Fare, and is in what Smith's biographer calls his 'Tudorbethan' style.

McCombie was no absentee landlord as many other town businessmen were. He himself said that he considered his tenants more as friends. At a dinner of tenants in 1870, his own cousin, McCombie of Tillyfour, commented, *"he lives in his own country and amongst his own tenantry, and he spends his income amongst us. I wish there were more proprietors that did the same."* By this time McCombie of Easterskene had inherited Lynturk from his Uncle Peter, the tobacconist. Consequently his more famous cousin became one of his tenants, renting Bridgend, the largest farm on the Lynturk estate. McCombie's love of his area and its people led him to establish the Skene Games around 1869, quite appropriate for someone whose father had been a champion stone putter on the links at Aberdeen.

A Justice of the Peace for about 60 years, and chairman of Skene Parochial Board for many years, at the age of 65, he took on the role of captain in the recently formed 3rd Aberdeenshire Rifle Volunteers. *"When nearly 70 years of age he stood as straight as many in the ranks, and was the tallest man in his company of 100 volunteers."*

McCombie had a keen interest in history and genealogy, building up a substantial library of antiquarian books. He visited Glenshee on several occasions to find out more about his own clan ancestry. He was *"fond of the local dialect, of which he had a mastery, and of our national music"*. McCombie was a patron of fiddle players, one such being John Strachan, known as Drumnagarrow. John's son, James, worked for 46 years at nearby Garlogie Mills and inherited his father's musical skill, but his shyness meant that he didn't play in public, only for such as his chief patron, McCombie.

During his lifetime, however, McCombie was perhaps best known as a major breeder of black polled cattle, the Aberdeen Angus. His herd was established around 1845 and became a major prize-winning one, including at the Highland Society and the Royal Northern show. As late as 1887 Black Beauty of Easter Skene, a heifer, won first prize in its class and Champion Scot at both Smithfield and Birmingham. Indeed his cousin at Tillyfour admitted that he frequently lost out to him in cattle-breeding, pointing out that, for its size, the herd had produced more prize winners than any herd in the north. At his death the herd was sold off, some of it going to the north of England, but most of it staying in the north, including the top sale Adonis of Easterskene 6517 which sold for 35 guineas (£36 15s).

McCombie died in 1890 aged 88. His funeral was attended by numerous dignitaries including the Earl of Caithness and ex-Lord Provost William Henderson. Twenty carriages conveyed the party from Aberdeen. The ABERDEEN JOURNAL reported his coffin being carried down the tree-lined avenue by relays of the tenantry to "*the quiet little God's acre just outside the policies*". As the cortege passed, the shops in the village were closed and blinds drawn, the church bell ringing every half minute. In 1831 he had married Katherine Ann Buchan Forbes of Invernernan, a Forbes by both her parents. Their joint heraldry can be seen in Kirktoun of Skene. Katherine died young, in 1835, and was followed six years later by their only child Thomas. He did, however, leave an illegitimate daughter. William and Katherine's massive monument of red granite stands in Skene Kirkyard. The McCombies of Easterskene also have a stone in St Nicholas Kirkyard in Aberdeen.

McCombie was succeeded at Easterskene by his nephew, Peter Duguid of Cammachmore, an advocate and expert on heraldry, who added McCombie to his own name. His son, Colonel William Duguid McCombie, was a colonel of the Scots Greys, serving in South Africa and throughout World War I. He lived at Easterskene until he died in 1970 at the age of 96. Some in Skene still remember that, several years before, the regimental band marched up the driveway of Easterskene on the occasion of his 90th birthday. For the last 46 years of his life he was a life tenant of Dunecht Estates, having sold the estate to Lord Cowdray in 1924. It is still owned by Dunecht Estates, the house currently being let out to BP.

The Leddach of Skene

Leddach is a very ancient name, recorded in medieval charters. We have already seen earlier variations of the name as 'Leyddacht' and 'Leddauch',' 'Liddoke' and 'Liddach'. It is thought to derive from Leth – Dauch or Leth – Davoch, dauch being a specific measure of land and leth being half, so half a dauch. THE LEDDACH LAND DISPOSTION, dated 1790, gives the boundaries of Leddach as defined by a series of "cutt march stones". It was bounded on the east by Lott Third, Blackhills (Westhill), and on the west by Lott Fifth, Easter Kirktoun (Kirkville).

From east to west Leddach comprised from Elrick to just short of Mason Lodge, from north to south – Hill of Keir to Carnie Wood, with a wedge further to the south on the east edge of the Carnie Wood. It therefore encompassed Hill of Keir, Broadshade, Berryhill, Kilnhillock, Slack of Larg and Crombie crofts, Broadstraik Inn and Farm, Burnland, and all of present day Elrick.

Leddach: Alexander Crombie

Leddach was bought by Alexander Crombie (1766-1832), then a writer in Aberdeen, later an advocate. He was the only bidder for this lot and he paid £42 sterling plus 45 bolls and 3 firlots of meal. Bolls and firlots being measures of volume rather than weight. In 1806 the feudal superiority of Leddach was also rouped, at the Laigh Tolbooth in Aberdeen, and Crombie was also the successful bidder for that. Crombie was an important person in the burgh, elected President of the Aberdeen Society of Advocates in December 1803. As well as being an advocate he was also a land agent and must have been a very wealthy man because, as well as his lands at Leddach, he also bought Auchronie, and owned property in the city and various properties in Kincardineshire. Although no mansion was built at Leddach in Crombie's time and he never lived there, he was, nonetheless, one of the subscribers to the new turnpike road in 1800. Unlike his neighbour to the east, Alexander Smith of Blackhills, who refused to have the tollhouse on his land, Crombie was quite happy to have it on his. Hence the tollhouse was built further west than originally intended. He was also willing to give out land on very long-term leases – Malcolm Gillespie was given a 38-year lease at Crombie Cottage, as was a Captain Wyness at Earlick, perhaps an indication that he wanted long-term tenants who would improve the land.

While not neglecting Leddach, Crombie's properties in Kincardine were much more important since he owned Thornton Castle between Laurencekirk and Fettercairn. He restored the castle, but he also owned land in Fordoun Parish, and there he had John Smith build Phesdo House for him. A history of that parish records that Crombie was a man of *"invariable sweetness of temper"* and that *"few have led a more useful or honourable life, or died more respected or lamented."* He was also a benefactor to the poor and left a legacy for the Kirk Session in Fordoun.

Crombie left no direct heirs when he died in 1832, so his estates went to his cousin, the Reverend Alexander Crombie. This Crombie had been born in Aberdeen in 1760 and educated at Marischal College. Although licensed by the Church of Scotland he was never ordained, and having run a school in Aberdeen, he subsequently moved to London where he ran private schools, particularly at Greenwich where he had his mansion house. He also acted as a pastor at a Presbyterian meeting house. After 17 years he retired from the school and sold the mansion and its grounds at considerable profit. Crombie was a notable scholar, publishing several books and articles. He died in 1840 at his home at York Terrace, Regent's Park, London, and is buried in Marylebone Church, his obituary appearing in THE TIMES as well as other newspapers throughout the country. Leddach and the other estates passed on through to the reverend's son, another Alexander.

We do not know much about the management of Leddach during these years, although there is evidence that he carried out significant drainage work. When the Reverend Crombie's grandson was married to the daughter of John Marshall of Chatton Park in Northumberland in 1870, his loyal tenants at Leddach in Aberdeenshire, Thornton, Pittarow and Loirston in Kincardineshire, all combined to send the couple a present of a beautiful locket and bracelet set with diamonds and emeralds costing £150. Each group of tenants held a celebration of the event, although without the happy couple, who had headed south from Northumberland after the wedding.

Crombie junior was a Writer to the Signet (W.S.) or advocate in Edinburgh and, as such, managed most of father's estates, including Leddach. The ABERDEEN JOURNAL records that he was well thought of by the Leddach tenants, gaining the love and esteem of them all. He attended to the tenants' needs and never interfered with their freedom of action, meeting them twice a year and wining and dining them at Broadstraik. One tenant in a cottage at Leddach is recorded in the 1861 Census as being a Chelsea Pensioner, Alexander Milne, then aged 79. He is buried in Skene Churchyard where he is described as having been in the 92nd Foot Artillery (later to become the Gordon Highlanders). He died in 1864, Skene's earliest recorded Gordon Highlander. Given his age he most probably served in the Napoleonic Wars. His wife, Elisabeth Watt, was much younger, since she died in 1889 at the age of 75!

The wedding celebration for Crombie junior at Leddach was held in the barn at the Broadstraik Inn and served by innkeeper John Milne and his wife. With the harvest newly in, the company were able to enjoy themselves. Around 50 attended, including tenants and neighbouring lairds such as McCombie of Easterskene, and Rust of Auchinclech who chaired. Also in attendance was Alexander Pirie, tenant of 80 acres at Nether Crofts and Kilnhillock, who acted as ground officer under Crombie and his successor. Flags fluttered from many of the tenants' houses and a bonfire was lit on the Hill of Keir. Once the dinner and toasts were over the ball commenced, the young folk having returned from the bonfire on the hill.

Leddach: Peter Jamieson

By 1878 Leddach, at 622 acres, was advertised for sale by public roup in Edinburgh. The laird had died the year before and presumably his son did not want to keep the property. It didn't sell at first and was re-advertised. The sale notice in the ABERDEEN JOURNAL mentions that on the estate were an inn (Broadstraik), a merchants shop (in Elrick) and a post office (probably not the later one at Mason Lodge, since this was not on Leddach land). Eventually the estate was bought by Peter Jamieson for £16,000.

Jamieson was born at the farm of Nether Cortes near Lonmay in the parish of Rathen in 1817 (although his obituary gives 1818). The farm is still there. His obituary records that he lost both his parents while still young and that he came to Aberdeen at the age of 20. Initially he worked for Alexander (later Sir Alexander) Anderson as a groom or coachman. Anderson was an advocate and businessman and was to become one of Aberdeen's most notable and controversial Victorians, serving as Lord Provost and being commemorated in the naming of Anderson Drive. In turn Anderson would later act as factor and legal advisor to Jamieson. After a few years Jamieson went to work for Isaac Machray who ran mail coaches from the Palace Hotel on Union Street, near Market Street. David Robertson took over the hotel and part of the coach business and Jamieson worked for him. The Palace

THE NEW ESTATES AND SOME OF THEIR OWNERS

was Aberdeen's most famous coaching inn, the building later becoming Falconer's shop which many people still remember.

All Jamieson's working life had involved horses and, while working for Robertson, he devised a unique blacking to give harnesses a shine and to help preserve them. Around 1850 he set up a business to manufacture the blacking, in a small way, in St Nicholas Lane. In 1860 he built a house at 9 South College Street, and a few years later moved production to a factory at 8 South College Street, between Affleck Street and Marywell Street. The business prospered and expanded to worldwide sales, Jamieson patenting his product in America as well selling it in Europe.

Although still involved with the company for a few more years, Jamieson built a house at Leddach, which Mary McMurtrie informs us was

**Peter Jamieson
The Leddach**

always known simply as 'The Leddach'. This was for himself and the five of his daughters who were as yet unmarried and still living at home. Son Peter and eldest daughter Helen were already married, and his wife had died some years before at the age of 40. His great-great-granddaughter has a family tradition that he built Leddach House with a flat roof in imitation of an Italian design that he admired.

Jamieson did not stop there; one of his obituaries records that a number of cottages were built on the estate, from Elrick and Broadstraik up to Hill of Keir under the personal supervision of the laird. These buildings were also flat roofed. Local tradition is that the locals did not approve, viewing the new laird as somewhat eccentric, and the roofs unsuitable for the local climate. After his death the roofs were gradually converted into pitched roofs, but it is possible to see that a few of them were originally flat roofed – the blacksmith's house at Broadstraik, at Hill of Keir Farm, and at Kilnhillock next to Leddach House, now a guest house.

Jamieson was involved with the local community. He attended the Skene Games/Picnic with his daughters, and Peter Jamieson junior (the grandson?) entered pigeons in the Skene Horticultural Association show in 1889. Jamieson died at Leddach in 1887. His funeral carriage left Leddach at 12 o'clock on Saturday 10th September and, at two o'clock, friends from Aberdeen joined the cortege at Queen's Cross. There was a large attendance of relatives and friends from town and county and Jamieson was buried at Nellfield Cemetery.

Leddach: consumption dykes and drainage systems

As mentioned earlier, drainage improvements were carried out under the Crombies. Jamieson also carried out considerable improvements to the estate lands, most notably beginning an elaborate system of drainage, employing 20 men permanently for that purpose. The consumption dykes which survive at the north edge of Carnie Woods and behind the houses opposite the Westdyke Leisure Centre could date to either period. Bill Rose from Aldersyde, Elrick, remembers that the dyke at Westdyke had steps you could climb to walk along it. As far as I can tell virtually all the consumption dykes in the parish were on the Leddach Estate, certainly all that have survived.

It may also have been during Jamieson's time that the dyke features at Broadshade, up the hill from Leddach House, were constructed. These have been surveyed for the recent developers by Murray Archaeological Services

Ltd. Here the field boundary dyke has been built on huge slabs over a box-like culvert, taking the burn from the mill dam and lade at Broadshade, then down the hill towards Leddach and Kilnhillock. Built into the dyke are stone watering troughs for animals, both at ground and dyke level, fed from the culverted water below. There are openings through the dyke, possibly to allow for inspection, as well as access to fresh water for the farm.

Archaeologist Hilary Murray, writing in SKENE HERITAGE NEWSLETTER (No.17, July 2010) comments, "*Dykes, culverted mill lades and even culverts below dykes are known elsewhere in Aberdeenshire, but to date we know of no other example where these are combined with original 19th century livestock watering troughs set in the dyke. Recording these dykes, troughs and culverts, we were constantly struck both by the amount of back-breaking work that had gone into their construction and by the ingenuity with which the natural water supply had been harnessed not only for the mill but also for livestock and human use*".

Tradition has it that the ruined bulding at Foresterhill, just below Berryhill Farm, was built for the dykers.

Some of the features mentioned here are shown on the first OS map from the 1860s and therefore date to the Crombie period. Hilary Murray thinks that the slightly different construction of the troughs to the south of the farm may indicate that they were established by Jamieson, as also the linking of the water system to Leddach House and Kilnhillock. Jamieson's FREE PRESS obituary records that, as well as Leddach House, he also occupied one of the farms at Leddach, 100 acres. THE ABERDEENSHIRE VALUATION ROLL does record him as the occupier of Broadshade in 1886, so he may well have built the dyke and other features on that farm. This area has been developed by Stewart Milne Homes and the remains of the mill dam and lade at Broadshade are now lost, but the dyke features survive. At Kilnhillock stone channels carry the water from Hill of Keir to a mill dam which has been restored. Bill Rose remembers painting a huge water tank behind Leddach House, presumably for the water supply.

Leddach: into the 20th century

The estate was put up for sale in 1891 when it is described as "*divided into convenient farms, fairly housed and let to good tenants. Most of the soil is sharp and easy, and is well watered and drained.*" It did not sell and the family kept it for a few more years.

As early as 1894 Dr Bell had run the Skene surgery from Leddach House and he was followed by Dr Skinner, both probably renting the house. Skinner eventually moved to Westhill House and, in 1901, the Jamieson family put Leddach up for sale. The sale notice describes the house as having three public rooms, seven bedrooms, two dressing rooms, two bathrooms, three WCs, kitchen, servants' and other accommodations, and a fireproof safe. There were gas fittings throughout, with a gas machine and gasoline tank. Outside there were stables for four horses, a coach house with harness room, and a hay loft. Eventually Leddach was sold to Henry Mitchell, formerly of Elmbank, Aberdeen and Inverteith House, Callendar.

In 1921 Mitchell put the estate and house up for sale in individual lots, some being bought by sitting tenants such as Alexander Craigmile, tenant of the Broadstraik Inn and Farm. Elizabeth H. N. Coutts from Kintore bought various crofts and the carpenter's shop at Wester Earlick; she also owned the smithy and a croft at Broadstraik. John Rose, tenant of Mains of Westhill, bought large parts of the estate including Berryhill, Wester Earlick, Hill of Keir, parts of Leddach Farm, Slack of Larg and Broadshade. He also owned various houses at Wester Earlick including Aldersyde. John Williamson bought Leddach Farm and Kilnhillock, though he died shortly after. Burnland was bought by William Melvin from Leggerdale, Dunecht and was then owned by George Leith before being bought in 1937 by William Duguid, whose daughter, Elsie, still lives there. At the time of the sale Crombie Cottage Farm was called New Knabs. By 1940 Charles Anderson, Douglas Anderson and Fanny Anderson were living at different cottages at Crombie.

Around 1930 Doctor Skinner moved back to Leddach House and, after his death in 1937, Doctor Junor bought it and continued it as the surgery. At some point an extension was built at the back of the house to act as a surgery which remained there until Doctor Junor died in 1966 and it became a family house once more. It has remained as such with a series of owners since then.

Kinmundy

Kinmundy is an an old name, recorded, as we have seen, in early charters.

> "In the last generation, legends wild and vague were rife, anent sheeted forms, seen at the most approved ghostly hours, gliding about the policies. Modern skepticism has consigned most of that lore to oblivion, and the house and premises lately enlarged and improved by the present proprietor, present a neat, sunny appearance."

THE NEW ESTATES AND SOME OF THEIR OWNERS

Thus did James Fowler Abernethy speak about Kinmundy House in a talk he gave c.1878. The legends persisted, however, and Mary McMurtrie was told by Mrs Malcolm, who lived there in 1964, that *"she used to find she was apt to stand to one side of a passage as if to let someone pass"*. This was supposed to be the green lady. Other recent tales are of horses refusing to advance towards the house. Mary also said that she had heard tales of a religious foundation at Kinmundy, although I have never seen this recorded in any documented source. The garden contains an 18th century

The Shrine at Kinmundy House

"Legends wild and vague were rife, anent sheeted forms, seen at the most ghostly hours, gliding about the policies."

dovecot, most likely built after the Easter Kinmundy Estate was created in 1789. There is also a 19th century gothic folly known as 'The Shrine'. Maybe it was that which gave rise to stories of a religious foundation and ghostly goings on.

As noted earlier James Davidson, who had bought Easter Kinmundy in 1789, had financial difficulties 10 years later because of a poor harvest. By 1807 the estate was up for sale, though it didn't sell. It was of 412 Scotch acres including the farms of Broadiach, Burnhead, Crabrae, Northside, Lawsondale and Southside, as well as several other crofts, nearly all enclosed and divided with dykes. It also had a plantation of 15 acres. The house stood in a lawn of four acres and had six apartments (rooms) beside garrets. In the 1801/2 window tax it is recorded as having seven windows, not very large. Davidson himself died in 1827 aged 72.

Kinmundy had several owners during the course of the 19th century. These included David Blaikie, advocate and merchant. He had bought the estate in 1830 from various brothers called Thomson, two of whom had been captains in the East India Company. Another of these brothers had been a surgeon in the East India Company, while the fourth was a writer (advocate) in Aberdeen.

William Gibson bought Kinmundy in 1840 and he stayed there until his death in 1865. Born in Lonmay, Gibson had been in Calcutta before buying Kinmundy, several of his children having been born there. Gibson is buried in Skene Churchyard along with his wife and seven of his children, most of whom died in infancy or in their teens. There is also a separate stone for his daughter, Isabella Fowler Gibson, from her bible class and former girls.

Gibson carried out several improvements to the estate including, in 1847, borrowing £1,550 from the Inclosure Commissioners for drainage improvement on his land. Gibson had put the estate up for sale in 1862; it then amounted to nearly 530 acres. In 1866, the year after his death, the estate was put up for sale at a reduced acreage of 444. The next owner seems to have been a widower from Aberdeen, John Webster.

In 1875 the mansion house and combined estates of East Kinmundy and Fiddy were up for sale at 744 acres. The house is described as recently having been added to and improved. It was bought by Mansfield Forbes of Woodend on Deeside and, when he died, it passed to a family member, Lieutenant-Colonel Henry Erskine Forbes (sometimes given as Forbes-Mitchell). He was the son of Henry David Forbes of Balgownie and had served in the East India

Company during the Indian Mutiny, ending up in the 21st Hussars. He had earlier rented Kirkville House for a time. Although a Justice of the Peace, he did not take part in public affairs, and was described in his obituary as being of a retiring disposition. His obituary also says that as a landlord he did much to improve the estate. Forbes died in Germany in 1891, but the estate was owned by his daughters and then his trustees until the 1940s. They didn't actually live there, though, and the house itself was rented out.

Fiddie

George Moir, a vintner of Aberdeen, had been the first owner of the estate of Fiddie after the Dean of Guild, but by 1806 he had sold it to David Low. In 1809 Mr Low of Fiddie advertised for a contractor to build 800-1000 ells (around 1000 yards) of stone dyke on the boundary march between Fiddie and Easter Carnie. In the 1850s it passed from David Low to his son Robert. By 1870 the Lands of Fiddie still belonged to the Low family and were put up for sale after the death of Robert Low. The estate was now about 278 acres and came into the possession of the Forbeses who owned Kinmundy. In 1927 it comprised three farms and some shootings and was owned in life rent by Miss Margaret Isabella Forbes. She also owned Sclattie Brae, which had been part of the Kinmundy Estate. As with Kinmundy, after her death Fiddie continued to be owned by the trustees of Lieutenant Colonel Henry Erskine Forbes.

Brodiach: the Fowler family of doctors

In early documents Brodiach is described as a pendicle attached to Easter Kinmundy. A document of 1692 defining the lands of Easter Skene refers to Easter Kinmundy comprehending the pendicle called Broadiache and Easter Carnie. A pendicle is a small piece of land attached to a larger estate, though it can refer to an ecclesiastical dependency, and, as we have seen, there are persistent stories that Kinmundy was an ecclesiastical foundation at one time. At the time of the sale of the Easter Skene lands, Brodiach was tenanted by the Fowler family who had farmed there since at least the mid-18th century. Andrew Fowler of Brodiach was a member of the Kirk Session in 1757, and the Fowlers seem to have bought it as a separate holding from James Davidson of Easter Kinmundy.

Brodiach was a very small property, only 30 acres at the 1851 Census, though somehow employing three labourers. Andrew Fowler, the first owner, was also described as a merchant, though it is not clear what kind of merchant, and he must have had income from more than just his farm. Andrew died in 1827 and was succeeded by his son, also Andrew. In 1845 this Andrew was appointed first Inspector of Poor for the parish of Skene for an annual remuneration of £10. Like his father, he must have had income from sources other than his farm. This was a small farm rather than an estate, but he called himself a landed proprietor in the Census and he seems to have acted like a landowner – being a subscriber to the Aberdeen Town & County Banking Company, for example, and owning property in Old Aberdeen. He is recorded donating to the Royal Infirmary funds and the Chicago Relief Fund following the great fire there.

Andrew was obviously educated and this helps explain the remarkable fact that four of his sons became medical doctors. Two of them died in their mid- thirties, John Smith Fowler MD, in 1878, and George William Fowler MD, in 1887. The other two sons lived to old age and one, James Elsmie Fowler, became a very well known figure and is written about in a later chapter. Andrew himself died in 1884 at the age of 92 and is buried with several of his family in Skene Kirkyard.

Brodiach: the building, the sundial and the curious arched bridges

Brodiach was visited by City Librarian and local historian, G.M. Fraser, in 1918 and again four years later. The farmhouse still survives, described by Fraser as "*a fine farm house – unusually long with front of dressed granite.*" It was originally the Six Mile Inn on the Old Skene Road, though never a coaching inn as has sometimes been stated. It has an eight-foot high cellar for storing barrels of wine and whisky. When the turnpike was opened in 1803 it would have ceased to be an inn, just as happened to the old Broadstraik. Brodiach also had a large horse watering trough against the dyke near the steading, but it had gone by 1969 when Mary McMurtrie vistited, though she remembered it. Further west from the steading there was a threshing mill later used to generate electricity. The mill building is still there, now a private house, and the old wheel lies buried under the drive.

The Brodiach sundial is a huge stone, originally built into a dyke in the cornyard of Brodiach Farm. The date 1790 is carved on it and also engraved on the metal gnomon. The gnomon also has the name Jos. Allen, which gives a clue as to its origin. Cuthbert Graham speculated that he might have been a ploughman. The truth, however, is rather different. A gravestone in Skene Kirkyard reveals that Joseph Allan was the schoolmaster at Skene for 62 years, dying in 1819 aged 87. His daughter, Elizabeth, married Andrew Fowler from Brodiach, though she died quite young aged 34 in 1799. Perhaps her father made the sundial as a wedding gift.

On his visit in 1918 G.M. Fraser met Mr and Mrs Alexander, tenants, who said they had been there for 30 years, probably following the death of Andrew Fowler. Bert Rennie, self-taught mason, inherited part of Brodiach from his wife, who was an Alexander. He subsequently built houses for himself, his daughter and his brother-in-law, all to the north of the original farmhouse. Bert determined to take the sundial with him and it is now in the garden of his house.

The Brodiach sundial being moved

Bert reckons that the sundial must weigh around four tons, since he had a digger able to lift two-and-a-half and it could not budge the sundial. He told me that there was a story that the sundial had come from Skene House, transported on a sledge. James Cruickshank, writing in DEESIDE FIELD in 1959, said that it had supposedly been transported from Skene (not Skene House) by sledge in frosty weather. A sundial is marked on the first OS map of 1869 on the site where the original Skene School and schoolmaster's house were situated on the Half-Milie. (see the section on Skene School). This would have been where Joseph Allen lived, so maybe the Fowler's of Brodiach moved the sundial from there at the time when the new Skene School was built. If so, this would have represented an impressive achievement in the days of horse-drawn carts and sledges. I still think it more likely that it was built *in situ*.

Also at Brodiach there are at least three curious stone arched bridges commented on both by G.M. Fraser and Mary McMurtrie. They consist of a single line of flat stones sat edge-ways in an arch over the various burns. Fraser says that they were made by Fowler some 80 years before he visited the farm. On the gable of Brodiach farmhouse there are clear signs that a second storey was added and on the upper part is the date 1850. Another curiosity associated with Brodiach is a small granite trough that I found being used as a plant trough in the Cruickshank Botanical Gardens of Aberdeen University. This has the old spelling 'Broadiach' on one side and the date 1848 on the other. When I asked the head gardener how it came to be at the Cruickshank, he didn't know, although he did say that it had the initials GF on the base. This gives a clue as to its origin and perhaps also the person who built the bridges and worked on the extension to the farmhouse.

The 1851 Census tells us that living at Brodiach at that time was George Fowler, unmarried brother of Andrew. George was a retired merchant and it seems that he might have had the time to make the trough and bridges Some have tried to treat the bridges as actual bridges, but I feel they are really follies or for children to play on. Bert Rennie has restored the arched bridges from time to time, with two being re-done in 2011. Mary McMurtrie mentions that there were several small troughs at Brodiach, and a further sundial on the wall of the farmhouse made by James Milne of Inverurie.

Wester Kinmundy / Blackhills / Westhill

Alexander Smith is described as a merchant at Silverburn of Counteswells, where his father farmed. He bought both Wester Kinmundy and Blackhills in 1788 and presumably he built himself a house at Blackhills, hence he was known as Alexander Smith of Blackhills, rather than Wester Kinmundy. That house later became Westhill House and seems to have been a relatively simple, farm-house-type building with seven windows at the time of 1801/2 window tax. It has been gradually added to over the years. No mansion house was built at Wester Kinmundy. Alexander lived to the ripe age of 88 and died in 1837, "*among the first to die from influenza which appeared in the district at that date for the first time*". One his sons, also Alexander, inherited the two estates. He seems to have had financial problems and, in 1859, he sold the two estates to John Anderson, a factor from Strichen, and cousin to Aberdeen's most controversial provost, Sir Alexander Anderson. At that time the two estates seem to have taken the main name of Blackhills, and Anderson, not liking either of the original names, took part from each and came up with the name Westhill. In the words of the SASINE REGISTER from December 1859, the two lots of Easter Skene "*now conjoined in one estate presently known as Blackhills is to be henceforth designated Westhill*".

Under Anderson in 1870 the estate comprised:
- Westhill Mains

- Three farms of Wester Kinmundy
- Crofts of Wester Kinmundy and Bridgefoot
- Five crofts of Westhill
- Crofts of Mains, Mosside, Brae
- Cairnton Cottage (occupied by William Williamson)
- A shop and land (occupied by William Williamson, merchant)
- House at Westhill (occupied by David Williamson, flesher)

Anderson was married to a sister of Doctor Farquhar of Rubislaw Terrace, and the latter ultimately heired the property. His son, Reverend William Muir Farquhar of Harwell, London, inherited it from his father.

In 1900, when Westhill House was to let, it is described as a desirable country residence with three public rooms, six bedrooms, servant's accommodation, a four-horse(?) stable, coach house and large, productive and well-sheltered garden. Wester Kinmundy farmhouse was known by locals as 'The Brae'. The croft house was known as Brae Croft up until the building of modern Westhill, hence the street name Braecroft.

Carnie

As we have seen already, Carnie has a pedigree as old as Skene and was probably not part of the original grant of land to the Skene family. In fact it was not even part of the Sheriffdom of Aberdeen until the 17th century. By the end of that century it had been acquired by Burnett of Craigmyle and subsequently became part of the Dean of Guild lands. It was variously spelt Cardeney, Carny, Carnie, Cairnie, the latter particularly in the 19th century. Today it is pronounced locally without the 'i', perhaps reflecting the older versions.

The two Carnies, Easter and Wester, were fairly large estates, though with a considerable amount of poor ground and moss. Perhaps because of this there were no offers for either of the Carnies at the initial roup of 1788. At a subsequent roup in 1825 Easter Carnie still didn't sell and much of it remained in the town's ownership until the latter half of the 20th century, with Carnie Wood still owned by the City of Aberdeen today. Perhaps for that reason there was less improvement done in Easter Carnie and, as late as 1825, a valuation for the land still referred to infield and outfield.

Wester Carnie (also known as Hillcarnie) was eventually sold to James Knowles of Kirkville in 1824. The estate comprised a considerable amount of woodland as well as the farms at Gask, Springhill of Carnie, Hatton of

Carnie, Latch of Carnie, etcetera. As well as carrying out improvements to the land, Knowles was something of a conservationist The ABERDEEN JOURNAL for 24th August 1825 records how he tried to conserve wild-life on the new lands. *"Cautions to sportsmen. The muir of Carnie in the parish of Skene while the property of the town of Aberdeen for many years having been much infested with poachers of all kinds, notice is hereby given that the present proprietor, Mr Knowles, is desirious to preserve for some time the few remaining there, and he will not allow any person whatever to shoot wild duck or other waterfowl there, or game of any kind to be killed on the lands of Kirkville without written authority. Trespassers may rely upon being prosecuted."*

In 1847 as Hill Carnie it was put up for sale by William Knowles. It then consisted of 830 acres with 470 arable and 180 in planting, the remainder improveable pasture, a considerable difference from what it had been when it was for sale in 1788. The wood, enclosed by stone dykes, had been planted between 1826 and 1832. The estate, as eventually bought by the Society of Advocates, was 1037 acres, bought to provide revenue for their fund for *"needy members, widows and orphans"*. They carried out considerable improvements to the estate as well; for example, advertising in 1854 for contractors to trench five acres of moor and mossy ground at Hatton and Little Gouk of Hillcarnie, and again in 1870 for the mason, carpenter and slater work needed to build a new farmhouse at Broadwater. Most of the farms on the estate were very small, and in 1843 they were advertised for rent as follows:

- Standing Stones 29 acres
- Little Gask 21 acres
- Springhill with additional ground at Leuchar-Burn 60 acres
- Hatton 46 arable, 35 moor or pasture
- Harryholme and croft at Carnie Village 15 acres
- Latch 16 acres, though land from Eastside could be added

In 1870 the estate comprised Little Gask; East and North Gask; Standingstones; Burnside; Hatton and Halebutts; Inverord; Springhill; Village Lands; Broadwater; Farm of Carnie Village; New Croft; crofts of Carnie Village, Brae of Leucher, Braes, Woodside and Howcroft.

In the early 1920s Hillcairnie or Wester Carnie was sold to Dunecht Estates who still own most of it.

Ord

Ord, as we have seen, was mentioned as belonging to the Earl Marischal in the late 16th century. In 1619 William or Walter Ord was described as the proprietor of Ord, but holding the lands from the Earl Marischal. The same year Alexander Ord was granted the right by the earl to dispone Ord to William Davidson to be held blench (at a nominal or small quit-rent). In the 1680s Captain James Basken of Ord, possibly from Ireland, was one of the three heritors in the parish and gave mortification to the Kirk of Skene. His ownership was not very long and I presume that Ord came into the hands of the Burnetts of Craigmyle and hence to the Dean of Guild.

John Smith had bought the lands of Ord in 1790, possibly because it adjoined lands he already owned at the Hole Mill in the next door parish of Peterculter. He also bought a *"haugh called Meadow of Lasts"* across the Ord Burn in Peterculter. At some point around 1880 Andrew Fowler's family from Brodiach fell heir to the estate of Easter Ord, the site of one of the parish meal mills, and this continued to belong to Doctor Andrew Smith Fowler into the 1920s. Jean Smith Fowler, unmarried and living on her own means, occupied Easter Ord House in 1901 and was still there in the 1920s.

Concraig and Auchinclech

I apologise for the confusing nature of the following section. It has been quite difficult to piece together the history of these two properties and the sasine record is complex to follow as the original estate of Auchinclech became divided up. Auchinclech seems to have been the older name of the whole area. Auchinclech and Concraig were not part of the Dean of Guild lands, and strictly speaking should not be part of this chapter. They did experience considerable change in the 18th century, however, and so it is convenient to deal with them here. They are both mentioned in the Dean of Guild documents for 1788, in connection with peat casting rights in the Moss of Easter Carnie, away to the south. At that time both Concraig and Auchinclech are listed along with their pendicles of Souterhill, Bottomford and Clockmore, suggesting that these three were fermtouns of some kind at this time.

Originally Auchinclech belonged to the Earl of Kintore, son of the Earl Marischal, recorded as Auchincloich in the REGISTER OF THE GREAT SEAL for 1506. It still belonged to him at the time of the 1696 Poll Tax. The three fermtouns named at that time are Auchinclech, Boddomfawld (Boddemford), and Brissock with its mill (later called Birsack); there is no mention of Concraig. The Earl of Kintore connection may explain why the original house of Concraig was built by Patrick Sympson (Simpson). His father Alexander was chamberlain or factor to the Earl of Kintore, and Alexander's brother was Robert Simpson of Thornton. Alexander acquired Concraig before 1713, presumably from the Earl of Kintore, and Patrick is described as "younger of Concraig" in 1729. Patrick died in 1762, aged 73 and his heir, Alexander, died just six years later. The estate seems to have passed to Patrick's sister, Margaret and her husband Lieutenant Colonel (later Hon. Major General) Mark Napier, a younger son of Lord Napier.

In 1778 Margaret Simpson and her husband, Lieutenant Colonel Mark Napier, sold the Auchinclech part of the estate to George Wilson of Glasgowego, a merchant in Aberdeen, who also bought the Dean of Guild's 16th lot, Rotten, in the neighbouring parish. Auchinclech subsequently passed to John Wilson. In 1783 Margaret also sold part of the estate to David Menzies, son of William Menzies of Pitfodels. In his obituary in 1788 he is described as David Menzies of Concraig.

So we have the original estate of Auchinclech split into two. The Menzies part was advertised for sale by John Menzies of Pitfodels in 1801, though David's widow, Henrietta, seems to have occupied it at this time. It was not yet enclosed or improved since it contained 116 acres of infield, 120 of outfield, 104 pasture and 21 of moss. At the same time John Robert Smith, a merchant from Trinidad, bought part of Auchinclech called Souterhill, Boddamford and Clochmore, also consisting of Mains of Concraig, Broadtree, Craigston and the Mill of Birsack. Some of these Wilsons and Menzies are buried in the Snow Kirk in Old Aberdeen, so they may have been Catholic families – the Menzies of Pitfodels family certainly were. The ruined Snow Kirk became a burial ground for some of Aberdeen's more notable Catholic families.

In the 1801/2 Window Tax Concraig had 13 windows, suggesting it was quite substantial, only Skene House in the parish having more. Keith, in his GENERAL VIEW OF AGRICULTURE OF ABERDEENSHIRE in 1811, describes it as "*a very good modern house, the property of John Smith esq, with some patches of wood, and a farm, well cultivated*".

The house of Concraig was advertised for let in 1843 when it contained a sunk floor with kitchen, wash-room, etcetera; a first floor with a parlour, three bedrooms and four pantries; the second floor had dining and drawing rooms as well as a pantry, a closet and a further two bedrooms. There was also a coach-house and a two-stalled stable. At that time it belonged to Gavin Mitchell Smith, and he is described as proprietor and farmer, but also as a merchant and druggist in Aberdeen. Gavin's heir was his second cousin, John Fleming Smith, living in Brandywine, Delaware. The estate, when it was up for sale in December 1846, was 466 acres. It included Mains of Concraig, Hillhead, Mill of Birsack, Craigston and Broadtree.

Sometime around 1847 King's College received the lands of Concraig under the will of Alexander Murray D.D, of London and then Philadelphia, and the will of George Hutton of Deptford, Kent. Murray and Hutton seem to have bought the lands for the university from John Fleming Smith. Or perhaps the university initially just received the revenues, as the ownership of the estate was referred to as the Trustees of Murray & Hutton's mortifications. The lands at this time comprised Souterhill, Boddamford, Clockmore, Place of Concraig, Broadtree and Craigston, the Mill of Birsack, and a share of the mosses of Easter Carnie and Arnhall. At some point, perhaps after the death of the two men, the university came to own Concraig and it continued to belong to the university until well into the 20th century. In 1847, as proprietors of Concraig and therefore a heritor, the advocate for King's College attended the meeting of the Parochial Board. Part of the walls of a walled garden still survive, just south of the present Concraig House.

The lands and estate of Auchinclech, when up for sale in 1821, consisted of 360 acres held of the Crown. There was at that time a granite quarry on the estate, apparently undeveloped. John Wilson is described as the tacksman of Auchinclech in the early 1800s. He may have bought the north half of Auchinclech and parts of Broadtree, because in 1836 it was seised in life rent and fee to James Rust, merchant at Cotton and Williamson Rust, his son, by John's daughter Elizabeth Wilson.

William Carnegie, who had farmed at Easter Ord, owned the southern half of Auchinclech in the middle of the century and lived at Newton of Auchinclech. He had bought the land from the sequestered estate of a John Aberdein in 1840. In 1850 he sold it off in lots with the Rev. John Souter, then schoolmaster at Drumblade, buying the south half which contained the farm of Souterhill. One might think that the Rev. Souter gave his name to Souterhill Farm, but it seems to have had that name well before Souter's ownership. Souter also bought another lot containing the New Croft and Gallyfarm.

Just over 10 years later, Souter sold his lands to Alexander Johnston of North Broadford, near Aberdeen. Johnston created a mini-estate which he called Johnston. The properties on this small estate took the name of it – thus

87

Galleymoss of Johnston, Souterhill of Johnston, etcetera. He had to borrow money, however, perhaps to fund his purchase, but at any rate using the land as collateral. Although it passed to his son Alexander, a surgeon in the army serving at Cape Coast Castle in South Africa, the estate was sequestered and sold to Ewen Macdonald, a merchant in the Gallowgate in Aberdeen, who owned it until his death in 1897.

In the early 20th century Robert Barron was the tenant of Concraig and also owned South Auchinclech. Benjamin Cassie tenanted Auchinclech. By the 1930s Benjamin had bought Auchinclech, including the Crossroads.

The Parish Church of Skene

The church of Skene is said to have been dedicated to St Bride. It is possible that a chapel existed here in the 12th century, when Skene was probably part of the Earldom of Mar, and parishes were established as part of the Normanisation of Scotland. In 1466 the Lady of Echt drew up a divorce document in what was called the Chapel of the Holy Trinity of Skene. Skene was not a separate parish in medieval times, but rather one of the six chapels or pendicles of what was effectively the large parish of Kinkell, the others being Drumblade, Dyce, Kemnay, Kinellar, and Kintore. The revenues from these chapels seem to have gone to the Knights Hospitallers at Torphichen in the early 14th century. In 1420, however, Kinkell and its chapels were made a prebend of St Machar Cathedral by Henry de Lychtone (Leighton). This meant that the bulk of revenues would have gone to support an official of the cathedral based in the Chanonry.

In the 1530s Bishop Gavin Dunbar endowed an almshouse, known later as the Bedesmen's Hospital, at the end of the Chanonry near the cathedral. Part of the endowment for this hospital, £20 Scots, came from the lands of Skene. Kinkell itself may have had a senior official, such as Alexander Galloway mentioned below, especially as it was connected to the Thanage of Kintore and the Keith family. The other chapels, if they had a separate official at all, would have been served by a vicar pensioner, or junior official, often an impoverished one because of the siphoning off of revenues to the cathedral. For example, we hear that in 1574 Skene had Thomas Bissait, a reader. At the time of the homage done to Edward I we know that two Skenes affixed their seal to the Ragman Roll. One of them is described as "*clericus*" and it has been assumed that he was vicar of Skene and owned land in the area. However it seems unlikely that if Skene was only a pendicle of Kinkell, a senior member of its main landowning family would serve as vicar.

In 1539, as we have already seen, Alexander Galloway, rector of Kinkell, received a croft next to the church at Skene from the Earl Marischal to build a manse for the vicar (croft here meaning the land on which the house was built). Galloway was an important figure and had acted as overseer on several building projects for the Bishop of Aberdeen, including the bridge over the Dee. We can deduce, then, that there was some kind of a vicar at Skene at this date. In medieval times the number of parishes fluctuated, however, and it is not certain that Skene had an uninterrupted line of vicars or parsons from 1539. It may have continued to share its parson with other chapels, even though it had a manse for one. John Quhyt (White), for example, served Skene, Methlick, Fintray and Kintore, from the 1570s until 1607. By that time he was described as being of "*gryte aige and faillit in doctrine*". Although he was admonished not to read homilies at the kirk under pain of deprivation, he continued until 1609.

Alexander Youngson was appointed to assist White in 1599, and he is named minister at Skene in the action against Mathew Stenchin, kirk officer, mentioned in the section on Skene and the Keith family. That action centred on John White's croft, so White must have continued to live at Skene despite having an assistant there as well. It would appear that White couldn't be shifted from his church or his croft. Youngson was to preach one Sunday at Skene and the next at Durris, so there was no requirement that the ministers had to serve only within the various chapels coming under Kinkell. Also overlapping with White was Alexander Scrogy in the early 1600s. He was one of a number of ministers charged with taking part in an unlawful assembly in Aberdeen in July 1605, i.e., they were trying to hold a General Assembly. Scrogy and nine others acknowledged that this was unlawful and were admonished.

Although not yet a full parish church, Skene was not neglected by the Presbytery. In 1599, for example, David Rait, minister of St Machar Cathedral and principal of King's College, "*makis next (next exercise, or took the worship) at the kirk of Skeyne, quilk is ordenit to be visit that day, togider witht Kinnelar this daye*".

In 1649 the Parliament of Scotland passed an Act of Dissolution "*dissolving, disuniting and separating*" Skene and the other chapels under Kinkell and erecting them into six separate parishes. William Chalmer or Chalmers, the existing minister of Skene, was ordained to be the parish minister. As we have seen, Chalmers was the minister at the time of the Civil War and his house had been "*plunderit*" by some of Montrose's men.

The old church

The old church of Skene stood just to the south of the present one. Although no real description of it exists we can get some idea about it from the Kirk Session records and from details in the Skene Estate records. Some of these records testify to the poor state of repair of the church. The minister at the time of the first STATISTICAL ACCOUNT says that no one knew when it was built, but that it was very old and had not been repaired for a long time.

In 1676, "*it being a rainy day, the roof of the kirk was so ruinous that the raine descended on the table and abused the table cloath so yt the holy symbol of the blessed lady and blood of Jesus Chryst were in danger to be dropped on by the raine, had they not been carefully covered, and that the minister was necessitate to change his usual posture – place of administration and goe from the east end of the tables to the west end of the church which was safest from raine*".

The following year the heritors, minister and elders met to inspect the church and found that "*the roof and quire did neid present reparation*". A payment was made to contract the "*sklaiter*," and he was subsequently also paid to demolish the old bellhouse. Country churches were often thatched until the mid 18th century, but Skene was certainly slated well before that time. In 1677, 500 slates were supplied and a further 1,000 ordered, every two plough teams in the parish being told to join together to help transport them. Six Norwegian daills (planks) were also bought and the smith made 860 nails. In addition, 15 bolls of lime came from Strathisla. The whole cost is itemised in the Kirk Session records including £2 13s. (Scots) for meal for the slater, and 13s. 4d. paid to Elspet Hall for drink for him. A bell tow (rope) was also bought, a payment having also been made to "*ye merchant*" for bringing home a new bell.

Only five years later, in 1682, the church needed a major rebuilding and the new bell tower had still not been built. On this occasion the material needed was 300 daills, 2600 single nails and 400 double nails for new work, and 500 nails for old work. 8,000 slates were also ordered from Culsalmond.

New communion tables were also made at this time, it taking two wrights two days to make them. The bell tower was not built until 1695 *"on the western gavel of the kirk"*. It had been paid for mainly by the minister, Ludovic Dunlop, who did not live to see it being built. He died in 1691, having left 100 merks towards the cost. His son and successor, John, also gave money towards it.

Obtaining money or assistance from the heritors was often the cause of delays in improvements to the church. On this occasion the heritors did agree to help, with the Laird of Skene ordering seven horses to be sent to Crathes for timber for the scaffolding, and seven for stone; the Earl of Kintore's tenants at Auchinclech sent five horses for timber and four for stones; Andrew Burnett of Craigmile, for Easter Skene, promised to send twelve horses for trees and fourteen for stones. Finally, in August 1695, £1.4s (£1.20p) was given to James Booth for making a new bell tongue, and 15s (75p) for a bell rope. The following month the tower was completed by Kenneth Fraser, mason in Old Aberdeen.

Other problems faced by the church in the 1680s were people leaving their horses in the churchyard and several men being called before the session for *"abuseing the churchyaird with the foot ball"*!

In the 18th century the church was still in constant need of repair. In January and April 1723 the scripture reading was cancelled because of the cold day and the ruinous condition of the church. The same thing happened in November 1725.

The church was probably a simple rectangular building aligned east–west. The bulk of the seats would be assigned to each heritor's tenants. It may have had a loft in the 17th century and in the 18th century it certainly had several. Lofts at each end of a church were common. In 1747 the minister spoke to the heritors living in the parish and to Aberdeen Town Council, to get permission to build a new loft at the back of the church, and also to reduce the seats belonging to the Laird of Ord from three to two. Presumably extra seats were needed for general use. The loft was built and the seats let out at a charge of six pence for the front row, five for the second and four for the third. Each pew contained 15 seats and the money from these open rental seats went to the poor fund.

This loft may have been the common loft which, by 1764, was described as being in a perilous state. Application was made to the magistrates of Aberdeen *"in whose part of the kirk it now is, either to repair it themselves or let the session repair it and set (rent out) the seats thereof to the behoof of the poor"*. The Skene House papers refer to the seats let to Skene of Skene's tenants. In 1774 they mention the pews in the loft, the gavel seat and the low kirk – north side and south side. The 1788 accounts mention the long loft as well as the south side and the north side, which does suggest an east-west axis for the church. The Town Council allowed the session to repair the loft, but claimed preference for their tenants in the letting of the seats. This loft is described as the "*gavill*" or gable loft, so must have been at one end of the rectangular church.

An inventory of the church "*utensils*" in 1747 lists four silver cups and two pewter for the communion, a communion table cloth, a mortcloth of plusk, a parcel of between 300-400 tokens, a basin and cloth for baptisms, and an old folio Bible. Three years later they needed new cups for the communion wine, two of the silver cups being no use. They were given to William Forbes, copper and silversmith in Aberdeen, to make into new cups. Another problem the session had in the 18th century was "*bad copper*". This could be old coinage no longer valid, or foreign coins, put into the collection. They were also sold to the coppersmith for melting down.

Ludovic and John Dunlop: national events come to Skene once more

Ludovic or Lewis Dunlop was born in 1620 and educated at King's College. He became minister at Tarland in 1649 and moved to Skene in October 1664. He was married to Elizabeth, daughter of William Douglas, Professor of Divinity at King's College. Ludovic is the first minister of Skene to be recorded in a volume of the kirk session records, and some of these records may even be in his handwriting. As we have seen he was responsible for a bell tower being built at Skene Church. This was actually recorded on his gravestone in Skene Kirkyard as transcribed by Andrew Jervise in the 1870s. It read, "*to say much in his praise would perhaps savour of vain glory; but amongst other laudable actions, it is deserving to record that the belltower of the church was erected in great measure at his expense. His better part now dwells in heaven with Christ He died 6th February, 1691*".

Jervise records that the tabular stone of a much later minister, James Hogg, was placed over Dunlop's one, but obviously Dunlop's could still be read at that time. Curiously, although Hogg's one is still there today, there is no trace of Dunlop's below it.

Ludovic was succeeded by his son, John, in 1686, though from just before that time, and for several years after, both men shared the duties. The kirk session minutes record that one Sunday the "*minister older*" preached, the next

Sunday that the *"minister younger"* preached. John's brothers Alexander and George also preached on occasions, as did their relative Alexander Douglas.

Events nationally were announced in the church at this time and these would have major consequences for John Dunlop. On May 12th, 1689, for example, a proclamation was read for prayers to be said for King William and Queen Mary, as ordained by the Convention of Estates. The following Thursday was appointed a day of thanksgiving, *"for our late delivery from popery and arbitary government by King William"*. This was repeated in September and, in October 1690, there was thanksgiving for King William's happy success in Ireland (the Battle of the Boyne took place in July that year).

John Dunlap (sic), minister, is recorded in the Poll Tax book of 1696, along with his mother, Elizabeth Dowglas, Margrat Dowglas, and his servant Thomas Burnet, as well as three other servants who may also be his. The kirk session record stops in November 1695, then it jumps to June 1696, when the minister is recorded giving some of his own, and a friend's, and part of his late father's mortification, to the relief of the poor. The last entry is June 18th, 1696. John Dunlop was deprived of the benefice for non-jurancy, though this was not noted in the kirk session minutes. This means that he refused to swear the oath of allegiance to King William. After the restoration of the Stuarts following the Civil War, Episcopalianism was made the state religion of Scotland. When James II was overthrown and the crown offered to William of Orange, part of the agreement for Scotland to accept William as King was that Presbyterianism would again become the official religion of the country. Many ministers refused to take the oath, either because of their episcopal beliefs, or because they felt that they had already sworn an oath to King James. They were removed from office until such time as they did take the oath. This may explain the gap in the records between November 1695 and June 1696.

It actually took around 50 years before every episcopalian minister was removed from what had been the diocese of Aberdeen. Throughout Scotland several hundred ministers were deposed. It seems that John Dunlop never did take the oath (his epitaph says that he would not violate his duty to God or his loyalty to his King, nor approve of those changes that had been made to government of both church and state). He lost his position and would have been evicted from the manse. It would be interesting to know what his congregation at Skene thought of this. His brother secured a position as rector in Nunnington, Yorkshire. We do not know what happened to John, though his epitaph says that he retired and employed himself in the service of God. The epitaph also records that he suffered from a long painful disease and that he died, unmarried, on the 27th April 1714, aged 55, being buried with his grandfather at St Machar's. A collection of over 300 volumes donated to Marischal College by John Dunlop are in Aberdeen University Library. A huge memorial gravestone in St Machar Churchyard commemorates Professor William Douglas, Ludovic Dunlop and John Dunlop.

Mortifications and other money

Mortifications were used for payments to the poor as covered in the section on poverty in the parish. Money was also collected in the church, and from hiring out mortcloths, etcetera. This money was sometimes held by one of the heritors, usually the Laird of Skene. The laird looked on this as money he could use for whatever purpose and then pay back when asked. Sometimes this was recognized as a loan and interest was specified, at other times he just used it and the kirk session had to petition him to get it back. In the 1670s Captain James Basken of Ord had left a mortification of 100 merks. This had been in the care of Jean Burnett, Lady Skene. When she died in 1688 the session seems to have had trouble getting access to the money from her son, Alexander. He said that in law he was not obliged to pay it, but did agree to pay "*anrent*" (annual interest) on the sum. This amounted to £4 Scots in 1692. In 1742 £449 Scots was in the hands of the Laird of Skene and a further 200 merks in the hands of Patrick Symson, Laird of Concraig; both of them had left a bill or receipt in the session box. As late as 1747, George Skene borrowed £55 from the minister, Arthur Mitchell, and the loan document was signed by the members of the kirk session. When Patrick Symson died in 1762 he left 200 merks to the poor. No sooner was the money paid over by his daughter Betty, than it was lent to his heir, Alexander, at four-and-a-half per cent interest. Even into the 19th century the Laird of Skene was borrowing the money at four per cent interest.

The Kirk Session

From the Reformation until at least the Disruption of 1843, kirk sessions had considerable power. They were responsible for education, poor relief and moral discipline. They could interrogate people suspected of having sex outside marriage (or even being seen alone together), as well as other offences such as public order, profaning the Sabbath, etcetera. They could fine them and require them to appear before the congregation over a period of several Sundays. This applied to people from other parishes guilty within Skene, or with someone from Skene, and those from Skene who fled to another parish.

We read in, 1681, of the session buying a sack-cloth for repentance. We also read of a pillar of repentance, no details of the pillar are given, except it seems to have been in a public place. Some churches had a stool of repentance and at others you might have to appear at the market cross. In 1747 a pillory is mentioned at Skene. The session could also pursue women suspected of having illegitimate babies, even into other parishes. It is surprising to us in these days of defaulting fathers and DNA tests that the moral pressure applied by the kirk session could make a man admit to being the father of an illegitimate child. Similarly, we cannot imagine the stigma in the 18th and 19th centuries of having your church membership withdrawn. Among other things, the church would provide you with a reference to take to a future employer. To have that withdrawn could make life difficult.

Some examples from the Skene Kirk Session minutes can illustrate this:

June 3, 1677 "*The said day John Walker was delated (accused) to have walked scandalouslie with Helen Able before her marriage and also upon the day of her marriage.*" John followed this up two weeks later when he confessed, "*he was overtaken with drink on that day of Helen Able's wedding and that he drew an durk the said day against the brother who was intending to separate John from the said Helen qu he was openlie kissing and embracing*". A few years later John was summoned again for having rung the church bell at midnight!

November 1679 "*George Johnston for scandalous conversation with Margaret Ord his servant-woman and which Margaret is reputed to have dyed in child-birth in the parish of Echt in the house of William Harthill in Finercy.*" The minister wrote to the minister at Echt to find any witnesses. Several advised that there was "*scandalous conversation*" between the two and that George came to Echt to bury Margaret. Further witnesses reported that they "*did both ly within an locked room together alone, her bed being at the foot of his, during the whole winter time till the end of the barley harvest*". Eventually he confessed that he did lie in the same room, but that his present and previous harvest women did the same and would continue to do so. Alexander Aberdeen, his manservant, swore that he and his neighbour slept in the barn, but that George and Margaret "*lay in the fire house with an locked door*".

April 1681 Elizabeth Skene professed repentance for her adultery in sackcloth.

August 1681 Alexander Ardes and Janet Davidson "*confessed their fornication.*

Ordained each to pay five pounds of penalty and to appeare on the pillar the place of publick repentence".

December 1721 Andrew Begg and Mary Cruickshank of Auchinclech guilty of antenuptial fornication. In April the following year they were guilty again and Margaret was to be seriously dealt with "*to bring her to a sense of her shame*". Andrew had to appear five times before the congregation.

May 1724 "*Several elders reported that John Gray and William Killans in Easter Kinmundie had profaned the Lord's Day by struggling and beating one another.*" They were cited to appear the next Lord's Day and admitted their guilt.

July 1724 "*The minister represented to the session the great dishonour done to God by profaning the Lord's Day in people wandering through the fields and visiting one another.*"

1730 "*James Henderson in Easter Kinmundy guilt of profanation of the Sabbath Day by marking sheep. Confessed that with his knife he had cut one lamb's ear. Alleged that there was no great fault in so doing. Proceedings against him delayed until he came to some sensze of his crime.*"

1739 "*William Milne, tenant in Blackhills, one of the members of the Church Session, had given great offence, both himself and his servants, by leading in a bigging upp of corn from Saturday night 21st October until Sabbath morning about the time of sunrising, and that having only intermitted some short while for refreshing themselves and horses, they had again yoked, continued the foresaid work until about 10, the time of ringing of the bell when people were convening to church.*" The unfortunate William was stripped of his eldership.

May 1760 Anne Davidson suspected of exposing a new born child in the parish of Newhills. A considerable effort was expended to question witnesses and find Anne. She was found and confessed that the baby's father was James Donald, now a servant with the Laird of Monboddo in Fordoun. She said the "*guilt had been contracted in Skeen about the week of Lowrandfair*" (Lowrin Fair at Old Rayne). James admitted his guilt but said he had no part in exposing the child.

March 1743 "*reported that William Kemp, a married man in Garlogie, and Barbara Alexander, a young woman in the parish of Echt had been carrying on a criminal intrigue giving great offence to the neighbourhood.*" This case involved a lot of witnesses including Barbara's master, John Ross, who had followed her one night to William Kemp's barn, listening at the door. She had stayed out all night. Ross' wife testified that Kemp, "*had not been in his own house with his wife for a considerable time before the nights done, but that he used to lie for ordinary in the said barn. This was known to the whole Toun of Garlogie*". A version of being sent to the dog house, perhaps. Despite other witnesses being called, the couple still denied the offence and they were sent to the Presbytery in Aberdeen. The Presbytery concluded there was enough evidence of scandalous and offensive behaviour.

February 1744 Infant child found exposed at Nether Affloch. A servant of Mr Gordon, Laird of Cluny, had been drunk in Bervie the same night. Highly probable from what she had said that she was the mother. In the meantime the child was given to a nurse. With the Laird of Skene being out of the county a warrant for her arrest was obtained from the Provost and Baillies of Aberdeen. Gordon of Cluny stood bail for her and ensured she appeared before the Justice of the Peace. When she did appear the evidence was thought to be defective and she was absolved. The child was left as a burden on the parish.

November 1744 One of the elders reported that Margaret Taylor in Garlogie had milk in her breast. She was cited to appear before them and confessed she was with child.

July 1760 "*Margaret Menie, an unmarried woman, had acknowledged herself with child. A man with black hair and blue clothes had met her at Bishopdams Moss, took her plaid and carried it for her. They passed by Newton of Concraig and Auchrony, and upon the Hill of Blackchambers he began to speak ill words to her and threw her over and was guilt with her. When she asked where she should seek him he said the Isle of Skye.*"

September 1826 Isobel Macdonald confessed she was delivered of a child and named George Black Esq., Garlogie Mill. On this occasion the 'gentleman' was not required to appear before the session or the congregation and was allowed to acknowledge himself as father by letter. George was guilty again in 1833, but had moved to England and had to be written to. He was then guilty a third time in 1835, each of the three times being with a different woman.

September 1829 "*A child believed to be a fortnight old was found exposed at the kitchen door of the manse. A woman of suspicious character has been seen lately by Millbouie, Auchronie and Rogiehill.*" The woman was later found and the child returned to her in the presence of the Fiscal.

March 1839 James Lamont, aged 72, confessed himself the father of Ann Milne's child, born in 1810, and he wanted to submit to the discipline of the church. The Session considered this a case of adultery as he was a married man. They should both have been sent to the Presbytery in Aberdeen but were excused because he was too old and she was of weak intellect.

1844 George Ingram admitted "*a trilapse in fornication*".

McCombie of Easterskene's illegitimate child

In April 1830 Jane Westland was asked to attend Skene Session by the

Presbytery of Aberdeen. She had an illegitimate child, but a letter was produced from William McCombie of Easterskene acknowledging himself to be the father of the child, in consequence of which Jean Westland was absolved from church censure. In the letter McCombie had enclosed a bank note for £5 in name of penalty. McCombie was a pillar of the community, a major landowner with business and other interests in Aberdeen as well as Skene.

As we have seen with George Black, it was normal for men of substance not to have to attend the session. McCombie's case was adjourned until the next meeting when the session decided not to accept the £5 as his penalty, and wrote to the Moderator of the Kirk Session of St Machar asking them to cite him to appear before Skene Session. McCombie said he was agreeable to attending, but didn't turn up at the next meeting. In January of the following year he did appear, was interrogated, and confessed himself the father. He was exhorted and absolved from church censure, so he did not actually have to appear in front of the congregation. Nevertheless, it was a significant act on behalf of the session to compel him to appear in front of them in person. McCombie must have kept in touch with his illegitimate daughter since, in later life, he had a grand-daughter staying with him and I believe she was acknowledged in his will.

By the mid 19th century cases of illegitimacy seem to have been on the increase, partly caused by the more mobile population. This also meant that, increasingly, the offending parties were no longer in the parish and had to be pursued through other parish sessions. The picture became more confused with the arrival of the Free Church from the 1840s, though in Skene there is evidence of co-operation between the churches over the pursuit of offenders. The role of the established church session was very much changed during the century, however, with the introduction of the parochial board, the competition from the Free Church, and eventually the establishment of school boards in the 1870s. Of course the kirk session and the minister were represented by right on these bodies, at least initially, but in Skene these boards became almost a battle-ground between the two churches.

The new church building

In August 1799 the heritors agreed to replace the old church with a new one. In September that year a notice appeared in the Aberdeen Journal which said that the new building was to be built the following year and was to be substantial and commodious, providing accommodation for 750. Tradesmen were invited to lodge plans and estimates with Charles Bannerman, advocate in Aberdeen. The contractors were to get the materials from the old church. It was to be 1801 before the new church was actually built and it is very frustrating that the Kirk Session minutes hardly mention this event. All we get from them is that in July 1801 the church was down (presumably the old one), and the day rainy so there was no sermon. We also know that in October 1801 the sermon was again cancelled because it was rainy and the church was not roofed (the new one). Prior to that, another announcement had appeared in the ABERDEEN JOURNAL for 30th March 1801. It stated that the plans had been approved by the great majority of heritors in the parish, and by the Presbytery of Aberdeen, and that tradesmen who wanted to tender for the contract to build the church should again apply to Mr Bannerman.

The architects are not known for certain, but it has been suggested that because of similarities to Echt Church, they were William and Andrew Clerk. Stones from the old church are thought to have been used in building the new one, and the wood for the church was given by George Skene of Skene, who claimed the greater part of the seating for his tenants. In 1840 John Smith, City Architect, did some alteration work on the south façade. According to Smith's biographer, David Miller, he slightly advanced the centre, reinserting the original windows and crowning them with a gable with a quatrefoil, surmounted by a lovely bellcote. The church was remodelled in 1930, but in the 19th century it had doors on two sides, east and west and, in stormy weather, sometimes the congregation had to go round to whichever door was on the lythe side. Above each of these doors there was a small round window, to give extra light to the gallery.

The minister who secured a new church for Skene was James Hogg, author of the account of the parish for the first STATISTICAL ACCOUNT. A story about him used to circulate in the Skene area.

> "One of the naturals – those picturesque vagrants who, in the days before they were immured in the lunatic wards of the poorhouse, must have brightened up the lives of the workers on the land in rural regions – figured in the tale as told by one who witnessed the incident. He was one of the peripatetic 'feels' common in every district of Scotland. This man's name was Jamie Nicoll. He imagined that he could preach, and often tried his hand at extorting. One Sunday morning he stole into the pulpit, and was seated in the minister's place when Mr Hogg emerged from the vestry. The minister was a very dignified man, and when his eye caught the intruder, he said – 'come down, James!

THE PARISH CHURCH OF SKENE

That's my place.' The rejoinder was very much to the point – 'na na, Maistr Hogg; come ye awa up. They're a stiff-necked and rebellious generation, the folk o' Skene. There's wark eneuch for's baith.'"

The watch tower and body-snatchers

"In consequence of an attempt to break into the churchyard of Skene, having been detected – a spade and a sack found at the time – it has been proposed and agreed upon with consent of heritors, to build a watch tower. Subscriptions will be received by Messrs Lewis Smith, bookseller, Aberdeen.; William Malcolm, schoolmaster at Echt; William Smith, merchant at Kintore; William Marshall at papermill of Culter; Andrew Fowler, Brodiach; William Marshall, School Croft; and Marshall Keith, Lyne of Skene.

NB: None will have the use of the said watch house who do not contribute for the same."

ABERDEEN JOURNAL, January 1829

The watch house has long disappeared. It stood just inside the churchyard gate, on the north side, where the war memorial is now. Mr Philip (minister 1870-1893) used to put on his gown there until the present vestry was built in

Skene mortsafe

101

1874. John Watt, once coachman at Kirkville, and for a time *"minister's man"*, was brought up at his father's croft, the house of which was at the end of the Kirktoun and looked over to the kirkside. His father was often one of the watchers who kept vigil all night in the church before the building of the watch house. On one occasion they had left their post to get some refreshment in a house nearby and returned to see men going about the churchyard; they fled over the dyke, leaving a rope and tools behind them. Another story relates how one of the young gardeners at Kirkville or Easterskene tried, for a joke, to give the watchers a fake alarm by entering the churchyard at night. He took a shot in the leg for his pains! The church also had the mort-safe, which still survives. This would be placed over the grave end and left for a while until the body was no use for the resurrectionists.

The Mission Hall at Lyne of Skene

Services were held at the Lyne of Skene in the original school building. When this was replaced by the Free Church School, the Free Church refused its use to the Established Church. The kirk session secured a feu and set about raising money to build a mission hall – both Mr Anderson of Westhill and Miss Farquhar of Westhill making contributions of £10 each, along with many donations of £1 each from Lyne folk. It was built in 1872 by Sandy Scott, mason, from Lyne of Skene. The joinery work was done by a joiner from Kintore because the Lyne joiner was Free Church. However, before the First War the Free Church also held services in the hall, paying a sum towards its upkeep.

Even earlier they were using it for weddings, such as in August 1898, when one of the Free Church school teachers, Miss Wilkie, got married there. The whole of the Lyne was decorated with flags for the occasion, and Mendlessohn's wedding march was played on the hall organ as the couple left. Dinner was served in the school house, decorated with flowers by Mr Ritchie, the Skene House gardener. The day ended with a fireworks display organized by James Watt, junior. Miss Wilkie was obviously highly thought of, and, on leaving the school, she was presented with a silver tray and massive silver biscuit box. In those days she would not have been allowed to carry on working after marrying.

In the late 19th century regular musical concerts were held in the hall, including by the Skene Church Choir. An account of one from 1896 gives a flavour of the kind of music and songs enjoyed at the time. A local performer,

THE PARISH CHURCH OF SKENE

Miss Copeland, sang *O Rowan Tree*; Miss Donald from Aberdeen sang *Lochnagar*, *Marguerite* and *I'm ower young to marry yet*; Miss Falconer from Easter Ord sang *Cam ye by Athole* and *Caller Herring* and, as an encore, *Coming through the rye*; and Mr Kemp, with his deep, rich voice, gave them *Off to Philadelphia*, and *The skipper*. In 1898 the parish minister, Mr Robertson, gave a talk on *Scottish Wit and Humour*.

After World War II the hall was also used for social events, though not for dances. In 1951 the word 'Mission' was dropped from the name. Electricity was added in 1959, and through the 1960s the social use was greater than the use for worship. Suggestions were made that the hall become a public one and be taken over by the District Council. There were several obstacles to overcome before this could happen, relating to the original conditions when the hall was built. By the time this was done the Lyne School had been closed and the District Council bought the school to convert into a public hall. In 1970 the mission hall was sold off for conversion into a dwelling house.

Skene Church in the early 1900s

Sundays in Skene c. 1910

The following account by Mary McMurtrie gives a vivid idea of what a Sunday was like in Skene at the beginning of the 20th century. I dare say it would not have been much different 30 or 40 years before that time.

"My father, George Mitchell, was schoolmaster, the 'dominie', as he was always called, of Skene Central School, and also an elder of Skene Church, and session clerk for many years. We walked regularly to church along the narrow road from the schoolhouse to the Kirktoun. The road is known as the Half-Milie, but in earlier times I was told it had been called the Loaning. As we walked the farmers passed us in their high gigs, called 'machines', they too were very regular in their attendance, and there was quite a procession of gigs; Mains, i.e., the Smiths from Mains of Skene, Lyne of Skene; Drummie, Mr Laing from Drumstone, who often gave me a drive home; the Massies from Terryvale; Mr and Mrs Machray from Howemoss; the Gerrards from Newton. They all stabled their horses behind McPetrie's shop (later Ogg's).

"By the time we reached the little steep brae to the church gate the bell would be ringing. We went past the farmers having a 'news', standing in little groups, or sitting on the flat 'table' stones that were on the mound of higher ground which marked the site of the ancient pre-reformation kirk.

"We walked on past the beadle, old Macintosh, tugging at the bell-rope; the little belfry was mid-way along the south wall. As usual he wore an old black tail-coat, green with age, and an old flat 'minister's' hat, and his steel-rimmed spectacles well down on his nose, so that he peered over them at you. We always went in by the east door, unless it was closed because of storms or easterly gales and rain. There was a little stone-flagged porch, with the Skene House pew on our left, a box pew with a high door and a railing along the top of the partition at its front. Inside it was lined with faded red cloth and there was a row of elegant drawing-room chairs with a footstool at each. The partition with its little railing formed the back of the seat in front. Other box-pews were – Kirkville, to the right of the west doorway and porch, it had a long seat upholstered in shiny black horsehair; – the Easterskene pew was near the vestry door, also high-backed, lined with faded green cloth and its railing too.

"The pulpit was in the centre of the south wall, with the choir below, and to the right was the manse seat, the last of the box pews, with a red cushioned seat and a narrow table. As we sat upstairs, we turned to the right in the porch and climbed the curving stair which took us to the top of the gallery which went round three sides of the church. Here we were very near the roof as the gallery was so high. We went down a flight of shallow steps to our seat at the front, on our left. From here we looked right down on the manse pew, and on the choir, who were arranged in a kind of box around the little American organ bought in 1890, which had by now replaced the precentor. Mr Laing of Drumstone was

THE PARISH CHURCH OF SKENE

Skene Parish Church Festival Choir 1910

the last precentor, now he sang in the choir and I remember his long drawn out 'A-a-a-m-a-ai-n'. Our pew stretched to the arched top of the high side window, there were only a couple of boards between the end of the seat and a sheer drop; the seat was high and narrow, the wooden front had a foot-board which my short legs could not reach and so I used to get pins and needles which I tried to relieve by swinging them; sometimes I swung them too energetically and kicked the front of the pew with a loud bang. The book-board (covered with a red cloth) had no raised edge, so if you pushed a book too far it fell over, I wonder if it hit anyone!

"When we stood up to sing I could see right down 'the body of the Kirk', down to the choir, with Miss Falconer, the choir leader, who always sat in a corner leaning against the pulpit; and the little organ in the centre where the precentor would have stood; and the rest of the choir grouped around. A long passage ran down the church between the porches, close to the front of the choir, and opposite the pulpit there were two square pews, with seats all around and a square table in the centre, one section of the seat was hinged so that a small door could be opened. Miss Davidson from the Kirktoun sat in the first of these – I remember how she raised the hinged seat and stepped into the pew, closed the door, lowered the seat and sat down firmly with her back to the pulpit! At one time these must have been the 'tables' for the Communion services. I have seen the same arrangement in the old church at Glenbuchat.

The seating of Skene Church was very quaint and typical of the period, and I have often wished it had not been swept away. The seats were all arranged to face the pulpit, between its four tall arched windows. The unusual feature was that the diagonal seats on each side of the central square pews were curved, with a partition running from back to front, so that the front pew only had room for one. Most of the pews had doors, with the names of the estates or farms in black paint, such as 'Blackhills', 'Wanton Walls', 'Line of Skene', 'Dean of Guild, Aberdeen'.

"The steps leading up to the pulpit were on the opposite side from where we sat, so I couldn't see them but I remember old Macintosh (the beadle as well as tailor and merchant), carrying the big pulpit bible, 'the book', up the pulpit stair and placing it on the red velvet cushion of the book board. Then he went back to the vestry, preceding the minister to the foot of the stair, stood aside to let him ascend, then firmly shut the pulpit door behind him. One time Dr Anderson was taking the service and absent-mindedly shut the door behind him so that Macintosh went up the steps to find it already closed. His face became grim. After the service he went up to Dr Anderson, full of wrath, and said 'Maister Anderson, it's your duty to preach the wirrd o' God, an its mine tae steek the poopit door'.

"In those days the offering, the 'collection', was taken up after the sermon by the elders using long-handled ladles. They were said to practice round the stalls in the byre when new to the job! Each elder got up, picked up his ladle, and went to his own set of pews, deftly wielding the long handle. That done he laid down the ladle until the end of service, when they were taken to the vestry and the money counted. Macintosh had some of the downstairs pews, the choir, I think, but always the pulpit, and he used to be told firmly that on no account was he to collect an offering from any visiting minister. But he had his own ideas about this, and without fail he went up the pulpit stair and firmly thrust the ladle in front of the visiting minister – and waited.

"When the church was first built there was no vestry, this was not built until 1874, by Sandy Scott, who also built the spire of the Free Church. Before that the minister, Mr Philip, used to put on his gown in the old watch-house.

THE PARISH CHURCH OF SKENE

The watch-house was built in 1829 when body-snatching was rife. It stood just inside the church gate, on the north. The churchyard at this time still had railings round many of the graves. There was one in particular, close to the south-east corner of the church, which had a high railing surrounding a square of bare gravel – we knew it was the grave of the Wizard Laird 'where no grass would grow' – and we looked at it with awe. There were many of the flat 'table' stones, originally supported by four pillars, but some had gradually sunk to the level of the ground, and even lower, so that grass was creeping over their edges. The oldest stones were all to the south of the church as in olden times people believed the Resurrection would be there, and the ground to the north was filled last, and all faced east.

"Close to the church door now, the old heavy stone mortsafe lies, but it used to be near the east boundary dyke, grass-grown and neglected. There were more trees around the churchyard when I was small, I think mostly ash, and possibly one might have been the 'bell-tree' where the church bell was hung when the old bell-house was demolished in 1677 – how long does an ash tree live? In the garden of Easterskene House there is a small stone belfry or 'bell-house'. I think it is most probable that it may have been taken there when the old kirk was pulled down in 1801, but no one has verified this. There is another in the garden of the Free Church Manse, possibly in use there before the steeple was built. (Author: I disagree with Mary on this, the bell-cote at Easterskene seems too large and of too well-finished granite to be from a 17th century church).

"The Old Skene Road ran close behind the schoolhouse along the line of the narrow wood between drystone dykes which was always known as 'the Beltie'. I played in this little wood constantly and ran down it to the farm, Miss Williamson's, to walk along with old Johnnie Fraser as he ploughed, and have rides on the horses, and hear the story of the big pike that lived in the loch from the cattleman. The loch was open to all, I used to go there to draw the lovely old pines, there was a little sandy beach at one point. It was altogether a delightful place, quiet and unspoilt. I remember too, in summer, my father took the upper classes from Skene School to the loch on expeditions for us to make maps of the countryside, marking the woods and fields, and of course the loch itself. He also took the older boys out and taught them how to measure fields and acreages. I remember the flocks of swans and wild duck that frequented the loch. In the evening, up in the schoolhouse garden, I would listen to the continuous, high, mournful calling of the birds as they gathered to settle for the night, geese, ducks, gulls and smaller water birds."

The fields of the glebe originally ran to about 12½ acres with a further three acres with the garden and surrounding area. In earlier times it would have been worked by the minister assisted by the 'minister's man'.

Stooks in the manse glebe

The manse and glebe

As we have seen the original manse was built near the church. Whether that was still the location of the manse in the late 18th century is unclear. At any rate a new manse was built to the north of the village in 1779. As noted earlier, John Smith did some alterations to the church in 1840. At the same time he made an addition to the manse. This was basically to add a new house on to the front of the original, thus doubling it. It had corbie-stepped gables with an advanced central gable and Smith also added the stable block to the east.

The house was sold by the church in 1980, when a new manse was built further east. The old manse is now a private home, but the manse sundial is still kept there. This is a listed sundial with a freestone top, inscribed Manse of Skene 1810. The top is taken inside every winter to protect it

THE PARISH CHURCH OF SKENE

Ploughing the manse glebe in 1920

from the elements. The fields of the glebe originally ran to about 12½ acres with a further three acres with the garden and surrounding area. In earlier times it would have been worked by the minister assisted by the 'minister's man'. In the 20th century it was generally let out to local farmers, though the horses for the hearse were also kept in the glebe fields. Adam Craigmile's father, from Broadstraik, worked the glebe and two of their Clydesdales stayed there. The houses of Glebe Land, etcetera, are built over parts of the old glebe.

Church artifacts

As well as the mortsafe among the artifacts belonging to the church are the following:
- Two large rough stone basins outside the church, probably the font and piscina of the older church
- The church bell was made by John Mowat at the Old Aberdeen Foundry in 1735, one of his earliest bells. The inscription on it reads 'To the Kirk of Skene. John Mowat. ME. FE.OLD.ABDN. 1735'
- Four silver communion goblets made from two older cups in 1750
- Two silver flagons each inscribed 'Presented to the Church of Skene by John Anderson esq. of Westhill, July 1868.'
- Several long handled collecting ladles survive. These were used up until the alterations in 1930.
- Several beggar/pauper badges. Two of these are in the National Museum

in Edinburgh. There are also several communion tokens dated 'Skene 1821'. Earlier communion tokens were sometimes diamond shaped and one is known dated 1767 with the minister's initial (AM) on it.
- Pulpit. Made in 1924 in memory of George Mitchell, schoolmaster, elder and session clerk. Given by his widow.
- Communion table. Given in 1932 by Brigadier General Hamilton and his sisters in memory of their father and mother.
- Communion chair. Given in 1932 by Mrs Low, Fernbank, Kemnay, in memory of her husband and parents.
- Baptismal font. Made of Kemnay granite. Presented by Mrs Hamilton of Skene House in memory of her husband, who died in 1945, and her son Captain John Hamilton, who fell in battle in Crete in 1941.
- Lectern. Gifted by the Women's' Guild to commemorate their 80th birthday. Made by Robert Fraser and dedicated in November 1993.
- The oak table for collection plate was made by the Rev. John McMurtrie from Skene grown oak.
- Tapestry of the Last Supper. Made in 1986 by a member of the congregation
- Cross. A wooden cross, gifted anonymously
- Clock. Originally in the Free Church, it then went to the Mission Hall at Lyne of Skene, when it was bought by David Mitchell. Donated by his relatives.

The original organ had been added in 1889, taken on a month's trial. The present Johannes electronic organ was bought in 1982.

The churchyard

In the graveyard many of the graves would have had railings round them. These included the Skene Family vault and the grave of William McCombie of Easterskene, the latter undoubtedly the most impressive gravestone in the churchyard. Made from pink granite, it contains heraldry from both his and his wife's families and is copied from the 16th century monument to William Forbes of Tolquhon in Tarves Churchyard. Close to the south wall was the square, with a high railing all around, of the Skene family. One curious gravestone is situated opposite the church door. This is in a phonetic script developed in 1847 by Isaac Pitman and Henry Ellis.

In February 1911 the Parish Council drew to the attention of the heritors

Sunday school picnic 1920

the neglected state of the churchyard and respectfully urged them to take steps for its improvement. This would be a prelude to the Council taking over the care of the churchyard. Two years later David Brownie from West Fornet, one of the councillors, moved "*that a special committee be appointed and report to the Council whether it would be practicable to have the management of the churchyard transferred from the Heritors to the Parish Council.*" The heritors replied the following year, but declined to hand over management to the Council. They finally agreed, in July 1920, to transfer the management of the churchyard to the Parish Council.

At the same time Rev. Walter Ireland, Free Church minister at Garelochhead, wrote to the Council regarding access to the graves of his grand-parents, Captain and Mrs Shepherd and Mrs Ireland. He proposed to surrender the right of way on the east side of the churchyard to the present proprietors of Kirkville provided the Parish Council preserve and keep in order the graves. Presumably this was a right of way restricted to himself and his family. The Council agreed to this proposal.

George Stuart, the well-known blacksmith at the Kirktoun, was appointed sexton in 1920. The same year, following a public meeting, the Parish Council decided to take possession of the parish hearse. In the tradition, a necessity, of rural men having several jobs, George was appointed custodian of the hearse with use of it being 6/- (30p), 3/6 (17p) of that being his fee. George was not the best of sextons, as a year later there were complaints that at least two internments had been in the wrong graves; this despite Walker and Duncan, surveyors, having drawn up a plan of the churchyard at a cost of £25. George was warned to exercise great care and refer to the plan and the index book. Later that year three bodies were re-interred following a warrant from the sheriff. Walker and Duncan's plan still survives in the old hearse building next to the Red Star.

In February 1925 Lord Cowdray's factor, Mr Morris, indicated that Cowdray was willing to grant land for the extension of the graveyard. The Parish Council at first decided to wait, but then accepted the offer a year later. However, the negotiations were drawn out, with the Council wanting half an acre to the east of the present graveyard. The situation was not helped by the death of Lord Cowdray in 1927. It was to be May 1928 before they reached an agreement with Lady Cowdray for a third of an acre. In 1925 the upkeep of the church and manse buildings passed from the heritors to the Church of Scotland.

The 1932 remodelling of the church

As well as planning some improvements to, and an extension of the churchyard, Lord Cowdray had plans for the church. He intended to renovate the interior and add electricity. At this time the church had no form of lighting whatsoever, and consequently no evening services could be held. Cowdray's death meant that his scheme did not come to fruition, but a renovation of the interior did go ahead a few years later, largely funded by money raised by the Women's Guild.

The old church interior was to be completely changed and the old pews, with the names of the farms or estates on them, removed. The plan gives some idea of how the seats were arranged in a fan shape, facing the pulpit which was on the south wall. The laird's box pews were also removed.

We have already read Mary McMurtrie's description of the old layout. Work began on 8 December 1931, the architects being George Bennett Mitchell & Son from Aberdeen. The old pews were rouped at the yard of local joiner, Willie Durno, who was also involved in some of the interior woodwork. The new pews were of pitch pine, bought from the Free Church at Kintore in 1930, and stored at the Skene House stables until needed. The

THE PARISH CHURCH OF SKENE

communion table, chair, pulpit, and font were of unstained oak. Only the west gallery was retained. Some years later, in 1937, electricity was added, the gift of George Ogg, an elder of the church.

The interior of the church before remodelling

Plan of the old seating arrangement

113

Re-dedication of the church with from the left Mr Allison, Dr Hetherwick and Mr McMurtrie

The Skene Kirk Session in the 1950s

On 27 June 1932 the service of re-dedication was carried out by the Reverend Dr Hetherwick, moderator of the Presbytery of Aberdeen, assisted by church's own minister, John McMurtrie, and Mr Allison from Lochside Church. The service closed with the baptism of Mr McMurtrie's daughter, Elspeth Anne.

The 20th and 21st centuries brought Skene its two longest-serving ministers, both of whom were very highly thought of by their parishioners. Firstly John McMurtrie served from 1911 to 1949. He oversaw the internal renovation of the church and the merger with the former Free Church at Lochside. His record of service was eclipsed by Iain Thomson who served from 1972 until his retirement in March 2011. He oversaw the growth of Westhill and the establishment of the shared Trinity Church there.

The dissenting churches

In April 1723 several people in the parish are recorded as having attended a Quaker's meeting in the area. The Kirk Session made efforts to find out who had attended these "*heretical*" meetings. John and George Clarks *(sic)* were said to be among the guilty parties and they were called before the Session. They did not turn up at first but, when they did appear, they were interrogated and they promised to "*abstain from such attendance and were rebuked by the session*". It was to be into the next century before the established church was challenged again.

Westhill Congregational Church

Westhill Congregational Church lasted for just over 150 years. It was never a very big church in terms of membership, but it was for many years important in the community and had several notable men as ministers.

The church had its origins in the religious movement which led to the formation of independent churches at the end of the 18th century. In Aberdeen in 1797 "*three friends met to look at religious matters*". These three friends subsequently established the first congregational church in Aberdeen, in George Street in 1798. This church, known as the Loch Kirk, lasted until 1861, when the congregation moved to Belmont Street. The George Street Church sent "*missionaries*" or evangelists to other areas of the city and beyond to help establish other independent congregations.

It is not clear who in Blackhills (as Westhill was then known) encouraged

Westhill Congregational Church and Manse, the fields now containing streets and houses

the missionary work; it may have been the Laird of Blackhills, Alexander Smith. He may have known the George Street men as he seems to have owned a property in the Gallowgate (his son certainly did) and one of the three, Alexander Innes, a dyer, had Innes Street in the Gallowgate named after him. In any case the laird allowed them to come and preach in the stackyard of Blackhills Home Farm, later known as Westhill Mains, roughly on the site of the current scout hut. He subsequently gave them land on favourable terms to build a small chapel in 1803, and the church was formed in 1804. Although he remained a member of the established church, the laird took a great interest in what he called "*oor ain kirk*" and often worshipped in it. He remained an honorary trustee until his death in 1837.

It was not an easy thing to leave the established church. In July 1804 the Presbytery of Aberdeen had ordered some elders suspended for "*dishaunting*" (staying away from) the parish church and attending a missionary meeting. These included at least one in Skene Parish, an Alexander Waraks.

Westhill Congregational Church: the pastors

In 1806 John Smith (no relation to the laird) was appointed its first pastor. The Rev. Smith worked hard preaching to the local population and when he died in 1835, at the age of 55, it is said that he was worn out by his efforts. He

THE DISSENTING CHURCHES

travelled throughout the area and had various preaching stations where he would talk to people, though often the response was poor. These preaching stations were not necessarily outdoors; often they were in people's houses. Rev. Smith also helped set up Sabbath schools and libraries. At his own request John Smith was buried in front of the pulpit in the original chapel, which became part of the manse garden when the replacement chapel was built in 1872.

Smith was succeeded in 1836 by Anthony T. Gowan who married his predecessor's daughter. Gowan was an academic man who stayed for seven years. He was really only a student minister in his time at Blackhills, although during this time the church reached its highest membership levels. He eventually moved to Dalkeith, subsequently becoming a professor at the Theological Hall in Edinburgh. The STATISTICAL ACCOUNT for the parish, written by George Mackenzie, the Church of Scotland minister, comments, "*the present pastor is well educated, and is an acceptable and faithful labourer among his people*".

The third minister of Blackhills was Alexander Munro. He was from Moray, the son of the Congregational minister at Knockando, and came to Blackhills in 1843, having previously been at Banchory. It is recorded that at his inauguration the parish minister, George Macpherson, and the minister of the newly-formed Skene Free Church, William Trail, both spoke. "*It may give you some idea of the spirit of the times when told that while harvest was pressing they (presumably the church congregation) sat for four hours and listened to addresses on subjects such as* The principles and laws of fair discussion, Moral greatness, *and* The duties of Christian citizenship"!

Rev. Munro stayed for almost 20 years and, in a period of doctrinal controversy which saw his church split from the city churches, led the now Westhill congregation into the Evangelical Union in 1862. This was just before he left to move to Forres in 1863. Westhill remained in the E.U. until re-unification of the Congregational Church in 1897.

Munro had a great interest in physiology and hydropathy – treatment of a variety of medical complaints using water, internally and externally. He advocated fresh air as well as hydropathy as a treatment for T.B. His interest in hydropathy perhaps partly came about because his own health was not good. With the support of his congregation he undertook a four-year medical degree at the University of Aberdeen, at the same time as acting as minister to Westhill. He was not allowed to graduate, as he was already engaged in hydropathic practice, though a New York college subsequently awarded him an M.D. He apparently carried out water treatment at home for friends, though it is not clear in what way, as the manse at that time was tiny.

In 1851 he established larger premises at Angusfield, near Rubislaw Quarry, before buying Loch-head in 1853. In this substantial property, lying between the Westburn Park and what was the Royal Lunatic Asylum, he set up a variety of baths, including Turkish ones, and had between 50 and 70 patients at any one time. Dr Munro also lectured and wrote on hydropathy, as well as editing THE ABERDEEN WATER-CURE JOURNAL AND FAMILY HEALTH GUIDE. He continued with his hydropathic work after he left Westhill. He was very much involved in the temperance movement, doing work for the Band of Hope and the International Order of Good Templars, as well as representing Aberdeen at meetings of the Scottish Temperance League. Obviously the small church at Westhill was not a full-time occupation! Although it should be said that Dr Munro was helped during his ministry by a local man, Alexander Wisely, as lay helper. Wisely kept a notebook detailing the work he did and who he visited. He left for America in 1872 and wrote back to the church from Ohio. He died in America in 1900.

Membership at this time came from a wide area including Blackhills/Westhill, Garlogie, Echt, Peterculter, Newhills and Drum – Mrs Johnston, a member of the church from Milton of Drum, dying in 1889 at the age of 100.

There followed a fairly long period of short ministries, often because of the failure of the health (and indeed death) of the pastor, and also several lengthy pastor-less years during which the manse and its land was often rented out. Finally the Rev. George Wisely from Montrose became pastor in May 1881, and remained in the post until his retirement in 1900. Mr Wisely was already 65 when he took over the pastorship and he celebrated his 80th birthday still in post. To mark this occasion he was presented with an address by James Barclay, president of the Westhill Church. By 1899 Mr Wisely's health was beginning to deteriorate; in fact in the middle of the year he had had to rest for five Sabbaths in a row. The following July he announced that he intended to retire on the 30th September, that being the date of the jubilee of his being ordained as a minister – 1850–1900. Rev. Wisely retired to a cottage at Kinmundy and died in February 1905.

In January 1901 the Rev. William Cran took over the church at a salary of £80. We have a much clearer picture of his life and work, not least because

THE DISSENTING CHURCHES

he left a large collection of lantern slides. William Cran was born in 1854 on the farm of Mains of Lesmore (or Lesmoir) near Rhynie. Educated at

The Reverend William Cran in his study

Rhynie, then the Grammar School in Old Aberdeen and King's College, he went on to study for his B.D. at the Congregational Church's Theological Hall in Edinburgh, under the aforementioned A.T. Gowan. From there, in 1883, he went to Antigua to teach at the Wesleyan Seminary, Coke College, returning to Scotland a couple of years before being appointed minister at Westhill. Mr Cran, as well as his work for the congregation at Westhill, was a brilliant palaeobotanist, particularly studying Mycetozoa, or slime moulds, and discovering numerous new species in Aberdeenshire. To quote one article on him in the SCOTTISH CONGREGATIONALIST: "*the visitor to Westhill must not expect to find him on the way to the nearest golf course with a bundle of golf sticks on his back. If not in his study, he will likely be found somewhere about in the byways, lens in hand, eagerly searching for treasure which nature discloses only to such as he.*"

Mr Cran had an algae named after him. Gulielma Lister from the British Museum, who followed her father in corresponding with Mr Cran, described his works as follows: "*Our knowledge of the Mycetozoa of Aberdeenshire is due almost entirely to the Rev. William Cran, whose industry and magnificent powers of vision have made known to us several new species, and have brought to light a number not previously found in Britain.*"

Mary McMurtrie records that Mr Cran was also an excellent violinist. She says that he was especially kindly to young people and she remembered happy evenings as a child in his little study overflowing with books, being shown "*marvels under his microscope*". He always ended by showing a slide of the mites on blue cheese. Crippled from boyhood, he rode a tricycle around the area, this appearing in some of his lantern slides.

Under Mr Cran the church celebrated its centenary in 1904, when the Northern Association of Congregational Churches was held over several days at Westhill, with 17 ministers attending, including those from Avoch, Elgin, Forres, Huntly, Insch, Inverness, Macduff, New Pitsligo and Rhynie. Afterwards the group went on a two-hour drive to the Loch of Skene, Skene House grounds, Easterskene, and received afternoon tea from Mrs Proctor at Kirkville. In 1906 Rev. Cran celebrated five years in charge of the church. Edith Abernethy and Ivie Stuart (the latter being the daughter of the tailor and grocer at Earlick House), in the name of the Sabbath School and Band of Hope, made a short speech in rhyme and presented Mrs Cran with a teaset. The secretary of the church, James Abernethy, presented the pastor with a dining room clock and aneroid barometer.

In 1922 Mr Cran celebrated 21 years as pastor. A social was held to mark the occasion with addresses given by Rev. J. G. Drummond and Mr James Carle, advocate, Aberdeen. Also attending were the Rev. John McMurtrie, Rev. W. G. S. Plowman, Doctor Skinner and Mr D. R. Brownlie, Skene. A substantial cheque was presented to Mr Cran by Miss Skinner, for adding volumes to his library. Mrs Cran received a spirit lamp and kettle. Mr Cran remained as pastor until he retired in January 1931, subsequently moving to Findhorn where he died in 1933. Incidentally Mr Cran's parrot, which is included in one of the lantern slides, lived to be 100.

Two further ministers followed Mr Cran: Charles Lynch from 1932 until his death in August 1944, and Mr C.F. Graham who came in 1945, and promised the congregation five years but gave them 13, retiring in 1958. This was a period of decline in church membership, with 14 members at the end of Mr Graham's time. By that time the church found it difficult even to get temporary cover for the minister, and a meeting of members was called on 20 July 1960 with a view to dissolving the congregation. Edith Abernethy proposed the motion and it was seconded by Alfred R. Williamson. A photograph taken at one of the last services held in July 1960 shows Miss H. Cheyne, organist, Alfred Williamson, Sunday School superintendent, William R. Smith, treasurer, his wife and daughter, Alex Williamson (not related to Alfred), Edith Abernethy and James Paterson. The building was sold and converted into a family home, before becoming Kirkside Guest House.

Westhill Congregational Church: the building

The original chapel at Blackhills stood almost on the site of the later chapel with the manse joined to it on the west side – "*the manse a cosy little thatched cottage of four rooms to which was later added a back kitchen at right angles. It had four windows to the south and two to the east. The chapel had its door to the east, two windows to the north and three to the south*". For the first 20 or 30 years the chapel was thatched with heather from the Hill of Fare, then "*heavier material from Glenfoundland*" replaced the thatch, i.e. slate. Apparently it was modelled, on a smaller scale, on the parish church – pulpit on the south side and a small gallery on the other three. At the time of the re-roofing the pulpit was moved to the west and only the east gallery was retained. According to the second STATISTICAL ACCOUNT of 1843, it seated 200. The manse was "*modest*" and "*the rooms were wee*". A new manse (now Church Cottage) was built in the dry summer of 1868, 10 yards west of its original site, described in the church records as being halfway between the chapel and the west dyke. Mr Anderson, the then laird, gave stones and sand for building where these could be found on the estate. The first meeting in the new manse was held in May 1869. In collecting funds from the congregation for the building, it is noted that John Lawson, Lawsondale, could only give £15 as three of his cows had died.

By 1871 the old chapel needed re-roofing, but further investigation found that decay meant that it was beyond repair and a new one would have to be built. The site chosen was immediately in front of the door of the old building. i.e., just to the east of the old chapel which had its door on the east side. Consequently Rev. Smith's gravestone, which had been in the original chapel, was then in the manse garden. It now lies virtually concealed under decking attached to a modern house built between the chapel and the manse.

Westhill School was used as a place of worship while it was being built. The last service in the old chapel was on 28th January 1872. The following week it was dismantled and on 18th April a memorial stone was laid resting on the south end of the door lintel of the new church. It was finished in early June and formally opened on 25th June by the Rev. A. Stewart of Aberdeen. During the following winter a porch was added.

Harvest thanksgiving at Westhill Church c.1910

In 1903, just prior to the celebrations for the centenary, plans were agreed to add a hall at right angles to the chapel. On 7th September a memorial stone for the new hall and vestry was laid, and a manuscript history of the church and other papers and magazines were put into a tin case and placed in a recess at the east end of the outer door lintel. This ceremony was carried out by Mrs Proctor of Kirkville, widow of the founder of Proctor's Orphanage. Mrs Proctor had joined the church in 1905 and, following her death in 1913, she left the proceeds from the sale of her estate, such as they were, to Westhill Church.

Westhill Congregational Church: people associated with the church

Westhill Church was fortunate to have a number of members who gave it many years of service:

The Lawson family were all members in the mid 19th century. They

Westhill Welfare of Youth with Miss Lawson, James Abernethy, Mrs and Mr Cran

farmed at Lawsondale farm and gave it its name (the entrance marked by the very large stone built into the dyke in the lane, just up from Berriedale Funeral Home). In April 1896 John Lawson died, aged 84, having spent all his life in Westhill, 77 years of it at Lawsondale. He was appointed treasurer of the church in November 1850 and kept that post until August 1895. He was also involved in more than one literary society as well as supporting temperance and Dr Munro's hydropathy. Miss E. A. Lawson, his daughter, died on 4th October 1951, aged 91. She had been a member for 73 years, having joined in 1878. She was also church officer for 65 years, and Sunday school teacher for 50. She appears in some of Mr Cran's slides.

James Cooper died in 1898. He was a senior member and office bearer of the church. Born at the foot of Bennachie, he moved to the farm of Tulloch, Newhills, in the late 1830s and for 50 years was connected with Westhill Church. His house was for many years one of the regular preaching stations.

James Fowler Abernethy was a crofter and farmer at Wellcroft, which he later renamed Wellgrove, and he was undoubtedly the greatest servant of Westhill Congregational Church. His whiskered face appears in most of Mr Cran's photographs of the Westhill Welfare of Youth. His family were early members of the church and he himself joined in 1861. He was secretary from around 1876, and also leader of praise (precentor) and superintendent of the Sunday school. In fact he "*took the lateron*" (the precentor's desk) in 1868, firstly by voice alone and later with the aid of an American organ. Around 1914 it is noted that in the first 110 years of the congregation's existence it had only had four precentors – William Marshall from Culter, William Crombie, Kirkville (who later became Rev Crombie of Melrose), David Abernethy and his son James. James, whose wife was one of the Lawson family, died in July 1926 and was succeeded as church secretary by his daughter, Edith Eliza Abernethy, who held that post until the church closed in 1960. She had already been involved in the Sunday school and can be seen in several of the lantern slides. James's other daughter, Mary, was also involved with the church and married James Burnett who became Provost of Banchory. *(see under Skene Worthies for more on J. F. Abernethy)*.

Other people active in the life and history of the church were:

Moses Berry, blacksmith at Bridgend, Concraig, who was appointed one of the trustees in 1881.

Alex Barron, Burnside, Carnie, who left around £200 to the church in 1890.

Various members of the Barrack family, especially James and his wife Eliza. Robert Barrack became one of the church managers in 1934.

Various members of the Smith family from Backhills, Countesswells were long time members of the church.

The Wisely family from Fifeshill, Peterculter, William Wisely being a member for over 50 years as well as trustee. Mrs Wisely, a native of Skene, died in 1911 at the age of 92, having been a member since the 1870s.

Alfred R. Williamson was appointed trustee in place of James Abernethy in 1927 and was its last president. Before joining the church he had been asked by Mr Cran to help run the Sunday School. Various Williamsons were involved with the church right up to its closure in 1960.

Westhill had always been by far the smallest church in the Scottish

THE DISSENTING CHURCHES

Evangelical Union. The STATISTICAL ACCOUNT recorded 12 families from the parish as being members in 1843, although, as we have seen, membership did come from outwith the parish. Numbers could be large for particular events; for example, 230 were present at the fourth anniversary of the new chapel in August 1876, and at around the same time over 200 could attend a social. However, actual active membership was never very large and at the time of the centenary it had 21 members and 33 attending Sunday school. I suppose it is surprising that the church lasted so long and this was undoubtedly because of the dedication of some of its members.

Skene Free Church

The Annals of the Free Church say that the parish minister at Skene at the time of the Disruption "professed sympathy for the Evangelicals but after some vacillations stayed in the Establishment". However, a considerable number of his congregation did "*come out*," and by 1848 they had a membership of 313. This had reached 450 by 1856. The church and manse were begun in 1843, on a site near the main Alford Road and overlooking the loch. The site, less than a mile from the parish church, had been feued by the Skene Estate, but was later bought outright. The first service was held in July 1844, the minister being William Trail who had been ordained the previous year. The original church had a belfry, but a steeple was added later by Sandy Scott, mason from Lyne of Skene, with the belfry then being moved to the manse garden. The manse itself was also added to and a church hall built as well. The bell was made by Thomas Mearns of London.

The interior of the Free Church with lamps at the ends of pews

Prior to the building of the church, meetings were held at Mason Lodge and at Kirkville Cottage. Among the early elders and supporters of the church were Alexander Low, Easter Kinmundy; Alexander Davnie, blacksmith at Broadstraik; Alexander Mitchell, Lyne of Skene; Robert Milne, Fornet; John Valentine, Nether Affloch; John Stephen, Wester Carnie; William Wyness, Lochside; Alexander Smith, Bervie; George Low, Longcairn; Adam Reid, Garlogie; William Williamson, Wester Kinmundy; and James Fowler, Kirkville. As early as 1848 they had established Sabbath schools with 106 children. There were 30 scholars meeting at William Williamson's house at Wester Kinmundy and he was teaching them. Elsewehere there were 25 at Garlogie, 25 at Straik, and 11 in the Kirktoun.

Robert Ireland, a minister's son from North Leith, was appointed minister in 1850, and he married Christian Shepherd, the daughter of Captain Shepherd of Kirkville. Ireland began the process of the Free Church challenging the Established Church in the running of the parish. This is covered in other chapters, but the Free Church was also instrumental in supporting the temperance movement and Captain Shepherd was a strong supporter of both.

The Reverend James M. Mackintosh was minister from 1861. Born in Nairn, he studied at Aberdeen and Edinburgh before joining the Free Church Mission in Madras. He returned for health reasons in 1859, and was appointed to Skene two years later. In 1873 Mackintosh was given permission to recruit a student missionary to work at Garlogie, presumably among the millworkers. Mackintosh died in 1879 and was succeeded by William Innes. Innes had been born in the year of the Disruption, 1843, and was ordained at Torry in 1873. He served Skene for almost 60 years, becoming Scotland's longest serving minister. For 35 of those years he was sole minister, thereafter senior minister. He lived until well into his nineties and his daughter Elizabeth, a doctor, became Lady Provost of Aberdeen as the wife of Tommy Mitchell. W. G. S. Plowman was appointed minister in 1915, and served until 1925.

James Proctor of Kirkville, along with his wife, was admitted to the congregation in 1880. James was actually elected as an elder, though he may not have taken office. In later life his widow was associated with the Congregational Church.

After the union of the Church of Scotland and the Free Church in 1929, the Skene Free Church became the Lochside Church. The last minister was Thomas S. Allison who came to Skene just before the union, in 1926, when he was 70 years old. During his ministry the congregation more than doubled, but when he retired in 1941 the two congregations were united under John McMurtrie. Mr Allison, who died at the age of 90, is credited with *"a spirit of kindly co-operation that did much to prepare the way for the harmonious union of the two congregations"*.

On a Sunday morning in 1927 the roof of the Free Church caught fire. The fire was caused by an overheating stove pipe which had been too near the

THE DISSENTING CHURCHES

woodwork. Buckets of water were used to control the fire until the fire brigade arrived from Aberdeen. The small private fire apparatus from Dunecht House was also called out, though by the time they arrived the fire was under control. The interior of the church was also damaged by smoke and water, but services managed to go ahead in the church hall. A cartoon of the event by D. R. Leslie appeared in the newspaper, depicting a well-dressed elder speaking to the fire master with locals sitting on a dyke watching the firemen at work. The caption was, *"Ye saved that Aiberdeen dancin'*

The fire at the Free Church

"Ye saved that Aiberdeen dancin' palace on Setterday, but ye've fairly atoned by savin' oor kirk this Sawbath day"

palace on Setterday, but ye've fairly atoned by savin' oor kirk this Sawbath day". Tibbie Reid thinks that the steeple was re-built at this time, but not to its original height.

The small hall at the back of the church was used for a few years as a meeting place for the Women's Guild and the Bible Class. It was also used as an extra classroom for Skene Central School. Eventually the Lochside buildings were sold to local joiner, Samuel Wyness, who converted the manse into two houses and the church into a joinery workshop. Today it is home to John Findlater, blacksmith. One of the conditions of the sale was that the 60-foot-high (18 metres) steeple should be demolished, to lessen the impression of the desecration of a place of worship. This event took place in 1946 when it was found to be impossible to remove the steeple stone by stone, so it was demolished by blasting, the event being photographed for the local Press. The church bell was gifted to Northfield Church.

Lyne of Skene must have had a strong Free Church presence, since as we have seen elsewhere, there was a Free Church school there and a refusal to let the Established Church use the school for services. Regular Free Church social activities did take place in the school and, at one such in 1863, hosted by Skene Free Church minster, Mr Mackenzie, addresses were delivered by ministers from Free St Clements, Echt, and the Northfield Mission (Gilcomston). The building was packed and the members enjoyed an evening of vocal and instrumental music, with fruit and cake being given out by stewards.

Baptist Church

There seems to have been a Baptist Church based at Echt in the middle of the 19th century. One of their number, Mr Wight, established a preaching station at Garlogie. In 1861 a presentation was made to him for his 20 years' service at Garlogie. This is the only information I have on the Baptists, but I presume that Mr Wight was working among the millworkers.

Education in the parish

The Reformed Church in Scotland in the post-Reformation period aimed to have a school in every parish as part of a national system of education. In reality this didn't happen, for various reasons – continual turmoil in the country, the poverty of the country, and the lack of educated teachers. It was to be well into the 17th century before real progress was made. Even then the schoolmaster's post was to be a poorly paid one; in poor rural parishes he would be dependent on the goodwill of the heritors. Moreover, parents had to make a contribution to their children's education, not easy in times of rural poverty.

Despite claims made for the universality of the Scottish parochial school, in Skene in 1751, for example, of 23 tenants who subscribed to the yearly vicarage on the Dean of Guild's lands of Easter Skene, seven could not sign their name. It was not until 1803 that Parliament established a minimum salary for teachers of £16.3.4 plus fees. The act also said that the teacher's house should not be more than two rooms and a certain amount of garden. This was not always implemented immediately, however. In Skene the heritors were called to a meeting in January 1829 to consider the 1803 Act!

More often than not, the schoolmaster was a probationary minister who would also preach the sermon in the minister's absence. As late as 1823 George Mackenzie, the schoolmaster and session clerk at Skene, was authorized by the Aberdeen Presbytery to preach on Sundays following the death of the previous minister, James Hogg. The congregation was to pay him whatever extra they could afford. As an educated man in the parish the schoolmaster often took on other rolls, such as session clerk, as Mackenzie did. Mackenzie was eventually appointed as minister. Both William Cruickshank, who left office in 1729, and his successor, John Smith, described as a young man, were schoolmaster, session clerk and the precentor who led the singing in the church. Perhaps a schoolmaster's education also included a musical one.

The Parish School

The earliest reference we have to a school in Skene is from the kirk session records in the 1676, when the session owed money to the schoolmaster for his position as session clerk. Then in July 1681 – *"this day the people are exhorted to send their children to school"*. This was to be a recurring theme right up to the end of the 19th century when school attendance supposedly became mandatory. As well as the cost of the fees to be paid for the schooling of their children, in rural areas the children were an important part of the rural workforce, especially at harvest time, hence attendance could be sporadic. That same year £4.13.4 (Scots) was paid to the schoolmaster as part payment of his salary. As with the minister, the schoolmaster received a money payment, but also payment in kind. This would usually be meal, and peat for his fire. Right down to the early 20th century there are memories of children taking a lump of peat or coal for the school fire as part of the payment of their fees. Of course, the schoolmaster would have some land as part of his croft and would also have an area in the peat moss. John Walker is mentioned as casting 'peets' for the school in the 1680s.

We can deduce from the poor condition of the school that it had been there for some time prior to the 1680s. In November 1681 the session book records a payment of 12 shillings (60p) for repairing the middle wall in the school and eight shillings (40p) for *"a lumb to the schoolmasters chamber"*. It is likely that the school and the schoolmaster's accommodation would be in the same building. As we will see, this was the case in Westhill School built much later in 1834.

In June 1681 James Smith of Wester Carnie gave some money on behalf of his late father for repairing the school *"and other pious uses"*. Soon after, the minister spoke to Stephen Mackie, *"one of the husbandmen of the town about materialles to the schole being at that time ruinous, which he obliged himselfe to furnish for the gooding of the schole. That said day Patrick Walker condescended to cast faill and divots to the schole"*. Faill and divots are turf, used for the walls, or for the roof prior to thatching. The walls could be made wholly of divots or, hopefully, stones with divots in between or on top. In fact Walker cast 4,000 faill and divots for the school.

EDUCATION IN THE PARISH

Quite a number of men worked on the school as well as Walker and Mackie. John Nevie is described as the builder, he had two workmen; Arthur King, the Kirktoun smith was also involved, making couples (for the roof), nails and "*staples for one of the broades of the window;*" and John Allardes was paid for "*ropeing of ye school*" – probably tying down the thatched roof. From the description of the work done we can surmise the following – the school had at least one timber wall; it had a window with shutters; the roof was thatched; there was a partition, probably separating the schoolmaster's quarters from the school; there was a lock on the school door (this is mentioned under a payment in the year 1693); both the schoolmaster's chamber and the school had a chimney.

The session did keep an eye on the school and what was being taught; it is recorded in April 1682 that the minister and some of the elders visited the school. There they found that, "*both Latine and English scholars (blessed be God) had attained and were attaining to a great proficience, and exhorted all parents of children to send them to the schole*". The session minutes do seem to suggest that the schoolmaster often had to wait for his salary.

In general, the heritors or landowners of the parish appointed the schoolmaster. Thus in 1744, "*the minister acquainted the Session that the heritors had appointed Mr William Morice, a young man well known in this place, he having resided in this parish for some years, to be schoolmaster in room of Mr George Abercromby who had demitted office*". Abercromby had been appointed in 1735. The session went on to appoint Morice as session clerk at the same salary as his predecessors. They also agreed to repair the partition wall and windows of the schoolhouse before he could teach in it.

The earliest mention I have seen of Joseph Allen in the session minutes is in 1762 when he was also session clerk. He served for 62 years as schoolmaster and was also an elder of the church. He died in 1817. It would be nice to know more about such a long-serving schoolmaster. Why did he stay so long when most other schoolmasters at the time served for a much shorter period? All we really know about him is that his daughter married Andrew Fowler from Brodiach, he made the massive sundial there, and his grave and stone are in Skene Kirkyard along with those of several members of his family.

Where was the original parish school?

This is a question that vexed Mary McMurtrie quite considerably. For a building that had presumably been in existence until the 1860s, it is strange that no one was able to tell her where exactly it had been. She did speak in 1955 to an elderly lady, Miss Lawson, whose father, Doctor Lawson, had attended it for a short time.

Mary had been told that the schoolmaster's house was in the Fiddle Wood, along the Half-Milie, and she found various plants growing there which suggested a garden. Other villagers said it was nearer the village, one informant telling her that the second field on the right along the Half-Milie was known as the school field. In fact the name Old School Field survived in valuation records into the 1920s.

In the division of the lands of Easter Skene owned by the Dean of Guild the schoolmaster's croft is mentioned in the boundary descriptions and it is clearly between the village and Dykenook (where the present school is). Joseph Allen was the schoolmaster at that time. At the division of the Guild lands into lots, the schoolcroft was eventually included in the lot bought by the McCombies, but the schoolhouse and schoolgreen were not included. Mary wondered if the square enclosure shown on the first OS map of 1864 was the school. This is about two-thirds of the way along from the Kirktoun and before the Fiddle Wood. An access track is shown from the Half-Milie, though originally the school would have been accessed from the Old Skene Road, to the north. The Half-Milie was made as an accommodation road by William McCombie because he did not like the old road passing so near to Easterskene House.

The OS map was surveyed almost at the same time as the new school was built, and it shows the new school. I think that Mary's square enclosure was certainly the site of the old school. One further piece of evidence is that the 25 inch to the mile OS map shows a sundial in that enclosure and I have shown elsewhere that schoolmaster Joseph Allen made the Brodiach sundial. This may even have been the Brodiach sundial.

The new school

In July 1864 the Kirk Session received "*two roods*" of land on Lochside Farm from the trustees of the late George Skene, "*to be used in all time coming as the site of the said parish school and schoolmaster's house*". This is where the present Skene School was built, along along with the separate schoolmaster's house. They are both still there, although with alterations and extensions, the house now a private dwelling.

EDUCATION IN THE PARISH

Dames' Schools

These were run by untrained, unmarried or widowed women in their houses, and more often than not they were simply paid babysitters with little actual teaching being done. There was said to be one in Westhill and one at Lyne of Skene, in the old schoolhouse. At Kirktoun the dame school has been identified as the house with the gable end on to the road. It was run in the 1820s and 1830s by two sisters called Collie, daughters of a local farmer. The story is told that one of the sisters went to the manse as housekeeper. One day when she was cleaning the silver the minister, George Mackenzie, asked her if she would like to call it her own and she became his wife.

Westhill School

This was built in 1834 as a subscription school. As with the first parish school, the schoolmaster lived at one end of the building and taught at the other end. It was known as Kinmundy School, sometimes as Wester Kinmundy School, even after the estate itself became Westhill. It had become Westhill School at

Prospect Cottage, the first Westhill School

the time of the establishment of the School Board. A report on a social event that took place at the school in 1863 thanks Mr Anderson, Laird of Westhill, for the school-room and the rest of the premises having undergone considerable repairs and enlargements, and presenting a greatly improved appearance. It must have been quite small before that! The money from the social went to the school funds. The school was replaced shortly after being taken over by the School Board, and was sold off. It survives today as Prospect Cottage on the Old Skene Road.

Lyne of Skene

Roy Lyall (senior) recorded that there was a dame's school at the Lyne which was then replaced by a more formal school with a dominie. The first school was a thatched one with very small windows, owing to the window tax. He first came across a mention of a schoolmaster around the time the new road was built from Lyne Smiddy to Dunecht (the 1820s), followed by a note of "*schoolmaster's dews*" about 1830. I have found the following advertisements:

> **1837 Aberdeen Journal,** for a teacher at Lyne of Skene School.
> Applications to Rev. George Mackenzie, minister. Marshall Keith, merchant, will show applicants the premises.
>
> **1844 Aberdeen Journal,** for a teacher at the Lyne school, applications to Marshall Keith, merchant, or George Mitchell at Skene House.

Roy also wrote that Charlie Milne from Moss-side attended this school. He was always getting up to mischief and would climb onto the couples of the roof and throw spiders at the dominie's bald pate!

Free Church schools

Following the establishment of the Free Church in 1843, two Free Church schools were built in the parish. The church received land at Mason Lodge in 1851 from Captain Shepherd of Kirkville, and built a school and dwelling house for the teacher. A school was also built at Lyne of Skene. Roy Lyall (senior) gives the date 1854 for that school, but Mary McMurtrie gives 1861. The latter date is the one I have seen on a sasine from the trustees of the late George Skene for 39 poles of ground for a school and dwelling house. Just before this, in May 1860, Captain Shepherd of Kirkville made a payment to the Skene Estate for ground required by the Free Church. However the Skene Estate rentals do record a payment made in 1857 for heathering the old schoolhouse which had been let out to tenants. Although run by the Free Church, these schools still came under the authority of the School Board when it was established, and the board inspected them periodically.

Miss Lawson, daughter of Doctor Lawson, later recalled that when scholars going to the Parish School met those going to the Free Church School at Mason Lodge, there used to be battles between them. Miss Lawson actually carried a stick under her "*pinnie*" for fighting with.

The ABERDEEN JOURNAL, in 1868, has a lovely account of an outing by the children of the Lodge and Lyne Free Church schools. It was to Dunecht House and the children were transported in farmer's carts – Messrs Leith, Lyne; Abel, Wester Fornet; and Milne, Easter Fornet for the Lyne children; Wyness Smith, Hillhead and Low, Kinmundy for the Lodge ones. They had their own piper playing and, courtesy of Mr Farquhar, the gardener, they had a tour of the hot-houses and the house. Games and refreshments were taken on the lawn, including strawberries courtesy of the teachers. There were three cheers for Lord Lindsay, owner of Dunecht, before the day ended at five o'clock.

Garlogie Mill School

Garlogie Mill provided a school for the children of the millworkers. This was not done out of benevolence. The 1833 Factories Act allowed employers to employ children from the age of nine but, in return, they had to provide them with a certain amount of schooling. At Garlogie the children are said to have worked one day then gone to school the next. As they got older it was week about. Younger children attended during the day and older ones in the evening after their day's work. In 1843, 50 children were attending the school. The school was simply one of the small mill cottages similar to those still in existence. It was slightly further along the road from the others and its ruins can still be seen.

The School Board

The Education (Scotland) Act 1872 brought in compulsory education between the ages of five and 13 (later increased to 14 by an act of 1883 which also allowed 'half-time' attendance after the age of 10). School building was expanded and more teachers were to be trained. It also brought the schools under the control of an education board elected by local ratepayers. School boards had the power to levy rates for school provision and they also received government grants. Education was still not free, however; unless they were receving poor relief, each pupil had to pay a fee in addition to what was raised from ratepayers. It was not until later acts of 1889 and 1890 that fees could be abolished in elementary schools. In Skene the first meeting of the School Board was held in the parish church on Thursday, 10 April 1873. The board then comprised John Anderson of Westhill, Captain Thomas Shepherd of Kirkville, John Valentine of Affloch, William Taylor of Southbank, and Rev. William M. Philip, the parish minister. At the second meeting they drew up a table of the schools then in the parish

	Salaries	**Fees taken in**	**Number on roll**	**Actually present**
Parish School	£75	£65.12.10	147	125
Mason Lodge	£35.12.6	£55.9.1½	107	88
Westhill	£12	£22	58	50
Lyne of Skene	£19.15.0	£21.5.7½	58	50
Garlogie Mill	£25		41	41

The School Board calculated that £170 would be needed to run the schools in the first year and informed the Parochial Board that this should be added to the sum raised by assessment for the poor. In September 1874 the Parish School was renamed Skene Central, a name it would keep for almost 100 years.

There was a problem with the Free Church agreeing to hand over their schools to the new board. Initially the church intended closing the Lodge School and keeping open the Lyne one. They did offer to hand the school and playground at Lyne of Skene to the School Board, but not the schoolhouse, and with the additional conditions that the congregation could still use the school and that the existing teacher be retained. This proposal was rejected by the board. It would take until the beginning of the next century before the Lyne School was transferred to the board. In fact when the Free Church school at the Lyne closed, there were a couple of years when there was no school at the Lyne until the board took it over. In those few years the scholars went to Dunecht or Ley Lodge. The School Board were also offered the Mason Lodge School, but thought it was in the wrong location.

There were also problems with Garlogie where, initially, the mill owners were going to hand the school over. The board was unhappy with the physical condition of the school and the Haddens, the owners, decided not to close it immediately. Thereupon the board intended to build a school at Carnie, *"where there is a sort of village population"*. A school was opened there using an existing building, and a teacher was appointed, but it only lasted a year or two. They also agreed to lease the Mill School. However the Board of Education refused to allow more than four schools in the parish, so the temporary school at Carnie was closed and the teacher transferred to Garlogie. The existing teacher at Garlogie was simply dispensed with.

Within a few years a new school was built at Garlogie, at the east end of the village. The reasons given for the siting of the Garlogie School so far from the mill were, *"that discipline would be improved, and cleanliness of the scholars encouraged, by removing the school from the immediate vicinity of the cottages in which they reside, the present school, besides, being too near the borders of the parish for the maximum benefit to the parishioners being obtained from it"*.

The School Board itself, like the Parochial Board, became a kind of battleground between supporters of the dissenting churches (Congregational and Free) on the one hand, and Established Church on the other. This is something I will discuss more fully in Chapter 12.

In 1877 the School Board proposed a new school at Westhill, the existing school being virtually condemned, and the Board of Education agreed. Mr Anderson of Westhill agreed to give land for the school on the site proposed by Rev. Philip, 250 yards west of the existing school at the point where the road from Auchinclech intersected with the Old Aberdeen road (the Old Skene Road). It was to be big enough to accommodate 100 scholars. There was a slight delay because of the high cost of the building but, in 1878, it was built, by George Ogg & Son, masons. It was opened on the Monday, 2 December 1878. The old school building was rouped for £97 to John Hird, Lavenie, Afforsk. The board then agreed to build the new school at Garlogie and it was ready at the end of 1880.

The School Board, in 1886, agreed to architects' plans for an extension to the south-west end of Skene School with separate playgrounds for boys and girls. The extra accommodation was to take up to 40 pupils. William Angus from Letter of Skene objected in a letter to the Scotch Education Department because there was surplus accommodation elsewhere. The Lyne School could accommodate 109, but had an attendance of 52. The accommodation was in the wrong place, however, and, in addition, parents from the outlying schools often sent children who had passed fourth or fifth Standard to Skene

Central in order to get a higher level of education. Hence the extra accommodation was needed there.

Life at school

One requirement of the new school authorities was that each school had to keep a log book as well as a register. These had to be signed off by inspectors from the Board of Education, and members of the Parish School Board also regularly visited the school, by way of inspection, but also to show an interest in the children and sometimes bring them gifts. The log books give us some idea as to what school was like in the second half of the 19th century.

As with the earlier period, attendance was still governed by farm work despite being nominally compulsory. Harvest time always saw a reduced attendance. In addition children were often absent at term time when their fathers were moving to a new toun. At Lyne of Skene children were often absent when there was a feeing market at Echt. At the other end of the parish, children at Westhill were absent when it was the Muckle Friday market in Aberdeen (amusingly anglicised as Big Friday by some teachers in their log). At Skene School there could be absences for either or both markets. Garlogie millworkers' children got the Aberdeen holidays.

For Christmas the children at all schools were given a Christmas tree with presents, but not until their Christmas holidays which were at the very end of December – 30th or 31st, not on the 25th. In fact, the old Christmas was celebrated in Skene on 5th January, until World War I. This is often known as Auld Eel and related today to New Year, but it was originally the Christmas celebration.

The board appointed a compulsory officer to chase up children who did not attend. In the North-East this person became known as the "tak-a" or "tak-all", a term used today by Adam Craigmile when talking about James Fowler Abernethy from Wellgrove and Dick Smith from Westhill, who were both compulsory officers. The dividing line, as remembered by Adam, for whether you attended Skene or Westhill school, was from Broadstraik to Souterhill. East of it went to Westhill, west to Skene, so that Slack of Larg children went to Skene. Adam, from Broadstraik, went to Westhill.

In the 20th century if you lived more than three miles from the school you were given a bike by the local authority. Parents were responsible for the maintenance of the bikes and the parish bobby went round checking on their condition. After a number of years you got to keep the bike. A stone marking

EDUCATION IN THE PARISH

the three-mile boundary can still be seen at Lyne of Skene.

Queen Victoria's Jubilee

The schoolchildren at all the Skene schools celebrated the Queen's Diamond Jubilee in June 1897. Those at the Lyne of Skene went to a picnic at Skene House where they were each given a jubilee mug. A bonfire was lit at Broomhill. Those at the other three schools (around 250 with adults) were taken by horse drawn "*busses and brakes*" to Queen's Cross in Aberdeen. From there they travelled slowly down Union Street so that the children could see the decorations. They had tea in St Katherine's Hall, then marched to the beach. On returning to Skene they were given tea at Easterskene, where around 100 younger children were already gathered.

Some notes from the minutes and log books:

July 1865: Rain falling in torrents today, only 20 present (Lyne)

October 1865: Half-holiday given in honour of the marriage of Lady Anne Duff, Lord Fife's eldest daughter (Lyne)

June 1866: One of the boys left today in a manner not altogether creditable to him (Lyne)

March 1866: Fast day in connection with the cattle plague (Lyne)

January 1867: Severe snow storm. One scholar, two the next day (Lyne)

August 1867: Boy severely punished for bringing gunpowder and matches to school (Lyne)

April 1869: Miss Laing resigned with the view to going to Bombay to labour in connection with the Free Church Ladies Association for Female Education in India (Lyne). (She later returned as Mrs Stephen to talk about her work in India)

October 1873: Received intimation that Board do not intend paying for cleaning the school nor affording coals as formerly. Teacher had to clean the school and afford coals and charge scholars accordingly (Skene)

June 1878: Elizabeth Milne, Terryvale, was at school on Tuesday, seized with fever between Tuesday and Wednesday, died on Friday (scarlatina). Fear of infection keeps families from sending children to school. The following December one of the girls died of diptheria (Skene)

May 1879: Many flagrant cases of violation of the Education Act. Children of ten years of age who are only in their 3rd Standard and are engaged for the summer (Skene)

September 1879: Jessie Black died of diphtheria (Westhill)

December 28th 1883: Scholars had a Christmas tree with presents for them. Each one got a bag of bread, fruit, tea and a toy (Lyne)

June 1885: Annie Stuart, Kirktoun, and Helen Scott, Lyne, sat preliminary papers for Aberdeen University Local Examinations (Skene)

June 1887: Clerk to authorize Mr Hunter, advocate, to take legal proceedings against various parents who had been withholding their children from Garlogie School (School Board)

October 1891: School closed at dinner time to allow the children to meet at the Hall with other schools in preparation for the foundation stone laying at the Kirkville Orphanage (Lyne)

July 1893: Had a visit from some members of Aberdeen St Nicholas Parochial Board (Garlogie). This was because many of the mill workers came from Aberdeen

July 1894: A half-holiday to allow the children to visit a menagerie (Lyne)

November 1896: Impossible to adhere to timetable in the afternoon as it is too dark after the dinner hour (Westhill)

November 1900: Several absences – potato lifting the excuse (Westhill)

March 1904: Half-timers are making three attendances in the week instead of two as the mill is stopped on Fridays because of scarcity of work (Garlogie)

November 1904: Number on the roll is gradually decreasing owing to the closure of Garlogie Mill (Garlogie)

September 1906: School closes Thursday and Friday on occasion of King's visit to Aberdeen to open new buildings at Marischal College (Skene)

July 1908: Scholars invited to tea by the officers of the Gordon Highlanders Camp (Garlogie)

October 1914: Attendance irregular owing to the operations of the threshing mills in the district (Westhill)

September 1915: Sad incident cast a gloom over the school and neighbourhood. One of our youngest pupils, James Bartlett, run over by a motor car and died soon after. Only had five weeks of school life (Skene)

September 1918: Miss Badenoch appointed. She appears in some school photographs, taught at the school until at least the 1940s and is remembered today being driven to school on a tractor (Skene)

August 1928: Now 50 pupils in the Advanced Division (Skene)

August 1928: Education Authority granted holiday in order that pupils may go to Aberdeen to see Prince of Wales, at Lady Cowdray's expense (Garlogie)

EDUCATION IN THE PARISH

Skene School c.1912 with George Mitchell, headmaster, Miss Banchop and Miss Anderson, Mr Lawrie, janitor

January 1936: Funeral of King George V. School closed and scholars attending service at Lochside Kirk (Skene)

May 1938: Empire Day. Address by Mrs Hamilton. Flag unfurled and the children saluted it (Skene)

June 1938: 17 pupils of Advanced Division and Headmaster visited Empire Exhibition in Glasgow (Skene)

September 1939: School closed by order of the Clerk to the School Management Committee to facilitate the billeting of evacuated children who will come from congested areas (Skene)

September 1939: A few families have come into the district from Edinburgh and seven pupils were today admitted. Roll now 153 (Skene)

August 1940: Two Aberdeen evacuees left (Skene)

January 1941: Three evacuees returned to Edinburgh (Skene)

February 1941: Three air raid warnings during school hours (Skene)

April 1941: Milk under 'Milk for Schools' scheme is now being supplied (Skene)
June 1941: Policeman called today and examined the gas masks
September 1942: Marched to Westhill Congregational Church for service in response to King's appeal for a National Day of Prayer (Westhill)
May 1960: School closed tomorrow due to wedding of Princess Margaret and Anthony Armstrong Jones

School rolls in 1911 were: Central 81; Garlogie 70; Lyne 94; Westhill 86

In 1900 Rev. William Christie retired as headmaster of Skene Central. He had been headmaster since 1877 and was presented with an illuminated address by the Skene Mutual Improvement Association. His successor was George Mitchell, chosen from 36 applications, and he is the first teacher of whom we have a photograph taken with his teachers and pupils. He was also, of course, the father of Mary McMurtrie. The era of photography brings alive the schooldays of the early part of the century and, thankfully, Skene folk have kept quite a number of their old school photographs.

Writing in 1995, Adam Craigmile remembered his first days at Westhill School, beginning on 11 July 1918.

"First day was a big event, and I was escorted by my two brothers, Frank and John. A neighbour, joiner's wife Mrs Cruickshank, gave me a penny which delighted me. My brothers took me to a classroom where I met the Head Teacher, Miss Duncan. There were two other teachers, Miss Lowson who became my teacher for 5-8 years, and Miss Alcock. There were three rooms and about sixty pupils. I was given a satchel, like stiff cardboard, with leather shoulder straps and buckles, which held my slate, white chalk, duster and my lunch. Every child brought their lunch, and mine consisted of a bottle of milk, two slices of plain bread and syrup.

"School started with assembly in one room for Bible stories and catechism. Children could then buy, if required, an HB pencil, rubber or jotter for one penny. Reading books had to be bought and were covered with brown paper to keep clean and mine was kept for my younger sister. Children walked from a wide area, Erick, Black Top, Old Skene Road, Carnie and Brimmond Hill. In winter rooms were heated by a coal fire for which we helped bring in the fuel. Schoolboys wore short trousers with long woollen socks until the age of

EDUCATION IN THE PARISH

Garlogie School 1934

fourteen. I had boots with studs in the soles and steel toe and heel caps, some boys had long wearing tackety boots which I envied. Girls wore long button-sided boots which needed a button hook to fasten. In summer some children walked barefoot. The annual school picnic was held at Kinmundy Farm with catering by Robbie Allan from Garlogie. After reaching twelve years, some children attended Skene Central School where Dominie Mitchell was Head Teacher, but some children remained at Westhill School until aged fourteen."

Skene Central struggled to get recognition for an Intermediate Department in the school, to provide more advanced education akin to later secondary education. The chief inspector visited the school in January 1907 to interview the headmaster and members of the School Board. In 1910 the School Board received a communication from the Education Department giving its final decision in refusing such recognition. Three years later the board had taken steps to provide suitable accommodation and equipment for effective supplementary work to secure full recognition as qualifying for the Intermediate Certificate. Pupils would later have to go into the Central School in Aberdeen for more advanced work, but Skene had its secondary school.

Just after World War I there was a new Education (Scotland) Bill which Skene Board strongly opposed because it proposed transferring education to the County Council. Nevertheless the bill went ahead and, on 12th May, 1919, the School Board held its final meeting.

In the years after World War II, Skene Central, Lyne of Skene and Westhill had their own kitchens and provided school meals. At Garlogie the meals came over from Skene. Just before the growth of Westhill, in 1969, Skene Central stopped being a secondary as a result of decisions made by the Aberdeenshire Education Department. Pupils then had to go to Bankhead Academy for secondary education and numbers at Skene declined. John Duthie was headmaster at the time, and some say the move broke his heart. He resigned soon after and died a year later.

Westhill and the need for new schools

Very early in its development it was realized that the old Westhill School at the roundabout was no longer adequate. A new Westhill School was built on what was described at the time as "the perimeter road of Westhill". It was prefabricated and open plan, with accommodation for 300 pupils from Primary one to seven. The school was opened on the 21st November 1974 by the County Convener Maitland Mackie. Ian Walker, the head teacher of the old school, oversaw the move to the new one and was its first head teacher. In that time of limited provision elsewhere in Westhill, the school also met some of the needs of the wider community with young mothers, guides, scouts, dancing classes, badminton and chess clubs all meeting there. Dates for the opening of the other new schools in the new Westhill are given in the final chapter.

Poverty and medicine in the parish

Poverty

As late as August 1851, Alexander Wisely, the lay helper to the minister at the Congregational Church, recorded the following poignant story which hints at the condition of rural labourers at the time.

> "Went to see and console a poor heart-broken wife whose husband had gone away in search of employment, about 11 days and no word was heard of him. She is almost frantic with grief. Has four children and one at the breast, with the charge of a croft. O, what misery is to be found in this vale of tears."

As late as 1911 the Inspector of Poor reported that he had made 25 official visits; numerous visits had also been made to him; 105 letters had been written with as many received, while details too numerous to specify had been dealt with as circumstances demanded.

As late as 1917 a woman in Aberdeen fled to America leaving baby twins, one in Aberdeen Poorhouse along with an older brother, and one in Govan Poor House where she had relatives. The woman married a Skene man in Glasgow, Montana; she presumably knew him already, and he may have been a farm servant with her brother in Skene. Because her husband came from Skene, Skene parish was liable for the children, and the inspector was about to go to Govan to bring back the baby, but unfortunately the child died. The other two children were brought up in Skene, one boarded at a house at

Easter Carnie, and the other brought up by Mrs Stuart, the blacksmith's wife at Kirktoun.

Tales such as these may seem extreme to us today but were far from that. Poverty was all-pervasive in the parish until well into the 20th century.

Prior to the Poor Law (Scotland) Act 1845, responsibility for the poor fell to the kirk session of a parish. In effect this meant charity or begging, the latter being regulated to an extent with the issue of beggar's tokens. The Skene Kirk Session collected money from various sources to distribute to the poor as it saw fit. Part of the collection on Sundays would go to the poor. In the mid-18th century the rental of the loft seats in the kirk also went to the poor box, as did the money from the hire of the mortcloth for use at funerals. Sometimes people left mortification money to be used for the poor, e.g., in 1676 Captain James Basken of Ord and Fiddy left 100 merks for the poor in the parish.

Payment would not, of course, be automatic. Claims for money would be investigated by the minister or one of the elders and the claimant could face interrogation to ensure that they could not support themselves.

The number of poor in the parish could be considerable. In 1742 the Commissioners of Supply for the County of Aberdeen requested a list of all the poor in the parish. This amounted to 31 people, plus 12 boys who helped at harvest time, but had to beg the rest of the year. Of the 31, six were on the lands of the Laird of Skene and 25 on the lands of the Town of Aberdeen. Whether this discrepancy in numbers was because the laird was better at looking after his tenants or whether the Aberdeen lands were more populous is not clear.

The great majority were aged 55 and over, with one man and two women aged 80 (ages were probably approximate, most being given as ending in a zero). There was one girl of 15 in Letter and one young man of 27 in Wester Carnie, the latter described as being paralysed and almost blind. Of the total, 19 were women and 12 men. As well as these mainly elderly people, others, while able to work when fit, would have had to claim poor relief when sick.

The poor did not always receive money. In 1765 the kirk session, considering the helpless condition of Rachel Stephen and her children, agreed that pocks (sacks or pouches) should be hung in the mills of Ord, Garlogie, Birsack and Craigiedarg, to hold whatever meal charitable people should think fit to put in them. They also had to find somewhere for her to live. Alexander Grigg of Blackhills took her boy in, but demanded a peck of meal

POVERTY AND MEDICINE IN THE PARISH

a week, a firlot of seed a quarter, and a pair of blankets which he would return when the boy left his house.

The Poor Law Act (Scotland) Act 1845 and the Parochial Board

In the 19th century conditions changed on the land, with the enclosure of land and the move towards a more capitalist system of farming. More and more people were employed as farm servants rather than having their own share of the land on which they might hope to grow enough for their needs. In effect subsistence farming was replaced by a more commercial system. This still left those at the bottom of society vulnerable to poverty. In the 17th and 18th centuries the rural poor were severely affected by poor harvests. In the 19th century they could be as badly affected by economic conditions – war, trade slumps, price fluctuations, etcetera. And, of course, old age and infirmity were constant factors in both eras. The greater movement of people was also a factor and perhaps contributed to a lessening of religious authority.

There is some evidence of increasing numbers of rural poor in Skene Parish in the 19th century. In 1830 there were growing problems with vagrant beggars. The problem was so bad that the kirk session asked the heritors to support some constables to check "*all vagrant and sturdy beggars*". Although beggars' badges existed from the late Middle Ages, those surviving from Skene are inscribed 'Pauper Parish of Skene 1830'.

Skene pauper's badge 1830

This may be when they were first used in the parish, to help combat the rise in itinerant begging. The following year session was trying to find accommodation for four paupers, and James Knowles of Kirkville donated 86 yards of flannel to be given to the poor. This was to be cut into two-yard lengths, suitable for making an under jacket with sleeves and enough for all 40 people then on the register. In 1832 the session reported an increase in paupers on the roll and there was "*great distress,*" the heritors being asked to release £20 from the funds to alleviate the situation.

In 1832 David Blaikie, the new owner of Kinmundy, proposed an

147

extraordinary collection be made quarterly in aid of the Poor Fund and the Congregational Church be contacted for a contribution. Blaikie, an Aberdeen advocate and merchant, was no philanthropist, since he also proposed reducing the amount given to each of the poor because provisions were cheap at that time, and that the allowance be proportionate to the fiar prices of meal. Both motions were eventually defeated. There certainly seems to have been some tension between the heritors and the session over meeting the needs of the poor. In 1833 the session were trying to get a response from the heritors to define their powers over pauper housing and they resolved to apply to the Presbytery in Aberdeen if they got no response. A few years later the Poor Fund was £17 in arrears with no prospect of remedying it. A reduction in allowances was made at this time. There was actually enough money to bring down the deficit, but they were reluctant to touch this invested money. Instead they made an appeal for contributions to those heritors not resident in the parish.

By 1837 they were still struggling, not helped by poor collections on Sundays due to sickness in the parish, the severity of the winter, and a heavy demand on the fund. One heritor, at least, was willing to contribute, as one of the trustees for Kirkville said he would contribute if the others did, according to the rental value of each estate. Eventually the other heritors agreed and Haddens, owners of Garlogie Mill, said they would endeavour to prevent any of their work force from claiming poor relief. The heritors contribution either didn't come in, or was not enough, because in 1838 the session had to borrow money. They also sent a statement of income to all heritors and asked them to attend the next time it was being distributed to the poor. In addition they said that if the money wasn't made up they would have to take back the £24 invested money which was currently with Alexander Crombie of Leddach. This seems to have prompted some of the heritors to attend the next few meetings and the trustees of George Skene, the trustees of Kirkville, and the Town of Aberdeen all agreed to pay their contribution to the shortfall. The town, through the Dean of Guild, was also asked to provide houses for paupers on their Easter Carnie estate.

All this points to a system in crisis, and in the towns the rise of factories and the population increase meant that older mechanisms for relieving poverty were no longer sufficient. Eventually the Poor Law Act was brought in, quite a number of years after the one in England.

Under the act, parishes were required to establish a parochial board with the power to raise taxes for the poor and appoint an inspector of poor to establish the validity of claimants. For Skene Parish a meeting was held in the Lemon Tree Tavern, Aberdeen, on 16th September 1845. At the meeting were the kirk session and some of the heritors or their agents: William McCombie of Easterskene; William Gibson of Kinmundy; James Smith of Wester Ord; Robert Low of Fiddy; John Smith, advocate, as mandatory for Skene of Skene's trustees; David Kennedy, writer, as mandatory for Alexander Crombie of Leddach; and Andrew Murray, advocate, as mandatory for William Pitcairn Knowles of Hillcarnie (Wester Carnie). For the kirk session the following attended: Rev. George Mackenzie, Andrew Fowler, George Mitchell, John Milne, and David Smith. The composition of the board was to include all the heritors by right, as well as the kirk session. In addition, however, there were to be elected members and this would lead to some controversies, especially once the Free Church became involved.

Andrew Fowler of Brodiach was appointed the first Inspector of Poor and Treasurer at a remuneration of £10 a year and he served for 16 years. This was not a full time post and Fowler continued with his other interests. Robert Low of Fiddie was elected chairman of the Parochial Board. Dr Lyon was appointed to attend to the poor and was remunerated with £3 per annum, with the board paying for any medicines needed. The board already had some funds, the former money from the kirk session, then in the possession of the trustees of Skene of Skene, from whom they moved to get it back. They also suggested a voluntary contribution of £40 in total from the heritors, each individual contribution being based on the size of their estates. Subsequently they raised money annually in the proportions – half from the heritors, and half from their tenants, though some tenants were exempt because of their own poverty and some were also granted a reduced assessment. This proportion continued until the end of the century. Perhaps surprisingly, Captain Shepherd of Kirkville, very active in charitable causes throughout the North-East, brought a legal case to claim exemption from poor rates because of the terms of the charter granted to his predecessor by the town of Aberdeen when they had sold the land.

Robert Ireland was appointed Free Church minister in 1850 and he very quickly got himself elected to the board. The Rev. Ireland was not one to bow down to the wishes of the formerly all-powerful heritors. Almost immediately he raised the issue of where the meetings of the board were held. Most of the meetings took place in Aberdeen, because it suited the heritors who either lived in the town, or sent their Aberdeen lawyers to the meeting. Ireland's argument was that the board officials lived in the parish and, with the meetings announced in the churches, the paupers should be given their opportunity to attend and state their case. He was defeated at this point: "*the convenience of the farmers is not the only plea. It is not against the interests of the poor or the working of the Poor Law to hold statutory meetings in Aberdeen*".

Gradually the board was given more powers and, at the end of 1854, they elected a Registrar of Births, Deaths and Marriages, official registration being another duty taken away from the church at that time. David Smith, the schoolmaster, was elected. He was already secretary to the board as well as session clerk. The election of a medical officer would continue to be a divisive issue.

When Andrew Fowler resigned as inspector in 1861, David Smith was elected to that post as well, despite Mr Smith of Wester Ord proposing that they advertise the post. This election provoked a major row since it seems that not all the members attended, and Rev. Ireland asked on whose authority the papers for the meeting had been sent out, since some members had not received them and some non-members had. This resulted in some people missing the meeting and perhaps invalidating the election of David Smith. Some of the voters were also challenged. The confusion seems to have arisen because Andrew Fowler was stepping down as inspector, but he felt he should send copies of the minutes to those responsible for the resolutions passed at the meeting and, in any case, as he said, the minutes were not secret.

Various resolutions were subsequently passed aimed at the objectors. They including the following:

- The voting for inspector was 18 to 8, so even if the five objectors had been there, Smith would still have been elected.
- Mr Fowler had given plenty of notice regarding his resignation on the grounds of advancing years.
- That Mr Fowler's resignation was accepted and therefore he was allowed to vote. (As Inspector he would not). He was also mandate for Mrs Moir, who was rated at £30 and entitled to a vote. Garlogie Mill was rated at £250 a year and consequently had four votes for each of its joint proprietors.
- "The allegation about securing an unusually large attendance of members – a common resort of those who find themselves in a minority – is almost unworthy of notice." The resolution then dismissed the objectors assertion

- of "repugnance by the great body of parishioners" and the assertion that many members of the board objected to the appointment of Fowler's successor – "said many being seven or eight".
- That the board had no alternative to the immediate election of an inspector, otherwise Mr Fowler would have been blamed for the delay in preparing a new rate assessment.
- Even some of the objectors had praised Mr Smith's qualities in the past and now they were stating he was unsuitable under any circumstances. It was distinctly stated that he would be retiring from the school post and they were mistaken in suggesting the school would thereby lose the Milne Bequest, because it still has it.
- The board has not doubt that the heritors will dismiss suggestions that Smith was given the inspector's post so that they would avoid having to pay him a pension from his teaching post.
- That the majority feel no less interest or responsibility as guardians of the poor than the objectors who seem to claim for themselves the sole possession of these qualities, also the majority are much larger ratepayers than the objectors. "It is no easy matter to find someone in a rural parish to carry out a post requiring keeping of books, dealing with correspondence, moreover the majority – not a few of whom have business experience – are equally able to judge someone capable of these tasks."
- That the Board adhere to the election of Mr Smith.

These resolutions were approved, with the dissenters being Rev. Mr Ireland, Robert Milne, John Valentine, Peter Lang and William Smith. Similar objections to the appointment of Dr Lyon were also dismissed.

Some of the comments made above indicate that there was a degree of bitterness between the two sides. The winners write the history and what we have here is only one side of the story as recorded in the minutes of the Parochial Board. However the battle lines had been drawn and the Free Church and other objectors were not about to go away!

A further special meeting was called in March 1861 when David Smith was again proposed by Mr Anderson of Westhill, seconded by McCombie of Easterskene, both major landowners in the parish. Robert Milne, mandatory for Captain Shepherd, proposed Alexander Wright, Netherton of Garlogie. Again Smith was elected by 17 to 6. Mr Ireland went as far as to ask that the Board seek opinion of legal counsel as to the validity of some of the votes, but the Board declined saying that this represented a "*mis-application of the funds under their management*". The issue continued to be contentious, especially when the Free Church subsequently had their own schoolmaster who they wanted to put forward for the post.

In the midst of these disputes the work of the Board still had to be carried on. The range of occupations of paupers was considerable – farm servants, tailors, weavers, millworkers, a hen-wife at Skene House, and a policeman. Even someone like Patrick Osbourne, a medical practitioner, sought poor relief in 1840. In 1874 William Sherret, who had been a teacher at Garlogie for 18 years, was in Nazareth House in Aberdeen and Skene Parish paid for his upkeep.

Stocking knitters were common recipients. These were women, often unmarried or widows, who supplemented what they could grow on their small pieces of land by knitting stockings. Normally a merchant would come from Aberdeen and distribute wool to the knitters in the area. A few weeks later he would return and collect the finished stockings, paying the women a pittance which got less throughout the century as mechanization increasingly produced cheaper stockings. In 1851, for example, there were three elderly women in the Kirktoun, either unmarried or widowed, engaged in knitting and spinning. One, aged 81, is described as a pauper, as is another woman engaged in domestic duties. The conditions which made people claim relief included paralyses; frailties of old age; lunacy; illegitimacy; bodily strength failure; ulcerated leg; bilious dyspepsia; consumption; lumbago and rheumatism.

Poor relief was classed as indoor or outdoor; indoor being in a poorhouse or equivalent, outdoor being support in their own house. For example, Jane Duncan from Wester Carnie was admitted to the register in 1841, and removed in 1870 when she was placed under the charge of Mrs Chisholm at Lyne of Skene. The board would also advertise for someone to attend to a housebound pauper in their own home. In Skene there were not the resources to build substantial poorhouses such as existed in Aberdeen. However, certain people did take in paupers, either as lodgers or like Mrs Chisholm whose house was, in effect, a poorhouse on a small scale. There were other premises in Easter Carnie and Wester Carnie. These rented properties were inspected by the Inspector and, in 1871, the board resolved to have the houses rented from Aberdeen City at Easter Carnie "*put into a proper state of repairs without further delay*". The 1901 Census shows Ann Kynoch, a widow of 75 years of age, was a boarding house keeper with four boarders aged from seven to nine.

POVERTY AND MEDICINE IN THE PARISH

In 1901 repairs were still being carried out to the roof of the "*House for Casual Sick Poor*" at Easter Carnie. The then Parish Council tried unsuccessfully to find a new house on the Westhill Estate. This became more urgent in 1906 when the Council received a letter from the City Chamberlain saying that the casual sick house was needed for estate purposes. Three years later they rented from Henry Mitchell the old tollhouse at Broadstraik on the Leddach Estate.

Children could be given relief until aged 14, when girls were put into service and boys to farm work. This would continue into the 20th century, as we will see with the section on Proctor's Orphanage.

The inspector was expected to investigate and pursue claimants. In 1870 he was given 25 shillings (£1.25p) to help him become better acquainted with the Poor Law. That same year he was instructed to investigate the case of Alexander McDonald, who was reported to be working in the Red Lion Inn in Aberdeen, and therefore earning enough to support himself. McDonald had been the blacksmith at Broadstraik, and had applied for relief because he had moved to Aberdeen with his family. His wife had refused to go with him. As a consequence he couldn't attend to his work, presumably because of the children. The inspector refused to have anything to do with the case and he was backed by the board.

Two years later, however, it was reported that Mrs McDonald had been in receipt of poor relief in Skene, but had gone south to look for work, leaving a child with Alexander. He had left one night, leaving the child in bed, and the child was sent to the poorhouse for St Nicholas Parish. Skene admitted liability for the child, who was to be removed from the poorhouse as soon as a nurse could be found in Skene. Cases such as this give some idea of the desperation that extreme poverty could produce.

The husband or father's parish determined who was responsible for a pauper, even after his death. The Skene roll of paupers contained quite a number of paupers living in other parishes. Thus Betsy Rae from Perth, but married to a Skene man and living in Kinnoull, Perth, was given relief by Skene Board. Her husband was actually in the 79th regiment in India and she received relief until he returned in 1867. Mary Aiken or Black, living at East Kirkville, was refused help in 1870 because she had a claim on Cluny parish through her dead husband.

In another case John Morgan at Berryhill was described as aged 56, in ill-health, totally destitute and confined to bed. He had been born in Ireland, but had wandered through Scotland for the last 20 years and had not acquired a residential settlement in any parish. He was visited by the medical officer who ordered that he be supplied with a nutritious diet, wine and cordials, and also that he be removed from Mr Urquhart's barn to some place where he could be properly attended to.

The board was also responsible for pursuing defaulters from other parishes or Skene folk who had responsibilities in other parishes. For example, in 1850 they took action against Archibald Strachan from Letter of Skene who refused to pay for the upkeep of his son in Aberdeen Lunatic Asylum. This case ran on for a number of years and was still not resolved by 1856. In 1869 Strachan was also being pressured to support his daughter-in-law, her husband having deserted her and her three children. The family were given money and added to the roll of paupers, though George Strachan returned the following year.

As we have seen with the kirk session, it was not only money that the board dispensed. It could be provisions or clothing. At the time of the potato failure in 1846 they were asked to make extraordinary provision for the paupers and were recommended to lay in stores of provisions – oatmeal, etcetera. The board declined to do this at that time, because the cost of provisions was too high (perhaps inevitably if the potato crop had failed!). Money could be given for specific purposes, such as buying shoes for children, and the inspector could also buy blankets and other bedding. In 1895 widow Farquhar claimed five boots and stockings for her children.

William McCombie of Easterskene was elected chairman of the Parochial Board in 1870 following the death of Robert Low. McCombie was to serve until 1885 when he stood down citing the state of his health and advancing years. Despite the contentiousness of the activities of the board and the appointment of its officers, for much of McCombie's time as chairman ratepayers seem to have been reluctant to attend election meetings. On several occasions none of them turned up, there was no election, and those proposed went unopposed. John Forbes of South Auchinclech was unanimously elected in McCombie's place, though only for a couple of years, being replaced by George Hamilton of Skene House in 1887.

Proctor's Orphanage

James Proctor was the son of a clock and watchmaker from Tarland, and he carried on his father's business as well as farming at Braerodach in Cromar. After inheriting £35,000 in the acrimonious and controversial Aberlour

Succession Case, he bought the Kirkville Estate from Captain Shepherd's trustees in 1879. James died in 1888, having made provision for the establishment of a children's home on his land. He is described as being a very public-spirited man, *"always revolving in his mind schemes for the improvement and benefit of his fellow-men"*.

He set up a board of trustees for the proposed home, comprising the Lord Provost and four senior baillies of Aberdeen, ministers from Skene parish, Migvie and Tarland, chairman of the School Board, two resident sheriffs and the procurator-fiscal of Aberdeen. It was some time after his death before any progress was made, due to a problem between the trustees of his estate and those of the proposed orphanage, which was resolved after legal pressure was put on the former.

In October 1891 the foundation stone was ceremoniously laid by Mrs Proctor, witnessed by local residents. The children of the parish sang, *"There's a home for little children,"* with *"their fresh young voices ringing out clear and harmonious"*. The home was to be conducted on the family principle, "ordained by God for the bringing up of children".

A case containing a facsimile of James Proctor's deed, as well as copies of Aberdeen newspapers and coins of the realm, were placed in the cavity and, in an old Masonic ritual, Mrs Proctor gave three knocks with a mallet and poured corn, wine and oil over the stone. A silver trowel was presented to her to mark the occasion. The home was in the tradition of Victorian philanthropy and was to be called the Proctor Christian Industrial Cottage Home, or some variation on that. Described as being in the cottage style, it is, nevertheless, an imposing house, built of red Corrennie granite by the architect George Marr of Jenkins & Marr.

James Proctor had left £3,500 for the building with a further £1,000 five years after his death. He gave the trustees the choice of a site on three farms on the estate – Whitestone, Rogiehill and Kirkton (or East Kirkton, later renamed Claylands). They chose Kirkton, just a few yards from the Old Skene Road, a short distance east of the village of Kirktoun of Skene. The accommodation was for 10 children and a house mother and father. The boys were to learn farming, gardening and carpentry; the girls dairying, housekeeping, sewing and knitting. The house sat in seven acres of land, along with a workshop, barn, stable, byre and other animal housing.

Two years later, in September 1893, the building was opened, again with some ceremony, presided over by Baillie Lyon, the future Lord Provost Sir

A History of Skene and Westhill

Proctor's Orphanage c.1905

Alexander Lyon. Mrs Lyon planted a silver tree in front of the house, supplied by the gardener at the Duthie Park, and luncheon was served in a marquee. A silver fir still stands there today, now considerably taller than the house. *"The visitors from Aberdeen drove to Skene by the Skene Road, returning via Culter and the Deeside Road."* Dr Lawson was appointed physician to the orphanage. Baillie and Mrs Lyon presented the orphanage with a large bible which is now in Aberdeen City Archives. In it are recorded the dates of birth of orphanage boys and girls, but only from the 1930s onwards.

The home had cost £1,600, leaving £2,900 for running costs, since the five years had elapsed and the extra £1000 was now due. There was £70 a year in income from the Kirkville Estate, with the local doctor and minister each being paid £10 for their services. William and Helen Bannerman were appointed house parents and they received £1 a week plus their food. The children admitted to the home were to be *"of poor but respectable parents; healthy and of good antecedents"*. Priority was given to two children from Tarland and the Vale of Cromar, and after that Skene and other areas. As it happened the home opened with just two boys and a girl.

Mary McMurtrie says that there was a family atmosphere under the Bannermans, always known as *"auntie and uncle"*. Mr Bannerman was very fond of the children, especially the little ones. Mary remembered being with him in the governor's car when they met the children coming home from school. He halted the pony and said to the youngest, a fat little dumpling, *"Weel, Jeanie – hae ye been gweed the day? Gang hame an tell Maggie to gie ye a jeely piece and min an tell her to spread a the corners."* The governor's car was pulled by a fat pony and Mary said that he made them lean to the front when going uphill and then to the back when going downhill – all to help the fat pony.

James Proctor's estate had difficulty meeting the annual allowance he had made for his widow, Ann, and seems to have had to borrow to money for this purpose, leaving it in debt. After her death the orphanage trustees had to take legal action to maintain their annual payments.

Orphanage children had to work before their school day began: boys milking the cattle, cleaning the byre and other farm work; girls cleaning the house. People from Skene today, including the former manse children, still remember going to Proctors in the morning for milk and eggs.

Jessie Kesson was perhaps the best known person who attended Proctors. As Jess Macdonald she was taken from her mother, a prostitute in Elgin, and sent to Proctors in the 1920s with her head shaven. When she eventually left the Orphanage in 1932 it was to a life in service (though locals will tell you that Jessie more often than not had her head in a book, or was writing herself when she should have been working). She later married and subsequently moved to London before her talent for writing eventually brought her recognition and some reward. Jessie's biographer, Isobel Murray, says, *"Jessie's feelings about her time in the Orphanage varied enormously in the different telling"*. Jessie had two matrons in her time at Proctors, though she named neither of them.

A History of Skene and Westhill

Orphanage picnic with matron, Mrs Elrick at the back right, Jessie Kesson extreme right of the second back row, and Charlie Gibbon, third from the right at the front. Two of his brothers are also in the photograph.

The atmosphere in the orphanage changed, with gramophone music in the recreation room

In 1991, at the time of Proctor's centenary, she contributed two articles of memories of the orphanage to the PRESS & JOURNAL. In them she speculated that the first matron had been there for some time, but the description she gave certainly does not seem like the description of Mrs Bannerman. Jessie says that the matron and her husband were a childless English couple in their sixties, and that the matron was Victorian in her attitudes. The place itself she described as having a bleak interior with drab fawn and green walls, stone flooring in the utility rooms, drab linoleum in the dormitories and public rooms, black linoleum of a rubber texture in the recreation room, a floor Jessie had to clean every Saturday. The recreation room was never used for recreation and its bookcase had "*an ethos of Victorianism in the books on its shelves*". The books "*implied it was better to die young but saved than to grow old and become a sinner*". After three years the matron had a stroke and retired, taking one of the older girls with her as a companion.

The next matron Jessie experienced was from the country, also in her sixties, but with a grown-up family. Under her the atmosphere in the orphanage changed, with gramophone music in the recreation room. The matron's husband also sang while he went about his work. He had been a grieve and he made a considerable difference to the farm produce of the Orphanage – growing their own fruit and vegetables and taking their oats to Garlogie where Mr Davidson milled them. They also bartered produce with the grocer's van. Jessie makes it clear that the children were really part of Skene life.

"We got neither more nor less than the local children, sharing their treats – the school Christmas tree and party, church socials, summer show and annual amateur play in the Milne Hall."

Under both matrons Jessie reacted against the ethos of the place, which was to train girls for service, either domestic or on the land. This was perhaps inevitable in the society of the time. To read Jessie it seems that the personality of the matron was responsible for the atmosphere in the place, rather than any dictates from the governors. Jessie, though, did see it very much as institution. This she contrasted with a recent visit to Proctors where she found that the place was home, "*a comfortably furnished, lived-in, private house*". Times had certainly changed. Jessie eventually overcame the trauma of her childhood, though her early life was a hard struggle.

Another success story from Proctors concerns Charlie Gibbon. He and his brother both went to the orphanage before World War II. Charlie was keen on gardening and, through the efforts of Hugh Munro, headmaster at Skene Central, he eventually got a gardening job at Dunecht House. In the war Charlie served on *HMS Queen of Kent* and wrote back to Mr Munro saying how crazy he was about gardening, reading all the gardening books and magazines he could get. According to Leslie Durno, Charlie went to Australia after the war and eventually became a professor of botany at a university there.

Generations of children passed through the orphanage, fondly remembering house parents such as Mr and Mrs Kennedy in the 1930s and 40s, and Mr and Mrs Wight in the 1950s. During that decade the orphanage had to use its capital for running costs and it also increased its charges, most of the children coming from Aberdeen City. It was eventually taken over by social work departments at Aberdeen County Council in 1969, and then Grampian Regional Council in 1975. Further reorganisation in the Nineties meant that it was again managed by Aberdeenshire Social Work Department. Proctor's managed to celebrate its centenary in 1992, but since closing shortly afterwards it remained boarded up until 2011 when it was sold.

The little wood behind the orphanage was at one time called the Bride's Wood. Apparently this had nothing to do with Saint Bride, but earned the name because a bride had met her tragic end there.

Medicine in the parish

The earliest reference to any medical care for the parish is 1759, when the Laird of Skene proposed appointing a midwife. She would be educated by a doctor and live in the parish. Skene was to pay half her charge and the kirk session the rest. The following year Elizabeth McDonald was appointed for a period of five years. There is also reference to a doctor's croft in the Kirktoun at the end of the 18th century.

In 1832 the ABERDEEN JOURNAL reported that, "*a Board of Health and other procedures had been established*". This followed a recommendation of the Justices at Aberdeen to adopt "*precautionary measures against the introduction of the eastern pertilence.*" The latter usually refers to the plague of Black Death, but here might mean some kind of flu epidemic. This temporary board divided the parish into 13 districts, each visited by "*intelligent individuals*", referred to as visitors, so presumably they were from Aberdeen. They overcame the "*canna be fashed*" attitude of some of the Skene folk. Dunghills were removed from the entrances to poorer houses and the inhabitants advised of the advantages of cleanliness. The Mason Friendly Society of Skene had raised money through a musical event, and blankets and bedding were distributed to the poor, and their houses were 'limed'. Here we have the town of Aberdeen taking it upon itself to try to improve health in the surrounding country areas.

Once the Parochial Board was established it became responsible for appointing a medical officer and the first one recorded was Dr Lyon. The post was to be an elected one, however, and Dr Keith from Newton Cottage was elected in 1850. After four years Keith left the parish and was replaced by Dr Lyon again. The appointment of medical officer was soon to cause considerable division and animosity among members of the board, just as we have seen with other appointments made by them. In 1859 Captain Shepherd proposed Dr James Laing, living at Nether Affloch, later at Wantonwells, instead of Dr Lyon, but he was defeated and Lyon was re-elected. Dr Laing had graduated from Aberdeen University in 1857 and was a member of the College of Surgeons in Edinburgh. He was later elected and, when he died in 1885, at the age of 56, he had served as medical officer for Skene, Kinnellar and Echt for almost a quarter of a century. His obituary described him as a hard working and successful practitioner whose "*geniality and kindness of disposition made him many friends*".

Following a very short appointment, Dr W. Oliphant Walker was chosen from among several candidates, with only the Free Church minister, William Innes, dissenting. Mr Innes's reasons are not recorded, but they were said to be injurious and offensive without a shadow of foundation and no vote was taken on the appointment. A few years later the controversies between established church members on one hand and the two dissenting churches on the other, arose again in connection with the appointment of a medical officer. Following Dr Walker's resignation there were a couple of short term appointments followed by Dr Lawson from Echt. Dr Lawson was from Westhill, being one of the Lawsons from Lawsondale Farm, and he served for many years as the doctor for Echt parish and the area round about. However, in 1892 James McIntosh, tailor (and later, merchant) in the Kirktoun, moved that because Lawson was not resident in the parish, his services be dispensed with and they advertise for someone who would live there. The issue would be voted on at the next meeting in February 1893. McIntosh was seconded by the Church of Scotland minister, William Philip. The Free Church minster, still Mr Innes, proposed that Lawson continue and was seconded by George Pirie. On this occasion Mr Innes's amendment won by 14 votes to six. McIntosh did not accept defeat, however, and brought up the issue again at the next meeting in August that year, where he was again defeated, each side ensuring that they drummed a full contingent of supporters or their mandates.

One can only imagine how unsettling this must have been, especially for Dr Lawson. McIntosh tried one more time, in February 1894. At this meeting there were problems with some of the mandates – McDonald of Johnstone (Galleymoss) gave two people his mandate and they were both rejected. McIntosh himself could not produce some of his mandates, but his motion this time was successful by 10 votes to seven. Rev. Innes dissented on the following grounds:

Because Dr Lawson, after having established a wide practice, and served the Board satisfactory for five years is dismissed without fault alleged against him.

Such dismissal is opposed to the spirit of the Board of Supervision Regulations – deprecatory needless interference with an officer who does his duty.

Because several attempts to establish a local practice having been made in Dr Lawson's time in vain, his dismissal now is fitted only to generate ill-feeling, but also to prejudice a satisfactory appointment – no self respecting doctor will care to risk such appointment except on his own terms

I think one can only be appalled today that parish politics can interfere with the working of the medical profession. William Innes's pleas were in vain, and Dr James Bell was appointed. Bell was renting Leddach as his surgery, and it was not to be the last time that the surgery was based there. Doctor Lawson, though, as well as his surgery in Waterton (Dunecht), also rented premises at Mason Lodge. Although Dr Bell was the medical officer for Skene dealing with public health matters, schools, etc., Doctor Lawson

Doctor Skinner and his wife

162

continued to have a surgery at Mason Lodge into the 1920s, and to serve the western half of the parish, as well as Echt and Kinellar.

Disease and illness were often fatal in those days. Some of this comes through in the School Board minutes, as we have seen. In August 1888 there was a virulent outbreak of scarlet fever in the family of Alexander Wilson, the blacksmith at Lyne of Skene. Two of the children died within a few days of each other and a further child followed a fortnight later. It is difficult for us to comprehend how it must have felt to lose three children to scarlet fever within a few weeks of each other. The same year there was an outbreak of typhoid at Garlogie Cottages, occupied by millworkers.

Dr Bell resigned in December 1896 on grounds of ill-health. In January 1897 Dr J. E. Skinner, who had taken over Bell's practice at Leddach, was the only applicant for the post of medical officer and he was appointed at £14 10/- (£14.50) p.a, plus 2/6 (12½p) per case as vaccinator. John Emslie Skinner is the first doctor of whom we have a real picture. He served for a long time and there are still people alive who remember him.

Water supplies in Skene

Prospect Cottage was the original school at Westhill and is occupied today by Mrs Sheila Kelly. When she came here with her late husband, George, in the early 1950s, they had to go down to Lawsondale Farm for their water (on the lane down to Berriedale). Water supply, which we now take for granted, was not so easily come by until quite recently, especially in rural areas.

In the 19th century the Skene Parochial Board came to have responsibility for environmental health matters. Thus in 1878 the sanitary inspector took action against Mr Spring, tenant of Auchinclech farm, in respect of a cottage occupied by one of his farm servants with his family. In the terminology of the time the cottage was "*causing a nuisance from want of repair, proper drainage, privy accommodation or cesspool, injurious to the health of the inmates*". The following year the inspector reported a nuisance at Kirktoun in respect that an ashpit and cesspool was situated near the public well. Water was tested by an analytical chemist from Aberdeen, but found to be of very good quality. By February 1880 the nuisance had not been removed, "*but on the contrary had rather increased*". Indeed the local authority paid a visit and found the nuisance "*to be of a very ugly nature*"! The inspector was asked to see to its removal.

Two years later, in August 1882, the board received a report which said that cesspools or ashpits are now scarcely to be seen near the doors of dwellings. "*Nuisances formerly met with are now almost entirely removed and not allowed to recur.*"

I am afraid this was a trifle optimistic because in October 1884, the board received a letter from James Macintosh, tailor and feuar in the Kirktoun, regarding the state of the water in the Kirktoun well. A committee was set up to look into it and reported back a few days later. The report makes grim reading.

> "On the north side of the well there was until lately an ashpit or cesspool filled with all kinds of filth. On the east side there is a byre or cow shed and dung heaps with the liquid manure in a rubble drain flowing within a few feet of the well. Alongside the Public Road there is a foul ditch partly covered with stones and earth within 5 or 6 feet of the well. The nuisance complained of occurs after a fall of rain – the water being highly discoloured and the taste obnoxious."

The committee infers that the well is saturated with sewage which finds its way into the well, especially in wet weather. The well was built of loose stones and covered on the top with cement. The committee recommended its removal and, in its place, a cistern be built with bricks and cement and covered on top with flagstones properly cemented and made water-tight.

A similar situation was found in 1886 when several families had severe cases of fever; four of the worst affected had their water supply from Wester Kinmundy Farm. There was a large amount of manure from which liquid escaped into the mill pond and, when water was let off, it overflowed into the well or cistern. Two children of Duncan McLennan, flesher, died. The board wrote to the Westhill proprietor, Miss Farquhar, and directed her to the 89th section of the Public Health (Scotland) Act. Miss Farquhar took immediate action. The cistern was removed about 200 yards to where a spring rose, and the water conveyed in a lead pipe from the fountainhead.

By 1887 William McCombie of Easterskene had provided his tenants in the Kirktoun with an abundant supply of water from a well in one of his fields, about 200 yards from the pump. The latter was placed at the north end of the merchant's shop and attached to the shop. It can be seen in an old photograph of the shop.

Some of these pumps were made from trees sunk into the ground, twelve feet or more in length. The bark was taken off first, and an auger or drill was used to bore out the centre of the tree. At the joiners in Elrick this process took three men two days to complete; two of the men turned the auger, one emptied the shavings. Powered sawmills could do it faster. If the depth was great enough, then two trees were joined together using pitch.

An example, still *in situ*, can be seen at Burnland and there is a discarded one lying at the end of a track at Gask. At Broadstraik Inn Adam Craigmile says that they had their own well and two pumps in the wash-house with hand-operated wheels to fill the two tanks in the loft. There was also a 'tree' pump outside the inn. Elrick had one village pump beside the joiners and it supplied the joiner, blacksmith, shoemaker, Elrick farmhouse, the shop with tailors above it, the toll-house and the tinsmith. Further east there was another at what became the cement works, with another one at Bridgefoot and at Moss-side. At Burnland croft running water was brought as far as the porch just at the outbreak of World War II. They had to wait until well after the war before it was brought into the house.

Water pump made from tree trunk at Burnland

The Parish Council

The Local Government (Scotland) Act 1889 set up county councils in Scotland with a wide variety of powers. This was followed by the Local Government (Scotland) Act 1894 which replaced the parochial boards with parish councils, elected according to the franchise that existed at that time. Area groupings of parishes were also formed with these being represented on the County Council. Skene was in the Aberdeen District Committee. The first meeting of the Provisional Skene Parish Council took place on 11th April 1895. The elected councillors at that time were James Fowler Abernethy, Westhills; William Adam, Broadwater; Alexander Gavin, Wester Ord; James Legge, Craigstone; Alexander Massie, Milton of Garlogie; Rev. Robertson, Skene Church; Peter Smith, Mains of Westhills; John Valentine, Upper Affloch; and James Watt, merchant, Lyne of Skene. The first meeting proper took place on 18th May that year, when James Watt was elected first chairman.

Although having to answer upwards to the County Council, the new Parish Council had more extensive powers than the Parochial Board. They were consulted, for example, on the subject of a light railway between Echt, Skene and Aberdeen, something to which they gave their support.

In 1903 John Wyness, Graystone, retired after 30 years as Collector of Poor. He continued serving as Inspector of Poor until 1910. John Wyness also gave 36 years service as clerk and treasurer to the School Board and is buried in Skene Kirkyard. James F. Abernethy, another great servant to public affairs in Skene, was appointed as inspector, having first resigned as a councillor, a condition of the appointment. His story is told in later chapters.

Aspects of rural life in the 19th century

Meal mills

There were four meal mills in the parish – Garlogie, Easter Ord, Birsack, and Craigiedarg. They are first mentioned as follows: Garlogie in 1456, Ord in 1591, Birsack in 1612, and Craigiedarg in 1542 (though that might just be the place-name rather than the mill). According to Roy Lyall (senior) the mill for Skene House Estate was originally at Fernlea, near to the house. He was told by Hugh Gillespie, the blacksmith at Lyne in the 1930s, that power came from the Gashley or Lochans Burn (also known as Jamie Bells), running down from Newton. This had originally run through Lyne of Skene, but was diverted and brought into Skene House grounds via Mary's Widdie. From there it went via the picnic park and a dam was made to drive the mill at Fernlea. The burn subsequently supplied water to a fire reservoir at Skene House, then went on to join the Bogentory via Back Mains.

Tradition has it that there was a small lochan below Newton Farm, possibly created by the diverting of the burn, thus giving the name Lochan to the burn and to one of the houses at the Lyne. There is no trace of a lochan on the first OS map, though. Traces of the lade itself can still be seen within the grounds of Skene House, and of the mill building within the present house at Fernlea, including the kiln floor. This house is mid-18th century. At what date it was removed and Craigiedarg became the mill for Skene Estate is not clear. I imagine it would have been by the mid-18th century and Craigiedarg

Mill is recorded in the Kirk Session records in 1765 and in the Skene Estate rental for 1773. It may have been re-located at the same time as the tradesmen at the fermtoun of Hatton were moved to become the village of Line (Lyne) of Skene. Two 18th century cottages at Craigiedarg may date from the move of the mill there and other present day farm buildings may have been part of the mill. The mill building at Birsack is now a private home. Garlogie Mill is now part of Milltown of Garlogie Farm.

We have already seen that only two millers were listed in 1696, but the others were certainly in existence, perhaps temporarily lacking a miller at that time. Curiously the four mills are all on the boundaries of the parish. This may just be coincidence, because that's where the best power could be harnessed from the relevant burns. Or it may have been deliberate, and certainly at Ord and Birsack the parish boundary bulges so as to include the mill. They were all powered by different burns – Craigiedarg by the Corskie Burn, Garlogie by the Leuchar, Birsack by the Littlemill Burn, and Easter Ord by the Brodiach Burn which becomes the Ord Burn thereafter. The mill dam for Easter Ord was on the Brodiach Burn half-way between Mill of Brotherfield and Damhead. Between it and the road there was also a sawmill in 1900. A lade left the dam and ran off to power Brotherfield, the burn itself leaving the dam and heading to Easter Ord. Practically nothing survives of Mill of Ord today.

Up to around 1800, in a practice going back to feudal times, tenants would have been thirled or astricted to a particular mill. This meant that they had to take their oats and other crops to a specific mill for milling and these rights were jealously guarded. Ord, Fiddie, Easter Carnie, Leddach, Whitestone, Blackhills, Easter and Wester Kinmundy and Brodiach were all thirled to the Mill of Ord. The tenants on the estate of Fornet, which had not originally belonged to Skene of Skene, had to take their crop to Garlogie, even though Craigiedarg would have been nearer. The latter was on Skene of Skene's lands but, even after Skene bought Fornet, the tenants there had to continue to use Garlogie Mill.

As late as 1753 the miller at Garlogie wrote to the Laird of Skene complaining that there had been a drought and he couldn't keep up with demand. Robert Hunter at Fornet, "*came here without sending any room before as is usual* (i.e. booking a place in the queue) *and told us that unless we could grind his corn tomorrow he would carry it to some other miln*". He ends by saying, "*I hope you will send your officer and order him to bring corn to the miln*".

The miller was also entitled to multure – a payment as a portion of the corn ground at the mill, or of sheaves for thrashing. Therefore when Garlogie and the meal mill were being feued in 1788 they included, "*the multures of the lands of Fornet*". Tenants also had other duties relating to the mill – to keep the mill lade clear, to help transport new mill stones, etc.. These duties and taxes often made the miller an unpopular person in the community.

In the later 19th century corn mills began to decline as new technology meant larger mills owned by large firms, working continuously with larger quantities of corn, much of it imported from North America. The ones in Skene survived into the 20th century and closed down at different times and for different reasons. As will be detailed in the section on Dunecht Estate, the Garlogie one closed in 1940 due to the raising of the water levels in the loch for electricity generation.

The last miller at Garlogie was a Mr Davidson who continued to farm from the mill building into the 1950s. Craigiedarg may actually have closed before the end of the 19th century. In 1891 it was rented by James Rae, manure agent; before World War I it was rented to Aberdeen milling company, John Milne & Co. Ltd of Dyce and Palmerston Road; then to William Wisely & Sons Ltd, contractors and warehousemen, after the war. Whether or not these various tenants were actually milling at Craigiedarg is not clear. It was described as ruinous in the early 1930s and by 1938/39 it was under reconstruction. In 1901 the miller at Ord was Thomas Pirie from Belhelvie. Mill of Ord was the last mill in the parish to function as a meal mill. Birsack was still going in the mid-1950s and Gordon Argo remembers the miller at Birsack occasionally milling some pease meal even after the mill was officially closed.

Other smaller mills flourished in the 19th century as improved drainage systems channeled water courses to allow for the creation of dams and lades. A look at the early OS maps shows these at places such as Howemoss, Brodiach, Wester Kinmundy, Broadshade, Barnyards of Easterskene and Newton. These were used for threshing, bruising oats to feed horses, and cutting turnips. The buildings and lades for some of these can still be seen, e.g. at Easterskene and Brodiach, the latter being used to generate electricity in the 20th century.

For those farms which did not have a dam and lade an alternative was a horse mill and these can be seen as small circles on the OS maps, e.g. at Burnside, Southbank, and Nether Affloch. Adam Craigmile described the working of a horse mill in the early years of the 20th century.

"When Barrack's travelling threshing mill driven by a traction engine, was not available, the barn mill in the steading at Elrick was used. Driven by two horses in plough harness attached to a cross bar, they walked in a circle to turn the gears which drove the thrashing drum for oats and barley. A man stood by to keep the horses moving. One man put sheaves on a table next to the drum while another man fed sheaves into the drum. Straw was shaken and carried forward, the oats or barley fed into a sack, and the chaff fell to the floor."

Bookplate from Skene Reading Society

Skene Reading Society and Sir Walter Scott

We don't know much about the Skene Reading Society, in fact the main reason we know of their existence is because they tried to ban the works of Walter Scott. The ABERDEEN JOURNAL of November 19, 1834, carried reports on the attempt. The previous Monday a meeting had been held in Blackhills Congregational Church to discuss a ban. The meeting was "crowded to suffocation" with people coming from as far as Echt and Midmar to hear the debate! The novels, in 48 volumes, had been bought for the library. This would be the parish library mentioned by the parish minister in 1843. At that time it had over 600 volumes and was supported by an annual subscription of one shilling (5p) per reader.

The speakers against the novels were led by Rev. Smith of Blackhills, and the supporters of Scott by Rev. Charles Skene, parish schoolmaster of Skene. The charges against the novels were that they contained oaths, defamed the puritans and debased Christianity; that "*they were to the mind what cholera was to the body,*" and that "*many better books have been publicly burned*". Mr Skene defended Scott as being a Christian and a very worthy writer who defended true religion. After some debate a committee was formed to further consider the novels.

In Aberdeen University Library I came across a four-page pamphlet bound with numerous other publications. This pamphlet must have been prepared by the anti-Scott faction, and is addressed to the members of Skene Reading Society. In it various religious writers of the time are cited condemning novels in general and Scott in particular. A few quotes give the flavour of their criticism.

> "As to that class of novels, I join with every other moral and religious writer in condemning, as the vilest trash, the greater part of the productions which under this name have carried a turbid stream of vice over the morals of mankind. They corrupt the taste, pollute the heart, debase the mind, demoralize the conduct."

Relating to historical novels in particular:

> "And what is the general tendency of the great majority of such works. To distort and caricature the facts of real history; to gratify a romantic imagination; to pamper a depraved mental appetite; to hold up venerable characters to derision and contempt; to excite admiration of the exploits and the malignant principles of those rude chieftains and barbarous heroes whose names ought to descend into everlasting oblivion; and to throw a false glory over scenes of rapine, of bloodshed, and of devastation."

The final quote sounds like the kind of put-down some of us might have heard from our grandmothers. "*Had Sir Walter Scott blackened shoes at the corners of our streets, he would have done the world more service than by writing* OLD MORTALITY."

It is ironic that Sir Walter is little read today because he is seen as dull and worthy. Here he is, in the middle of the 19th century, being blamed for the decline in moral and religious values at that time.

Unfortunately I've not been able to find the outcome of this debate. The

ABERDEEN JOURNAL sarcastically ends by commenting:

"Tell it not in Scotland, publish it not in the civilized world, are eleven of the good men of the parish of Skene to sit in judgement on the works of the master-spirit of the age – the immortal Sir Walter Scott. Gentle Reader, is this the march of intellect, or the progress of cant?"

The Reading Society survived this controversy and, in 1865, its librarian, James Fowler at the Kirktoun, appealed in the ABERDEEN JOURNAL for the return of all books.

Temperance and the Skene Social Reform Association

Alexander Wisely, lay helper at the Congregational Church, records in his notebook: June 11th 1851, "*I addressed along with others a temperance meeting at Carnie. I am astonished at the apathy of our own church in this matter.*" However it was to be several years later before the temperance movement really got going in Skene.

Originally know as the Permissive Bill and Social Reform Association, the Skene Social Reform Association started early in 1859 at a meeting held in the Free Church School at which a lecture on the influence of alcohol upon the human constitution was given by Rev. Dr Longmuir of the Free Mariners' Church in Aberdeen. The association was part of the temperance movement, but had wider ambitions. It soon had 60 members, mainly farmers. Its main objectives were to reduce the number of public houses and to get rid of bothies and feeing markets. Captain Shepherd of Kirkville was a leading supporter who, in 1861, took part in a two-day Open Air Meeting for Religious Exercises, on the Links at Aberdeen.

At Skene, the same year as it was inaugurated, an open air meeting was held on the banks of the loch. Benches were set up for 600, but over 1,000 turned up. Flags flew at various points and an arch of evergreens and flowers pointed the way to the meeting site. Twenty-four stewards supplied tea and bread for the crowd. The secretary of the Royal Northern Agricultural Society spoke about the practicalities of abolishing feeing markets. A local farm servant, William Reid, was persuaded to give his experiences, and the overseers of Easterskene and Kirkville also spoke. The main argument against the feeing markets was their demoralizing nature and the amount of drink sold at them. William McCombie of the FREE PRESS, cousin of Easterskene, addressed the gathering, as did local farmers Low of Mains of Kinmundy, Valentine of Affloch, Low of Longcairn and Stephen of Carnie. Both Free and Established church ministers took part.

In 1860 over 1,600 people attended the main gathering and there were follow-up revival-type meetings at four locations in the parish, with a large one on the lawn at Kirkville. In the reporting of the time, "*a number evinced anxiety about their spiritual condition and many went home rejoicing, making the woods resound with the voice of psalms*". Meetings and social events continued throughout the 1860s, the last one I have seen recorded being in 1869.

The movement persisted, however, because Andrew Mathieson records in his diary entry for 28th November 1878 that, while ploughing, he saw all the Skene Free Church folk "*going down to sign the call but to their great disappointment he, the minister, declined coming*". Later in December he notes that it was the day of signing the call at Skene for Mr McInnes of Torry. It seems that the temperance movement was given a new lease of life with the appointment of William Innes as minister at the Free Church in 1879. Two meetings were held in March of that year, with addresses given by J. H. Smith of the Scottish Temperance League. At the meeting at the Mason Lodge about a dozen people took the pledge. However at the Lyne of Skene, "*although there was nothing like disorder, there was more liveliness and several of those appealed to quietly uphold their belief that there was no evil in taking a glass now and then. It is hoped that the formation of a Total Abstinence Society will not be a mere flash in the pan, and will accomplish much good among the young if it should be found that auld sparrows are ill to tame*".

The Free Church minutes for 1885 include a request to all willing to join a Temperance Society and Band of Hope. That same year the annual temperance soiree was held at Mason Lodge and again was addressed by someone from the Scottish Temperance League. The committee is recorded as comprising: President, Rev William Innes; Vice President, Rev. Wisely of the Congregational Church; Treasurer, G. Leslie; Secretary, J. F. Abernethy; Committee Members, William Williamson, William Abel, J. Urquhart, A. Stuart, and J. McLennan.

Skene Mutual Improvement Association

One of the admirable features of working men in the 19th century was their desire for self-improvement even after a long and hard day's work. In the town it might have been to attend classes at the Mechanic's Institute in Market

Street. In the rural areas it would be the Mutual Improvement Association which began in Rhynie in 1830s, spread throughout the North-East, and became closely associated with the Liberal Party and the Free Church, as well as the Temperance Movement. An association was not formed in Skene until 1874, but it was to last for more than 30 years. There was also a Cullerlie and Garlogie Mutual Instruction Class which was in existence earlier, since at least 1860.

The Skene Association held meetings weekly, the kirk session minutes recording in October 1882 that the association "*has resumed its sittings each Monday evening at 8 o'clock in the Old School at Mason Lodge.*" Individual members or invited speakers spoke on a defined topic and a debate ensued. In 1884, for example, the subject was, "*Is the drunkard more sinned against than sinning*". Mr Mackenzie of Northbank spoke in favour; Mr J. F. Williamson of Crombie Cottage spoke against, Mackenzie winning by one vote. At the annual festival in January the same year, 160 people turned up despite the stormy weather and the slushy state of the roads. As well as readings, recitations and songs, the Rev. Wisely of Westhill Church spoke on 'Habit' and Rev. Innes of the Free Church spoke on 'Punctuality'. In October 1885 the topic was "*Has Conservative or Liberal government done most for the working classes*," the vote being 3-1 in favour of Liberals. In March 1885 the topic was "*Should art galleries and museums be opened on Sundays*," with a majority of seven for the negative. In 1877 they held various events such as concerts to raise money to donate clocks to the schools of the area.

Andrew Mathieson, whose diaries are mentioned later in this chapter, records going to the Mason Lodge in October 1878 to hear Charles Thompson giving a lecture on chemistry "*with experiments*". On another occasion they debated "*whether is there most knowledge derived from observation or from reading*". As one might expect in a practical farming community there were eight votes for observation and none for reading! At the same meeting the Rev. Innes from Skene Free Church gave a lecture on the Orkney Islands. Andrew also went to the Waterton Mutual Improvement Class where the gardener at Dunecht gave a talk on potatoes, a more practical topic, but also "*Mr Stopani gave a reading upon I don't know what*"! Andrew himself read an essay at one of the meetings, though unfortunately he does not say what it was about. Andrew's dedication to learning can be seen when he describes going to a conversazione at Skene Free Church. The speakers were all local men: Rev. Wisely of the Free Church; John Bruce of Fornet; Mr Abel of

Whitestone; Mr Mackay; Mr Winchester; and James Abernethy. Andrew says it was a very good meeting and it was nearly 12 midnight when he got home. This from someone who would probably have to be up around five the next morning.

By 1890 they still had 50 members. In 1900 the president, Rev. William Christie, schoolmaster at Skene, retired from both posts. He presided at the annual festival before retiring. A musical evening was held, where ex-Baillie Kemp from Aberdeen sang patriotic songs which were well received. However he also gave a short address attributing the war in South Africa to the machinations of Stock Exchange speculators which was met with "*marked disapproval*". The Free Church minister, Mr Innes, spoke patriotically on the same subject and was warmly received. Alexander Murdoch from Mason Lodge gave a humorous reading of local interest entitled 'Jock's courtship'.

The last reference I have seen to the activities of the association was in 1908, when Skene schoolmaster, George Mitchell, gave a talk on the Puritan movement in England, with James Abernethy presiding.

Agricultural Association

In 1873 Skene and Midmar joined the exisiting Echt Agricultural Association, thus becoming the Echt, Skene and Midmar Agricultural Association. The ABERDEEN JOURNAL commented that this led to a larger show than normal with more classes and exhibitors. Among those from Skene winning in various classes, with some attending the dinner, were Valentine, Affloch; Thomson, Newton; Milne, Northside; Ewan, Lochside; Spring, Auchinclech; Smith, Wester Ord; and Dr Laing. This organization is still in existence today and organizes the very popular Echt Show.

The Milne Hall

Three brothers and one sister, John, Helen, James and David Milne, all lived at Leucharbrae, Skene in the 1870s. They came from Aboyne originally, and Helen and John may have been twins. Their gravestone in Skene Kirkyard reads as follows; "*erected in memory of Helen Milne d. 13 Jan 1873 aged 72 – she did what she could; John Milne d. 27 Dec. 1879 aged 79; Rev. David Milne A.M. formerly schoolmaster of Fintray d.14 Jan. 1884 – a superior scholar, a successful teacher, an amiable & kindhearted man; James Milne d. 9 Mar 1889 aged 86.*"

David would have been around 75 when he died, so they were a fairly long lived family for their day. They are remembered, however, for their benevolence more than their longevity. David left £200 to the minister and kirk session for the benefit of the poor of the parish, the money being invested in the Harbour Commissioners of Aberdeen and the interest only used. He had lived for the last 12 years of his life at his brother's farm at Leucharbrae and was a church elder.

James Milne would probably have put up the memorial stone to his siblings and modestly left his own inscription understated. However in 1885 he gave £300 to build the hall which bears his name.

A feu disposition with the ground connected with the building was obtained from Mr J. McIntosh, tailor and merchant in the Kirktoun. To quote from the minutes of the first meeting of the hall managers held in the church vestry on 20th August 1885: "*it was the wish of Mr Milne that the whole property should be vested in the Church of Scotland*". Consequently the managers were to be the Minister, Rev. W. M. Philip, as chairman, the kirk session and five members of the congregation.

The building was to cost at least £400, and Mr Philip received donations from several individuals, as well as a promise of £75 from the Baird trustees once the hall was opened. In all £426/7/7 was raised. The architect, James Watt, gave his service free of charge and local farmers carted the materials, also for nothing. The hall opened on 2nd September 1885, with a social soiree and musical evening. Mr Philip was presented with his portrait painted by Joseph Salmond, Adelphi Court, Aberdeen. Mrs Philip received a Singer sewing machine! As we shall see in the chapter on parish politics, the building of the hall and the minister's role in opening it was not universally popular.

Some of the uses of the hall in the first year were dancing classes, the Volunteers Ball, Oddfellows Ball, Ploughmen's Ball, a Farmers Land Meeting, and Volunteer Force meetings. Divine Service was held there 14 times and the bible class also met there; the Easterskene Games Committee met twice. James Scott Skinner, the famous fiddler from Banchory, played there in March 1893. Musical events were always popular, with a large attendance reported for the cantata *Eva* presented by the Skene Parish Church Choir in 1895.

Concerns over smoking and drinking echo similar problems today. The third meeting of the hall committee was called by the chairman because he had heard that there was dissatisfaction in the parish that a resolution had been passed prohibiting the use of "*intoxicating drinks*" in the hall. The earlier resolution had been brought forward with no prior notice and was replaced

ASPECTS OF RURAL LIFE IN THE 19TH CENTURY

The Milne Hall before World War II

by one which stated that the prohibition would be relaxed for the games committee's annual ball and in other special cases as judged by the management committee, provided that the privilege was not abused.

In 1895, after lengthy discussion, smoking was banned in the hall on a vote of five to two. This issue rumbled on because, in 1898 at a meeting of the Oddfellows Ball committee, they were told that they could have the hall on condition that they prevent smoking in the building. At this one member of the committee defiantly lit his pipe and was followed by several others. After this "*cowardly defiance of the rules*" the managers wrote to the Oddfellows committee asking for an apology and assurance that they would prevent smoking in the hall. In the event of smoking being discovered, they would pay an additional five shillings (25p), and may also face a ban from use of the hall. Eventually, around 1907, a lean-to shed of corrugated iron was built for smokers.

> The Oddfellows Ball committee were told that they could have the hall on condition that they prevent smoking in the building. At this one member of the committee defiantly lit his pipe and was followed by several others.

177

Tibbie Reid remembers that during World War II the hall was used for showing films, including public information films, saving people from having to travel into Aberdeen. Two men came from Kemnay, she thinks, one called Jim Cruickshank. Until the war, what is now the car park in front of the hall was a field, part of the blacksmith's croft. Entrance to the hall was via a lane between the field and the shop (Red Star). The hall remained church property until after World War II. In 1949 it was in need of improvement, but couldn't get a grant from the Education Committee of the local authority because of the fact that it was church property. One of the conditions of such grants was that ownership should be vested in a committee representative of the whole community and a kirk session was not considered sufficiently representative. Consequently the hall committee – Messrs Brownie, Collie, Durno, Lyall, Mathieson, Ogg, Porter, Smith, Sey and Troup, along with the new minister, Rev. David Johnston as chairman, began the process of transferring the hall to local authority ownership. This process was completed in 1951 and the final meeting of the Milne Hall managers took place on 10th May 1951.

The Skene Games

The Skene Games probably began around 1869. The 1870 announcement of them in the ABERDEEN JOURNAL says that the games are open to the parishes of Skene, Cluny, Monymusk, Kemnay, Kintore, Newhills, Peterculter, Echt and Drumoak. The first secretary was Alexander Pirie junior, of Leddach. The early games are called 'Games and Picnic' and were held under the auspices of William McCombie of Easterskene and Captain Forbes of South Auchenclech. They were held in a park at Easterskene, near the Barnyards, and the crowds at the first two games were 800 and 1,000. Local farmers and landowners mentioned as being present were Major Robertson, Counteswells House; George Hamilton of Skene House; Colonel Forbes of Kinmundy; Alexander Edmond of Aberdeen; Andrew Fowler of Broadiach; and the Rev. W. M. Philip.

Events were similar to modern highland games with, for example, Alex. Fraser of Kintore throwing the 22lb. (9.8kilo) heavy hammer 74ft 3ins (22.57m); D. Donald from Greenburn throwing the 20lb (9k) heavy ball 33ft 3in. (10.07m); and Lewis Stewart of Kemnay long leaping 18ft (5.5m). Among Skene competitors mentioned are Stewart Adams, John Lawson, Alexander Laing, John Mathieson, and Helen Ross from Fiddie in the girls' race. Three elegant brooches were the prizes for the ladies' dancing and running. Mr Williamson from the bakery and shop at Westhill provided the tea (nearly 1,000 sitting down to tea in the afternoon of the 1871 games).

Mr Burnett was secretary to the 1870 games, and Mr Alex. Pirie to the 1871 ones; Mr McCombie and Captain Forbes acted as judges; and Mr Grant, pipe-major of the Royal Aberdeenshire Highlanders, acted as superintendent. There was a large muster of powerful amateur athletes to compete for the prizes which included four very handsome silver medals. At the 1870 games the winner of the girls' race was *"borne off in the arms of her beaux and was an object of interest for the rest of the afternoon"*. She received an elegant silver brooch from Mrs Forbes, but unfortunately her name is not given in the list of prize winners.

"Mr McCombie of Easter Skene, who kindly grants free use of his fields for the celebration of these games, appeared everywhere on the scene in his towering straightness, and looked as young and supple as he did half-a-score years ago." A note from 1889 records that by kind permission of Colonel Ogston, the City Artillery Band will perform. *"No hawkers or sweetie vendors allowed on the policies."* Buses were to run from Aberdeen and from Cluny.

Towards the end of the century numbers were as high as 3,000, with 2,500 sitting down to afternoon tea. In 1899 the cycle competitions were a source of great attraction, one winner being R. Cruickshank of Blackburn who rode a bicycle specially built by Arthur Sangster of Aberdeen Cycle Works, George Street, the latter being a native of Skene parish. Among local landowners present as well as Duguid McCombie, were Mrs Pirie from Dunecht House; Major Brooke, Fairley, Newhills; Charles Forbes, Auchinclech; the Misses Falconer, Ord House, Skene; Mr and Mrs Allan, Broadshade; Mr and Mrs Low, Easter Fiddie; and Mr Shirras, Schoolhill, Aberdeen (presumably of Shirras Laing).

Secretary and treasurer of the games were John Williamson, Crombie Cottage and Peter Mackie, Westhill, with William Adam, Broadwater, president of the Skene Athletic Society. No Skene winners at this games, although John Tawse from Brae, Kinmundy, came third in the trotting match for roadsters, and James Hay from Garlogie came third in the quoits. Winner of the quoits was Alexander Forbes from Bucksburn with the remarkable score of 58 out of a possible 60, despite it being *"perfectly dark at the time it was made"*.

During the day the Grandholm brass band played, including for the dancing which went on until nine o'clock. The Oakbank pipers, with conductor and drummers, also played "*and the Easterskene Games Committee are to be congratulated on being amongst the first to appreciate the value of the Oakbank pipe band at such gatherings. This band, we understand, is to be still further augmented next year, and should prove a great attraction all over the country.*"

A different era indeed

I had originally thought that the Skene Games was eventually replaced by one at Skene House. However, it seems that this was a separate games, overlapping with the one at Easterskene. It started at Skene House around 1884, moving to Dunecht House shortly after and being known as the Dunecht Highland Games. The parish minister from 1893-1911 was Robert Robertson, a well-known piper, who for many years acted as a judge of the piping and dancing competitions. The Skene Games finished in 1929.

Independent Order of Oddfellows

The Oddfellows was a friendly society and I have come across various references to the Skene Lodge (Excelsior) in the late 19th century. They held meetings in Skene School and hired the Milne Hall for social events, where they caused trouble with members smoking in the hall. In 1905 the Excelsior Lodge of Oddfellows (No. 1080) held their annual ball in the Milne Hall and, despite it being a stormy night, 80 couples turned out, so they must have had considerable support in the area. Brothers Bandeen, Mackay, Mearns and Croft acted as masters of ceremony and Thomas Johnston is recorded as being secretary.

Other societies

Various other societies were around in Skene towards the end of the 19th century which seems to have been a lively time for social interaction. The Skene Literary Society was formed in October 1895 and by the following year had 65 members.

In that year over 80 attended their first drive, but I don't know how long it lasted. There was also a Skene Athletic Association which owed its existence to McCombie of Easterskene. It was presumably connected with the Skene Games and, although it survived his death, it probably didn't survive the ending of the games. The Skene Horticultural Society lasted longer, organizing displays and shows, and their prize lists can be read in the ABERDEEN JOURNAL.

ASPECTS OF RURAL LIFE IN THE 19TH CENTURY

Cinema comes to Skene

In January 1896 the cinema first came to Skene when Mrs Hamilton of Skene House sponsored a cinematograph exhibition for Skene Estate tenants by Messrs. Walker & Company, Aberdeen. The event was held in Skene Central School, and it was packed with old and young "*many of whom had never seen the moving pictures before*". Mr Hamish Beveridge of Walkers gave a summary of FARTHEST NORTH by Fridjof Nansen, the Norwegian polar explorer, so we must presume that the film related to that.

Andrew Mathieson and a farm servant's diaries

Andrew Mathieson was born in Forgue parish around 1843. In the 1870s and 80s he lived at Balmuir cottage and croft, near Affloch, with his father-in-law, William Moir, a retired farmer, Andrew's wife Isabella (Bella), and their family. Andrew kept a very detailed diary of his time at Balmuir, and continued when he moved to Kemnay in 1887. These diaries give us some idea of what life was like for a farm servant in the second half of the 19th century. The first 13 diaries cover his time at Affloch where he worked for Valentine of Nether Affloch, then J. Duthie at Nether Corskie.

For part of his time at Balmuir, Andrew worked for John Valentine, farmer and manure agent at Nether Affloch. He delivered coal as well in the area, commenting that Mrs Calder, the sawmiller's wife, would only take half his load, as she wanted English coal for the other half, not Scotch! On a day when he had to go into Aberdeen, Andrew rose at 2.30 in the morning. He would usually take a load in and one back. The load going to Aberdeen could, for example, be corn to be shipped south by the Newcastle & Hull steamboat. Sometimes he delivered oats to Mr Alexander at Nether Justice Mill, below where the Odeon Cinema was later built. He also took hay to the tramway company's stables. For the return load he might carry bran or lime. On one particular day he had time to see the first race at race-day on the Links. On another trip he had an accident and the cart slipped into the ditch. He had to take the whole load off before he could get the cart out. On Sundays he got up late at seven, and fed and watered the horses before having his own breakfast.

Andrew describes new machinery – a new reaper demonstrated by a Mr Walker, from the manufacturers in America. He also went to Kintore with a Royal Royce Reaper one day in September, though he doesn't say why, possibly for repair. The same day he went down to Lochies (Lochead) with the clyack and they had their clyack supper, describing the supping of the meal and ale as "*a real kirn* (mess), *raking through the dish with their fingers. Little Andrew got the ring*". The clyack refers to the last sheaf at the harvest, usually collected by the youngest girl in the field. Sometimes it was decorated and then kept to feed birds or cows at Old Yule. The meal and ale contained stout, whisky, ale, sugar and oatmeal, with perhaps a ring and button put in the bowl, hence the mess trying to find them. Old customs such as these survived in Skene until at least the end of the century. Andrew writes that "*this being Old Yule didn't rise till half past six*"!

When he moved to Kenmay Andrew was presented with a barometer, gold clock and book by the congregation of the Free Church at Echt. He attended other churches as well, however, going to Skene to hear candidates preach, for example. He also attended the Free Church at Skene and the Mission House at Lyne of Skene (as he calls it).

Some entries in his diary give an idea of the working day of farm workers at the time.

> At the smithy in the forenoon getting the mares shod. Drove two loads of turnips from the Doctor's park after I came home. (this probably refers to Doctor Laing who lived on the croft at Wantonwells). Was at the plough in the afternoon. The traction was up this afternoon with two tons of English coal. Had to clean my harness and prepare for going to Aberdeen. Was home a little past nine.
>
> At the plough in the forenoon. Lowsed at half past ten to go to the smithy with my socks and culter to get them sharpened. Got back from the smithy about twenty minutes to one. Was very angry at the strapper. Neither cleaned the horses nor mixed up their meat. (*The strapper was the man who drove the farmer's gig.*)
>
> The strapper and I went up to cast a wreath of snow between us and Uppries (Upper Affloch). We scarcely had begun to cast when they came up to us with the plough. So we stopped the casting and sat on the plough. Went along with them to the Free Church of Skene, when they turned. Came back with them to Nicol's Lodge.
>
> After dinner went up to Sutherland the tailor, got measured for two pairs of moleskin trousers and a pair of drawers.
>
> Slept too long this morning. Twenty five minutes past five when I rose. (*When ploughing in February he got up at half past four.*)
>
> Driving coals all day from Kintore to the smith. Five tons of them, four

cart loads in the forneoon, three in the afternoon. *(Kintore was where the nearest station was.)*

Rose at quarter to five. Thrashed out a rick for George Coutts till piece time. From piece time till dinner time pulled some turnips. Then shifted and set up some stooks. In the afternoon took in two loads of corn and fodder into the barn, cut some thatch about the dam, then thrashed.

Ploughing lea all day. Great party and ball at Corskie at night. Danced till between three and four o'clock. I left a little past two, went to bed a little before three. *(Old Yule next day so he didn't rise till eight.)*

Went down to W. Taylor, Southbank, registrar, and got baby registered. Then went and paid the doctor. *(This was following the birth of his daughter in November 1881.)*

This being Echt feeing market, went down to Affloch at the usual time, sorted the horses, oiled my harness, came home then went to the market. Didn't manage to make an engagement.

Saw Hamilton's groom. He asked a favour of me, to take the letter from the post when he came. Which I did. Went up to Skene House. Saw Mr Hamilton himself, had a conversation with him for a short time, got a glass of whisky from him.

(Extracts from Mathieson's diary reproduced by kind permission of Special Collections, University of Aberdeen Library)

Despite the long working day Andrew went to classes at both Skene and Waterton (Dunecht) as described in the section on Skene Mutual Improvement Association.

Most of Andrew's days are routine, but he records them anyway. What is infuriating is that when he goes to something a little more out of the ordinary he says very little about it. He records going to the races in Aberdeen, but says nothing about what it was like. The same applies when he goes to the feein market at Echt, the Easterskene Games, ploughing matches, the Lawrence Fair at Rayne (Lourin' Fair), or the cattle show in Aberdeen.

After leaving Valentine at Nether Affloch, Andrew only stayed two years at Nether Corskie. He gives no reason for leaving and he didn't have another place to go to. Thereafter he did some casual work for Mr Hamilton of Skene House, sorting the mill lade at Craigiedarg and cutting hay at Mains of Skene, before he got a job with the roads. At that job he sometimes had to walk for an hour-and-a-half to get to work if the road gang were at Concraig, for example. The chapter on transport gives some examples of the kind of work he did on the roads.

Andrew left Skene parish in 1887 and subsequently rented a farm at Mosshead, Kemnay. He must have been well remembered in the Skene and Echt areas because several men from those parishes attended his funeral at Kemnay in 1909. These included Lessel of Waterton; Wilson of Broomend, Skene; Duthie of Nether Corskie; and Valentine of Affloch. We can presume that there was no bitterness behind his leaving the latter two places earlier in his working life.

Established Church versus Free Church: parish politics and John Bruce of the Fornet

In Skene during the 19th century the breakaway Free Church gradually came to challenge the position of the Church of Scotland in parish life. Hitherto, as we have already seen, the parish church and its minister, along with the heritors, had been the leading force in education and in the care of the poor. When official bodies such as the Parochial Board were established, the Kirk Session of the Church of Scotland had a right to a specific number of places on the board. The Free Church in Skene began to challenge the role of the Established Church, especially after the appointment of the Rev. Robert Ireland as minister in 1850.

The Parochial Board
We have already seen that Ireland got himself elected to the Parochial Board and made his presence felt by trying to get the meetings of the board held in the parish, possibly as a way to make the body more accountable to the parish. Perhaps also to lessen the influence of the heritors, members by right not election, many of whom were based in Aberdeen. In 1861 there was a dispute over the replacement of Andrew Fowler of Brodiach as Inspector of Poor, and Ireland questioned the validity of the election of his successor – David

Smith, retiring parish schoolmaster. As we have seen in chapter 10, Ireland questioned the validity of those allowed to vote; why some members had received papers and minutes for the board meeting while others had not and why some non-members had received papers; and there were suggestions that Smith was given the post so that the heritors didn't have to pay him a pension, etcetera. The majority on the board refuted these points and also stated that the majority were as concerned about the poor as the dissenters, that they were larger ratepayers and many of them were men who had experience of business and were more than able to decide on the worth of an individual for a particular post.

We can see in the last point that the objectors were up against the power of the establishment and the larger landowners. Smith was appointed as inspector, with the objectors being Rev. Ireland, Robert Milne, John Valentine, Peter Lang and William Smith. Against them were leading establishment figures, including landowners such as McCombie of Easterskene, Anderson of Westhill, Crombie of Leddach, Rust of Auchinclech, and corporate landowners such as the Dean of Guild, Society of Advocates, University of Aberdeen and representatives of the Hadden Family, owners of Garlogie Mill, who had four votes for their joint proprietors because of their large rateable value. On top of that, the Kirk Session had five or six members.

The Session Minutes for 1861 record that, "*The Session impressed with the importance of being fully represented at the Parochial Board and taking into consideration that at present only four members of session are as such members of the Parochial Board, while by the Act six are entitled to a seat.*" The number of members actually elected openly by the ratepayers was only usually three, so even with the Free Church minister on the board as a well, and one or two landowners, such as Captain Shepherd of Kirkville, being Free Church, the latter was bound to be outvoted. Perhaps this explains ratepayer apathy, since several times in the 1870s and 80s no ratepayers turned up at the elections.

The dispute rumbled on, and the appointment of the medical officer also became a contentious one. Ireland even tried to get an agreement for opinion of legal counsel being sought as to the validity of some of the votes ranged against him. The board declined this proposal as being a misapplication of funds under their management. In 1869 the appointment of registrar became a straight choice between the parish schoolmaster and the Free Church schoolmaster, with the former inevitably being appointed.

Education as a battleground

Education was another area where the Free Church and the Congregational Church challenged the Church of Scotland. Perhaps this was a partly a result of the ill-feeling that had built up at the Parochial Board, such that when the School Board was formed it, too, became an area of conflict between the churches. In February 1873 a meeting of ratepayers was called to set up a school board for the parish, with George Hamilton of Skene House elected to chair the meeting. Captain Shepherd of Kirkville (a Free Church member) proposed that they should come to some agreement as to the membership of the board so as to avoid the expense of a ballot.

To this end Mr Williamson, Free Church precentor, rose and said that the best men should be chosen and all sectarianism set aside. He then produced a list of 10 names as being the best in the parish for membership of the board. However four of these were from Williamson's own church, two from the Evangelical (as the Congregational was known at this time) and only four from the Established Church. This was despite the Established Church having 99 ratepayers as against the Free Church's 66 and the Evangelical's six. The Established Church supporters wondered how it was that while Mr Williamson professed to be non-sectarian, almost all the best men in the parish belonged to his own church. A couple more names were added to the list and Williamson pointed out that he had deliberately excluded any ministers from the list "*as he considered they ought to have nothing to do with the educational interests of the people*". This issue would also come up in later years.

At this time a vote was taken on the inclusion of any minister in the list of possible members. Fourteen voted in favour of their inclusion and 20 against, according to the pro-Established Church ABERDEEN JOURNAL these were "*the precentor and his prompt and energetic friends*". However there were nearly 200 people present, so the vote meant little. James Smith of Easter Ord then proposed a motion that the now 12 names be written down "*on bitties o' paper, and the bitties pooten intil a pyokie, an' shaken throwither, and that the Chairman, in presence of the meeting, should draw oot five o' them, the five to be the School Board.*"

The JOURNAL comments slightly sarcastically that, "*Mr Smith, who is an active and down-right man of business, and never shrinks from declaring his thoughts or performing his duty, was in deep earnest with respect to his motion, but as it received no seconder, unfortunately, it fell to the ground.*"

Mr Lawson then moved that the election be carried out under the rules laid down by the Education Board in Edinburgh. Finally the parish minister,

William Philip, rose and authoritatively said that as the last motion superseded all others and was carried unanimously, the business was ended.

As I said in the chapter on education, the first School Board comprised John Anderson of Westhill, William Taylor of Southbank, the Rev. William Philip, John Valentine of Affloch, and Captain Shepherd of Kirkville. On issues that were in any way controversial it split along religious lines, with the first three being Established Church, Taylor's obituary describing him as a staunch conservative. Valentine and Shepherd were members of the Free Church. For example, the Free Church offered to transfer their school at Lyne of Skene to the board, but wanted to retain the teacher's house and gardens and also to be allowed to use the school for meetings, etcetera. This was accepted by Shepherd and Valentine, but opposed by the others. A lengthy letter appeared in the ABERDEEN JOURNAL accusing the Free Church of wanting to block any future sale or transference of the buildings, something the letter writer said made the transference illegal. The letter further accused the Free Church of wanting to transfer to the parish the burdens of ownership, while retaining the rights of ownership, and have the parish maintain two preaching stations at the expense of the wider parishioners. Finally the letter claims to have exposed the selfishness of the Free Church and that the church "*has often boasted of what she has done for the education of the country. The mask has fallen from her brow*".

The letter was from an anonymous member of the Skene School Board, but I have no doubt it was from the parish minister, Mr Philip, who made a habit of not giving his name when sending letters to the press – something exposed by John Bruce of South Fornet who had no such qualms. It was to take 30 years before the Lyne School was eventually transferred to the School Board.

Similarly, when it came to appointing an officer for the board, Mr Philip proposed George Pirie of Wester Carnie, while John Valentine proposed James Abernethy of the Evangelical/Congregational Church. The former was elected. Abernethy was later elected to the board itself and became an important figure in the on-going disputes between the two religious factions.

Tenant farmers' meeting

In August 1881 a meeting of tenant farmers in Skene was held as part of a movement to discuss the depressed state of agriculture and to ask the landowners for help. The account submitted to the ABERDEEN FREE PRESS ended:

ESTABLISHED CHURCH VERSUS FREE CHURCH

"much dissatisfaction, however, was expressed with the members of the School Board for having denied at the eleventh hour the use of the schoolhouse for the meeting. A deputation was appointed to wait on the Board, and ask satisfactory reason".

A few days later a letter appeared in the paper saying that use of the schoolhouse was not denied as no application for its use had ever been made. It goes on to say,

"the author of the meeting, of the much dissatisfaction, of the deputation, and of the report in your paper was one and the same person, an eminent reformer of this parish,"

It was signed by a member of the School Board of Skene.

John Bruce of Fornet replied:

"…the letter in your issue of Wednesday signed by a member of the School Board of Skene, which is merely a thin disguise for the minister of the parish. Matters affecting the wellbeing of a community ought to be discussed in a free and straightforward fashion, and it would have been more becoming in the gentleman above to have come forward *in propria persona* than to have acted the part of an ecclesiastical detective. It would have been still more becoming in him to have appeared as the champion of the harassed parishioners, and to have attended the meeting in question in the interests of peace and unanimity than to be conspicuous in the ranks of opposition and discord. The display of sting at the tail end of the letter is such as we would expect from one who is himself a *ci-devant* (former) reformer. Those who change their opinions are ever more energetic in the new cause than in the old, from the fact that the old coat has given place to a garment of better texture, requiring more careful defence. If the rev. gentleman will attend a meeting to be held at Fiddy on Monday next, his doubts will be cleared up in a more satisfactory fashion than through the agency of a newspaper correspondence, and he will thereby earn a large measure of respect and honour from his flock as their shepherd who guards their welfare, instead of earning enmity and distrust as the wolf which attacks the fold."

Here we have a dispute between two of the main protagonists in the parish and I have no doubt that Mr Philip did not attend the meeting at Fiddy.

The Milne Bequest

A further dispute between the various factions occurred in 1883 when the ratepayers met to consider the future of the Milne Bequest. Dr John Milne of Bombay was born in Gilcomston. At his death in 1841 he left £47,000 to improve education in Aberdeenshire. This was to be used to improve the salary of parish teachers and pay for the education of 25 children in parishes where the parents were too poor to pay, these to be chosen by the kirk session of each parish. Skene School was admitted to the Milne Bequest in 1846. Changes were proposed to the administration of the fund in the 1880s, with the fund's governing body controlling all the awards, a limited number of bursaries to be distributed by them to children of potential, and the money paid to teachers ended as their conditions had now been improved by other means. Prior to this the Kirk Session of the Established Church had selected the children who would receive the bequest.

At the very start there was disagreement over who should chair the meeting – William Christie, parish schoolmaster, being proposed, with John Bruce asking for a non-sectarian approach and proposing James Abernethy. Unfortunately Abernethy was not present, so Mr Christie took the chair unopposed and said that he had experience of two parishes and had never encountered sectarianism in the selection of children to benefit from the Milne Bequest He then said how fortunate they were to have one of the trustees present, Rev. Philip, and he was called to address the meeting. Philip sought to demolish Bruce's sectarian argument by saying that two of his (Philips) opponents in the board of trustees were actually Church of Scotland stalwarts, one of them being Principal Pirie of the University. Philip went on in detail to talk about the Milne Bequest and what it had done for education in Aberdeenshire. He said that the proposed changes would in all likelihood award two bursaries to a parish such as Skene, whereas hitherto 25 children had benefitted.

John Bruce jumped to his feet to defend Principal Pirie. Philip commented that, "*Mr Bruce always likes to get his steam blown off*". Bruce was met by hisses and boos, but said he was not afraid of them. Philip went on to say that the real aim of the changes was to get absolute control of the scheme in the hands of "*Aberdeen gentlemen*". I would propose, though, that his own aim was to keep control in his own hands as far as Skene was concerned, since it enhanced his own patronage, and thereby his authority in the parish. John Bruce, when he was allowed to speak, did not enhance his argument by harking back to so called happy days when the needs of the poor were met from the plate at the church door.

Finally the Free Church minister, Mr Innes, spoke in favour of the changes for two reasons – that because a man was fit to be a member of a kirk session did not mean that he was the best person to manage a trust fund; and secondly that the present system *"secured a respectable mediocrity, but the new system secured a chance of excellence. It afforded an opportunity for bright scholars to become great men and perhaps bequeath similar benefits"*. Reith of South Auchinclech, supported by Scott of Concraig, moved that they oppose the changes since the existing method had benefitted 25 children in the best school in each parish, i.e. the main parish school. John Bruce moved to support the changes proposed by the trustees who *"are all excellent men even though they are thorough-going Tories"*. This comment was met with hisses and interruptions. Reith's motion was carried by 52 votes to eight.

The matter did not end there, though. Following a lengthy letter by William Philip, minister of Skene, in the ABERDEEN JOURNAL, an anonymous letter appeared in the ABERDEEN FREE PRESS in January 1883. It stated that *"after reading the minister of Skene's ponderous letter and your report of the Trustees meeting I think it would be interesting to have a statement of how the Trust is administered denominationally by kirk-sessions, or what proportion of dissenter's children participate in the benefits."* The letter goes on to say that in Skene the aim of elevating talented teachers and educating poor children was plainly unfulfilled. A further anonymous letter also stated that the terms of the Milne Bequest gave parish ministers the power of patronage and while it may have improved teachers' conditions, it is questionable if it has raised the standard of education or benefitted the poor. The letter, signed Clodhopper, ended: *"the minister of Skene who has acquired his courteous style in the bear-garden of the Aberdeen Presbytery or some other ecclesiastical gathering, may be left to demolish himself. He had had a long say on the subject and has certainly had little success in modifying, far less melting, the city dignitaries whom he was so fain to overthrow"*.

Westhill School

At the same time as this controversy was going on there was a smaller one in Westhill where James Abernethy proposed replacing the male teacher with a cheaper female one. He claimed it cost £40 a year more to run Westhill School as compared with Garlogie. Abernethy was told by two other members of the School Board that these figures were misleading and that instead of saving money the change would cost more and cause problems for senior scholars. Abernethy commented that he had to accept accounts as circulated to ratepayers and that causing senior scholars to go elsewhere for their education was not a problem at Westhill, because *"senior scholars beyond the capacity of a female teacher have not hitherto been very plentiful at Westhill"*. Abernethy's motion was defeated with the voting going along the usual sectarian lines.

John Bruce joins the School Board

In April 1885 there was a new school board, an election described by the PEOPLE'S JOURNAL, with supreme understatement, as a *"brisk and breezy contest"*. The ABERDEEN JOURNAL commented that *"there had not been such a determined party spirit exhibited in Skene since the memorable year '43"*. (The year of the Disruption which led to the establishment of the Free Church). At the election meeting James Abernethy had proposed that, although he was pressed to stand, he would withdraw if Mr Philip did as well and thus *"make a clean sweep of the old Board in the interests of harmony"*. This obviously alludes to sectarian tensions within the board. Mr Philip did not respond to the proposal and the election proceeded. John Bruce was elected, joining Abernethy and Philip as well as two supporters of the Established Church – Peter Smith of Wester Ord, and William Hall of Claylands. There was no love lost between Bruce and the parish minister and it did not take long for their animosity to surface on the new board.

At the very first meeting there was controversy and petty squabbling as John Bruce proposed that each meeting start with a prayer. The chairman, Rev. Philip, took this as mockery and said that if Bruce and Abernethy would not come to church on Sundays to hear him pray, why were they so keen to hear him pray on a weekday when they were meeting for business purposes. Bruce offered to open with prayer himself, and the chairman said he did not want to hear him pray and advised Bruce and Abernethy to pray before they came to the meeting. The meeting also considered the dismissal of the compulsory officer, George Pirie, who Mr Philip accused of stirring up rebellion amongst the children against the new teacher at Garlogie. Pirie was further accused of going to the teacher and dictating her teaching arrangements. Bruce objected that some of the evidence was hearsay and Abernethy wanted more time to gather evidence. The chairman, however, pushed through the sacking of Pire and his replacement by James McIntosh,

Kirktoun tailor and a staunch Established Church man.

The PEOPLE'S JOURNAL of 13 June 1885 reported a meeting of ratepayers held in Westhill. At the meeting resolutions were passed expressing strong dissatisfaction, both with the existing state of affairs at Westhill School and with the proposals for reform put forward by the chairman of the School Board. These resolutions were raised by James Abernethy at the meeting of the board a few days later. John Bruce requested that the government reports on Westhill School for the last few years be examined. He seemed to suggest that these reports were not genuine. Peter Smith presented a number of testimonials from ratepayers expressing high satisfaction with the education at Westhill School. The PEOPLE'S JOURNAL further reported, on 18 July, that a meeting of ratepayers had taken place under the presidency of William Abel of Whitestone Farm to discuss education in the parish and particularly at Westhill School. George Shand, from Westhill, said that the Government Inspector's report on Westhill showed a *"miserable state of matters in the higher branches and reflected most seriously on the headmaster"*. (He used the term advisedly.)

John Bruce then made a lengthy speech in which he said, to applause, that the parish minister had *"uttered and repeated threats unworthy of a man and a so-called Christian"*. He charged him with having taken advantage of his position as chairman of the School Board, and as leader of a servile majority, composed of two men who by their own confession were ignorant of the merits of the case, to follow up these threats by driving, in the most arbitrary fashion, a deserving young woman from her position, thereby injuring her scholastic reputation and her future prospects. In doing so he refused to allow Mr Abernethy and him the least opportunity for the thorough inquiry so urgently demanded. (Hear, hear!)

At issue here was the future of Miss Reith, sewing teacher at Westhill, but said to be only capable of teaching the first standard grade. The chairman of the board wanted to replace her with an ex-pupil teacher and he was supported by the head teacher at Westhill, Mr Masson. Miss Reith was to be dismissed after the beginning of the harvest vacation. Masson later claimed that Miss Reith refused to do any work after four o'clock each day. Subsequent to this Miss Reith was dismissed with immediate effect and the board split on sectarian lines with Abernethy and Bruce supporting her, Smith and Philip voting for her dismissal. Only four members were present and she was sacked on the casting vote of the chairman.

In July 1885 a letter appeared in the ABERDEEN JOURNAL. It stated: *"Your correspondent wonders what mania has got into the Skene School Board. He does not seem to be aware that Mr John Bruce has got to be a member of it"*.

One issue of the SKENE TIMES accuses Mr Philip of saying *"that poor Mr Masson was quite unfit for the Westhill's School, and his wife was of no earthly use to him; he would have to be removed. Now he says he is the best and worst used man in all Westhills. Fancy such weathercock sayings of a minister."*

This is interesting because in 1891, with Mr Philip still as chairman, the School Board gave Mr Masson notice that he was to be replaced by a cheaper female teacher. Masson described it in the school log entry for 29th April 1892 as *"leave today on account of illegal dismissal of the School Board"*. So Masson suffered the same fate as Miss Reith, whom he had conspired to have dismissed seven years earlier.

The Skene Times

At the height of the dispute between John Bruce and William Philip a series of curious publications appeared in the Skene area, eventually these were entitled the THE SKENE TIMES. The authorship of these was variously given as A Ratepayer; Truth; and *Pro Bono Publico* (for the public good). Only one of them is dated and it relates to the opening of the Milne Hall in 1885, but it seems likely that the others were also published that year. At this distance these publications can be difficult to follow because of the way they are written, the issues they refer to, and the disguised way they refer to certain people. For example one of them said – *"we have at considerable expense been supporting a* 'Caleb Quotem', *so to speak, a pedagogue somewhere in the West Highlands of the parish, generally considered lamentably incapable of the duties generally devolving on him: as witness the progress of our little folks, whose efficient education it is our duty to advance."*

A *Caleb Quotem* is a literary allusion to a parish clerk/jack-of-all trades, and would seem to refer to John Wyness of Graystone near Lyne of Skene (in the west of the parish). Wyness was for many years Inspector of Poor as well as Clerk and Treasurer to the School Board, despite calls for him to stand down from the former when he was appointed to the latter. This particular SKENE TIMES also refers to the education disputes mentioned earlier, including commenting on the letters appearing in the ABERDEEN JOURNAL. It attacks the parish minister referring to the "*C.S.B.S (Chairman of the School Board of Skene)*" as Mr Philip called himself in his letter in the JOURNAL. It does not actually name him, but says of him that he *"is evidently writhing in agony at the fact of his refusing to open the meetings with prayers; and his summary uncalled for dismissal of the late Compulsory Officer being exposed.*" It goes on – "*There is a feeble attempt to cloak a high-handed and tyrannical policy, with semi-circulated rumours and half-substantiated statements, with a hidden view to the attainment of certain ends; and the good folks of Skene may look out and be prepared for greater changes still – changes which will be the least to be desired in certain quarters. Mean attempts are made, with or without cause, to get up charges against officials, manufactured or otherwise, which the community would do well to observe, and do what they could to prevent, so that should there be changes they should be for the better and not for the worse. Even in terror of disestablishment, surely one old wife is not enough to leaven the whole parish of Skene.*" This last comment is certainly being directed at the parish minister.

The next issue entitled LOCAL AFFAIRS IN SKENE further discusses the sacking of Miss Reith from Westhill School while keeping Mr Masson "*a dominie who can neither teach nor let alone teaching*". It refers to the parish minister as the Mahdi (see comments in the next section) with his "*two Apostles*", Peter Hall and William Smith, who "*out of spite and sheer ill nature*" have dismissed Miss Reith from Westhill. It also calls the trio the "*Chairman and His Mechanical Majority*" and "*an ecclesiastical bully and a pair of duffers who hardly know a B from a bull's foot*". It further suggests that Messrs Hall and Smith simply do what their wives tell them, the two ladies being great favourites of the minster! It then refers to "*our West End representative remembering the incident of his illustrious and historical namesake and the climbing spider*" and says "*well done Bruce and Abernethy. A few more issues of LOCAL AFFAIRS, a few more stormy meetings, and you will bring the stricken bucks to bay at last*". A further issue analyses the different financial proposals put forward for teachers at Westhill School and how they would affect the ratepayers.

Then an issue appeared that aimed barbed comments at the minister – "*I hear it rumoured that some benevolent 'People of Skene' are to have the Mahdi examined by two medical men from Aberdeen, prior to suggesting his removal to a local institution. I hear it also suggested that part of the money subscribed for the famous picture should be laid out on a full-sized representation, in wax, of the Mahdi of Skene, to be ready for McLeod's exhibition of notorious characters, in the Wax Work, Aberdeen*". The picture referred to was a portrait of Mr Philip presented to him on the occasion of the opening of the Milne Hall. This issue also included the following mock advertisements:

WANTED, a Mahdi to smash for the Parish of Skene, the present one having smashed himself.

WANTED, a Caleb Quotem for Westhills, warranted to tell the truth; not to bully female teachers according to order, nor to trump up charges against brother Elders in the Session

WANTED, a Joiner, with a history, to act as Chief Henchman, Private Secretary, and Scandal Monger to the new Mahdi

WANTED, a Tailor, warranted to read School Board's Reports backwards, misrepresent sentences and names, and faithfully second all motions at public meetings made by the Chief Henchman, as ordered by the new Mahdi. Salary, £5 per annum

WANTED, the Presbytery of Aberdeen to appoint a Committee of Inquiry into Ecclesiastical Matters in Skene

WANTED, a new School Board to look after the interests of the Ratepayers, warranted free from all personal spite

WANTED, Information sufficient to excommunicate certain, or any Elder in the Established Session, who may offend, evidence must be clear and effective, the last attempt having failed

WANTED, To know if the few that vegetate about the Glebe, of the Tailors, Joiners, and Blacksmiths, of the district, constitute the "People of Skene" referred to in the Minister's last letters

Opening of the Milneum (Milne) Hall

The final issue of the SKENE TIMES concerned the opening of the Milne Hall and was the most outrageous of all.

The Procession will start from the Manse at 7.30 p.m., led by a "Joiner, with a history," playing on a tin whistle the appropriate march, *See the Conquering Hero Comes* (we don't think) followed by the Mahdi in the glorified robes of Auchinclech & Coy., carried shoulder high by his faithful apostles, backed by the non-descript legion of the glebe, dressed in character, a-la-mode. "Christy Macintosh's scholars".

The Procession will be met at the avenue gate by the educated Tailor of that Elk, clad in the tartan of his clan, a lineal descendant, though much removed from the Macintosh of Macintosh, and by him will be led via Threadneedle Street to the Hall, where it will be received by the elder, Masson, who will say little and mean less, surrounded by the Kirk Session, who are requested to be present in black coats and white ties, Mr George Pirie included (in defiance of locked church-yard gates.)

Prayers being read, or as people are not expected to come in a prayerful spirit, they may be dispensed with as convenient.

Mr Milne of Leuchar Brae will then address the audience on the Inquisition; the power of the lever and screw for extorting money for public purposes, and tell them how he was led to see that the lesser of two evils was to build a hall than marry a wife. It is expected he may bequeath another £20 to each of a certain family.

SOLO… *The Merry Wives of Windsor*

The Mahdi will then give an address which will be much applauded, Corn-craik & Co. being there for the purpose. As usual, his utterances will be in praise of Wellington and himself and his good deeds done in the body, and in his blandest manner. The youth of the audience are specially requested to note how one with little brains and no religion can, by sheer impudence, rise to £150 a year!

QUARTETTE… *Three Blind Mice* By Ladies of the harem.

Then will follow the most interesting event of the evening – the presentation of the portrait by Mr Waterbroad, assisted by Hong-Kong. Ladies, have your hankeys ready, and this affecting scene will be more than your money's worth, and "Sair on your feelins." (N.B. We regret our inability to obtain better men to present the sewing machine.)

After which the Mahdi will lead off, in his favourite dance, *Burlesque*, followed by the Kirk Session and the School Board, in which Whitestones will be invited to join.

ANTHEM… *God save Skene*.

Come one, come all! Volunteers, in uniform; Babes in arms, half-price. Soda water for the Ladies, biscuits for the babies; stronger stuff may be had over the way. As the gathering will be great, extra accommodation will be provided. Shade of Burns assist me?

Here stands a shade to fund the show'rs,
And screen our countra gentry;
Macgregor, Gask, and twa-three mair,
Are blinkin at the entry.
Should Bruce or Spring be in the thrang,
Or in the barn present them,
The very sight o' Willie's face
Doon tae the Loch 'ill send them
Wi' fright that night.

Among the extras, Mr Postman will be there with a hammer and nails to hang the picture in its wonted place; the Factor of Skene will be there to state the exact terms of Mr Fornet's lease; the Sexton will be there to explain what he means by a highway robber; and Mr Pirie will make a few interesting remarks on Resurrectionists and Church-yard Dike Loupers, i.e. D.V. and time permitting

Skene, 1st Sept., 1885

So here again we have the Rev. Mr William Philip referred to as the Mahdi of Skene. The year 1885 was when General Gordon was killed by the Mahdist troops at Khartoum, so to refer to the parish minister in these terms would be incredibly severe, his ability as a minister and even his sanity are called into question. Among the others lampooned along with the unmarried James Milne, were Auchinclech; John Forbes of Auchinclech, a staunch Conservative and supporter of the Established Church; the tailor called Macintosh was James McIntosh who built the building now occupied by the Red Star; the elder called Masson was controversial Westhill teacher, John Masson; Whitestones was John Abel of Whitestone. There is also a hint in the last paragraph that John Bruce at Fornet was threatened by the factor of Skene House because of his outspokenness.

John Bruce of the Fornet

These propaganda sheets are absolutely wonderful in the insight they give to parish politics at the time. Thank goodness that one set at least has survived. It may be impossible after so many years to state for certain who the author of the pamphlets was. In one of the publications the author says that some say he is called "an impudent stranger in the parish; nay, I am well known in the parish". The copies that have survived were posted to Andrew Fowler, initially of Brodiach and then Ord House. Fowler was an elder of the Church of Scotland, so these pamphlets were not confined to Free Church members. Some parts read as though they were written by a member of the Established Church or have inside knowledge of that church's kirk session. There is also a suggestion, though, that some of the author's information came from Mrs Hall and Mrs Smith. However, the likeliest candidate for their authorship, one who was not afraid of speaking his mind, one who had a very tempestuous relationship with the parish minister, is John Bruce, even though he is referred to in the pamphlets. If he is the author he may have had assistance in publishing the pamphlets from James Abernethy who had a background in the distribution and sale of books, pamphlets, etcetera. Bruce certainly had the vocabulary to write these publications as can be seen by his many letters to the press. It is difficult to see anyone else with the fiery, headstrong nature. Could he have praised himself in his own publication? We may never know. One argument against him as the author is that he usually attached his name to his writings. A full account of the life of John Bruce appears in the chapter on Skene Worthies.

The Garlogie School case

The Rev. Philip stepped down from the School Board for a short time owing to illness. His return in 1891 caused immediate controversy. Peter Duguid of Easterskene had been elected chairman of the board in April, but at the end of the year he stepped down. At the meeting at which his resignation was presented Mr Philip was appointed to the board and to the chair on the casting vote of the vice-chairman, only four members being present: Alexander Massie, Milton of Garlogie, and James Legge, Craigston (vice-chairman), supported Philips appointment; William Adam, Broadwater, and James Abernethy opposed it, though Abernethy said he had no personal objection to Mr Philip, but did object to the way the procedure was carried out, it taking less than 15 minutes.

A letter signed by A Ratepayer appeared in the ABERDEEN JOURNAL saying that the procedure was not unconstitutional and that "*the return of Mr Philip to the School Board was a subject of general satisfaction throughout the parish*". However, even in the absence of John Bruce, who had now retired to Aberdeen, this was not true, and a meeting of ratepayers was subsequently held at the Mason Lodge Hall chaired by Free Church minister, William Innes, with several Free Church members speaking. The issue seemed to resolve around the fact that Duguid's resignation should not have taken effect for a month and that therefore Philip's appointment was unconstitutional. Despite ongoing protest about the appointment, Philip continued to chair meetings.

This became important because the new board went on to dismiss a teacher at Garlogie, Miss Isabella Anderson. Miss Anderson had been asked to move to Westhill, and had apparently agreed, but later said that she had done so on condition that she be given time to consider the move and the salary offered. She subsequently declined the move. Abernethy and Adam opposed the dismissal and Philip, in fact, ignored a petition signed by well over 80 ratepayers asking for the board to reconsider Miss Anderson's dismissal. Matters got quite nasty, as she was ordered to vacate the schoolhouse at Garlogie. Miss Anderson brought a case for wrongful dismissal, part of her case relating to the conditions on which she was offered and turned down a move to Westhill. She also contested the appointment of Mr Philip on the grounds mentioned already, as well as the actions of the vice-chairman in assuming the chair at the meeting where Philip was appointed. The issue was even raised in Parliament when a question was asked of the Lord Advocate. With the help of the Educational Institute of Scotland, Isabella Anderson won her case and was re-instated.

William M. Philip

William Philip, the minister at the centre of much of these controversies, was the son of the schoolmaster at Portsoy. He initially trained as a solicitor before studying for the ministry at Aberdeen University. He himself became a schoolteacher at Forglen before securing a ministry in Canada. He returned in 1870 to be presented to Skene Church by the Earl of Fife. He is credited in his obituary with the building of the mission hall at Lyne of Skene, though I think that fund raising for that building was under way before he came. He did, though, instigate the building of the vestry and the hearse-house, as well as, more controversially, the Milne Hall.

As well as being a minister, Mr Philip was also an author, both of poetry and prose. Some of his poetry appeared in *Modern Scottish Poets* by D.H. Edwards. Of his four sons, three became doctors and one, Hardy Philip, became a solicitor in Aberdeen. Rev. Philip died on 6th July, 1903, aged 74 years.

Bruce, Philip and Abernethy

None of the accounts of the various disputes in the parish in the last few decades of the 19th century openly state that the disputes were between the Established Church and the two dissenting churches. There were certainly, though, calls to be non-sectarian, which does indicate that people felt that there was a sectarian division at the time. To a certain extent the disputes over the School Board and other matters became very personal ones between Bruce and Philip. Nevertheless, the various issues initially arose as a dispute between the Free and Established Churches, and in many cases continued to divide the boards and the community along sectarian lines.

We might dismiss Bruce as a hot-head, a trait he seems to have shared with Philip, but both men did have considerable support in the parish. They also, of course, had many detractors. Crucially, perhaps, Bruce had the support of James Fowler Abernethy. No one could accuse Abernethy of being a hot-head and his letters to the newspapers are usually sober and factual, never resorting to personal attacks, unlike the other two. The esteem in which he was held can be seen in the fact that, despite being a leading member of the tiny Westhill Congregational Church, he was continually voted on to the School Board and the Parochial Board, chairing the former, and later being elected a councillor when the board became the Skene Parish Council.

He also overcame earlier sectarian opposition and, at various times, held the posts of Inspector of Poor and Clerk to the School Board. Indeed Abernethy was praised by the board in 1911 for his ability and fair mindedness and the great interest he took in education. At the last ever meeting of the board, in 1919, he had given it over 40 years of service. Abernethy even reached the heights of being made a Justice of the Peace. I would argue that his continual support for Bruce does give considerable credibility to the latter's criticism of the parish minister, who seems to have been just as controversial as Bruce himself.

The ill-feeling lingered for many years, to such an extent that even at Rev. Philip's funeral service his successor, Robert Robertson, felt obliged to comment on it, ostensibly to inform those new to the parish of the events of the past. He referred to the *"intensity of feeling and depths of evil passion that had been aroused by some differences of opinion that had arisen in regard to certain School Board matters that could be settled only by appeal to the law courts. What astonished me most was the tendency people showed to regard as a private and personal enemy any man who ventured to differ from them on a matter of public business"*.

Robertson also suggested that the ill-feeling generated by the various controversies was the reason for the poor turn out of parishioners at Philip's funeral. That the feelings did linger to this extent is testimony to the bitterness that had been generated in the past. The comments of Robertson also seem to indicate that it was not just Free Church people who had been alienated by Philip's actions and, effectively, boycotted his funeral.

Roads and transport

Old Skene Road

The Old Skene Road has interested many people over the years. G. M. Fraser mentioned it in his writing and notebooks and walked along it. Not surprising, given that he wrote a book on the OLD DEESIDE ROAD. Mary McMurtrie was fascinated by it, writing about it in the SCOTS MAGAZINE and the DEESIDE FIELD. Mary remembered it in her younger day and revisited in later years to see what survived. In recent years John Ritchie, a former member of the Skene Heritage Society, has traced some of the old milestones in and beyond Skene parish, even restoring two that had fallen over.

Referring to the Number Nine stone in the grounds of Easterskene, Fraser described it as "*tall, nicely squared and bevelled, with a much nicer presence than the dumpy round-topped ninth milestone on the turnpike below Easterskene*". Several members of the society have walked the section from Kingswells to Kirktoun of Skene, and I have myself taken groups along the section from Brodiach to Kirktoun pointing out historical sites along the way.

The King's Highway, as it originally was, is shown on Taylor & Skinner's map of 1776. It left

No. 9 milestone on the Old Skene Road

A History of Skene and Westhill

The Old Skene Road in 1776

Mary McMurtrie sketch of the old inn at Lochee

the Gallowgate in Aberdeen at about where Spring Garden is now. It went up Midstocket and along the Lang Stracht reaching Kingswells. There it went behind Kingswell's House where one of the milestones still stands. It passed near the Quaker graveyard, then passed the cottage built across the road in the 19th century by Francis Edmond of Kingswells to stop people using the old road. Part of the road can be followed from that cottage, a fairly rough track, then on the current road to where it enters the parish at the bridge over the Brodiach Burn. Just before Brodiach is the Number Six milestone.

There were inns roughly every two miles along the road. Before Skene Parish the old Four Mile Inn was to the north of the current one, on the road now only used by buses. Brodiach was the Six Mile Inn, and then there were the old Broadstraik, Lochee, and finally Bervie at the western edge of the parish. Both Brodiach and Bervie are known to have cellars where refreshments for weary travellers were stored.

The Number Seven milestone is in the lay-by opposite the police station in Westhill, the lay-by being the line of the old road. Number Eight is on the right side of the road just before the Broadshade development and the old Slack of Larg quarry. At the Kirktoun the road goes straight on down to the right of the shop, then

ROADS AND TRANSPORT

**Sketch by Mary McMurtrie of the Old Skene Road
going down to Bervie and on to the next parish**

partly up the drive of Easterskene where the Number Nine stone can be seen to the right among the trees just beside the drive. The road becomes a track leading off to the left and across the edge of a field to Skene School. This track, through what became Easterskene, was kept as path for parishioners to use to get to the church when the turnpike was created, the old road itself being shut up at Dykenook when the Half-Milie was built as an accommodation road by McCombie of Easterskene. There has been some debate regarding the line of the road after Easterskene. Mary McMurtrie said that it ran down behind the school following the line of trees between dry stone dykes, the section known as 'the Beltie'. Others have suggested that it ran slightly further north, at the bottom of the road from Drumstone, where there is a straight line of beech trees down to Lochside and Loch-head. Both lines look possible; however, a boundary stone part way down the Beltie mentioned in the division of the Easter Skene lands in 1789 seems to be mentioned in connection with the road, and would therefore suggest that this as the line.

At Loch-head the old road follows the new one for a time until just before Nether Affloch, where the new road turns sharply left, the old one carries on through trees to Nether Affloch. Thereafter its line is still a puzzle. It may have carried on through the woods behind Wantonwells, or turned right and gone up to Upper Affloch. From there it seems to have gone behind where Balmuir Croft was (a track still exists there), crossed the Skene House drive and then turned up to Crow Lodge. Part of the road can be seen beyond there, overgrown. It then led over the hill to Bervie, after which it crossed the Bogentory burn by the two-arched bridge so admired by Mary, though she had been told that originally it had been a humped back bridge. Beyond there the old road goes past the Number Twelve stone, still *in situ*, and on into the parish of Echt.

Other old roads

From the Kings Highway other roads branched off. Some of these, shown on *Taylor & Skinner's* map, still exist – the road from Westhill over to Auchinclech and Conraig, the road from Kirktoun to Concraig, and the road from Dykenook along to the north of Skene House and Lyne of Skene. Also shown, though, is a road from *'Bredstraik'* called the Echt Road, just beyond the Number Eight milestone (has this milestone perhaps been moved slightly further west?). The documents dividing the Dean of Guild's lands in 1789 actually list most of the roads in these lands and the description of the boundary stones also helps place the line of the old roads. The following are listed:

1. PUBLIC ROAD LEADING FROM ABERDEEN TO KIRKTOUN OF SKENE TOWARDS BERVIE (The Old Skene Road)
2. ROAD LEADING SOUTHWARD TO KIRKTOUN FROM THE LANDS OF CONCRAIG, THENCE GOING BY THE MARCH BETWIXT THE LANDS OF LEDDACH AND WHITESTONE AND KIRKTOUN OF SKENE SOUTHWARD THRO' WESTER CARNIE. Part of this road still exists from Concraig to Kirktoun.

ROADS AND TRANSPORT

Thereafter it is shown on the first two OS maps as a dotted track going south just before the line of trees by the Old Skene Road just before you enter Kirktoun from the Westhill side, i.e. one field west of Kirkville. Bill Troup remembers ploughing this when he farmed Whitestone and being told off by a woman who said it was a right of way. Before Mason Lodge and the turnpike were built it would have gone on and joined up with the other roads in this area.

3. ROAD LEADING THRO' KIRKTOUN SOUTHWARD TO THE MOSSES AND MILLS OF WESTER CARNIE AND GARLOGIE. This is the old peat moss road later named Barclay's Brae after James Barclay who lived at Roadside c.1900. It was made into a proper road by James Knowles of Kirkville and Hillcarnie in 1825.

4. PUBLIC ROAD LEADING FROM KIRKTOUN BY THE MARCH WITH THE GLEBE NORTHWARD TO THE MARCH WITH THE LANDS BELONGING TO FRANCIS LEY. This is an interesting road, one I've never come across on maps, or on the ground, or been told about by locals. It is mentioned elsewhere in the march boundaries and must have gone north to Auchronie Hill (to the west of Rogiehill and almost parallel to the existing road east of Rogiehill)

5. PUBLIC ROAD LEADING FROM DYKENOOK NORTHWARD THRO' THE LANDS OF MILLBUIES TO THE MARCH WITH FORNET BELONGING TO GEORGE SKENE. Dykenook is no longer a place name and its exact location has been forgotten. It must have had some importance, though, since it is marked on *Taylor & Skinner's* map. It is also mentioned in the Dean of Guild documents and was used as a reference point in the division of the Guild's lands. As we have already seen, it was preserved for some years as a small croft or holding. From this we can deduce that it stood roughly where Skene School was later built. It would have been positioned at the point where the Old Skene Road crossed the roads running north, north west and south, and would therefore have been a crossroads. Hence it is marked on the old road map. This road (number 5) must have run north roughly where the current road to Drumstone runs, with a branch off to Lyne of Skene.

6. ROAD LEADING FROM DYKENOOK SOUTHWARD TO MILL OF GARLOGIE AND THE MOSSES OF CARNIE AND GARROCK. This is not listed as a public road so it may have been a mill road, but where it went in relation to Number Eight is difficult to say. When the turnpike was under construction in 1802 the contractor was told not to shut up the road of commutation from

Dykenook as it was a mill road.
7. PUBLIC ROAD LEADING PAST BROADSTRAKE THRO' EASTER ECHT TOWARDS KIRKTOWN OF ECHT. This road is shown on *Taylor & Skinner's* map branching off at 45 degrees from the old Broadstraik Inn and just beyond the Number Eight milestone. The road is called the Echt Road. So it must have crossed to about Leddachcroft, possibly in a fairly straight line at the angle which can be seen on later maps as a field boundary. From there it would have gone roughly through Burnland across the other road to where a sign now points to a track leading to Springhill Farm. This is confirmed by the 1790 description of the Leddach Estate boundary which state that stone V is on one side of it and stone K/L (Kirktoun / Leddach) on the other side. These stones are still in situ, although the former one has been moved slightly as a result of recent road straightening. The old road itself can be traced as a dotted line on the first OS map of 1865 and on the ground today. It goes west to a point where one part turns left to Springhill and Wester Carnie (possibly road number two would have joined it here). The other part carries straight on. As late as 1824 it was mentioned in the sale document of Wester Carnie to James Knowles of Kirkville where it is called the Old Echt Road leading from Garlogie to Broadstraik. The main part of this road can be followed today, albeit through some fairly overgrown parts, crossing the old moss road just north of North Gask and contouring round Gask Hill as a track used today by dog walkers, through Gask Wood and Garlogie Wood, avoiding the boggy ground lower down. Again the boundary stones can help here since one in the Garlogie woods with a G/K/7 (Garlogie/Kirktoun) is described in 1788 as being on the edge of the road and so it is today (see the section on boundary stones).
8. PUBLIC ROAD LEADING FROM DYKENOOK PAST NETHERMILL OF GARLOGIE SOUTHWARD. This road must have gone to Kirktounbridge then bearing right to Nethermill.
9. WE ALLOTE A ROAD FROM THE MOSS OF GARROCK PAST NETHERMILL OF GARLOGIE AS MARKED BY PROPS ON THE GROUND TO THE MOSS OF WESTER CARNIE; AND A ROAD FROM THE KINGS HIGHWAY LEADING EASTWARDS FROM THE TOWN OF GARLOGIE TO THE SAID MOSS OF WESTER CARNIE.

Around the Lyne of Skene the roads took different routes from those we see today. The road from Broomhill to Dunecht was only built in 1830. It went straight through between the smiddy and the joiners, the space between them having previously been used for repairing and storing implements. According to Roy Lyle (senior), before that road was made it had curved north through Tappies, Shoemakers, Bruntland, Mainside, Back Ward and Back Mains to join the Old Skene Road at the bridge at Bervie. He also said that at one time a straight road ran from Affloch to the Shoemakers via Gas Wood, Fernlea and 'The Walk'. When the Duke of Fife took over the Skene House estate, The Walk was used only by carriage and pair and the gates were kept shut to other traffic. Heavy-wheeled vehicles had to go by Mainside and Back Mains to get to Skene House.

Moss roads were important to give people access to the moss for fuel. Hence the documents say that the moss roads are to be "*left patent and open to the tenants and possessors of the said lands*". There were several other roads to and through the moss, some of them surviving as paths in the Garlogie woods, such as the one leading south of Little Gask and on to Springhill farm. One old road in Elrick was a moss road, giving access to the moss where Carnie Wood is now. There was also a right of way running up the east side of the Broadstraik Inn to Crombie, roughly where the path goes today. The roads listed above were to be kept to a breadth of 24 feet, with the principal King's Highway to be of that breadth plus the ditches at either side.

These roads, even the King's Highway, were not constructed roads; they didn't take wheeled traffic, of which there was little in any case. Material and goods would have been transported by a litter pulled by a horse, or panniers or creels slung over a horse; even dung was carried to the fields by the latter method. Peat cast from the moss would also have been carried by these methods, or by wheelbarrow. The line of the road would have been created by custom and usage, keeping to higher ground to avoid boggy areas where possible, curving round hills to do that, in the way that we have seen with the Old Skene Road and the Old Echt Road. The gradients followed by these old roads also made them unsuitable for wheeled traffic.

The turnpike road

During the 18th century, prior to the building of the turnpike, some attempt was made to keep the main roads in a fit state. The Commissioners of Supply had responsibility for the condition of the roads and enforcing road improvement legislation. Money was levied from landowners and evidence of this can be seen in the Skene House accounts. In 1805 money was being spent "*scouring ditches on the road from Dykenook westward*" (roughly the road from

Skene School to Lyne of Skene). Money was also spent on 1,896 ells of road from "*Lord Kintore's march to Robert Mackie's house*" (one of the Main's crofts). A Scottish ell was 37 inches. Landowners' tenants would have to give so much service to the upkeep of the roads, or pay money instead (commutation). However, it was not enough, and with the agricultural improvements and the move away from subsistence farming there arose the need for properly constructed roads.

Turnpike roads were funded by landowners and other investors, and they would hope to receive a return on their investment in the form of tolls. The North-East was noticeably behind areas further south in the provision of turnpike roads. There was considerable opposition to them among some landowners and others in the area. Improving landowners needed access to material such as lime, however, and also needed to move their own produce to markets; until the building of the canal, roads were the only option.

One of the prime movers for the Skene Road was Skene of Rubislaw who wanted to get granite from his quarry at Hill of Rubislaw into the growing city of Aberdeen. The line of the road he wanted was through his lands to Union Street, then under construction. There were doubts as to whether or not Union Street would be finished and an offer was accepted from Crombie of Leddach to fund an alternative entry from Rubislaw to Woolmanhill. In return he was to be allowed to develop his land which bordered this section of the road.

A Turnpike Bill was pushed through in 1795, but it needed the corresponding Commutation Bill, which dealt with converting labour on the other roads into monetary payments. This was achieved in 1800, by which time meetings on the Skene road had already taken place. In fact the first one was held on 21 June 1799. Among those attending the second meeting, six months later, were Skene of Skene, Alexander Smith of Blackhills, Andrew Fowler of Brodiach, and Alexander Crombie of Leddach. They appointed Charles Abercombie as surveyor for the first section which was to be from Aberdeen to Kirktoun of Kinnernie.

George More of Raeden (twice provost of the town) proposed that the road follow the line of the old road more closely, including the section through Kingswells and on to enter the Kirktoun of Skene. It would also have passed More's own property at Raeden. This motion was ruled out of order by the chairman of the road trustees, George Skene of Skene, and so the line we know now was adopted, by-passing the Kirktoun. The initial subscribers were:

ROADS AND TRANSPORT

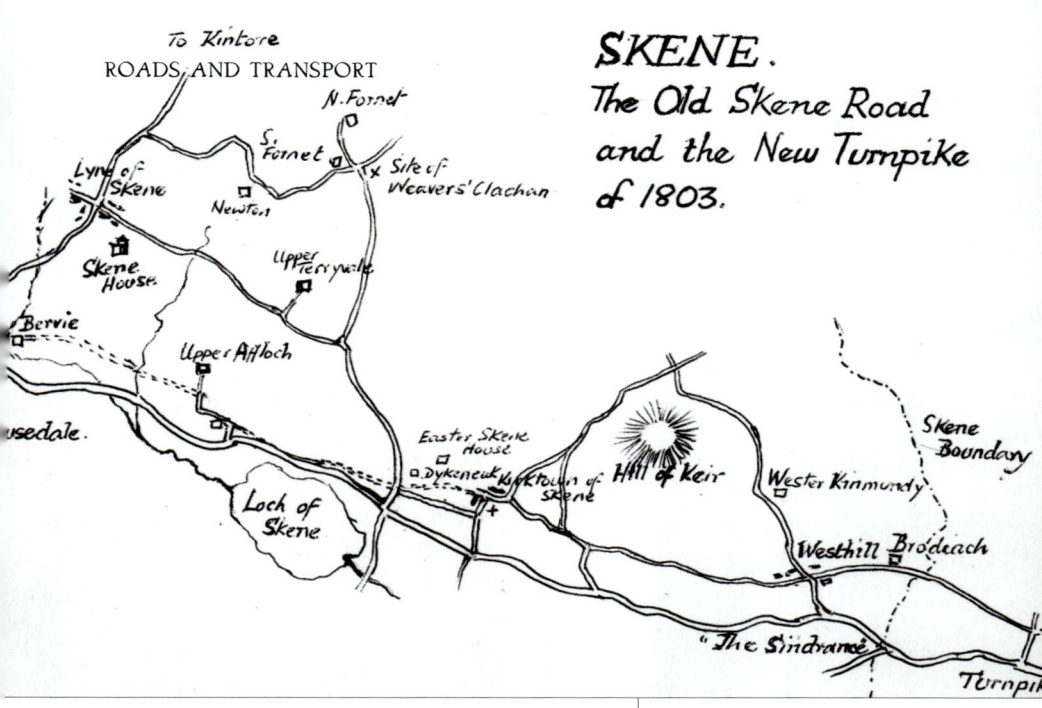

James Skene of Rubislaw	£1,000
Alexander Robertson of Hazlehead	£400
William Black of Cloghill	£100
George Skene of Skene	£300
Alexander Brebner of Learney	£200
Andrew Davidson, tenant of Skene, together with Joseph Allan, the schoolmaster	£100

A year or two later the following also subscribed:

Alexander Crombie of Leddach	£400
Dean of Guild	£400
Town of Aberdeen	£300

This was not enough, though, and £900 had to be borrowed in 1803 to finish the road that year. Skene of Skene's account for 1805 shows payments of £50 to Alexander Gildawe, mason, for building toll houses and bridges.

£1,012 was also advanced on an assignation of the tolls, no doubt money that was never paid back. The old road had to be closed off to make the new

Line of the old road alongside the new

George More of Raeden proposed that the road follow the line of the old road more closely. This motion was ruled out of order by George Skene of Skene, and so the line we know now was adopted, by-passing the Kirktoun.

211

one viable. In the parish the closure points were at the march between Dykenook and Wester Kirktoun, and on the march between Leddach and Blackhills. Further problems came from William Knowles of Kirkville who refused the compensation on offer for allowing the road to go through his land.

The Strake Toll

The case was to drag on for 12 years, going as far as the House of Lords who found against the trustees. The closure of the old road was not popular and the treasurer to the trustees was empowered to prosecute people who broke down the bar or railing. In fact a stone cyke was built at the bar at Leddach in place of the railing which had already fallen into decay by 1808.

Milestones were put up in 1809, measuring from the west end of Union Street, and were to be painted. By 1811 the section from Dykenook to Bervie was completed, with Skene of Skene giving up land to the road. In return a section of the old road, between Dykenook and its junction with the turnpike near Loch-head, was to be shut up and incorporated in his land. A new era could begin and it began with the stagecoach.

The Skene stagecoach

William Knowles had been one of the objectors to the new road, or at least to its passing through his land and the compensation on offer. By 1828 his son, James, had put Kirkville on the market and he included in the sale announcement that a post passed daily, and the coach to Alford and Strathdon every alternate day.

The coach through Skene to places beyond got off to a stuttering start. On 30 April, 1824, the ABERDEEN JOURNAL carried the following announcement.

> The public are hereby respectfully informed that a new coach called The Aberdeen & Alford Telegraph is to commence running between Bridge of Alford and Aberdeen through Skene three times a week on Mondays, Wednesdays and Fridays and starts from Dawson's' Inn, Bridge of Alford on Wednesday 5th May at six o'clock, arrives in Aberdeen at Cruickshank's, vintner, at 11 o'clock forenoon, for the first six weeks and every alternate six weeks at Ross's, vintner, Little Belmont Street: leaves town at 4 o'clock

afternoon, being the hour the North Mails are dispatched, and arrives at Bridge of Alford at 9 o'clock same evening. Seats may be taken and parcels left at Cruickshank's and Ross's during the six weeks the coach arrives at each of these places respectively.

The proprietors of this coach humbly solicit the numerous gentlemen residing in that part of the country and the public in general for their patronage and support in carrying on this undertaking and having resolved on moderate fares and engaged a careful Guard and Driver who will pay every attention to the comfort of the passengers and careful delivery of goods they trust to merit that patronage they thus presume to solicit.

N.B. each passenger allowed 14 lb luggage and all above to pay 3 pence per lb. And all passengers luggage if not sent to the coach office 15 minutes before the coach starts, the Proprietors will not be accountable for perishable articles nor for any parcel whatsoever, if lost or damaged above the value of £5 sterling unless entered and paid for accordingly."

This coach soon extended its run to Rhynie, but it did not last long because on 24 April, 1827, we read:

There will be sold by public roup at Liggerdale in the parish of Cluny, ten horses with two sets of harness complete belonging to the Aberdeen Alford Coach Company now about to be dissolved. The horses are of superior quality, generally 8 years of age, perfectly sound and in good condition, they are well worth the attention of gentlemen, coach proprietors and farmers. Arrangements are in the meantime in the course of forming to continue the said coach now called the "Lord Forbes" on the road."

Knowles's advertisement suggests that the latter coach did take the place of the earlier one.

At the time of the second STATISTICAL ACCOUNT in 1845, the minister, George Mackenzie, wrote that "*a stage-coach passes by every alternate day from Aberdeen to Alford. A mail-gig runs daily on the same line; and there is a sub-post office near the centre of the parish.*"

By May 29 1852 the JOURNAL had the following announcement:

"The Skene Star Coach. John Fowler, fourth Milestone, Skene Road begs to intimate to the people that he intends running between Aberdeen and the Loch of Skene, that beautiful coach that belonged to Mr Cruickshank, late of

Newpark, Newhills, for the accommodation of passengers etc. The "Skene Star" will leave Mr Sherriff's Inn, St Nicholas Street, on Monday June 7th at 8 o'clock, making for Skene and will leave George Philips, Innkeeper, Loch of Skene at 5 pm for Aberdeen.

P.S. William Fowler, the Guard, will pay great attention to passengers and parcels. Fare only 1 penny per mile."

To us five hours from Alford to Aberdeen would seem like an eternity. In the 19th century it would have been a tiring journey, as this story of one old lady's first journey to Aberdeen illustrates: *"when, no doubt waking from an uneasy doze, she saw the Loch of Skene and thought it was the harbour through the steamy windows, exclaimed – Aiberdeen an time tilt."* Poor soul, she had another nine slow miles still to endure.

The Skene, Cluny and Sauchen coach ran for 60 years before being superseded by a new form of transport. The bus had 31 seats and was hauled by either three, four or five horses, depending on the season. The bus left Sauchen at 7.30am arriving at 10am in St Nicholas Street in Aberdeen, returning at 5pm. It took mail to the villages and carried eggs and butter to

The old Skene bus c.1905

ROADS AND TRANSPORT

the city. It could be a dangerous form of transport as shown when, in 1857, a gardener from Aberdeen named Anderson fell from the top of the coach near Broadstraik. He was taken to the infirmary but his injuries were so serious that he died.

The following poem was written at the time the service ended in 1906, and credited in the ABERDEEN JOURNAL to Rab. Onlooker. Bus here refers to the horse drawn coach and motor car to the motorized bus:

> Nae mair we'll see the guid auld bus
> Come trundling in the road fae Skene
> Although for sixty years and mair
> A faithful servant she has been
> Year in, year out, she stood the test
> Nae stress o' weather could her bar
> But noo, alas, she maun retreat
> For we hae got a motor car
> The Allan liners days are deen
> Her toilsome journeys noo ar past
> We canna stan' the auld bus noo
> In modern days we travel fast
>
> Time was when we were weel content
> Tae gang wi' buses near and far
> Until the forward march o' time
> Provided us wi' a motor car
> But time and progress changes a'
> We' rapid strides in every clime
> We often note the wondrous charge
> That has been wrought by hand o' time
> One by one familiar objects
> Leave the ranks and tak' the rear
> At the forward march of progress
> Auld time stagers disappear

Roadwork

Andrew Mathieson's diaries record some of the work that a road gang undertook in the 1880s:

- Cleaning daubes off the road
- Metalling the road between the Free Church and Mason Lodge
- Mending water runs between the bridge at Bogentory and Wester Fornet
- Breaking stones at Gask Quarry
- Coating on the Taposheetie road and a piece of the Kirktoun Brae
- Driving stones from Paterson's park, Hill of Keir, to the Tirryvale road
- Braking stones on the Echt turnpike beside the Old Fiddie Toll House
- Cleaning drains
- Working at Broadshade Quarry
- Patched the road by way of Gellymoss and Brae of Kinmundy

Adam Craigmile remembers the roadmen breaking stones at the side of the road in the years after World War I. Adam's father had the contract for

Breaking stone at the Slack o' Larg Quarry

Road crew between Skene and Dunecht

maintaining a section of the road from the Free Kirk to the Six Mile, and on the Old Skene Road from Brodiach to Skene Central School. The stones came from the Slack of Larg or Gask quarries.

ROADS AND TRANSPORT

Adam described how the stones were crushed:

> "There were two stone crushers driven by steam engines at the quarries. Steam engines and wagons brought the crushed stone to the roadside to be broken down by workmen with hammers. A horse-drawn six foot brush swept the sand into the stones, followed by a water cart to wash sand into the stones, and by a steam road roller."

Early motorised buses had a speed limit of 12 mph because any faster and their solid tyres would dislodge the stones. Adam recently told me that the shafts of the hammers used to break the stone had to be flexible to avoid excessive vibration and that rowan wood was used. The late Bob Cruickshank remembered the main road through Elrick first being tarred in 1928.

A railway for Skene?

Skene's position between Deeside and Donside meant that it missed out on the railway lines to Ballater and to Alford. There were possibilities for the Skene area and as early as 1862, Captain Shepherd of Kirkville, William McCombie of Easterskene and Alexander Anderson, farmer at Millbuie, were on a committee to look into providing a spur line running from two-and-a-half miles north of Stonehaven, through Netherley, Maryculter, Skene and on to Kintore, under the auspices of the Scottish Northern Junction Railway company. Nothing came of this, but towards the end of the century a light railway was under discussion for Echt and Skene.

To improve transport links to the area, ABERDEEN, SKENE, ECHT & MIDMAR TRAMWAYS was floated in 1877. It was to be a 4ft 8½ (1.4m) standard gauge with steam motive power. The route was to be from Midmar, following the road to Echt, Rubislaw, Queens Cross, Skene Street, Woolmanhill and Schoolhill to a terminus at the north end of Belmont Street. The scheme never came to fruition because of a shortage of cash and reservations about using steam power on some steep gradients.

In 1896 The Light Railway Act was passed in Britain, which encouraged the building of railways with fewer restrictions than their main line counterparts. In 1896, Aberdeenshire Light Railway was floated by an independent consortium, with a route planned from Echt to the city boundary at Oldmill (Woodend). There was to be a branch line to Skene. The intention was to eventually join up with the railway lines in Aberdeen harbour via the public roads. Steam power was to be used.

The rival Echt Light Railway scheme was also floated in the same year, 1896, by the Great North of Scotland Railway. Their plan was to run from Echt parallel to the main road, then head past Scotstown Farm to the west of the Loch of Skene to join the Aberdeen road. From there the route was via Skene to Oldmill (Woodend) and then to the Bayview tram terminus. It was intended to obtain running powers over Aberdeen District Tramways track via Queens Road to Union Street and George Street. A connecting line was also planned to King Street via Nelson Street. Again steam power was to be used. The standard gauge of 4ft 8½ (1.4m) was chosen, since this would allow transfers to the rest of the railway system and Aberdeen tramways which used that same gauge.

A meeting of Skene folk to consider the schemes was held under the chairmanship of the parish minister, Rev. Robert Robertson. Robertson commented that only those inhabitants living between Affloch and Brodiach could look at the two schemes in an unbiased way:

> "the promise of a branch line to Waterton (Dunecht) was a sufficient bribe to secure the blind and unreasoning support of the inhabitants of that district. The private company was as anxious to promise anything and everything to secure support as a Parliamentary candidate before the poll."

Nothing new there, then, nor with the worries raised by some as to what effect the schemes might have on the rates. Robertson also dismissed the suggestion that the G.N.S.R.C. had put forward a bogus scheme to keep their rival out of the field. They were honourable men, he insisted. The fear that once the G.N.S.R.C. had their scheme they would be able to raise fares as much as they liked was also dismissed by Robertson – "*if people thought the rates were too high they could walk into town; Skene was not a great distance from the city*." Despite some criticism the meeting agreed with the chairman and the following resolutions were passed:

> That in view of all the circumstances this meeting expresses its opinion that the light railway to Skene and Echt promoted by the G.N.S.R.C. is that which will serve best the interests of Skene, and give most guarantee for an efficient and permanent train service without detriment to the ratepayers
>
> That this meeting forms itself into a committee to watch over the interests of the parish in connection with the proposed railway

Aberdeen Corporation opposed both these schemes. Objections were

ROADS AND TRANSPORT

lodged against the laying of additional tracks along streets in the fast developing residential areas. The use of tramways for goods traffic was also objected to. This opposition caused the promoters of the Aberdeen Light Railway to abandon their scheme. The G.N.S.R. was not discouraged though. At this time the horse-drawn Aberdeen District Tramways was a privately owned company. Aberdeen Corporation made an offer to purchase the tramways system, but it was rejected. This did not go unnoticed by the G.N.S.R. who then made overtures to purchase the tramways.

In August the general manager stated that the tramways would be an important acquisition as *"they might be worked in conjunction with the proposed railway to Skene and Echt"*. It was planned that city routes were to have through cars to Skene and Echt. Some building development was planned along the routes and the Loch of Skene was to be developed as a leisure and recreation area. Steam would be used outwith the city and electric or compressed air within the city. The G.N.S.R. offer was accepted, but required approval from Aberdeen Town Council. Aberdeen Corporation informed the G.N.S.R. that they wished to have a tramways system run for the benefit of ratepayers rather than shareholders. They then re-opened negotiations with Aberdeen District Tramways who, of course, had been able to raise the stakes. The offer made by Aberdeen Corporation was formally accepted in March 1897.

Next month, in April 1897, the Light Railway Commissioners approved the railway as far as the outskirts of the city, but the objection to the use of tramways was upheld. This was despite the G.N.S.R. making undertakings that they would use special goods wagons and engines which consumed their own smoke. Next the G.N.S.R. tried to overcome objections by promoting some alternative routes within the city. One was from Oldmill northwards to join the main railway line at Kittybrewster, and also a route to Mannofield and Holburn Street. High costs of purchasing land, and building overbridges and a tunnel, caused the whole scheme to be abandoned in 1898.

In 1900 the Skene & Echt Light Railway was floated by Aberdeen District Committee of Aberdeen County Council. The route was to be similar to the previous G.N.S.R. one from Echt via Skene to Woodend. There was also to be a branch line to Waterton (Dunecht). Estimates were given for both electric and steam traction on standard gauge 4ft 8½ins. and also 3ft (0.9m) or 3ft 6ins (1.06m) narrow gauge. It was suggested that a steam locomotive of a six-wheel tank type, weighing about 24 tons (24,385k) would be suitable. It would haul one bogie passenger carriage weighing 90 tons (91,444k) capable of carrying 40 passengers in first and third class accommodation. (This was in accordance with the practice adopted by the local railway, the G.N.S.R., which had abolished second class). Goods wagons to be used would weigh about two tons, each able to carry a load of five tons. Brake vans and cattle trucks would need to be procured.

In 1904 a three-foot gauge electrified line was mooted, running alongside the public roads. It was hoped that through working would be possible along the Aberdeen Corporation Tramways, but the costs of laying mixed gauge track proved to be insurmountable. Costs proved to be prohibitive, however, for all the schemes.

As late as August 1919 the chairman of the Parish Council, as representative on the District Committee of the County, reported the failure of the Transport Committee to encourage the scheme for the light railway and that their alternative, a concrete track for motors, was unanimously disapproved by the County Council.

Bus services

The Great North of Scotland Railway did not lose out, though. The company was very innovative with regard to bus services acting as feeders to their railway system. They built and operated their own motor buses and were one of the largest owners of buses in Britain. On 1 June 1905 a motor bus service running from Culter railway station to Echt and Midmar was started. On 1 May 1906 a new service started from Aberdeen to Dunecht and Cluny via Skene. The routing was from Aberdeen Schoolhill station via Oldmill, Kingswells, Skene Road, Elrick, Mason Lodge, Skene (United Free Church), Dick's Lodge, Waterton (Dunecht), and Cluny. This duplicated the service operated by the horse-drawn Cluny bus which made its last trip on Friday, 31 August 1906.

On 1 September 1906 a G.N.S.R. bus service started between Aberdeen and Midmar via Echt. This new service also took passengers right into town to the Schoolhill railway station beside His Majesty's Theatre, so the feeder service to Culter station was discontinued in October. The vehicles had solid rubber tyres and mostly seated 18 passengers. They were legally restricted to a maximum speed of 12mph (19.3k). They were painted in a livery of purple lake, which was the same as used on the company's railway carriages. The railway operated bus services lasted into the 1920s.

Just as in more recent years, there was dissatisfaction with the bus service and a deputation went to the general manager of G.N.S.R. to press the need for a more efficient and extended service for passengers and luggage. Various companies ran bus services after World War I – notably Goodalls. Gradually they were all taken over by Alexanders.

Steam engine at the entrance to Westhill House driveway c. 1920

Goods transport

In December 1906 the G.N.S.R. bought over the business of Robert Smith, the carrier of Echt, who owned a five-ton Yorkshire Steam Wagon Company vehicle. Smith was kept on as agent. More steam vehicles were bought during the next couple of years. All these steam lorries could haul a three-ton trailer and were thus eminently more suitable than motor lorries for goods haulage in the country districts. The lorries were to leave Echt every Monday, Wednesday and Friday and go via Waterton, Craigiedarg and Broadstraik. Every Tuesday, Thursday and Saturday they went via Garlogie and Carnie. Goods pickup points were Allan's shop at Garlogie, Rae's at Mason Lodge, Broadstraik Inn and Mr Bains'shop, Crommie Cottage, at the junction of the Echt and Skene roads. Special runs could be made for coal, grain, feedstuffs, and manure. This was the forerunner of later independent hauliers such as

Charlie Anderson from Moss-side, Farquharson Pope and, more recently, Bill Leslie (W. & H. Leslie).

Polling day at Broadstraik with the Dickie Family

The arrival of the motor car

One of the first cars in the parish was an Argyle bought by the Hamiltons of Skene House in 1912. Doctor Skinner also had a car quite early on, which can be seen in a photograph of him and his wife outside Westhill House. His car was an Albion from around 1907, though Grampian Transport Museum tell us that it had a *"strangely improvised rear body"*.

John Rose of Westhill Mains and Willie Hogg of Standing Stones both had early cars. John Rose's was an Austin, one of the first ever made. Willie Hogg had a Model T Ford. John's was called the Aldersyde Express and Willie's the Silver Bullet, though in truth neither could manage much above 10 mph (16k)! The minister, John McMurtrie, and Alexander Craigmile from Broadstraik were other early car owners.

Skene House and estate

Skene House

We have already seen that the main Skene family was involved in national affairs from time to time, but that they were never a major family in the North-East. Consequently they are not well known, even within the Skene area.

The same could be said about Skene House. Hidden away among the woods near Lyne of Skene, it has been neglected by most writers on Scottish castles and houses. THE VIEW OF THE DIOCESE from 1732 does not mention it in listing the castles and gentlemen's houses in the province of Mar, despite listing the ruined Hallforest Castle nearby. MacGibbon & Ross do not mention it in their CASTELLATED AND DOMESTIC ARCHITECTURE OF SCOTLAND. W. Douglas Simpson does not have much to say about. Even Historic Scotland paid it little heed until as recently as 1996 when

Skene House before Archibald Simpson's alterations

they visited and immediately realized that it should be upgraded to 'A' Listed. Perhaps had it retained the term Castle or Tower of Skene it might have been viewed differently.

Often described in family tradition as the first stone and lime castle in Mar province, the original part of Skene, the north wing of the present building, is usually compared with the Hallforest near Kintore. Along with Hallforest and Drum, Skene was one of the castles guarding the royal route over the

Mounth and through eastern Mar to the Garioch. This road led from the fords at Drum and was later known as the 'Couper Road'. Current thinking is that, in the second half of the 14th century, Hallforest replaced a timber hunting lodge built by Robert the Bruce.

The same may have applied to Skene. Presumably John of Skene, at the end of the 13th century, had some kind of stronghold at Skene, though no castle is mentioned in the charter Robert of Skene received from Robert the Bruce in 1317. Consequently Skene probably dates from the middle to late 14th century, rather than some of the more fanciful very early dates given for it, especially on some websites.

A description is given in MEMORIALS OF THE FAMILY OF SKENE OF SKENE of the old tower.

> "The Tower, or old house, still stands, which was originally built of three arches or stories, and entered by a ladder on the second story. It was covered with a mound of earth upon the top of the third arch, and is all built with lime, quite run together or vitrified, and the walls about ten feet thick. It continued in its original state till about the year 1680, that the arches being taken out, it was roofed and floored by Jean Burnet, Lady Skene, Relict of John Skene of that ilk, in her widowhood, and makes now a part of the accommodation of the present house."

Jean Burnett had 11 children, with seven surviving past childhood. She is described as a frugal lady who transformed the old tower in difficult times. Prior to that the family had "*always lived in low thatch houses, like the better kind of their common farm houses.*" These houses would have been within a barmkin wall with the family retreating to the tower in times of trouble.

Had Jean decided to build a new house, then Skene today might have been a ruin like Hallforest. Instead she took out the vaults of the old tower, and floored and roofed it, leaving the basement vault which was used later as a wine cellar. She also added a new building to the tower, the middle part of the later house. The original tower, much modified, is the north part of the house. Portraits of Jean Burnett and John Skene hang in Crathes Castle, Jean's childhook home and where she died in 1688.

The family fortunes seem to have suffered during the 17th and into the 18th century, despite the marriage of John and Jean's eldest son, Alexander, bringing the lands of Wester Fintray to the family in 1690. Alexander married Giles Adie (or Aedie), daughter of David Adie of Newark and Easter Echt, baillie and burgess of Aberdeen. The Adie's were a prominent Aberdeen merchant family, with Andrew Adie's house in The Green, at the foot of the Back Wynd stairs, a landmark until it was demolished in 1914. The Skenes were connected to the Adies. Skene's kinsman, George Skene of Fintray and Rubislaw, later Sir George, Provost of Aberdeen, was apprenticed to George Adie, a trader with Danzig. George Skene's niece, Katherine, married a son of George Adie.

One might have expected the marriage to Giles Adie to have revived Skene's fortunes. However, a short note in the SKENE PAPERS records a list of books with the message "*list of all the books in the family of Skene at the Union (1707) which shows the low condition the Covenant had brought the family that all was sold and the lands wadset (mortgaged) to pay debt. Nor was there wherewithal to give the heir education.*" The list has eight books for James Skene, all of them religious tracts; and 21 books for his brother the Laird of Skene. A letter from Giles to Alexander, also in the SKENE PAPERS, ends "*my dearest heart, your affectionate wif till death*". She died in Aberdeen in November 1750, aged 75, her death notice appearing in the ABERDEEN JOURNAL.

Thereafter things did improve for the family, as George Skene (1695-1756) inherited Skene from his father and the lands of Careston (or Caraldstone) from his uncle, Major George Skene. He also married his cousin, the Major's daughter Elisabeth. Careston is near Brechin and was originally in Forfarshire; now it is in Angus. Much of the SKENE PAPERS relate to the administration of that estate with the castle there referred to as Castle Skene. George also inherited business interests in London from his uncle. This George seems to have been responsible for the revival of the Skene fortunes. He was elected on nine successive occasions as Lord Rector of Marischal College, ironic considering that Marischal College was established by the family's old nemesis, the Earl Marischal. His obituary in the ABERDEEN JOURNAL says that he was a "*man of superior capacity; fitted for business; remarkable for doing good*". He was thereby able to further extend Skene House, adding the south wing. This was probably done by 1745 although entries in the Skene accounts show that, in 1753, he received 20,000 slates, presumably for use on the house as most of the farm houses on the estate would have been thatched at that time.

An interesting account exists for building work done for George's successor, also George. This is from 1779 and concerns the building of a portico at Skene. The account is quite detailed on the work done and the

Skene House

cost – taking down and rebuilding a part of the walls for the portico; cutting and ragling six inches deep in the walls of the mansion house round the portico; and also slating work. However, the most interesting comment is in a letter from George where it seems that it was Lady Skene who wanted the portico, George describing it as a *"damned useless bauble!"*

This lady was George's cousin Mary, daughter of George Forbes of Alford. Mary was said to be very beautiful, but she was also dumb according to Memorials of the Family of Skene, though other sources say she was both deaf and dumb. Family legend has it that George seduced Mary, and was forced to marry her after fighting a duel with her brother who he wounded. Mary's father is said to have cursed the Skene line. One reason for George objecting to his wife's portico might have been his parsimonious nature. Alexander Duff of Housedale (Dunecht) wrote about him thus: *"the Laird of Skene must draw his purse at last and I dare say that the money comes from him like drops of blood!"*.

The final major addition to Skene House was carried out after it had come into the possession of the Duff Family, Earls of Fife. The oldest child of George Skene and his cousin Mary Forbes, inherited the lairdship as George Skene, known as 'The Last Laird'. George and Mary's sixth child, also Mary, married Alexander Duff in 1775.

The authors of the BOOK OF THE DUFFS comment that a portrait of Mary Skene in their possession shows that she did not inherit her mother's beauty. Mary herself wrote in a letter to Lord Fife about a piece of silk he was sending for a gown, that she will need a full quantity, "*for what I have not in height I have in breadth*". When the last laird, who never married, died in 1825, he was nominally succeeded by his brother, Alexander. Alexander was born deaf and dumb and became blind owing to an illness. Cruelly known as 'Dumbie Skene', Alexander was not thought fit to heir the title properly and, in any case, he died only two years after his brother. James Duff, son of Mary Skene and Alexander Duff, and fourth Earl of Fife succeeded to his uncle's estates at Skene in 1827. James Duff lived at Duff House and had no direct heirs following the early death of his wife. His heir was his nephew, also James, and when the latter married Lady Agnes Hay in 1846, it was decided that the couple would make Skene their home. Lady Agnes is credited with much of the interior decoration of the house, some of it still surviving. Archibald Simpson, then one of Aberdeen's two leading architects, was chosen to alter and modernize the house.

Simpson is said to have had the plans of Skene House on his drawing board when he died suddenly in 1847 at the age of 56. Simpson added new or extended wings, including a large dining

Impaled arms of Alexander Duff of Echt and his wife Mary Skene, from inside Skene House

> Mary Skene did not inherit her mother's beauty. She wrote in a letter to Lord Fife about a piece of silk he was sending for a gown, that she will need a full quantity, "for what I have not in height I have in breadth".

Old entrance archway at Skene House

room, the old dining room and bedroom above being converted into a substantial library. The most notable and noticeable feature externally was the moving along of the existing entrance archway, with its bellcote, to screen a service court. A new entrance was then created, flanked by round towers

SKENE HOUSE AND ESTATE

Skene House new entrance

A History of Skene and Westhill

Skene House mausoleum (the howff hoose)

The walls are granite and it has an arched roof made from brick. There are 16 coffin recesses. The lintel has the inscription *17 GS 69* (George Skene).

with witches' hat roofs. Following Simpson's death his assistant, William Ramage, faithfully saw the work through.

An account in the ABERDEEN JOURNAL from March 1849 describes celebrations held at Skene for the wedding anniversary of James and Agnes Duff, and lists the following local companies having carried out work on the house in the previous two years – Mr Kemp of Inverurie contractor for the mason work; Messrs Buyers of Aberdeen for the carpenter work; Messrs Blaikie the plumbing; Mr Begg of Elgin for the painting and decorative work; Messrs Hay, the carving and gilding work; sculpture executed by George Russell of Aberdeen. At the same time two cart loads of beautifully ornamented stones and a valuable sundial were removed from Careston and brought to Skene House. Whether or not these are still at Skene is unclear.

Simpson also seems to have left Ramage plans for the stable block which were also carried out well after his death. This massive block, in baronial style, has a central tower with battlements and cap-house. It had stalls for 12 horses, a byre, lofts, two coach houses, harness room and two coachmen's houses. In 1984 it was converted into separate houses.

The Skene mausoleum, if indeed it can be called a mausoleum, is situated on an elevation to the south-west of the house. The walls are granite and it has an arched roof made from brick. There are 16 coffin recesses. The lintel above the entrance has the inscription 17 GS 69 (George Skene). Nearby lies a large stone with oblong indentations where timber blocks would have been driven in, soaked, and allowed to swell to split the stone. There was a small quarry just beside the mausoleum so the stone may have been from there. In 1775 John Barron, mason, was paid 11/6 (55.5p) for pointing and sneck pinning the victualhouse and burial place, the latter presumably the mausoleum. Known as the 'Howff hoose', the wood in which it stood was the Howff Wood. It was originally surrounded by yew-trees, cut down in the late 1940s, and an avenue of yews led to the house. A pair of columns originally flanked it, but these are no longer there. The 1863 plan of the Skene lands has monuments marked beside it which I assume are the columns. It was never used, except possibly for dogs. Sometime after it was built the door blew closed on a groundsman and he was stuck there for two days. Thereafter the door was removed.

Skene of Skene's lands in the 18th century

There is evidence that the 18th century lairds of Skene carried out some agricultural improvements on their part of the parish. In 1723 a society of improvers was set up in Scotland, called THE SOCIETY OF IMPROVERS IN THE KNOWLEDGE OF AGRICULTURE IN SCOTLAND. Seven years later, when a North-East society was established, George Skene of Skene (1695-1756) was one of its members. It does not seem likely that this was a society of serious improvers along the lines of Cockburn of Ormiston; perhaps more of a gentleman's talking shop. Grant of Monymusk is the best known improving laird in the North-East and he was certainly known to George Skene. Letters survive from Grant to Skene in the 1750s and in, one of them, Grant hoped to meet Skene in Aberdeen. Skene would most likely, therefore, have been aware of what Grant was doing, although it is difficult to say to what extent Skene carried out his own improvements.

In his account of a journey he made on horseback to London in 1729, published by the THIRD SPALDING CLUB in 1940, he does take a great interest in agricultural conditions in the areas that he passed through. He records quality of the land, the nature of the crops and pasturage, the methods of cultivation and the price of crops. He was, then, very much interested in agriculture.

There were three lairds of Skene called George in the 18th century. Under the third of them there are accounts from the 1780s of land improvements being carried out on the Skene estate. New dykes were built and improvements carried out to existing ones; stones and weeds were removed from fields; and drainage work was also being done. Gunpowder was bought to blow up and remove stones at Affloch; new dykes and drainage improvements were carried out at Terryvale; and there were some plantations at the Loch of Skene. Seven bolls of English shells were received in 1788 for use as fertilizer.

The same year there is an account from John Adam, nurseryman, for the following:
- 32,000 two year old Scots fir
- 1,000 thorns
- 200 elms
- 2,000 beech
- 1,000 seedling ash
- 3,000 three year old spruce fir

This planting is confirmed by the parish minister, James Hogg, writing in the STATISTICAL ACCOUNT in 1795. He says *"on the land belonging to Skene only have trees been hitherto raised"*. However, he is not that impressed by any improving that has been done as he goes on to say *"No plantations have till of late been made, and even that to no great extent, nor improvements indeed of any kind, owing to invincible obstructions"*.

So, some improvements were being carried out, but not enough to excite the parish minister. Incidentally, Skene or his servants must have been actively using the Loch of Skene, as an account survives, also from 1788, of the carriage of a boat from the dockyard in Aberdeen to the loch, the cost being eight shillings. (40p). The boat-house itself was thatched with heather.

Love poem to a lady

In a bundle of Skene House papers I found this LOVE POEM TO A LADY, which begins:

> *O with those too, too happie glowes I*
> *Could nou transmitt some secret sympathy*
> *Whose powerfull nature might your hands inclyn*
> *Never to joyn with any mans but myne*
> *Or if they on your hand shall touch that pairt*
> *Of your fair breast that's nearest to your heart*

It ends

> *Though lots denyd you at this solemn tym*
> *I bought you from another so youre myne*
> *Ane surer way than any else can bee*
> *Unless you would bestow yourself on mee*
> *Who am Maddam*
> *The submissive admirer of your vertue and*
> *A most humble servant*

Then it is signed G (heart drawing) G, almost certainly George.

An earlier line refers again to gloves and runs *"Which were the gifts ordained by Wallentyne"* (Valentine).

There is no date on the poem and the bundle of papers it is contained in has material from 1753 and 1804. My own feeling is that the spelling makes the earlier date more likely. Gloves were of old a traditional Valentine gift. But who was the poem written by and addressed to? If we assume the earlier date then it would be George Skene, who became laird in 1756 following the death of his father. It would be delightful to think that the poem was for his cousin, Mary Forbes, who he seduced then married. Was it ever sent? Again we have no way of knowing, but we can hope that it was.

The last Skene laird

George Skene, the last laird, was an altogether different figure from his grandfather. Although educated as an advocate, he never practiced. He was for some time in the army and served one term as Member of Parliament for Aberdeenshire as a Whig. The election in 1786 was described as a trial of strength between the Tory Gordons, supporting James Ferguson of Pitfour, and the Duff Family on the side of their Whig relative. Skene spent over £60 in pre-election entertainment which included magnums of claret, as well as port, gin, punch and entertainment for the servants of those attending. The total account for the election seems to have come to £364, around £23,000 in today's money; a fair amount, given that the electorate would have been very small at that time. Skene won by a small majority and a poem celebrates the event, the last verse being:

And a joyful day it was to be sure
For the victuals were good and the claret was pure
While the rabble roared out – such roaring was never
For Skene and Lord George, beef and porter for ever

Skene lost out to Fergusson at the next election, though he was elected to represent the burghs of Banff, Cullen, Kintore and Inverurie in 1806.

William Forbes Skene wrote of him:

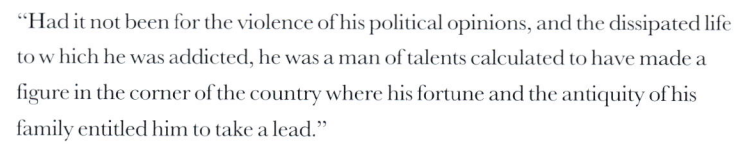

"Had it not been for the violence of his political opinions, and the dissipated life to which he was addicted, he was a man of talents calculated to have made a figure in the corner of the country where his fortune and the antiquity of his family entitled him to take a lead."

Forbes Skene goes on to talk from memory of when, as a child, he witnessed some of the drunken behaviour of his relative, his own father jumping out of his bedroom window at Skene and walking 17 miles home to Inverie to escape from George's drunkenness. Forbes Skene remembered seeing the laird at six a.m, walking round the courtyard *"clamouring for another bottle"*, as his Swiss servant vainly advised him to go to bed. He borrowed considerable sums of money, as much as £15,000 – a huge amount – from his relative, the Earl of Fife, using his lands at Skene and Fornet as collateral. At least his behaviour did not lead to an end like that of his cousin, also George Skene, executed for forgery in London in 1812.

George Skene never married, but he did love his dogs, puttin up a monument to them in the grounds with the bitter inscription:

Tartar, Fury, Ginger, Viper, Bess, Vixen, Mufie, etc., etc. My faithful dogs, by whose inviolable attachment I have been induced to banish from my mind for a time the disgust occasioned by the Vices, Follies and Ingratitude of Mankind. They never anticipated evil. A sad reverse is the fate of man.

Cur Non. G.S. 1808.

Glimpses of life from the Skene House papers

The parish minister, writing in 1843, recorded that the library at Skene House contained over 6000 volumes, well arranged and carefully kept. Catalogues still exist of the library as it was in the 18th and 19th centuries. A note laments the sparsity of the library just after 1700, but one important item did survive. This was a manuscript copy of Spalding's MEMORIALLS OF THE TRUBLES, his account of the Civil War, dating from the 1640s, and more complete than two other surviving copies. It may have been in Spalding's own hand, and is listed in one of the catalogues of the library at Skene House. The Earl of Fife found the manuscript in the library when he took over the estate and contacted James Skene of Rubislaw, who was preparing an edition of the work to be published by the Bannatyne Club in Edinburgh. Skene of Rubislaw had already published Volume I in 1828, but used the Skene House copy for Volume II. The receipt for the volume, from him to Blaikies the advocates in Aberdeen, survives in the SKENE PAPERS.

As well as the mental stimulus of his library, the laird had a physical one. A letter to him in 1753, from David Dalrymple of Old Aberdeen, talks about golf: *"I am overjoyed to hear the good effects of the golfing scheme – exercise is certainly necessary both to procure and preserve health"*.

The tax returns for the late 1790s/early 1800s show that Skene of Skene had no wheeled vehicles, at least not at Skene House. He paid a house and window tax for 54 windows in 1812. (It had been for 43 windows in 1806. I wonder why the increase in only a few years?) He also paid a male servant tax. He paid no tax for wheel carriage, saddle and carriage horse, or draught horses. Nor did he pay a tax on hair powder!

He seems to have hired horses from the inn-keeper at Bervie when he needed them, a chaise and driver being hired in 1783. In 1874 he hired a chaise to take him to Balbithan, then on to Old Meldrum, Old Deer, and Moncoffer. The poor condition of the roads, until the building of the turnpike, made wheeled transport very difficult, and one cannot imagine that this would have been a comfortable journey. Horses even had to be hired for collecting taxes. By 1812 he was paying tax for eight work horses, and by 1822 he had an account book for John Taylor, coachmaker.

The account books for various tradesmen give some idea of the lifestyle in the 'big hoose'. In 1824 there is an account from William Duncan for the supply of oysters, barley sugar, ginger tablet, walnuts, French plums and St Michael oranges (an early M&S!). From William Fraser, grocer, Skene, he was buying raw sugar, plums, coffee, white and yellow London soap, black pepper, whitening, blacking, pipeclay, vinegar, prunes, lemons, nutmeg and mustard. From the baker, in 1822, bread, loaves, bran and French rolls. The fish book for 1824 lists ling, haddock, skate, finnans, lobster, and crab claws. Malt tax was paid for beer to the house and for coopers. They may well have been brewing their own, although there are also accounts for the Gilcomston brewer. Later this became the Devanha brewery in Ferryhill, from whom he bought brown stout and ankers of ale and beer. There are also accounts for wine: £45.7/- to Thomas Bannerman & Co, wine merchants.

Skene was a member of the Musical Society in Aberdeen and of the County Club. In 1774 Sara (or Sallie) Skene, daughter of George Skene and Mary Forbes, received dancing lessons from Francis Peacock, the well-known Aberdeen dance master after whom Peacock's Close in the Castlegate is named. As well as the lessons, Skene had to pay for a musician, concert tickets, tickets to Mr Peacock's Ball, song and music books, and a ticket to see the model of Paris – presumably being displayed in Aberdeen.

Skene Estate in the 19th century

George Skene Keith in A GENERAL VIEW OF THE AGRICULTURE OF ABERDEENSHIRE published in 1811, describes Skene House as a spacious old mansion, but says that George Skene has an excellent house at Careston in which he generally resides. Keith says that Skene has about 600 acres on his personal farm at Skene (the Mains) and adjoining Fornet in his own possession. On these lands he had already carried out some improvements with the rest in the process of being improved. At some point he also brought over a forester from Germany to work on the estate. Charles Hellmrech is buried in Skene Kirkyard, having died aged 39, in 1817. He must have died around the time his daughter was born as she is also on the gravestone, dying aged just 9½ in 1826.

The rents on the estate continued to paid part in kind, part in money. An account from 1815 notes that the girnal at Skene House received 16

Game larder at Skene House 1886

bolls of oat meal from James Smith of Nether Affloch, Skene of Skene's share of the 1814 crop. The girnal was a barn for storing rental payments made in kind, grain or meal that the laird could then use for his own household, distribute to his tenants, including selling back to them, or sell on the open market.

In 1826 the farm of Newton of Skene was advertised for let on a 19-year lease. It contained upwards of 150 acres of arable land sub-divided into fields of *"convenient sizes, substantially improved and sheltered in every direction by thriving belts and plantations"*. The dwelling house is described as modern, *"fit for the occupation of a genteel family"*. There is also a water-driven threshing mill on the farm. So here we see definite signs of agricultural improvements.

Farther from Skene House, at Nethertoun of Garlogie, the 1826 plan of the area shows what looks like an unimproved fermtoun with 15 buildings, some crofts or cottar houses, each with a yard, some with yards at a distance from their cottage. Some pasture is still common and some marked *"old folds pasture"*, but some is marked *"now ploughed"*. The Milltoun of Garlogie, just to the north, does not have the same pre-improvement arrangement. This seems to be a transition stage, with some areas enclosed and improved, others not. By the 1863 plan, the scene at Nethertoun had changed completely.

The gasworks

South-west of Graystone, and just under 600 metres south-east of Skene House, is a wood called Gas Woods on modern Ordnance Survey maps. This takes its name from the gasworks which supplied Skene House and Stables in the middle of the 19th century. The SKENE PAPERS record the cost of making a road to the gas house in 1849. The buildings are shown on the first OS map c.1870, and by the time of the second one in 1900, are marked disused, although still roofed. Both maps show a gasometer at the south west end of an L-shaped group of buildings. The earlier map also shows two other buildings lying just to the south. Perhaps one of these was the gasman's house. In 1857 the gasman was James Milne; in the 1871 census he was James Sangster, aged 62, from Oldmachar parish, who lived with his wife, Elizabeth, aged 58, who was from Old Monkland, Lanarkshire. The chimney for the gasworks could be seen from the Lyne of Skene. Nothing now remains of this short-lived method of providing lighting to the house, except some lumps of coal and some slates on the site of the buildings, but it obviously gave the name to the surrounding wood.

A History of Skene and Westhill

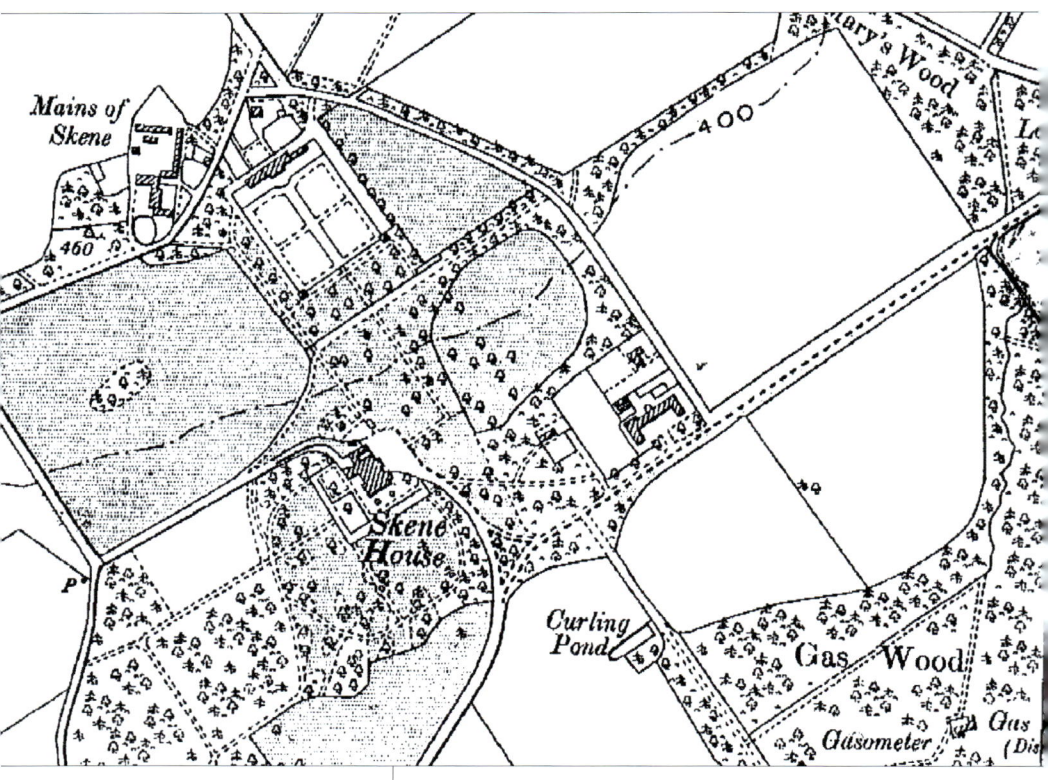

Skene House and the Mains in 1900

Only the really wealthy could afford gas lighting, which burned coal and was quite smelly – one reason why the gasworks was set at some distance from the house.

Private gasworks for supplying large country house came into prominence from the 1840s, initially mainly for service rooms and passages. Gas was used as early as 1778 to light Dundonald Abbey, and Walter Scott installed gas lighting at Abbotsford in 1823, but found it expensive and smelly. It was also used at Park House in Drumoak. Only the really wealthy could afford this method of lighting, which burned coal and was quite smelly and unpleasant – one reason why the gasworks was set at some distance from the house. The cinders were used to make the roads to the gasworks. I imagine it was not a pleasant occupation. Skene House at this time belonged to the Earl of Fife who could afford such a luxury.

Initially large amounts of gas were needed to

light rooms and they needed considerable ventilation. By the 1850s the invention of regenerative burners made gas more economical for domestic use; by the 1880s the incandescent gas mantle was developed, making it even more economical. Skene House gas was piped in three-inch (7.62cm) cast iron pipes and was replaced around 1890 when an acetylene gas plant was coupled up to the system, hence the buildings are shown as disused in the second OS map. In 1922 Skene House was wired for electricity.

The Rustic House

This summer house no longer exists, but it stood at the back of Skene House, near the walled garden, and had the date 1850 on a table and on a panel above the door. It was octagonal with pillars supporting the roof. According to Mary McMurtrie it was made with planks three-quarters of an inch thick, cut by pit-saw. Split twigs were used to decorate it, with thousands of smiddy-made nails to arrange the twigs into beautiful patterns – stars, palm leaves, diamonds, and so on. Inside there were patterns of white birch bark, and a bench seat round the walls with scroll ends, similarly covered in beautiful designs. Opposite the door was the Earl of Fife's motto VIRTUTE ET OPERA. The floor was paved with white pebbles and there was a circular pedestal table, later removed to Skene House for safe keeping. The roof was heather thatch but, sometime in the 1960s or 70s, boys from Aberdeen who had come to work at the farm began pulling it to pieces until it eventually fell apart.

The Hamiltons

George Hamilton was the son of a Glasgow merchant and, like many other 19th century Skene landowners, he made his initial fortune in India, working for the firm of W. & A. Graham, before moving to Liverpool with the same company. While in India he married Anne Elizabeth Shaw, a daughter of General Robert Shaw, who latterly lived in Westfield Terrace in Aberdeen. Still owning estates in Ceylon, Hamilton was able to retire from business in his early forties, and because of the family connection, moved to the North-East. He initially became tenant of Skene House and the Home Farm in 1872, renting it for £220 p.a. In 1880 he bought the estate from the Earl of Fife. Thereafter he followed other Skene landowners in becoming involved in local and regional affairs: Deputy-Lieutenant of the County, J.P., Commissioner of Supply, and serving on the County Council once it was

Skene House at the time of the Hamiltons 1886

established. Locally he was a not altogether successful member of the School Board; he was also involved in various bodies in Aberdeen.

George Hamilton also became interested in agricultural matters, establishing a herd of Aberdeen-Angus cattle which he bred and exhibited. He seems to have personally farmed his property at Nether Garlogie. He died in 1891, aged 61, and was succeeded by his son, John.

George and Anne Hamilton also left six daughters, none of whom married. They were a talented group of women, engaging in writing, art and ornithology. Most of them lived at Murtle and Mary, the artistic one, became friendly with fellow artist, Mary McMurtrie, to whom she eventually left the property of Sunhoney, Milltimber, where Mary McMurtrie's daughter, Elspeth, now lives. Thankfully she also left a photograph album from 1886 which shows the family and guests in and around Skene House. (For more on the Hamilton ladies see the article by Alan Knox in LEOPARD magazine November 2009). G.M. Fraser was told by one of the Hamilton daughters that her father had tried to buy books and papers from the house, but that these were taken to Duff House or to Mar Lodge. She said that the books were later sold in London for less than her father had offered. A number of Skene portraits were also taken to Duff House.

Brigadier General John G.H. Hamilton, who succeeded his father as Laird of Skene, joined the Black Watch in 1890. He served in the Boer War from 1899 to 1902, and in World War I. He was a lieutenant when he left for South Africa, and was promoted to captain after distinguished service at the Battle of Magersfontein. He was later wounded at the Battle of Paardeberg. He was second in command at Balmoral when his regiment acted as bodyguard to Queen Victoria. From 1904 until 1910 he was Adjutant of the third Battalion Black Watch at Perth, then he went to India on being promoted major. He returned home to command the depot at Perth from 1912 until December 1914, when he went to France to

Hamiltons on the Loch of Skene 1886

Hamiltons and guests 1886

join the first Battalion Black Watch. Promoted brigadier general to take over the 154th Brigade of the 51st Division, he was mentioned in several dispatches. After the Armistice he was in command of Caesar's Camp in Italy for four months, then returned to India to take command of a battalion of the Black Watch.

Skene Estate and house were put up for sale or let during John Hamilton's early years as laird. At that time it was described as being about 4000 acres, the house containing a dining room, two drawing rooms, library, business room, billiard room, 15 bedrooms, seven dressing rooms, bathrooms, etc., besides ample kitchen and servants' accommodation.

After the war a considerable part of the estate was sold to Lord Cowdray. Some other farms, including the Fornets, Broomhill, Newton, Upper Terryvale and Letter Brae, were sold to sitting tenants. Following his retirement from the army in 1921, Brigadier Hamilton moved back to Skene House and, in 1925, was elected to represent Echt and Skene on Aberdeenshire Council. He was appointed Deputy Lieutenant of the County in 1930 and was chairman of Huntly & Garioch Agricultural Committee from its establishment in 1939. During World War II he was in the Home Guard. When he died in 1945, aged 76, his obituary in the PRESS & JOURNAL recorded that "*by his quiet unassuming manner and his keen interest in everything to which he turned his hand he earned the deep respect and love of hundreds of people with whom he came into contact.*" Following his death even more of the estate farms were sold off, including the Lyne, Greystones, Nether Terryvale, Back Mains and Mainside.

Brigadier Hamilton's wife, Sybil, is still remembered by many in the Skene area. Like her husband, she involved herself in local affairs, founding the Skene SWRI, among other things. She was very involved in morale and fund raising activities in World War II, for which she received the OBE in 1943. Skene House itself was the venue for picnics and Christmas parties for children from Proctor's Orphanage and the area around Skene House. The Hamilton's only son, John, was a captain in the Black Watch during World War II. He was mentioned in dispatches while serving in the Middle East and was killed in action in Crete in 1941.

Skene resident Roberta Murray was just 16 years old when she went to work as house tablemaid at Skene House in 1946, cycling up from her home in Kingswells. There was a cook (Roberta's cousin) and a housemaid as well. Brigadier Hamilton died that same year. While he was alive three flats were converted for Black Watch soldiers, but Roberta does not think they were ever occupied. Brigadier Hamilton also had a butler, his batman from army days; according to him there had been 12 maids at the house in the couple's younger days. The Hamiltons owned most of Lyne of Skene and people came up to the house to pay their rents, but the properties were all sold off during Roberta's time, possibly to pay death duties.

Certainly Mrs Hamilton didn't seem to have much money. Every month she unlocked a cupboard and gave the cook and Roberta the ingredients for baking a sultana cake. It lasted a month, but the staff never got any of it. There was a collection of silver in a room with a steel door. If there were guests for dinner or it needed cleaning, Mrs Hamilton passed the silver out to Roberta. A huge wardrobe in Mrs Hamilton's room was filled with dresses which she had worn in her younger days.

Roberta remembers the huge entrance to the house, with paintings and curling stones which she thought would have been used on the loch when it froze over. There was a curling pond in the grounds at one time. One particular painting, on the right hand side, was of the Wizard Laird with what Roberta thinks was a raven on his shoulder. She went back when the house was for sale because Joe, the gamekeeper, wanted her to show him the picture. Everything was the same as 50 years earlier, even the carpet, but the painting of the Wizard had gone. Much of the house was in ruins, although the upstairs sitting room was still the same. This was the Brigadier's study, and Mrs Hamilton had wanted it left as it had been when he was alive, and took her tea in it every day. Roberta remembers a silver inkwell in the shape of a claw. The wine cellar and kitchen were in ruins – much of the wine had to be thrown out. In the huge drawing room at the time of the Brigadier's funeral there were large gold mirrors and whisky decanters with locks on them. In the room near the wine cellar where the servants cleaned the shoes, there was a hole leading from a cupboard. Roberta thought it was a passage and tried to crawl along it to see where it led, but got scared and turned back, as she did not have a torch. Again, Joe wanted to see this cupboard when they went back to the house, but that part of the house was in ruins.

Skene House garden

According to Edna Edmond, the Skene House walled garden was kept in beautiful order by a succession of head gardeners and their assistants. In the early 1950s it was leased out to a market gardener who ran a successful business employing a number of local women. For many years he had a stall in The Green every Friday. When he retired the garden was not re-let as a garden, but was offered for rent to the farmer at Mains of Skene who used to keep calves in it.

Skene House: a new era
Roberta Murray's memories give some impression of the decay into which Skene House had fallen, partly as a result of death duties. Sybil Hamilton died in 1974, leaving Skene House and the estate in the possession of her daughter Jean who was married to Captain Farquharson of Whitehouse. Jean died in 1985 and Skene House was sold in 1995. Most of the grounds and some of the farms round about, those which had not been sold off earlier, continued to belong to Captain Farquharson who died in 2010. The estate still belongs to his family. Skene House itself was bought by Nicholas and Fiona Renny. Since then they have embarked on a massive programme to restore Skene House to something like its former glory. Much of the work is being done by Nick himself, despite his having a demanding job as a leading maxillo-facial consultant. A great deal has been achieved, but there is still a huge amount to be done.

The Skene family vault
The Skene family vault, surrounded by a dyke with a gate and a railing, was in the parish churchyard. In the 20th century the vault is described as being 12ft x 12ft (3.65m) with a red door. During World War II the dyke and railing were removed and the vault filled in. Local children were told that no grass grew on it because the Wizard Laird was buried there. The current memorial stone to the Skene Family was paid for by Mrs H. Oberhummer of Vienna, a descendant of a line of Skenes who had gone to Europe many years ago. When she visited Skene in the 1970s she thought it was terrible that there was no memorial to the family. Edna Edmond arranged for samples and costs of stones to be sent to Mrs Oberhummer who chose the one she wanted.

The Kirktoun of Skene and other communities
Garlogie, Lyne of Skene, Carnie,
Elrick / Broadstraik, Mason Lodge, Westhill

Rural depopulation began towards the end of the 19th century and continued apace throughout the 20th. Prior to that, rural communities were in many ways self-sufficient and a large number of tradesmen existed to support those primarily working on the land. Today Carnie is not recognized as a village at all and the others named here are barely so. In the 19th century things were very different, and other significant communities existed that today are no more than farms. More than 80 people lived at Millbuie, for example, including tradesmen such as masons and blacksmiths. The same is true of its near neighbour Terryvale, where there was a shoemaker. Concraig also had a blacksmith, at Bridgend. Peter Berry was the blacksmith there in 1861, his wife, Martha, being a midwife. One of their sons, Moses Berry, ran the smiddy from the late 19th to early 20th century and he was followed by his son Robert. For a time there was also a blacksmith just along the road at the Auchinclech crossroads. In the 1780s a smith's fold and a smith's croft is recorded at Mackie's Steps. All of these villages had a reason for their existence, be it proximity to the church, castle or mill, encouragement by a landowner, or the positioning of a road.

Kirktoun of Skene
From the earliest times of the church of Skene, a hamlet grew up around it,

Kirktoun of Skene

despite the fact that there was no manse until the 16th century. There was a smith's croft and a brewhouse in the village in 1554, and in 1605 there was a substantial enough house in the Kirktoun for Robert Irvine to have a banquet there with his friends. In the late 17th century a variety of professions were being carried on in the village. Arthur King was the smith, receiving payments for making a *"sliveband to a cuple and three dizen of double plenshion nails"*. The Kirk Session records that there was more than one tavern in the Kirktoun in 1723, because the minister reported that some of the congregation were frequenting them during the sermon. The session records also name a James Ogilvie as an officer of excise in the Kirktoun in 1743, a forerunner of the infamous Gillespie the gauger.

It is difficult to visualise what the village might have been like in the era before the estates of Kirkville and Easterskene had transformed the area around it. A valuation from 1793 lists 15 crofts or houses in the Kirktoun. From reading the descriptions of the crofts I imagine that the village would have straggled along the old road, heading towards Dykenook. Perhaps the 'bowie lum' cottages were a survival of these. These two or three cottages stood on the line of the Old Skene Road down behind Ogg's shop. They can just about be seen in some early photographs of the village, and Mary McMurtrie sketched them in 1922. By that time the actual bowie lums had disappeared, but the cottages were still thatched.

The bowie lums were so called because they were made from strips of wood tied with straw and they had a barrel or bowed shape. Wood and straw could be used because the fires burned peat which doesn't produce the same flames as coal, though there was still some danger of them going on fire. The cottages survived until the 1930s, and they were somewhat sarcastically named 'Bowie Lum Street'. Unfortunately this has been corrupted in recent times into 'Bogie Lum Street' which does not convey the original meaning.

Kirktoun in 1865

Along at Dykenook in the 1840s there was a tailor and shoemaker, along with several other families, so a little community there. The original school, schoolyard and schoolhouse opened off the old road, so Dykenook was almost connected to the Kirktoun with the school occupying much of the area between the two. Further crofts seem to have existed to the south of the village, along the old road to the peat moss. Part of the description of the fifth lot of the Dean of Guild's lands, Easter Kirktoun, goes as follows:

> "up the brae to a cutt march stone marked 3 (still there), placed in the cornland called the peatroad bank, and on the east side of the peat road. Proceeding northwards up thro' the infield ground to a cutt march stone marked 4 placed in the north east corner of the yeard presently occupied by Alexander Ettershank in Kirkstile, turning eastward and running in a straight line thro' said yeard dyke and the house occupied by said Alexander Ettershank to the south cheek of the west gate of the Kirkyeard of Skene. Where there is a cutt march stone marked 5. From thence turning northward and keeping along the west dyke of said Kirkyeard and thro' the houses of the Kirktoun in a straight line to a cutt march stone marked 6 placed on the southside of the King's high way (Old Skene Road), near to and a little southwest from a well – and from thence holding still northward in a straight line across the road to a cutt march stone marked 7 placed at the south dyke of the Minister of Skene's glebe, a little eastward of Alexander Greig's shade or carthouse. And from

thence turning first eastward and afterwards northward and holding along the dyke of the Minister's glebe till it come to a cutt march stone marked G denoting Glebe on the West side and A denoting Aberdeen on the East side."

So here we have a description of part of the Kirktoun in 1788. Alexander Ettershank's croft (Kirkstile) must have straddled the peat road with his house near to where the buildings at the entrance to Kirkton Nursing Home are (these being originally part of Kirkville Home Farm). There is a suggestion that there were houses on the east side of the road, where the Red Star is now. Alexander Greig's carthouse would have been just to the west of the entrance to Manse Road, possibly where the smiddy was in the 19th and 20th centuries. The G/A stone marked the boundary between the glebe and the Aberdeen Dean of Guild's lands. However, as the Guild's lands were being divided up at this time the stone was replaced by one with G/K, dividing the glebe from the new estate of East Kirkton (later Kirkville). The G/K boundary stone still survives on the road up to the manse.

Each croft in the Kirktoun would probably have had a longer garden than they do now since even tradesmen had to grow their own crops and keep a few beasts. In 1826 Knowles of Kirkville had advertised a genteel cottage and garden lawn for let in the Kirktoun, so perhaps there were some properties that were more than simple thatched but and bens.

The shoemaker in the Kirktoun in 1785, William Collie, made a pair of shoes "*for a young gentleman*" at Skene House. In the 1851 Census the Kirktoun had two shoemakers – Alexander Chappell who employed two men, and John Glenny.

Alexander Archibald, a minister from Stirling, wrote to Mary McMurtrie in 1978: "*I was 24 when I left Skene to go to my first charge in the Borders. My grandfather came from Keig to the shoemaker's business in the Kirktoun in 1856, and my father kept the business going until he became a partner in an Aberdeen firm in 1915. So when I left the family had been in the parish for 73 years. I remember my two teachers – Miss Anderson and Miss Bauchop. Of course I remember your father and mother and Mr McMurtrie, although we belonged to the other kirk.*"

The 20th century soutar, Sandy Beaton, is mentioned in the section below on Jessie Kesson. In the 1881 Census the Kirktoun had a master wright employing one man, a master tailor/merchant (James McIntosh) employing a journeyman tailor, several knitters, a mason, a blacksmith, two shoemakers with one employing a journeyman shoemaker, a merchant/grocer (George

THE KIRKTOUN OF SKENE AND OTHER COMMUNITIES

McPetrie), and a carpenter. Quite a community of tradesmen, in fact.

From the division of the Dean of Guild's lands onward the village was more or less split between the estates of Easterskene and Kirkville, with the former owning the west of the village, including the original shop, and the latter the north and east, including the blacksmiths.

A shop is mentioned to let by William Knowles of Easter Kirktoun (Kirkville) in 1800. If it was on Kirkville land then it was probably not the later McPetrie /Ogg's shop. It is described then as a well frequented shop with a new house lately possessed by George Emslie, merchant. George McPetrie came from Midmar in the 1870s to run the main shop, part of the Easterskene Estate. He continued in the shop until around his death in 1913, and his widow carried on for a few years after that.

A photograph exists of the shop with his name on it and it is said that it is his wife at the door of the shop. For a time his son Alexander ran the shop before, on 29 May 1924, it was taken over by George G. Ogg. George had previously been a vanman for W.& J. Smith of Kintore. He came from

Kirktoun of Skene c.1920

249

George Ogg's first van

Under George the shop sold everything including petrol, the pump being added in the 1950s. The Oggs also ran a grocery van, a lifeline for rural farm and cottar houses.

Oldmeldrum and in his younger days had been a prize-winning ploughman. He served in the Gordon Highlanders in World War I, his wounds giving him permanent back problems throughout his life. The shop ledger records that George's first day's takings were eleven shillings and sixpence (57p) and that the first customers were Mr and Mrs Findlater of Barnyards of Easterskene, who bought a quarter of tea! George Ogg also took on other duties.

From 1934 until his death in 1961 he was registrar, but he was also a J.P, session clerk for 12 years, and treasurer of Skene Church for 23 years. Under George the shop sold everything including petrol, the pump being added in the 1950s and only removed in October 1997 when new EEC regulations came into effect. The Oggs also ran a grocery van, a lifeline for rural farm and cottar houses.

Often there would be a form of barter, with the farmer's wife exchanging eggs, butter and cheese for other groceries. After World War II, George obtained a hackney license, for private hire, sometimes even taking expectant mothers to the maternity hospital at Torphins. Son William was vanman, hackney driver, and mechanic. When school transport came along, Ogg's shop also provided that, including carrying school dinners from Skene Central to the schools that needed them. Grandson Alistair continued running the shop and undertaking much of the driving work until 2010. On 6 March, 2011, Alistair finally called it a day and handed the keys over to Peter and Gracie Adams, who modernised the shop but kept the name Ogg above the door.

A tailor is mentioned in the Kirktoun in the 1841 Census (James Lillyshire). In the 1870s James McIntosh, born in King Edward parish, came to the Kirktoun. McIntosh initially lodged with the merchant, William Milne, along with two young journeyman tailors. A few years later he feued land, to the north west of the church, from the Kirkville Estate. Here he built a shop with a house and garden and established a business as a tailor. By 1881 he was described as a master tailor and general merchant, though he also found time to be sexton and be involved in parish politics, as we have seen elsewhere. Was he now in competition with his former landlord across the road? McIntosh died in March 1920, his wife a few months later.

In February 1923, James Davidson, from Midmar, bought the shop. James had trained as a miller before emigrating to New Zealand in 1910. In 1922 he returned to Scotland, meeting Isabella Wishart from Edinburgh on the ship home. The two were married at Holyrood Abbey Church and moved to the Kirktoun of Skene. As well as running a grocer's shop, James carried out cycle sales and repairs in the part of the building that had probably been a stable originally (next to the hearse-house). The couple left Skene for New Zealand after nearly three years, selling the shop to John (Jack) Comfort in October 1925.

Comfort added a petrol pump and he may have converted the stable to a garage, though others say it was his successors the Lawsons who did that. The next owners were the Lawson Brothers who obtained a licence for the shop. It has been suggested to me that the back of their shop became an unofficial drinking den!

In 1962 Willie Lawson sold the house and shop to Charlie and Bunty

Kirktoun shop under Jack Comfort

Yule, though Willie stayed on in the garage for a year or two, living in a caravan round the back. Bunty had bred dogs in the village. On taking over the shop they got local builder/joiner, Sam Wyness, to convert the shop into a bar, the licence being granted in December 1962. Once this proved successful, they converted the garage into a lounge and built a function suite at the back. The inspection pit is still below the lounge area. The reason for naming it The Red Star is something of a mystery with Charlie and Bunty's two sons giving different versions of the story. One said it was because his mother read a weekly paper called THE RED STAR. The other son thought it came from Dryborough's Red Label Beer. Charlie and Bunty Yule retired in October 1988.

For some reason there was no inn in the Kirktoun for 100 years before the opening of the Red Star. James Knowles, proprietor of Kirkville, did advertise some of his properties in the village in 1824 and suggested that *"a respectable public house would probably serve well"*. The first OS has what became Ogg's shop marked with P.H. (public house) and the issue of the SKENE TIMES ridiculing the opening of the Milne Hall does say that stronger stuff can be had over the way. However, there is no mention of an inn in any of the censuses or valuation rolls and the P.H. was not marked on the second OS map at the end of the century. Although none of the inns on the Old Skene Road had been sited in the Kirktoun, there had been inns there in earlier times. You would have expected there to be one in the village where so many other tradesmen were situated.

William Fowler was the blacksmith in 1851 and he was born in Skene. The blacksmith also had his croft lands which ran behind the smiddy and across the road where the car park is now. They amounted to 12 acres.

Alexander Stuart from Keig was the blacksmith in the late 19th century and continued into the 20th century. His fine handiwork can be seen in the swey over Elsie Duguid's fireplace at Burnland. Alexander was succeeded by his son, George, whose hardy wife is remembered below by Jessie Kesson and Leslie Durno. Alf Williamson from Mason Lodge worked for him for a time after he returned from World War I. The smiddy was closed by 1940. The blacksmith's was where the men would gather for a 'news'. On the opposite side, round the corner from the shop, was the village pump where the women would often do the same. Mary McMurtrie wrote of the smiddy, "*the dark mysterious interior, with its glowing fire, big bellows and flying sparks, always attracted a crowd of wee laddies on their way home from school*".

Kirktoun smiddy

Lord Cowdray bought the estates of Kirkville and Easterskene in the 1920s. This gave him possession of most of the village and he carried out a certain amount of remodelling. The old narrow corner at the south of the village was enlarged to create an open space. This coincided with the conversion of Kirkville Home Farm at the edge of this space. The former steading became a laundry for Kirkville House, and the other buildings became houses for estate workers. A new approach to Kirkville was created from the field in front of the Home Farm. Various tenants occupied Kirkville House, one being the Honorable George Leslie Melville, factor to some Deeside estates. George's twin brother inherited, by a few minutes, the title Earl of Cawdor. Kirkville eventually became Kirkton House Nursing Home in 1986.

Electricity came to the Kirktoun on Hogmanay 1936. The year before that the Jubilee Cottages were built. Decline in the village was perhaps reversed by the building of a considerable number of houses in the South Glebe Field by the County Council in the late 1960s. In more recent times new housing was built on the road up towards Claylands – Carpenter's Croft, etcetera. Proposals have been put forward for many more new houses, proposals that would radically alter the nature and layout, including bringing the school into the village.

The Milne Hall has been mentioned already. For many years the present car park was actually a field, part of the blacksmith's croft. A path ran up the side of the field giving access to the hall. Alongside the hall, in 1947, the Skene cadets built a wooden army hut which had a 15-foot target range.

Jessie Kesson and the Kirktoun of Skene

When Jessie Kesson (as Jess Macdonald) was sent to Proctor's Orphanage she also went to the local school. Skene, the land round about it, its people and the orphanage were important in Jessie's writing. Jessie owed a debt to the encouragement of Skene dominie, Donald Murray, a debt she acknowledged in dedicating THE WHITE BIRD PASSES to him, even though he did not live to see its publication. Parish minister John McMurtrie and his wife Mary also encouraged the young Jessie and in five letters Jessie wrote to Mary, two in the 1940s and three in the 1980s, she talks about her time in the village. Through the letters and photographs taken by John around the same time, we get a glimpse of the real people who lived in the village at that time.

Jessie's feelings about her time in the orphanage, and about Skene generally, varied enormously in the telling. Just as Grassic Gibbon's Chris Guthrie could view life on the land as harsh and full of drudgery and the speak "*coarse*", and the next minute see the beauty of the land and the expressiveness of the language, so Jessie could write about Skene in different ways. It was a hard environment for the young girl who arrived there with her head shaven, having been taken from her mother. But it was also a place where she did not have to worry about her next meal or having clean clothes to wear. It features in several of her stories: STORMY WEATHER is set in the orphanage, part of the autobiographical THE WHITE BIRD PASSES is set in Skene, as is WHERE THE APPLE RIPENS. In the latter Isobel Murrray says the hymn *BY COOL SILOAM* is crucial. In the story, Jessie writes, "*They would sing BY COOL SILOAM for you when you were born: or if you died young.*" The young girl in the story has died young, by taking her own life.

In her letters to John and Mary, Jessie wrote about how Mr McMurtrie took the orphanage children on drives in his car, one of only three in the parish in the 1920s.

"I remember how you once took the Orphanage children to Potarch in your car – the lupins stretched so vast, and the blue solidly as far as the eye could see, they smelt spicy – like musk I think it was."

In a later letter:
"The most vividly remembered excursion – to the Brig of Feugh, but I remember the wild lupins along the banks of the river. Taller than men. Hot smelling and spicy. On another occasion up and over the Devils's Elbow via Moor of Dinnet- the heather there was not purple – but Blood Red.

"No one, it seemed to me, and indeed, still does, could read finer – nor sing sweeter than Mr McMurtrie. I always felt that Isaiah was his favourite Book – his beloved prophet. He did such justice to its wonderful words. His hymns, *BY COOL SILOAM* – I felt was his favourite. Blake's *JERUSALEM* another. Also – but I think this choice was for old Willie Laing – an Elder – who sang it so fervently – *THE SANDS OF TIME ARE SINKING*. Old Willie nearly "brought the rafters down" when it came to – "and glory, glory dwelleth in Immanuels Land." That old man had…"certainty". He was without doubt. His long swallow-tailed suit was green with age – betrayed outside in the sunlight. Strange that I, an agnostic, fortunately still hold on to the things that were beautiful then."

Isobel Murray also records Jessie's memories of Willie Laing.

> "When winter proved too severe for younger folk to attend, the old miller was all the choir there was, and all that was needed. He stood alone, a unique figure in his sweeping tailed-coat that years of Sundays had faded from black to dull green. His great white beard swept over his chest, and from somewhere under it, arose filling the Kirk with volume and beauty… We outlived the miller. We saw him carried into the Kirk for the last time."

There was indeed a William Laing in the Skene area at that time, a farm servant in the 1920s, possibly the husband of the Mrs Laing who can seen beside the village pump.

He then lived in a house at Milton of Garlogie in 1933, so he may have been a miller, though the main miller there was called Davidson. However, I am fairly certain that Jessie is confusing, or mixing two different people here. James Laing, farmer at Drumstone, was an elder of the kirk for nearly 30 years and he died, aged 87, in July 1932, just about at the end of Jessie's time in Skene. His obituary describes his long service as an elder and records "*of*

Mrs Laing at the Kirktoun pump 1922

a deep and simple piety, he loved the House of God and its services." He was for the greater part of his life a member of the choir, and on many occasions acted as precentor, as we have seen in Mary McMurtire's memories of the church. He possessed real musical gifts and had a wide knowledge of the old psalms. *"When over eighty years of age he was still to be seen in the church choir, an example of faithfulness."*

Elspeth Haston, born in 1932, remembers Willie Laing and that he also had a great singing voice (but no beard). She says that her father liked to sing with him. However, James is buried in Skene Kirkyard, William is not, and James's obituary also shows him with a beard. Surely James was the almost Dickensian figure who Jessie saw carried in his coffin into Skene church, but she may have merged elements of Willie into the figure she remembered.

In one of the 1947 letters Jessie also wrote about how Mr McMurtrie once sang Blake's *Jerusalem* –

"…the Kirk hadn't been renovated then, it was dark, dank and foosty – but because it was the first time I'd come in contact with the vivid imagery:

> *Bring me my bow of burning gold*
> *Bring me my arrows of desire*

…I remember not the dark, dank atmosphere, but the fact that the congregation still had the same, stolid, set look on their faces during Jerusalem – it just didn't seem to do anything to them – and myself was burning inside with sheer ecstasy. I was amazed that they could sit so still and untouched – but then, even now I am intolerant of human beings' 'unawareness'. They're not only dead, they seem to be buried as well."

Presumably Mr Laing, whichever one, was not present on that occasion. Finally on the subject of the kirk, Jessie writes poignantly from 1982: "*I suppose I remember these things so vividly because 'The Kirk' was literally a refuge, a place of affinity for me in those days.*"

Jessie's first letter to Mary McMurtrie in 1947 came, in her own words, "*out of the blue*". It was to let Mary know that BBC Scotland was broadcasting some of her work beginning with BLESS THIS HOUSE – A DRAMATISED PORTRAIT OF THE ORPHANAGE. Jessie wrote that she was not meant for a life in service.

"I'm not proud of the fact that I wasn't a good servant, but I'm not ashamed either. My teens were stormy. I was never 'bad' in the criminal sense of the word – but I was difficult. Rightly or wrongly I stopped attempting to be – and to do – what others wanted me to do. In some dim way I sensed that there were many thousands who could turn out a room well – and enjoy doing so – but there wasn't so many who could write a poem."

The second set of letters, after a gap of almost 35 years, Jessie sent after receiving a copy of NORTH EAST FOLK by Elizabeth Adair, which contained a short section on Mary McMurtrie and her restoration of the medieval garden at the House of Balbithan. Jessie wrote:

"I always knew you loved a garden. I remember the Manse garden. Never lush, the actual land of Skene always seemed bleak to me. A kind of "utility" earth. But the Manse garden… What I remember vividly about it was the Himalayan Cowslips – a flower I had never seen before. Nor – alas – since. Shakespeare wrote of wallflowers:

That smell so heavenly sweet
The senses ache at thee

"That applies equally to the Himalayan Cowslips I saw in the Manse Garden. So much so that I made them one of the 'turning' points in my short novel – WHERE THE APPLE RIPENS."

In a subsequent letter the same year she wrote of her own love of gardens. "For myself, my love for gardens came with my first awareness of the external world itself. The garden of the wood – in long early walks with my mother. Real woods. Not commercial afforestations. And then, of course, my Grandmother's garden and all the cottage gardens on the road to her house. Skene – the Kirktown I mean – never seemed to have "cottage" gardens like the ones I left behind in Morayshire. I wonder why. Shall we delve for reasons – half seriously, half in fun!

"The first Kirktown garden – passed for years on the way to school – belonged to the joiner's wife. A lady hard to avoid, she always seemed to be folded over the gate of her cottage, awaiting the unwary. A lady of intense curiosity. Highly skilled in the art of interrogation. One longed for Mercury's feet to evade her. That being so she didn't have time for the wordless occupation of gardening. No interest whatever in conversing with living things like flowers.

"In the next house, small, quiet, fragile, Mrs Greig. Three little girls –

THE KIRKTOUN OF SKENE AND OTHER COMMUNITIES

The Kirktoun smiddy with Alf Williamson and Dod Stuart 1922

doorsteps – two big lads – all clever children – but like Martha, she was natural – 'careful and troubled about many things'. So…no garden.

"Then, almost a cottage garden. Mrs Valentine. She was the aunt of one of your maids. A small trim woman. Neatly, soberly dressed. Her garden – neat, trim and like herself, sober in colour."

"Past the gates leading to the manse and bang into the Blacksmith's abode. No 'mighty man was he with large and sinewy hands' as Longfellow's blacksmith had. But a small, timid, dark man who also was the grave-digger. It was his wife who was the Amazon. And a joy to behold in her mob-cap – beating the daylight out of her 'Basks' – rough mats. As she stood on

> No 'mighty man was he with large and sinewy hands' as Longfellow's blacksmith had. But a small, timid, dark man who also was the grave-digger.

her doorstep, hailing all who passed by. There was a rough, kindly 'caringness' in her interrogations – one's life – public and private. So no offence ever taken. Since it was never intended. No garden there.

"Then 'The Soutars' small dark shop. How we loved our 'official' visits there. With heel-rings or toe caps needed for our boots – shoes were strictly for Sundays. An old man The Soutar – with a young apprentice 'Dod Yule'. We loved it – officially – and on 'un-official' visits. Because it was always warm in there. And the welcome always friendly. The smell 'homely' leather and paraffin stove. I was always greatly fascinated by the new shoes for sale. In long, polished, white boxes. The brand name of these shoes – 'Gipsy Queen'. The boxes had a vividly illustrated head of a dark be-ringed Gipsy Girl. I vowed then that one day – grown-up – I'd have a pair of 'Gipsy Queen Shoes'….Alas! Like many things the Gipsy Queen brand of shoes had disappeared from 'the trade' by the time I grew up.

"Then, last of all, 'The Beadles' house. Dick Smith, who, apart from ringing the Kirk bell, and preceding Mr McMurtrie up to the pulpit with the big Bible, also did a 'tidy trade' mending watches. In appearance he looked like one of Dickens's amiable characters from Pickwick Papers. But that was only a veneer – beneath which a sharp, thin man 'snapped' to get out".

Jessie may have used elements of real people in her writing, we will never really know now to what extent. In these letters she was writing about some of the inhabitants of Skene in the 1920s and 30s, albeit her memory of them at some years distant.

Photographs illustrate the village of Kirktoun of Skene and some of the people who lived there just a few years before Jessie arrived at The Orphanage. Willie Durno was the carpenter (and undertaker – common practice in country areas). Willie's house was the first you came to when arriving from the orphanage (Westhill) direction. It included a sawmill and, for a while, the "*killing hoose*". It was demolished around 2001 to make room for 'affordable' houses agreed as part of the nearby development to which it gave its name – Carpenter's Croft. Willie's son, Leslie, followed him in both occupations. Leslie was a good source of information on the village and the worthies who lived in the area. When describing a local character, Private Dickie, he would say, "*he was just a worthy*". Leslie remembered Jessie taking milk to his mother, just as Janie does in THE WHITE BIRD PASSES. His sister Mary is pictured in the same class as Jessie at Skene School. Willie Durno

THE KIRKTOUN OF SKENE AND OTHER COMMUNITIES

Mrs Stuart, blacksmith's wife 1922

himself lived to the age of 97, Leslie died in 2011.

George Stuart was the blacksmith, having succeeded his father, Alexander. We also have a photograph with his 'amazon' wife with her mob-cap. Leslie said she was a very hardy woman and, as children they were feart of her. When making horse shoes her husband used to shout in through the door of their house, "*Gie's a chap, wife,*" and she would come out and wield the hammer while her husband held the shoe. Leslie remembered that Dod Stuart was fond of a dram down at the Straik (Broadstraik). His wife would go down, give his face a slap, and drag him by the lug all the way back to the village. Dod Stuart was given Colonel Duguid-McCombie's horse, Warrior, and it pulled a cart. When Doddie got "*too fu at the Straik*" they sometimes put him in the cart, gave the horse a dunt, and it took him home. Leslie also remembered Dick Smith, the beadle (and registrar as well as watch-mender). Leslie later lived in Dick's house, the last in the village on the way to Skene School. Dick Smith lodged with two elderly sisters, Mrs Lesley and Izzy Duncan. He carried out repairs in an old shed which stood on the grassy area next to the house where Leslie's boat later rested.

'Soutar' Beaton lived into his 90s and is still remembered by some; his young apprentice mentioned by Jessie died of TB in his 40s. Alexander (Sandy) Beaton was born at Monkshill of Fyvie in 1861, one of 11 children. He later moved to America where he worked in Michigan for four years, then he walked to San Francisco where he had a shoemaking shop for 14 years. He left in 1906, just before the big earthquake. He returned to Britain and, just before World War I, he started in business in the Kirktoun. By 1956 he was still doing repairs for friends and neighbours at the age of 94. Various folk in the area have memories of Souter Beaton – that he never wore socks; that he was a great vegetable grower, running out of the shop every time a horse passed by in case it had left some dung behind; always having his mouth full of tacks as he worked; being asked to light the bonfire on the Hill of Keir at the Coronation in 1953, he was then the oldest person in the parish. He died in February 1957, aged 95. (For more see Skene Heritage Newsletter No. 20).

The centre of the village itself has not changed that much from those days, but, as Jessie goes on to say…

> "Few gardens but folk …" before as Lewis Grassic Gibbon might describe it – "the years that faded and fell" to – widen that world – leading out via the car – to bingo, discos, supermarkets. Time was when the only cars to be seen there belonged to the Doctor, the Minister and the wealthier farmers. I'm glad I lived in that other era – when the horse ploughed, and you could see the steam from its nostrils spread out and across the frosty mornings. When the hens clucked around your feet, When those who could sing, sang, and those who could dance, danced. And Main's Wooing performed in the Milne Hall, was the communal high-spot of winter. We are in danger, I think of becoming plastic people. No one in the Kirktown was that."

Mary McMurtrie records a rather poignant comment beside these letters. "We would have had so much in common if only we could have kept in touch." And I'm sure they would, but Mary and her husband should have been very proud of the kindness and encouragement they showed to the young girl from The Orphanage.

Lyne of Skene

Auld farran canty bodies / Better never hae I seen
Auld farran canty bodies / Dwals into the Lyne o' Skene

Lyne of Skene is at the north-west edge of the parish, but near the 'big hoose' (Skene House) and therefore would have been of some importance. Mary

McMurtrie found it a place where older customs survived. She recorded old traditions from the Lyne and also wrote that, about 1906, three old cottages survived at Back Ward, Brodies living in one, Davidsons in the middle one and an old saddler, James Hall, in the third one. They were thatched and had wooden lums (bowie lums) just as we have seen at the Kirktoun. At the time she wrote, in 1980, only one was left and the name had been changed to Back Mains. She also records that when Roy Lyall (senior) was renovating his house, originally the wrights or joiners, he came on the remains of a 'hingin' lum'. The wall at the back of the house was three feet thick and there was a circular hearth. The lum, about five feet off the floor, was over it. In 1917 there were still 27 thatched houses in the Lyne area, as well as some thatched farm buildings. Most of the houses had been re-roofed by 1938, though the byre at the smiddy was not re-roofed until 1959.

It is thought that the original name was Hatton, which is sometimes used to mean the fermtoun nearest the big hall (halltoun), and this seems the likely derivation. The fermtoun of Hatton is listed in the 1696 POLL TAX, with a blacksmith, a main tenant and several sub-tenants. Other tradesmen would also have been located there. Hatton seems to have been beside the current Mains of Skene farm and an old wall still standing is thought to be from one of the buildings. Another old wall, part of the joiner's, was demolished around 20 years ago, the stones used in a new house. The first OS map of around 1864 has five buildings at the end of 'The Walk' where the track forms a V shape going right to Mains and left past the walled garden. The Walk is the long drive leading from Lyne of Skene to the Mains and the Skene House walled garden.

By the second OS map of 1901 only one roofed building and an un-roofed one survive. Was this the original Hatton? Would it have been so close to the Mains? Without an early estate map it is difficult to be certain today and we have to rely on oral tradition for some of our information. The Maynes (Mains) is also recorded in the 1696 POLL TAX, Mains derives from domaine or demesne, being the land, usually nearest the castle or big hoose, kept under the laird's own control to meet the needs of his own household. Where the Mains and Hatton were in relation to each other it is difficult to say.

The Kirk Session records mention Hatton of Skene in 1753. An account for 1756 for straw bought for Skene House records that John Booth, Robert Walker, William Skene and Donald Low, all lived at Hatton. This is the latest use of that name that I have found and, in 1770, I found a reference to a roup of grass which mentions John Forbes in Line, the first reference I have found

to the name Lyne. There is an account from 1785 for the building of William Gellan's houses "*on the Line*", and from the same year, for "*appraising the houses of the Lyne*". So sometime between 1756 and 1770 the name changed, presumably because the fermtoun of Hatton was moved to become the Lyne.

Where did the name Line or Lyne come from? If it has a Gaelic derivation from meadow as has been suggested, the name might have been there all the time and when the fermtoun of Hatton was moved then the name was taken up for the new community. However Lyne is not mentioned in any of the early Skene Estate rentals or in the 1696 POLL TAX book. Perhaps the laird simply took the name from the Lyne (of Cairndae or Linton) just a few miles along the road in the parish of Midmar. Hatton may have been moved because of general agricultural improvements which enclosed fields and did away with the old infield and outfield system. Possibly the Mains expanded and enclosed the land that had formerly been farmed by the tenants of the Hatton. If so, this would have been quite an early improvement and enclosure compared to elsewhere in Skene Parish.

The Mains continued to be fairly near Skene House, with numerous

THE KIRKTOUN OF SKENE AND OTHER COMMUNITIES

Lyne of Skene farmers' outing 1921

Main's Crofts – 12 in 1804, compared with six crofts at the Lyne, and sometimes tradesmen are listed under the Mains.

The meal mill for Skene House estate seems to have been moved from Fernlea to Craigiedarg around the same time as Hatton. I think that there is an element of the Skenes, as they became more affluent and extended Skene House, choosing to move the mill and the hamlet of Hatton away from their mansion. The Skenes were certainly capable of radical actions. It is recorded that at Careston *"in consequence of a whim of Mr George Skene, the gravestones were turned out of the church-yard when the present dykes were built. After Skene's death a few monuments were recovered and replaced."* The new site at Lyne has a very poor water supply and so was perhaps not an ideal choice.

Older customs survived at Lyne of Skene. About 1906, three old cottages survived at Back Ward. They were thatched and had wooden lums (bowie lums)

265

Back Ward, Blue Park, the merchant's folk
Hae ever kind and cantie been
An' lang may Marshal's humour please
The bodies o' the Lyne o Skene

William Chisholm's poem refers to Marshall Keith, long time merchant at Mains, and at Lyne of Skene, in the first half of the 19th century. Keith is listed initially at Mains of Skene, then, by 1851, at Lyne of Skene. Whether or not his premises actually moved or the designation of the location changed is unclear, certainly from the mid-19th century onwards his shop was at the Lyne of Skene end of The Walk just along from Bluepark. It is the long building marked on the first OS map and on the 1863 plan of the Skene lands. This building was 90 feet long and thatched, with a house, shop and store. There was, though, also a shop at the actual Mains, since this is detailed in Skene Estate rentals, with John Gray the shopkeeper in the early 1850s. He was followed in 1857 by Alexander Singer, who was actually a soutar so it may have been a shoemakers shop.

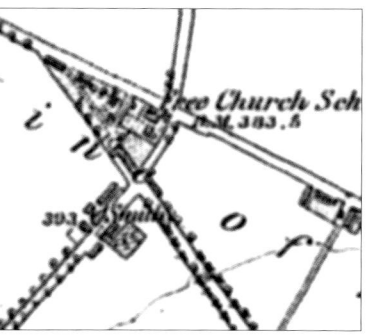

Lyne of Skene in 1865

Chisholm himself was a heckler or flax dresser, the heckle being a toothed comb used in the process. He was apprenticed to Leys, Masson & Co. As was common in this occupation, he suffered from bronchial trouble and had to give up the work. He subsequently went round the countryside selling stationery and other goods; he is described as a *"book hawker"* in the 1861 Census, his wife being a washerwoman. In 1854 he moved to Lyne of Skene with his wife, Ann, lodging with Jean Anderson. William Buchanan, in GLIMPSES OF OLDEN DAYS IN ABERDEEN, describes him as the most intelligent working man he ever met, a lover of Burns, Byron, Shakespeare and Scott. Buchanan said that it was a joy to hear him in discussion with William Thom, the weaver poet, capable of discussing any subject. Chisholm was nicknamed The Minstrel because of his sweet singing voice. He died in 1862, shortly after writing THE BODIES O THE LYNE OF SKENE, quoted earlier. The poem mentions many of the places in the parish and surrounding area, and Chisholm does seem to have been genuinely touched by the kindness of the people in the Lyne of Skene area. The farmers, crofters and tradesmen of the area around Lyne of Skene all attended his funeral. Ann Chisholm lived on there for quite a number of years after her husband. In the 1871 Census she was a lodging-house keeper, possibly looking after a small poor house, since three out of four of her boarders are described as paupers. Given his occupation it is tempting to speculate that Chisholm may have been the author of another song that mentions Skene:

When I was just a rantin girl
About the age of sixteen
I fell in love wi' a heckler lad
Upon the banks o' Skene

Bluepark was an old name with several tenants living there; Backward of Blewpark is listed in the Skene School Account for 1770. In 1773 Alex Mair had to give up his tack of Bluepark and Backward, not because it had expired, but because of old age. In 1807 William Davidson was a tailor at Bluepark, with eight acres. Shoemaker, John Farquhar, was also there with three acres of thin land. Robert Leighton was blacksmith there, with four acres, but his rent was not fixed yet because his house was not built. The Playhillock Park in the moss was to be divided up among the tenants of Bluepark for pasture to their beasts at a yearly rent. Mary McMurtrie records that when Roy Lyall (senior) took over Mr Thomson's croft around 1930, all the land round about was called Blue Park, so he called the house that.

The 1851 Census lists quite a number of stocking knitters and paupers in the cottages at Letter and at Lyne of Skene, just as there were at Kirktoun and Carnie. Roy Lyall (senior) recorded that Letter Brae was once the site of a *"clearance when fourteen reekin' lums were put out and only four or five left"*. Unfortunately he did not know when this had taken place, whether under the Skenes or the Earl of Fife, but this was when the old thatched moss cottages were built from stones taken from the destroyed buildings. I have found no record of this event, but it sounds like something that has been passed down by oral tradition and may well be true.

Mary's Widdie is the strip of woodland between the lodge for Skene House and Morven, the first house as you approach Lyne of Skene. Mary lived in a tiny cottage in the wood and was found dead there on the day of the ferryboat disaster in Aberdeen (5 April 1876).

Blacksmith at Mains of Skene in 1841 was Robert Leighton, aged 60, possibly born in Brechin. He had been at Lyne of Skene since at least 1806

Lyne of Skene smiddy

when, as noted, his house at Bluepark was not yet built, so possibly that was when he came to the Lyne. His son was also a blacksmith. Robert Leighton was still blacksmith in 1851, though he would have been quite elderly for such heavy work. There was also, though, a family of Booths as blacksmiths. In 1851 they were listed as being at West Mains, where there was also a mason. They were sons of John Booth, a wright/farmer at Mains of Skene. In 1851 his son George was blacksmith, with James a journeyman blacksmith, and John an apprentice blacksmith. Then in June 1853 an advertisement for a blacksmith appeared in the ABERDEEN JOURNAL, one experienced in horse-shoeing preferred, apply to Alexander Booth, nephew of James. James and Alexander were still at the Mains in 1861; perhaps James's two brothers had gone elsewhere. Alexander Wilson was the blacksmith in 1919 and in the 1930s it was Hugh Gillespie, who had served his time with Wilson. When the smiddy closed in 1951 the smith was Andrew Arthur. The blacksmith's old stone mould for making cruisie lamps has been built into the wall of a house in Letter Road.

Alexander (Sandy) Scott was a mason who lived at the crossroads in Lyne of Skene in the 19th century. As a young man he walked all the way into Aberdeen every day to his work. Later his handiwork would be seen all over the parish as he built such buildings as the Mission Hall at the Lyne, the vestry at the parish church, and the spire of the Free Church.

The Lyne also supported a soutar, with an advertisement appearing in the ABERDEEN JOURNAL, 5 September, 1855, for a journeyman shoemaker, who will find a *"good seat and light work"*. Apply to Alex Singer, who was presumably the existing soutar. It was not long after, in 1864, that David Lyall came to the Lyne as a soutar. He was originally from Fettercairn, but had been working in Aberdeen. On moving to the Lyne he married the widow of the previous soutar. His brother, James, also a shoemaker, later joined him.

Several tradesmen's shops are listed in the 1870s, testifying to how busy a place Lyne of Skene must have been then. A photograph of the tradesmen of the Lyne in 1872 has 14 men. It lists three carpenters: Alex. Williamson at Bluepark, Samuel Copland near the Mission Hall, and Sam Angus at New Mains; James Booth, blacksmith, with two journeymen and apprentices; Marshall Keith, merchant, employing two tailors; David Lyall, shoemaker with a man and an apprentice; A. Mitchell, carrier at the top of the Lyne.

In October 1878 an application went to the County Licensing Court for a dealer's certificate for new premises at Lyne of Skene. This was for James Watt, the merchant, who also employed two journeymen tailors and an apprentice. In 1875 Watt had followed Marshall Keith in the premises at the foot of The Walk. He moved to the shop at the crossroads which was built in 1885 using stones from the old shop. Behind that shop was where the tailors worked, with three windows, one for each tailor, positioned to allow them as much light as possible. The shop also housed the post office until the end of World War I. Watt was made a J.P. in 1893, was a member of the Parish Council and represented them on the Aberdeen District Committee of the County Council. He was also one of the prime movers who tried, in 1894, to get telegraphic communication brought into the Skene/Dunecht area. In 1919 the licensed shop and store was run by James W. Bell. For a time there was also a petrol pump outside the shop. James ran the shop with his wife Lizzie until 1964, when his daughter, Peggy Smith, took it over. It finally closed in 1987. At the closure, a customer of 69 years, Backie Watt of South Fornet, remembered that, lacking a bar, the locals used to have a dram or beer at the shop, though he went on to say that James Bell was strict with the licensing laws. "*You may buy the stuff out of hours, but never drink it in the shop – jist outside the doorie wis ok, though.*" More than 10 years later the premises became the Letter Tearoom for a number of years.

In 1969 Mary McMurtrie received information from Roy Lyall (senior) regarding a lost weaving colony at South Fornet. According to Roy, "*there used to be a clachan, about eight or nine houses, all trace of them gone. They stood where the burn wood road comes up to South Fornet, on the right hand side but possibly some on the other side of the road too. This was the weavers' clachan. There used to be one or two tablecloths of their weaving still at the Lyne, one was owned by Mary Copeland, it had the date woven in –17.*"

Elsewhere Mary states that there were 80 reeking lums at the weaver's clachan, which would be astonishing. Clumps of bushes are growing on the site of the clachan and Mary drew a map of it, based on the information she had been given. I have not been able to find any evidence for its existence. The fact that Mary produced the map and that someone had a tablecloth made there would suggest that it did exist and folk memories can be very strong. There was, though, a large chimney for a steam engine at South Fornet. The chimney could be seen from the Lyne and is marked on old OS maps.

In 1948, 12 council houses were built at the Lyne, on Letter Road, intended for agricultural workers, as were those built at Westhill at the same time. Electricity did not come to Lyne of Skene until 1959. It is difficult to believe today that, as recently as the 1961 Census, the population of Lyne of Skene was still 106, greater than any of the other villages in the parish at that time. Unlike Kirktoun of Skene, Elrick and Westhill, Lyne of Skene saw no major housing developments.

Garlogie and the mill

There may at some time have been a laird's house somewhere at Garlogie. A charter under the Great Seal, dated 1678 and referring to the lands of Easter Skene, says that "*the principal messuage* (dwelling house) *whereof is declared to be the manor place of Garlogie.*" All trace of this house has long gone and it is around the textile mill that the main community of Garlogie grew up.

The water of the Leuchar burn has been a source of power from medieval times. As we have already seen, the meal mill at Garlogie is mentioned in 1456 during Skene of Skene's dispute with the Keith family, and it probably existed well before that date. The leaflet produced by the North East of Scotland

Museums Service for the Garlogie Mill Power Museum says that a waulkmill is mentioned in a document dated 1568. Unfortunately they have no source for that comment and I have been unable to confirm it. However a charter relating to the Earl Marischal from 1592, recorded in the REGISTER OF THE GREAT SEAL, does refer to a corn and a fulling mill at Garlogie. A similar Keith charter for 1587 only records a corn mill, but both the mill and fulling mill are recorded in 1612. Another document relating to Alexander Burnett of Countesswells, recorded in the Register for 1653, also mentions the corn mill and the waulk mill at Garlogie. Fulling and waulk mills are the same thing. In a document dated 1696, relating to the Burnetts as owners of Easter Skene, it is described as a dye mill. So it seems that a textile mill of some kind has existed from at least the late 16th century, though perhaps not continuously.

It became part of the Dean of Guild's lands and the waulkmill continued in operation during the 18th century. In 1793 a John Walker was the tenant of the waulkmill and the croft at Garlogie. Shortly after it is described as *"formerly used as a waulkmill, at present possessed under lease to Thomas Black, merchant in Aberdeen."* Black subsequently bought the mill on behalf of himself, George Watson Black and John Black, presumably the '& Sons' later referred to. According to Aberdeenshire's leaflet on the mill, in 1799 he built a three-storey building which became part of the later, much larger mill. The Kirk Session minutes in 1808 call it a carding mill. He must have had a partner because, in 1810, the firm at Garlogie Mill is listed as Black & Moir (or More), and they advertised that they continued to card and spin and manufacture wool into cloth and blankets. Ten years later they were known as Thomas Black & Sons. Thomas Black is also listed in the Skene Estate rentals for 1804 as tenant of Burrowley and of Mill of Air and, by 1814/5, he was paying a very high money rent for Burrowley and Mill of Air. I think we can assume that this is the same Thomas Black who had the textile mill, since the latter lies

Garlogie Mill and the workers' houses 1865

immediately between the Mill of Air and Burrowley. In fact the name Burrowley was sometimes given to the Garlogie Mill. A sasine of 1827 refers to Over and Nether Garlogie, otherwise called Burrely.

Thomas seems to have difficulty in making money from the mill and, in 1826, he borrowed £1,000 from Finlay Finlayson of Aberdeen on the security of the Nether Mill of Garlogie. In 1832 it was put up for public roup at the Lemon Tree Tavern as part of the Blacks' sequestrated estate. The premises are described as having machinery, water-fall, croft of land, houses and yard, with the machinery being new and the water-fall one of the best in the country.

It was bought by Alexander Hadden & Sons in 1833. The Haddens were well known in Aberdeen, major employers, producing two provosts of the town and having Hadden Street named after them. The Haddens extended the mill buildings and installed the beam engine in the late 1830s, supplementing water power with steam. The mill had its own chimney stack, only demolished in the late 1950s. Under the Haddens the mill produced wool and also yarn, used in making carpets. Garlogie supplied wool and yarn to their other mills in and around Aberdeen.

At the time of the second STATISTICAL ACCOUNT (1843) the mill was employing about 120 people, young and old. As we have seen, by providing a school they could employ children as young as nine. Prior to the 1833 FACTORIES ACT younger children could be employed. In 1822 Thomas Black offered housing to a widow or family with children between the age of five and 12, with the children being offered constant employment at the mill. As late as 1896 the mill was advertising for young workers, saying that a widow could lodge cheaply there and obtain work for children over 11 years of age. In 1843 gas had recently been introduced for lighting and the company had recently built "*neat cottages*" for the workers. The minister in 1843 also reported that the schoolroom was used as a place of worship every alternate Sunday "*as they have not sittings in the parish church*" i.e., they were not entitled to any of the seats in the church which were taken up by tenants of the original heritors.

A writer to the ABERDEEN JOURNAL in the early 1900s remembered that Haddens also gave out worsted to the country women who knitted stockings, socks and gloves. The worsted was weighed out and the finished work weighed in. If there was a small deficiency then a fine was imposed. If there was a big deficiency the work was handed back and had to be done over again.

THE KIRKTOUN OF SKENE AND OTHER COMMUNITIES

Garlogie House, the mill manager's house

As there were many different sizes of stockings and grades of worsted, and no pattern was given, it was no easy matter to hit upon the exact size. He remembered that in the early 1840s, before he went to school in the morning, he helped his mother in counting the threads and winding the exact quantity of worsted that had to go to the making of a stocking. His final comment was, *"Hadden's work was no doubt a help to many poor old women who had nothing else to do, but the remuneration was not tempting"*.

The manager of the Garlogie Mill in 1856, giving evidence to a committee looking at Alford Valley and Deeside railway lines, said that the mill produced 201 tons of finished products every year. It also transported 232 tons of wool and waste, 287 tons of coal, 29 tons of oil, etcetera: in total, 756 tons of material that could be transported by rail. The Haddens, in common with other Aberdeen textile companies, often looked to England for expertise. The manager of Garlogie in 1851 was John Boyes from Bradford. He was still there in 1869, the year his wife died. The manager lived at Garlogie House, overlooking the mill from higher ground. The house still stands.

The late John Forbes of Garlogie recalled that his grandfather came to Garlogie in 1867 to *"fire the boilers for the steam engine"*. His mother later worked in the mill at the age of nine, working part-time and attending the school. In John's youth he used to ring the old bell which was on top of the mill. His mother left the mill in 1890 to go to Culter Paper Mill. This was because Haddens, in 1885, had installed ragging machines which teased out old woollen rags to economise in the making of wool.

"This new method made the wool so shoddy and resulted in the breaking of strands. The mill girls were broken hearted because being on piece work they couldn't earn a proper wage."

As we have seen with the school, Garlogie workers usually took Aberdeen holidays, such as they were in the 19th century. In 1868 Garlogie workers joined their fellow Hadden employees in the first Haddens' picnic at Culter House. The Aberdeen workers had marched to the station with banners flying, led by the band of the 1st Batallion City Volunteers. The Garlogie workers met them at Culter, to where they had been transported in spring carts. The picnic was held on a Saturday afternoon with the mills closing one hour early! On Christmas Eve that year John Boyes granted the schoolroom at Garlogie for the workers' annual soiree. Upwards of 150 attended with John Moir, the merchant at Garlogie, serving tea for everyone, and leading the choir. There were instructive talks on Water, Imagination and the Senses, and Agriculture v Manufacture, as well as humorous poetry readings.

In January 1891 a major fire occurred at Garlogie in the teasing department. The main mill and the smaller teasing department were at right angles to each other, connected by an outside staircase. The fire broke out on the ground floor of the teasing department at around five in the evening. Immediately the nearby gasometer was shut off. A messenger was sent to Culter where they phoned the fire brigade in Aberdeen. The steam fire engine arrived at around nine, but by that time the building was gutted and the roof had fallen in. By using buckets of water from the lade, the workers had managed to stop the fire spreading to the adjacent building. At the time 150 workers were employed at the mill and, of course, they were made idle until temporary repairs could be made. The cost of the damage was £2,000.

The mill could be a dangerous place. In 1898 a 63-year-old millworker, Alexander Stark, of Roadside of Garlogie, got the corner of his jacket caught between a belt and a loose pulley. He was dragged round the pulley and thrown to the floor, a distance of four-and-a-half feet (1.37m). He was lucky. Doctor Skinner attended him and he was found to have a broken collar bone, bruised back and ribs, and a few teeth knocked out.

In the late 1890s economic conditions led to a downturn in the industry and, in 1904, Haddens closed Garlogie along with their other mills. Some of the machinery was sold and efforts were made to find a buyer for the mill buildings. This proved fruitless and the property was eventually sold to Lord Cowdray. I have detailed elsewhere how he used some of the buildings with most of the actual mill being demolished.

Garlogie House and much of the workers' housing still survive, as does the beam engine. The latter is "*a house-built rotative beam engine of medium size, with a double-acting cylinder, separate condenser and air pump. The cast iron beam is 16 ft 3 in (4.95m) long. The only beam engine of its type in Scotland to have survived intact* in situ."

Part of Garlogie Mill

For much of the 19th century, Garlogie was the largest village in the parish, due to the sizeable workforce at the mill. Four shops are recorded in the 1870s, including a shoemaker. The closure of the mill meant that the associated workforce moved away and the Garlogie of the dark satanic mill became a more rural village.

I have been told that Robert P. Allan (Rob or Robbie) was the merchant at the grocer's shop at Roadside of Garlogie from the time of World War I. However, he must have been there much longer because, in April 1897, he applied for a porter and ale license for his premises at Garlogie. Alex Mair thinks that Rob's wife was called Agnes, but Rob always called her 'Lucky'. Adam Craigmile remembers that Robbie did the catering for the Westhill school picnic. For a while there seem to have been two shops tenanted by Robbie, since a licensed shop and a separate grocer's shop are listed for Garlogie in 1921. Rob and Agnes retired at the November Term, 1936, and built a new bungalow for themselves at Westmore, Fiddie. They named it Robag, and it was only demolished during recent construction work for the building of the Subsea Seven premises.

The shop and bar were taken over by their nephew, also Robert Allan (Robbie) and his wife Annie. Robbie, a champion ploughman, was the son of Johnny Allan who farmed East Finnercy, just along the road. The shop itself barely survived the war and had gone by 1950. After Robert's death his widow continued to run the bar, subsequently remarrying and becoming Annie Mackie. She retired in 1972. Two of Robbie and Annie's sons became champion motorbike scramblers, Vic Allan making history by becoming British Champion two years running, and being awarded the MBE. The Garlogie Bar later became well known as a venue for traditional music ceilidhs, with Robbie Shepherd really beginning his career there. It then became the Garlogie Inn, a popular eating place, as it is today.

Carnie Village and its weaving colony

Carnie Village was part of the estate of Wester Carnie or Hillcarnie, mentioned in an earlier chapter. Carnie Village itself comprised a number of cottages on the opposite side of the road from Hatton Farm, and extending along the old road that leads to Burnside and Mason Lodge. James Knowles of Kirkville advertised in 1831 a *"genteel cottage with a neat garden to let in the village of Carnie"*. In the 19th century it was a sizeable community. Twenty-four buildings are shown at Carnie in a plan dated 1827, this before the old fermtoun was enclosed. Even in 1832 there were 15 buildings. At the time of the 1841 Census 77 people are listed at Carnie Village. This does not include the neighbouring farms such as Hatton, Latch, Springhill, etcetera. Such was the size of the community at Carnie that it briefly had a temporary school after the Skene School Board was set up in 1873 because *"there is a sort of village population"* at Carnie.

The newspaper cutting shown mentions that Carnie had a lost weavers' colony. But is there any truth in that story? The heyday of the handloom weavers in Scotland was from 1790-1810, with a gradual decline until around 1850. In the period of decline many handloom weavers suffered extreme poverty after a few years of relative plenty. In rural areas they would almost certainly have maintained a small croft as well as their weaving. Much of their weaving would have been linen for the local community, but areas near town might have supplied local merchants. There was certainly a weaver at Easter Carnie because a gravestone in the old churchyard of Drumoak has a stone for David Stephen, weaver in Easter Carnie, who died in 1809. It has the following verse:

In Carnie sure did David die
We hope his souls in Heaven high
The body lies beneath this stone
To moulder there both skin and bone
It was his blessed will to wear
A coat without a seam
Which fitted well in every part
Wove in a wyver's leem

According to tradition the last four lines were chiselled out as being too irreverent.

In the third STATISTICAL ACCOUNT Mary McMurtrie says that at one time there was a flax mill at Carnie. I have found no evidence of this so far and it is not mentioned in the two earlier STATISTICAL ACCOUNTS. Perhaps she meant the one at Garlogie, as it is unlikely that there would have been two so near each other. There were some weavers in Wester Carnie, however. An advertisement in the ABERDEEN JOURNAL in 1828 mentions a shop to let *"lately occupied by W. Allan, weaver in the village of Cairnie."* Two weavers are recorded in gravestones in Skene Kirkyard. These are Alexander Rae, weaver in Wester Carnie, who died aged 42 in 1824, and William Rae who died in 1833 in his 84th year (possibly the father of Alexander). The 1851 Census also records at Wester Carnie – William Troup, handloom weaver, aged 62, and born in Skene Parish. None are recorded in the 1861 Census.

Mrs Murray at the Carnie pump

So there were individual hand loom weavers at Carnie Village in the first half of the 19th century, and the memory of their existence must have been passed down by the occupants of Carnie for over 100 years.

It is difficult today to imagine that there ever was a large community at Carnie. A few houses remain, including the long one by the road that had the shop at one end and a house at the other. Today it has been made into one long house. The present owner showed me a ruined wall covered in ivy, which he said had been the soutars. As well as the soutar, there seems to have been a shop since the early 19th century. There were a number of trades in the village then. By the middle of the century the shopkeeper, and also tenant of Latch Farm, was George Daniel, surely a brother of Alexander Daniel who had a shop in the Kirktoun of Skene at the same time. Both are buried in Skene Kirkyard. By the 1890s Andrew Donald, merchant, had a house and shop at Carnie Village. In the 1920s, before Mrs Murray, the shopkeepers were called Whyte and they also had a porter and ale license. Tibbie Reid, Mary Milne and Alex Mair remember the 'Carnie shoppie' under Mrs Murray, selling sweeties, lemonade and biscuits from a room in her small house. Tibbie remembers that they would walk there on a Sunday when the Kirktoun shop was closed.

The 1832 plan of Hillcairnie Estate shows that there was a blacksmith at Carnie, with the smith's croft to the south of the turnpike road, opposite Braelea. In 1845, Knowles advertised for a blacksmith for Carnie Village, and there certainly was one there in 1851. Earlier, in 1826, James Knowles advertised for a saddler and a shoemaker for the village, so he seemed intent on establishing it as a thriving village. In fact he re-advertised for the shoemaker three years later, with a newly-built house available with the position. There must have been a joiner or wright as well, because a Wright's Croft is shown on the Society of Advocates plan of the estate in 1862, west of Carnie Village. It later became known as Wright's and Cummings Croft.

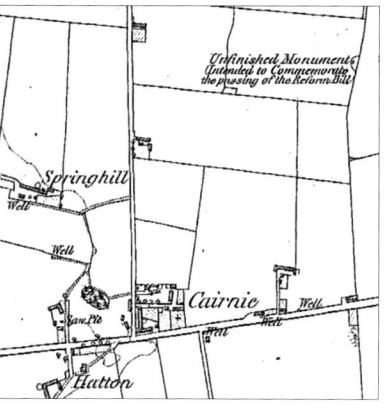

Carnie Village 1865 (also showing the site of the Reform Monument)

There was a fair amount of poverty at Carnie and several paupers are listed in the Census, as well as stocking knitters and pedlars. The Parish Board established a building for paupers at Carnie, listed in the 1881 Census with Jane Duncan, lodging house keeper, and five boarders all 10 years or under. This was possibly the building with the arched, almost church-style windows, that has now been converted into a family home. I have been told by Eric Thomson, who was brought up at Carnie, that it was a children's home of some kind, linked to one in Drum's Lane in Aberdeen, but as yet I have not found out anything about it.

Along the road that leads to Burnside and Mason Lodge you can still find, with the help of an old map, the ruins of two of the houses of Carnie Village. One of them still has the outline of the walls which ran round their garden. Of Standing Stones farm or croft, farther along that track, there is no trace. Bill Troup, who farmed at nearby Whitestone Farm, thinks it was ploughed over many years ago.

A lost weavers' colony? Perhaps not, but Carnie is certainly a lost village.

Mason Lodge

As the name implies this was once the location of the parish's freemason's lodge, situated in the building on the opposite side of the road from the later Free Church School, i.e., the north side. It was established in October 1824 and the ABERDEEN JOURNAL reported that it was constituted by the St James's and St George's Lodges of Aberdeen. Following that, and with a deputation from Newmachar Lodge as well, the new lodge went to the parish church and received a service from their chaplain, Rev. George Mackenzie of Skene, a collection being taken for the Bible Society of Aberdeen. They then returned to the hall *"where they sat down to most excellent dinner, prepared by landlord, Mr Webster. The ladies then joined them"* (who fed them I wonder?), and a ball ensued.

The hall consisted of a hall-keeper's house and shop on the ground floor, and above it the hall with a small kitchen and cloak-room. The hall was also let for social gatherings, dances and revival meetings. At a later date a building known as 'The Pavilion' was added at the back. This became a noted preaching station, but had disappeared well before 1900.

The ABERDEEN JOURNAL for August 5th 1829 reported the following:

"The Annual General Meeting of St George's Lodge of Free Masons, Skene, was held in their hall when after transacting routine business, the brethren walked in procession, accompanied by music, to the Bents of Skene, where each of the members was regaled with plenty of excellent whisky by their honorary R.W. Master, William McCombie of Easter Skene. They then returned to their hall where they sat down to an excellent dinner, prepared by Mr W. Webster, Broadstrake, and afterwards elected the following office-bearers:

William McCombie, Honorary R.W. Master; W. Cruickshank, R.W. Master; W. Wyness, depute-master; George Hunter, senior-warden; Andrew Massie, junior-warden; Alexander Gallow, treasurer; John Wilson, secretary; Rev. Mr George Mackenzie, chaplain; John Fowler, grand-steward; John Moir, senior-steward; Charles Wyness, junior-steward; Alex. Williamson, Robert Low, David Anderson, and John Leith, counselors; Alexander Mennie, clerk; and Alan Paterson, tyler. The evening concluded with a ball."

This large number of office bearers would suggest a significant membership but the society only lasted a few years. It was certainly still in existence in 1832, but they had had to borrow money to build the lodge and, after a few years, were forced to sell it to a Mrs Janet Skene, widow of George Skene, a farmer from Easter Echt. She converted it into two dwelling houses. Despite the Freemasons having the hall for only a few years, the name endured in the little community that grew up there. By 1837 Mrs Skene had sold it to John Moir from Cullerlie and Midmar. He died in 1852, but his descendants had it for several years after that, the creditors of John Moir, presumably his son, putting Mason Lodge up for sale in 1876.

Which building was the actual Mason Lodge? Mary McMurtrie was clear that it was the building, now three houses, lying next to what is now a carpet shop. Other people I have spoken to have given different answers. Most seem to think it was to the south of the road, possibly confusing it with the large Free Church school and school-house. A masonic plaque of some kind was discovered in the house adjacent to the butcher's shop. However, it is clear from other evidence that the lodge was indeed to the north of the main road. A sasine from 1838 spells out that it was to the north. The first OS map of 1864 shows two buildings on the north side of the road immediately opposite what was then a small post office. One of these two buildings, the one to the east, is divided into two, which matches the description of the lodge after it was turned into two houses. Kathleen Reid, daughter of postman Alf Williamson, lived in one of those houses until 2011, and said that the first date on her deeds was 1836. She also describes the thickness of the walls in her building. This all confirms that Mary was correct. Much later, perhaps towards the end of the 19th century, a third property was added and it was converted into six flats. It survived as six, with no indoor toilets, until the 1970s when it was converted into the three homes that we see today.

The community of Mason Lodge straddled the boundary between the Leddach and Kirkville Estates, with the Lodge itself being on the Leddach Estate and the Free Church School being on Kirkville. It is not altogether clear why Mason Lodge developed into a community with several businesses, especially as Straik/Elrick was just down the road. Perhaps its position at the crossroads helped, with the road leading to Culter and the older road across to Carnie, both leaving from Mason Lodge. Moreover, the turnpike road bypassed Kirktoun of Skene, which might have helped Mason Lodge to develop. Whatever the reason, businesses did spring up at Mason Lodge and by the 1851 Census there was a licensed grocer, a master tailor and a post master. A tailor was advertised for in 1863 and in the following year William

THE KIRKTOUN OF SKENE AND OTHER COMMUNITIES

George Rae and family at Mason Lodge c.1900

Christie, merchant at Mason Lodge, advertised for three tailors. James Thom, baker at Mason Lodge, advertised his business for sale in 1867. When the Mason Lodge itself was for sale in 1876 it included the merchant's and the baker's businesses. It was bought by George Knight, merchant. He is described elsewhere as a grocer and baker and owned six properties at the Lodge. His tenants in the 1880s included a shoemaker and pedlar.

In 1892 George Rae, a Gaelic speaker born in Clyne, Sutherland, and his wife Mary, from Caithness, took over the shop/bakery/post office, initially as a tenant. He was also a tenant of a house, garden and the old post office across the road. Later George bought the various buildings

George Rae, a Gaelic speaker born in Clyne, Sutherland, and his wife Mary, from Caithness, took over the shop / bakery / post office, initially as a tenant.

on the north side of the road. George died in 1925, but Mary continued with the business, helped for a time by her son, George, and Alfred Williamson, her son-in-law. She had eight properties in 1926, presumably including the six flats mentioned earlier and the post office itself. The second George Rae died relatively young in 1928, leaving a young son, George, who would become the third George Rae to run the shop and post office at Mason Lodge. Alf Williamson had fought in World War I and when he first came back from the war he came to Skene to work as a postman and lodged with the blacksmith, George Stuart, at the Kirktoun. Alf was very involved with the Westhill Congregational Church, and did a considerable amount of work to help the war effort in World War II.

The bakery closed in 1928, but the post office continued. The very first post office in Skene had been at Straik, but it soon moved to Mason Lodge, to a small building to the south of the road (this being one of the flat-roofed buildings built while Peter Jamieson was Laird of Leddach). Later it moved across the road. Adam Craigmile says that just after World War I he saw a group of army men with horse-drawn bogies replacing the plain telephone wire with copper wire. His father actually bought some of the old wire for fencing. Urgent messages depended on telegraph boys who wore uniforms with pillbox hats, and they delivered telegrams by bicycle. When the phone service was extended in 1923, a call office was established at Mason Lodge. We have already seen that Doctor Lawson from Echt rented a surgery for many years at Mason Lodge (this being distinct from the later surgery of Doctor Skinner at neighbouring Leddach House). The post office closed in 1993, the year that George Rae died. It was followed by an antique shop with a small tearoom. Now there is a carpet shop in these premises.

Elrick / Straik / Broadstraik

One of the main questions relating to Elrick is what is the village's correct name. The late Bob Cruickshank, carpenter in Elrick, joked in an article in the PRESS & JOURNAL that some council workmen mis-spelt Elrick as Earlick when putting up signs on the council cottages. The history of the parish published for the millennium says that Earlick was the original name, though without saying why they think that. Traditionally Elrick was to the south of the road and Broadstraik, or just Straik, was north. Older people still refer to the inn and the village as Straik. Here are my thoughts.

I can find no reference to either Elrick or Earlick being used for a settlement,

Elrick

croft or farm before 1800. The earliest name for the area was undoubtedly Leddach, used in charters from medieval times. Leddach (spelt Lennach) and Bredstraik are both shown on Taylor & Skinner's map of the Old Skene Road in 1776, with Leddach just to the south of the road about halfway between the eighth and ninth milestones. The east part of the Moss of Arnhall was called the Moss of Leddach, not Elrick or Earlick, again showing that Leddach was the main name. The area of the future Elrick was probably a strip of poor ground, sandwiched between the Moss of Leddach and Carnie Moss and the Earlick Butts. The latter were located "*betwixt the west end of that part of the Moss of Arnhall called the Moss of Leddach and the east end of the moss of Easter Carnie*".

Butts can mean an area where archery is practised. This is unlikely here, but other meanings given in the SCOTS DICTIONARY are, a ridge of ploughed land, an irregularly shaped ridge, or a small piece of ground cut off in some way from adjacent land. The latter two definitions seem more likely, as the Earlick Butts (roughly the area between the main road through Elrick and the Carnie Woods) drops off considerably down to the moss and woods at the south end. In fact in the 1789 document dividing up the Dean of Guild's lands, the Leddach boundary stone (still there at the entrance to the Carnie Woods) is described as being "*on the hard ground at the foot of the Earlick Butts*". The elevated butts may have been why the 1841 Census lists some houses as being at Elrick Hill.

Drainage in the 19th century improved the area of Elrick a little and there were small crofts to the south of the new road. Leddach and Broadstraik are shown on ROBERSTON'S MAP OF ABERDEENSHIRE from 1822, but now they are on the new turnpike road. As late as 1900 the toll house was still described as the Old Leddach Toll, though in 1841 it was the Toll of Strake.

There is no mention of Broadstraik or Elrick in the LIST OF POLLABLE PERSONS IN ABERDEENSHIRE dated 1696. Neither of them is mentioned in the list of subscribers for the yearly vicarage paid to the Dean of Guild in 1751. Nor are they mentioned in the Commissioners of Supply assessments list for 1801-2 (a forerunner of the valuation roll). By 1810, though, Broadstraik is mentioned. Even by 1830 there is no mention of Elrick. Neither does THE LEDDACH LAND DISPOSITION from 1790 mention Elrick as a place of settlement. There are few gravestones in the older part of the churchyard which use either name – there is one gravestone with Elrick on it dated 1812 and there are several with Earlick or Wester Earlick, the earliest being 1893. I am sure, however, that these are individual properties rather than the name of a settlement. The 1841 Census lists several properties as being at Elrick Hill, even the inn at that time is described as being at Elrick Hill.

We have long known that the original Broadstraik was on the Old Skene Road, and that it moved to the new site sometime after the turnpike toll road was opened in 1803. THE LEDDACH LAND DISPOSITION of 1790 describes the Leddach boundary as running past the houses of Straik, so there was a small community called Straik near to the inn. The late Kitty Howitt, whose family had lived at Crombie Cottage and then Mains Cottage on the old road since the mid-19th century, told Mary McMurtrie that some stones were taken from the old inn to help build the new one. Mary wrote in her article on the Old Skene Road in the SCOTS MAGAZINE that the old Broadstraik was at the highest point on the road (before it went down to Crombie Cottage) at the site of Mains Cottage, i.e., where Kitty Howitt lived until her death in 1951. However, this does not tie up with other evidence. The 1865 OS shows the old Broadstraik to be further west and by the 1900 map it has been renamed Crombie Cottage, i.e., the old Broadstraik became Crombie Cottage. This ties up with the 1859-60 valuation roll which, under Leddach Estate, lists both Broadstraik Inn and Farm and a separate Broadstraik.

If the old Broadstraik had been on the site of the later Mains Cottage, then it would have come under the Westhill Estate. A laird would not want to lose an inn from his estate, since it would bring in revenue and trade, therefore I think it likely that the original inn was slightly further west on the Leddach Estate, just as the new one was.

With the opening of the turnpike road in 1803 the Broadstraik Inn and the name Straik moved south to the new road where there would be more business and trade. Other crofts and traders also grew up on the road on the opposite side from the inn and it seems that they took their name from the two natural features mentioned in the LEDDACH DISPOSITION – the Earlick Stone and the Earlick Butts.

In 1828 the remainder of a 38-year lease was offered for sale at the 'Earlic of the Leddach of Skene'. This is the first use I have found of Earlick as a farm name, and the length of the lease does suggest that this was ground needing improvement. The names of physical features tend to be old, and in Scotland would often be derived from Gaelic or even Pictish. I think that

The Earlick Stone

Earlick became corrupted to Elrick in local speech, with the butts and stone perhaps commonly being called Elrick, while being written as Earlick in legal documents. It is also possible that there was a small croft or two in the area before 1800 that were too small to be recorded in official documents.

The name Broadstraik / Crombie on the old road is further confused by the fact that when Malcolm Gillespie, the infamous gauger, moved to Skene, he obtained a 38-year lease of 20 acres from Alexander Crombie. On this land he built a thatched house which he called Crombie Cottage (possibly after his landlord). He also built farm buildings and stabling for his horses. This would have been a fairly substantial property since it housed several of his assistants, as well as servants and his own children. In fact, he cited the length of his lease and the money spent on improving the property as one of the reasons he fell into debt. As well as being charged with fraud, he was also charged with getting his servants to set fire to the property which he had insured with two different insurance companies.

The same year that he was tried and executed (1827) he had advertised the cottage for let for the remaining 31 years of the lease. The advertisement describes it as a desirable little farm that would "*answer well as a country residence*" divided up by good stone dykes. It also says that a considerable sum is payable by the proprietor at the expiry of the lease for buildings erected by the tenant. So had Gillespie been able to stay for the full length of his lease he would have got back the money he spent on building Crombie Cottage. Unfortunately for him that never happened.

So far so good – the original Broadstraik would have been partly removed to build the new inn, Gillespie then built Crombie Cottage and other buildings on the site and the cottage was burned down. What I can't explain is why, in 1865, the OS gave Crombie Cottage its old name of Broadstraik, but by 1900 they had reverted to calling it Crombie. Of course the OS would probably have given it the name told to them by locals. The 1841/1851 and 1861 censuses all use Crombie Cottage, with several properties listed there, whereas the 1859/60 valuation roll makes no mention of Crombie Cottage.

Throughout the 19th century Leddach and Straik or Broadstraik are used for the village, the latter more often. It is never called Elrick. Individual farms or houses are called Elrick or Earlick on the OS maps, and in the Census. In fact the names are used almost interchangeably. The 1861 Census uses Elrick House, Wester Elrick, etcetera. By the 1891 Census they are using Earlick House, Earlick Mains, etcetera. Ten years later they are using a mixture, Easter Elrick but Earlick House. Neither name, though, is used for the community. The same applies into the 20th century. As someone born and brought up in the area, Mary McMurtrie, writing in the 1950s, never uses the term Elrick. In the third STATISTICAL ACCOUNT she calls the village Broadstraik. She does use Elrick in her much later OLD SKENE ROAD, by which time Elrick had grown. It is understandable why some would say that Broadstraik is north of the main road, Elrick south. All the properties with Elrick in their name were south of the road – Easter Elrick, Wester Elrick, the Earlick stone, the Earlick Butts, the later Elrick House, and the council houses called Earlick. However the use of Elrick for the whole village is a recent one.

Broadstraik Inn was the site of a market during the 19th century. A notice appeared in the ABERDEEN JOURNAL on 14th April, 1819, saying that, "*at the desire of several respectable dealers and the farmers in Skene three markets are to be held yearly at Broadstraik for the sale of black cattle, horses and merchandize*". The first was to be in May after the Greenburn Tryst and Inverurie Market, the second in August on the Tuesday before Lammas Greenburn, and the third in October on Thursday after Michael fair of Kinkell. It was also proposed to fee servants at the May and October markets. How many years these markets lasted I have been unable to find out.

The Straik or Broadstraik Inn was the centre of the village during the 19th century and into the 20th century. The innkeeper also farmed the surrounding fields, with the farm buildings being behind the inn where some

THE KIRKTOUN OF SKENE AND OTHER COMMUNITIES

Broadstraik Inn c.1900

Lizzie Watson of the Broadstraik with her granddaughter c.1889

survive today. Alexander Davnie was the innkeeper at Straik Inn in 1851, possibly succeeding his father, also Alexander. The younger Alexander died young, aged 30, and his widow ran the inn for many years. He was succeeded by John Milne, still tenant of farm and inn in the 1870 valuation roll. The inn was advertised for let on a 19-year lease at Martinmas 1871, when the farm is described as being 41 acres, with the buildings in good order and a considerable trade carried on at the inn. It may have been at this time that John Watson took over the lease. Born nearby in Newhills, he was certainly there in the 1881 Census and he also farmed 42 acres. His widow, Lizzie or Eliza, continued to run the inn until at least 1901.

During her time the inn became known as Mother or Ma Watson's and fortunately a photograph still survives of it then, as does a photograph of Mrs Watson herself. Eliza Watson,

287

The remodelled Broadstraik

with her son David, also tenanted the farm of Wester Earlick.

Around 1903 Alexander Craigmile took over the tenancy of the inn and farm. At this time the Laird of Leddach, Henry Mitchell, had it remodelled in the style of an English inn, "*quite out of keeping*" according to Mary McMurtrie.

Alexander still farmed the surrounding fields. At Broadstraik you could hire a gig. Two black horses for the hearse were also stabled there. A receipt for the wedding of John Smith's daughter from Mains of Skene in 1908 shows an inclusive cost of £11.10s for 46 guests. There were seven bottles of whisky, one of port and six dozen lemonades. The whisky was for the men, and the one bottle of port with lemonade was for the women! Close machines (covered carriages) were provided from Waterton (Dunecht), Lyne of Skene and Gask, with a waggonette from Carnie.

Adam Craigmile describes the excitement of a wedding at Broadstraik in the post-Great War years, with the lion rampant and union flags being flown to announce the occasion. The guests were collected by landau, or open carriage for 12, drawn by two hackney horses. Waterproof knee covers were provided for passengers in bad weather. Others came by bicycle, motorcycle or their own pony and trap. The men headed for the bar, which had fitted seats in the bay window, and wall spittoons and sawdust in front of the bar counter for pipe smokers.

The Broadstraik could accommodate up to 50 guests and the meal was usually Scotch broth, steak pies made by George Rae at Mason Lodge, or cold meat and veg. Trifle or jelly and fruit with cream followed, then tea and a piece of bridal cake. Men were given whisky and the women port, to toast the bride and groom. Lemonade and iron brew were on the table. Sweets were handed round. After Scottish country dancing there was tea with homemade pancakes, scones and cakes. Every guest received a piece of wedding cake in a bag. The bridal couple usually left in a landau with lots of cans tied to it.

The smiddy was the other centre of the village and, in 1891, the Broadstraik blacksmith was Peter Emslie from Tarland. In 1901 it was John Balneaves from Peterculter. The blacksmith's croft comprised three-and-a-bit fields behind the smiddy, running back to the large consumption dyke, parts of which are still visible. Alexander Carle came to the smiddy in 1912 with his wife Elizabeth.

Polling day at Broadstraik

Broadstraik smiddy with 'Auld Carle' in the centre over the anvil

> Auld Carle was a champion at making horseshoes, winning prizes at the Highland Show. During World War I as he employed 18 men and made a huge number of horseshoes for the military.

Known as Auld Carle, he was a champion at making horseshoes, winning prizes at the Highland Show in Aberdeen and elsewhere. This stood him in good stead during World War I as he employed 18 men and made a huge number of horseshoes for the military, the smiddy working from five in the morning until 11 at night. Carle left the Broadstraik smiddy in 1920 and was succeeded by Robert and James Macdonald who had been his assistants. Auld Carle returned in 1935 for a second stint at Broadstraik, and he worked on until the mid-1950s, by which time he was in his seventies and the trade was dying. He died at Broadstraik in 1962. (For a full article on Carle see SKENE HERITAGE NEWSLETTER No. 20).

Opposite the blacksmith's was the carpenter, Bob Cruickshank, who had the carpenters from before World War I. His son, also Bob, was born in Elrick in 1906, and left school at 14 to join him.

THE KIRKTOUN OF SKENE AND OTHER COMMUNITIES

Bob Cruickshank's workshop, Elrick

His croft ran quite far back, with three fields. William Christie was the tailor and general merchant at Elrick or Earlick House in the 1880s and, in 1891, his widow Elisabeth was carrying on the merchant's side of the business. They were succeeded around 1900 by James (Jimmy) Grant Stuart, tailor and grocer from Glenlivet. Adam Craigmile remembers the tailors being above the main shop, with access via an outside staircase. Bob Cruickshank also spoke of the tailors' workshop above the shop, where Jimmy, his wife and two assistants worked on two sewing machines and a wooden bench. Bob remembered the circus coming to Elrick every summer, putting on shows in the field next to Broadstraik Inn.

Leddach Old Toll housed a shoemaker in 1901 – John Reid from Aberlour. Later there were also various shoemakers at Earlick Cottage – William Fraser in 1920s and 30s, and Walter Geoffrey Emilsen in 1950. Both Adam Craigmile and Bob Cruickshank remembered the tinsmith who lived in a house next to the Toll House. He was known as 'Tin Jock' or 'Bissom Jock'. His wife was Gypsy Kate. No doubt originally travellers, they made basins, jugs, mugs, tie pins, socks, laces, ornaments,brooches, and the heather brushes that gave him his second nickname. Every summer they set off by horse and cart to sell their wares to farms inland, or sometimes Kate would push an old-style pram filled with goods to sell.

George Sangster was listed as a mechanic and cycle agent/repairer from 1901, presumably related to the Arthur Sangster of the Aberdeen Cycle Works mentioned earlier in the section on the Skene Games. He hired out bikes as well as repairing them. When the motor car came along he hired out cars instead, establishing a motor garage at Broadstraik as early as 1919. Bob Cruickshank said that he also sold gas lamps for vehicles and delivered papers. George was another one who went into the threshing mill business, covering the whole Skene area.

The south side of Elrick would eventually be where the main industry in the area was housed. I have written later about how Stewart Milne started off in Elrick. An earlier industrialist was David Gordon who lived at Bridgefoot. Born in Crieff, Davy Gordon moved to Elrick with his family at about the start of World War I, when he was aged four. He served his apprenticeship with the local joiner and set up his own joinery business just after World War II. A few years later he began to make concrete blocks, one of the largest manufacturers in the country. His son joined him in the business in 1964, and Davy died in 1983.

Old Westhill

Westhill, before the creation of the 'garden suburb', is not normally described as a village. Nevertheless it was a recognizable community, a collection of croft houses strung along the Old Skene Road and also along the road that curved down towards the turnpike road (now Arnhall Crescent). In fact it was to this latter area, around where Berriedale is now, that the 1st OS map attached the name Westhill. As early as 1841 the Blackhills part of what became Westhill had a tailor, mason, blacksmith and a midwife, and was described as the 'Town Head' of Blackhills. Later that century it had a school, merchant, baker, a wright with a small sawmill, a small independent church, and a killing house and butcher's shop run by a family of entrepreneurs named Williamson (no relation as far as I know of the Williamsons currently at Kilnhillock).

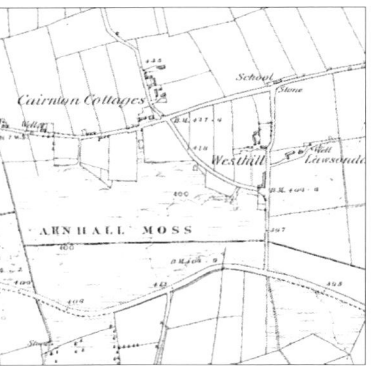

Westhill 1865

The Williamsons had farmed as tenants in the area since the early 1800s, but became well known all over the North-East as fleshers. As early as 1820 George Williamson, flesher, erected a gravestone to his son George who died that year, aged just 24. The 1841 Census records John, George and James Williamson, all fleshers at either Kinmundy or Wester Kinmundy. Several sons of John were also butchers and one, William, was a merchant and grocer at Kinmundy, probably the same Williamson who had the bakers at Westhill towards the end of the century. In the 1871 Census William had the shop and is described as a baker.

THE KIRKTOUN OF SKENE AND OTHER COMMUNITIES

Alexander Williamson moved from Wester Kinmundy and bought land at Cairncry near Aberdeen in the 1840s. Andrew Mathieson, in his diaries, records going down to Westhills in December 1878, with five cows for the Williamsons. Another of John's sons, also John and born at Kinmundy in 1825, moved to Aberdeen after his marriage in 1853. There he began an extensive business under the name Messrs. John Williamson & Son. He was also chairman of the Aberdeen Hide, Skin & Tallow Market Company.

James Williamson also went to Aberdeen and became a butcher, as well as farming at Cornhill, near Aberdeen. He died aged 91 in 1895. His son James was very well known among cattle dealers in the North-East as a cattle judge and as salesman for the Metropolitan Meat Market in London. His other son, John, set up as a butcher in the New Market and then on Union Street. His business became one of the biggest retail establishments in Aberdeen. Unlike their father, both sons died in their early fifties. Several of

Baker's cart at Brodiach c.1905

these Williamsons are buried in Skene Kirkyard.

John and Duncan McLennan seem to have taken over as fleshers in Westhill in the 1890s, Duncan living at Aquaville. John was listed as butcher/shopkeeper. He was down at Eastside, the property sometimes being called McLennan's croft. James Williamson was still there as a baker and grocer in 1901, having followed his father, William. I suspect that James or his father may have been the ones who built Berriedale towards the end of the 19th century, as his address is given as Lawsondale. In effect he moved the shop across the road from Eastside to Berriedale, which would have been beside Lawsondale Farm. There may even have been two shops operating at the same time for a while, since William Williamson is listed in 1896 as a merchant at Eastside, but also as a tenant of a house, shop and bakehouse at Kinmundy (presumably Berriedale). By 1911 the merchant was William Taylor. Adam Craigmile remembers the bakery being in the rear part of the present building. Charlie Stephen later said that the bakery was never as successful when it moved across the road, and the bakery part seems to have closed in the mid-1920s.

Also at Eastside was James Hunter, veterinary surgeon and general practitioner. This was in a group of buildings on the left as you go up the lane from Berriedale, beyond the entrance to Lawsondale Farm, the latter being marked in the dyke today by a very large triangular boulder. Hunter had been there since the 1890s and some alive today remember his daughter, Miss Hunter, living there into the early 1960s with her father's brass nameplate still on the house.

The Barracks also began at Eastside, with James, originally from Fyvie, a threshing mill owner in 1901. His son, John, was also an engine driver. Adam Craigmile remembers old Mr Barrack living opposite Berriedale, where he had a yard and shed for keeping threshing mills and engines. I have been told that Berriedale was at one time called Mormond House, possibly in the 1920s, and occupied by a Mr Ritchie who had served during World War I. His housekeeper was Miss Nelson. He did not work, but he used to walk to Broadstraik for a dram and a bottle of Bass. Later it was bought by a Mr and Mrs Pope who came from Caithness and renamed it Berriedale. They also ran it as a small shop, as did the Kinghorns, the latter from around 1959. From 1971 it also housed a post office.

Mains of Westhill was a substantial farm – 250 acres in 1871 when James Black was the tenant. In the 1920s the tenant was John Rose, who also bought

THE KIRKTOUN OF SKENE AND OTHER COMMUNITIES

John Rose harvesting at Mains of Westhill

a substantial number of the farms on the Leddach estate. Brae of Kinmundy or Wester Kinmundy farm was 100 acres.

The wright at Wright's Croft, Westhill, at the end of the 19th century was George Donald, who had a workshop and sawmill there. Unfortunately he had a drink problem which affected the business and tragically, one night in 1901, he died from exposure in the moss on his way back from The Straik. He left a wife and three young children (for the full story see SKENE HERITAGE NEWSLETTER November 2009). By 1932 the shed, sawmill and machinery were owned by Margaret Gow, widow, but they are described as in ruinous condition. Wright's Croft was on the site now occupied by the Holiday Inn.

In the 20th century Westhill House was rented by Doctor Skinner as his home and surgery, before

Fee'd loons at Mains of Westhill

295

Cairnton Croft, now the edge of the car park at the Westhill shops

he moved to Leddach. Thereafter the tenant for many years was Alexander P. Imlay. Initially, in the 1930s, he was Captain Imlay, but by 1960 he was Lieutenant Colonel Imlay D.S.O.. He had served in the second Battalion of the Gordon Highlanders and then the Indian Army, retiring in 1948.

In the 1930s the other tenants of the Westhill Estate were names that will be remembered by many today: Gordon Shaw (Aquaville), George Christie, D. Bruce, David Gordon (Bridgefoot), Alexander McGregor (Cairnton), Alice Hunter (Eastside), Archibald Smith (Eastside), William Middleton (Wester Kinmundy), Edward Christie (Wester Kinmundy), Arthur Stewart, John Spence, Mary Gammie, Charles Anderson, John Rose (Mains of Westhill), Eliza Lawson, John Burnett, Mary Young, James Robertson, John Robertson (tinsmith). Miss Henderson lived at Arnhall Croft across the road from Ben Ledi. Miss Cheyne, who taught at the school, lived almost in the moss, in an old army hut converted into a house. Some of these tenants were still around at the time the modern Westhill was built. In 1973 three were given new houses at numbers 17, 19 and 21 Kinmundy Drive, as their own cottages were demolished for the new streets and houses of Westhill. Gordon and Agnes Shaw, Annie Henderson and Jane Leslie, who with her husband had taken over Cairnton croft from the McGregors, all had streets named after them.

Further west along the Old Skene Road sat Kitty Howitt's croft, just

THE KIRKTOUN OF SKENE AND OTHER COMMUNITIES

Kitty Howitt at her cottage on the Old Skene Road

before the present junction with Hay's Way. Kitty's father had been a shoemaker there from the 1870s, his workshop just out the back. He regularly walked into Aberdeen along the old road to buy leather and he carried on working when he got back. Kitty's house was thatched up until her death in 1952. Leslie Durno and his father repaired the roof once, and the workshop still had all the old soutar tools, untouched since the death of Kitty's father more than 50 years before.

What is now Prospect Cottage or Prospectbank was originally Kinmundy School until the building of the new school further west at the roundabout. Prospect Cottage went on to house two families. In 1901, for example, there was James Simpson, retired farmer, with his wife, daughter and granddaughter. Next door was Alexander Mitchell, farmer, with his wife and three children. Later it became the cottar house for Westhill Mains, owned by Charlie Stephen. In the early 1950s it was bought by George Kelly and his wife Sheila, both artists. Sheila still lives there today with her son Paul, also an artist.

Charlie Stephen, along with John Alexander of Brodiach, is said to have had an illicit still, with the whisky being stored somewhere underground around Brodiach steading.

Westhill actually shrank before it began to grow as a new community. In her 1972 Scots Magazine article on the Old Skene Road, Mary McMurtrie states that *"Westhill was much larger in earlier times"*. This despite 12 council houses being built opposite the school in 1948.

Fiddie

There was never much of a community at Fiddie, but it was the location of the toll house on the branch of the turnpike road leading to Echt. In the first half of the 20th century there was also a shop there.

Aspects of rural life in the first half of the 20th century

In 1902 the ABERDEEN JOURNAL carried a small item headed 'Old World Harvesting at Skene'. This concerned an elderly crofter at Lyne of Skene who could not get anyone to cut her lea corn. She decided to cut it herself using a hyeuck or sickle. In two days, with the help of another elderly woman, she had more than an acre in stook. What particularly interested the newspaper was that within a few hundred yards could be seen the hyeuck, the scythe, the reaper and the self-binder. THE JOURNAL comments that although the shearer lacked the speed of the others, her work was far superior. Elsewhere it is recorded that this woman cut her crop on her knees when she was aged over 70, and carted it home by barrow.

The horse-drawn machines had largely replaced hand harvesting methods during the 19th century, just as the horse had replaced the oxen team for ploughing. On smaller crofts earlier methods might survive and sometimes horses were teamed with cattle for working. However, by the end of World War II the horse had largely been replaced, this time by the tractor. Fortunately the early years of the 20th century brought a big increase in the use of photography in rural areas and, though many photographs were posed, they also recorded the ways of working the land.

We are fortunate in Skene to have three particular sources of photography to help bring the era alive. Alexander Mackilligan was a photographer in

A History of Skene and Westhill

> We are fortunate in Skene to have three particular sources of photography. They help bring to life the era which saw the beginning of travelling photographers who gave us images of country people at work.

Sandy Leith at Burreley

Aberdeen, working for various newspapers and on his own behalf. He seems to have had friends and family in various areas of the North-East and took some marvellous photographs of them in rural settings. The original plates have been donated to the Aberdeen & North East Family History Society. In Skene he was friendly with the Alexander Family at Brodiach and took a number of photographs of them c.1910. The Rev. William Cran at Westhill Congregational Church was an amateur, but he took several hundred photographs of the Skene area, as well as his original home area of Rhynie. Slightly later, in the 1920s, parish minister John McMurtrie took a large number of photographs in and around Kirktoun of Skene. This era also saw the beginning of school photographs and of travelling photographers giving us photographs of country people in their working environment, rather than formally posed in studios.

RURAL LIFE IN THE FIRST HALF OF THE 20TH CENTURY

A horse yoked with two cows

Elsie Alexander starching or bleaching clothes at Brodiach c.1910

RURAL LIFE IN THE FIRST HALF OF THE 20TH CENTURY

ABOVE: **Tattie picking crew at Leucharbraes in the 1920s**

LEFT: **Jim Clark at Southbank**

FAR LEFT: **Making a straw rope at Brodiach c.1910**

Horse drawn binder at Burnhead, Kinmundy

Dragging the 'smiler' at Brodiach c.1910

Dunecht Estates

As early as 1911 Lord Cowdray had considered buying Skene estate instead of Dunecht. He received a report from Walker & Duncan, land surveyors, valuing it at approximately £60,000. The report went on to say that the buildings were not in a good state and that a substantial part of the rental value would need to be spent on them, as well as on drainage for the land. As it turned out he decided to buy Dunecht as his main estate in the North-East, but that did not stop him buying other, smaller estates, including some in Skene parish.

Only eight years later, in 1918/19, Cowdray bought various lands from George Hamilton of Skene House. These comprised Nether Affloch; parts of Upper Affloch; the Mill of Craigiedarg and parts of the farm of Craigiedarg; part of the farm of Bervie; Lochside; Garlogie, including the meal mill, Over and Nether Garlogie or Burrowley; and he also bought the former Garlogie woollen mill from the trustees of Alexander Hadden & Sons. He bought, too, some of Hamilton's lands adjacent to Garlogie at Air and Locheye in Echt Parish. This meant that the whole of the Loch of Skene belonged to Dunecht Estates. These extra lands near the loch led Lady Cowdray to have the landmark Tower Lodges built in 1922/23 as an entrance to Dunecht House. They are in the Scots Baronial style, the architect being Alexander Marshal Mackenzie who designed numerous buildings in the North-East, including Marischal College, the Art Gallery and Art School on Schoolhill, St Mark's Church on Rosemount Viaduct, Mar Lodge and Crathie Church. The stone for the towers came from Craigenlow quarry on the Dunecht Estate. The driveway from the towers was actually laid on bundles of saplings and bushes to counteract the boggy nature of the ground near the loch.

The illustration of the towers under construction shows a car with London number plates, perhaps Lady Cowdray inspecting the work. Adam Craigmile remembers their car as being a yellow and black Rolls-Royce, with brass fittings and white tyres, driven by a chauffeur and accompanied by a footman, both in uniform. The two headlamps were carbide, lit by a match, and there were two paraffin side lamps and tail lamps.

A tearoom existed for many years at the south tower which also acted as a boathouse, replacing

Tower Lodges under construction

Lodge for Dunecht House with Mr Findlater, Easterskene gamekeeper, and Rev. Cran's tricycle c.1910

the older boathouse that still stands, roofless, to the west of the tower. A further boathouse was situated on the opposite side of the loch, this originally being the boathouse for Echt. Near to the latter is the 'temple'.

The temple was something of a mystery, since I was told by someone at Dunecht that its columns were originally part of a *porte cochere* at Dunecht House, and moved to the loch in the late 19th century. Skene Heritage, though, has a photograph of them, taken early in the 20th century by the Rev. Cran, at what looks like the Old Aberdeen lodge on the main A944. Further evidence suggests that they were indeed part of Dunecht House, but were later moved to the lodge entrance and subsequently taken down a second time and moved to the south side of the loch just before the towers were built.

As noted already, in 1924 the estates of Kirkville and Easterskene were also bought by Lord Cowdray, with Colonel William Duguid McCombie remaining a life tenant at Easterskene until his death in 1970. Also in the early 1920s Dunecht Estates bought some of Wester Carnie or Hillcarnie from the Society of Advocates. This estate included Braes of Leuchar, Broadwater, Braelea, Cummings Croft, Gask, Hatton, Howcroft, Inverord,

Springhill, Woodside and five houses at Carnie village.

Dunecht carried out a considerable amount of work in rebuilding the roadside drystone dykes, still a feature of the area. They also gradually improved many of the houses on the various estates and in the villages. Perhaps the biggest change Dunecht made in these early years was to the old woollen mill at Garlogie where a hydro-electric scheme was created. The water from the Leuchar Burn was used to generate electricity, initially for Dunecht House. This was a significant project, involving up to 200 men, many of whom were housed in the old counting house for the mill. The first part was completed in 1923 and involved raising the water level in the loch. Wooden sluices that had regulated the flow of water to the woollen mill were replaced by a channel and weir. A balancing reservoir was created south of the meal mill and a five-foot diameter reinforced concrete conduit, 700 yards (640m) in length, took the water to a surge tank and then on to the turbine. Some of the stones from demolished mill buildings were used in the building of the dam, with granite facings over the concrete. The Leuchar Burn was also widened. The 120H.P. turbine was manufactured by Escher-Wyss of Zurich, and had an output of 60KW. A channel for the cable was hand dug all the way to Dunecht House, around two miles (3,218 m) away, and on to the estate workshops.

In 1935 most of the properties in Echt and Dunecht were covered by the scheme. This perhaps explains why I have been told that the work went on for 15 years, possibly the dam taking that long to complete, and that the level of the loch was raised more than once. Certainly Tibbie Reid remembers a beach at the east side of the loch where children played. Mary McMurtrie also mentioned it in her writings. That beach is no longer there. Most of the actual mill buildings were demolished, except for the part housing the turbine and another part that became Garlogie Village Hall in 1931. Another side effect of the raising of the water in the loch was that the meal mill ceased at around the time of World War II.

Dunecht Estates still own much of the area, including some of the original village of Kirktoun.

Skene Choral Society

During the 19th century there had been a Skene Musical Association and an account of a concert held at the Lyne of Skene Mission House in 1880 is given in the ABERDEEN JOURNAL. The Skene Choral Society was established in 1912

Skene Choral Society 1926 with conductor George Innes

by parish minister, John McMurtrie and lasted until 1931. The conductor was George Innes who lived in the area. George was a well-known music teacher, later advisor on music in Aberdeen, and he conducted many choirs in the North-East. His greatest success was to take the famous Hall Russell Choir to Glasgow where they won a national competition. John McMurtrie was first president of the Choral Society, with schoolmaster, George Mitchell, as secretary and treasurer. Initial patrons were Lady Cowdray, Mr and Mrs Hamilton, Rev. Cran of Westhill, Dr Lawson, Dr Skinner, Mr Mitchell of Leddach, and Professor C. Sandford Terry, professor in history at Aberdeen University, himself a notable musician and musical scholar.

The first concert of the society was held in the Milne Hall on 8th November 1912. At that time they had 11 sopranos, five altos, three tenors, and six baritones. The programme included teachers Misses Cruickshank and Bauchop singing *The Torpedo and Whale* with a quartet with Mr Ogg and Mr McMurtrie; Janet Burt, the main soloist sang *Ae Fond Kiss* and *My Dearest Heart*; and the whole society sang *There's aye some Water whaur the Stirkie Droons*.

Skene Choral Society with John McMurtrie kneeling

In 1914 they held a Grand Patriotic Concert with patriotic songs in aid of the War Relief Fund. Guests at this concert were the Aberdeen Tramway Male Voice Choir.

The Rural

On 16 May 1923 Mrs Sybil Hamilton called a meeting at Skene House with a view to establishing a Women's Rural Institute. Forty women attended, including two area officials, Mrs Moir-Byers and Miss Adams, who explained the aims and objectives of the society. It was unanimously agreed to form an institute in Skene and 36 women enrolled immediately. A committee was elected with the main office bearers being: president, Mrs Hamilton; vice president, Mrs Plowman, wife of the former Free Church minister; secretary, Miss Ellis, daughter of the local policeman; treasurer, Mrs Mitchell, wife of the Skene schoolmaster.

It was agreed that meetings would be held on the first Wednesday of the month in Skene Central School and Lyne of Skene School, on alternate

A HISTORY OF SKENE AND WESTHILL

Westhill SWRI 21st birthday, 1953

months. For three years the ladies cycled to and fro and then, in 1926, they became two separate rurals. Westhill was to follow in 1932.

The format of the meetings has more or less remained unchanged up to the present day – business, a talk or demonstration, cup of tea and a competition, with outings and a visiting rural at the AGM.

The Women's Guild

Formed in 1913 by the Reverend John McMurtrie's mother, it continues today. It helped raise considerable finance at the time of the church renovation in the 1930s.

William Black and Roby

William Black and Roby

In the days before fridges and supermarkets, farms in and around Aberdeen delivered milk to customers. This photograph shows William Black of Burnhead of Kinmundy on his milk cart. By

310

1930 he had been delivering milk to Aberdeen for over 50 years and, at 73 years of age, was one of the oldest dairymen on the Skene Road. As he was returning from his round the cart was approached by a police constable who thought there was something strange about the attitude of the driver. In fact, William was found to be dead and his horse, Roby, knowing the way, was continuing home on the correct side of the road.

Mary McMurtrie

I have already quoted at length from Mary's memories, but two more will take us back again to the early 20th century. Mary wrote in later life of the winters in her younger days. Real snowstorms, she said, where the snow was so deep that the field dykes were covered. She remembered that during one, when her uncle was staying, he set off for bread to the bakery at Mason Lodge, carrying a pillow case, and walking straight over the frozen fields. On the icy roads, Mary and the other children wore socks over their boots to prevent slipping.

Winter visits were always timed for a full moon, as were concerts and other entertainment. I have also heard it said that the same applied to the timing of the meetings of the Rural ladies. Years later Mary wrote about watching Halley's Comet from the schoolhouse at Skene, very clearly night after night with its two tails. This would have been in 1910.

Adam C. Craigmile

I have already quoted considerably, too, from Adam and he shared with Mary McMurtrie a phenomenal memory into his 90s. Adam was born at the Broadstraik Inn in 1913, his father being tenant of the farm and inn at that time, finally buying it in 1921. Adam's memories of his early days give a vivid picture of what life was like in the parish in the years between the two wars.

He remembers the fishman, Mr Fowler, coming out on the bus from Aberdeen with two baskets of fish. Fowler picked up his wheelbarrow at the end of Westhill Road and then called at Berriedale and the houses along the Old Skene Road, as far as the Kirktoun. He finished at Broadstraik where he had a drink or two before returning to Aberdeen. Adam's job was to push the barrow back to the bus stop at Westhill, as he made his way to school. He was paid seven old pence and he did it from the age of nine until he left school at 14, having succeeded his brothers Frank and then John.

Every Wednesday morning during winter two men with horse carts left

Broadstraik for Culter station where they collected barley draff. The draff came by rail from distilleries on Speyside and was used to feed the cattle at Broadstraik dairy. At Broadstraik in winter, when there was a shortage of milk, they were given lemonade or stout for their porridge. Adam's father was also the coal agent for the area and supplies came from Aberdeen by Super Sentinel steam wagons. From Broadstraik coal was delivered to the surrounding area by horse lorry. As well as farming Broadstraik, the Craigmiles ploughed the glebe, the joiner's croft at Elrick, the Howitt's croft on the Old Skene Road, the blacksmith's croft at Kirktoun and the one at Broadstraik.

Adam's father, Alexander, was a regular church-goer until saddened by the carnage of the Great War. He did love hymns, however, and every Sunday evening at Broadstraik, during winter, the family gathered with locals in the bar parlour. Adam's sister, Mary, played all her father's favourite hymns and everyone had to join in the singing. There was no Sunday licence then, so the drinking was illegal, but I don't suppose the local bobby up at the Kirktoun was in any way bothered. The piano at Broadstraik was hired out to the Milne Hall. It was transported by horse lorry and it took four people to lift it. Adam says that the wheels on the lorry had iron rims and, between that and the metal road, the piano played itself all the way up to the Kirktoun!

Around 1922 the first wireless in the area was bought by Postie Gordon at the Toll House in Elrick, and Adam and his sister were invited in to listen. The equipment consisted of a 20-foot (6m) pole at the back of the house, with an aerial and insulators carrying the radio wave signal into the house to the wireless which was connected to a battery and earphones. They each had a turn to listen and heard a talk and music, but it was very faint.

The village bobby

The first police station was in the Kirktoun at number four, the first policeman we know of being Constable Birss, born in Aboyne, who was there from at least 1896. Mary McMurtrie remembered Birss at his house in the Kirktoun, *"off duty, leaning against the side of the door, jacket unbuttoned and smoking his pipe"*. After World War I and through the 1920s the policeman was George Strath. Around 1926 the County Council bought Viewfield in Elrick and the police station was transferred there. Adam Craigmile remembers both Birss and P.C. Strath. Part of the policeman's duties included attending at sheep dipping, which was compulsory. He also had to check horse-drawn lorries and coaches for road tax (even then!). Carriages with springs paid 15/- (75p) a year. Box cars with fixed axles were exempt, but had to display a brass plate with the name and address of the owner.

Various other policemen followed, including George Wood in the 1930s and George Dalgarno in the the 1950s. Gordon Argo came in 1960 and was constable at Elrick until 1975. Gordon was also session clerk at Skene Church from 1971 until the end of 2010.

Skene in two world wars

World War 1

Fund raising during the war was carried on under the auspices of the Parish Council. Thus, as early as September 1914, a special meeting was called to raise money in response to the Prince of Wales's National Relief Fund. All members of the Council were given subscription sheets and £61.13.3 was raised. The same month the Council arranged a recruiting event for the Territorial Forces. At this event there were various speakers including Skene's own schoolmaster, George Mitchell, at that time Lieutenant in charge of the Territorial Headquarters at Banchory. A resolution was proposed by Henry Mitchell, Leddach House, and unanimously adopted to the effect that "*this meeting pledges itself to do everything in its power to find men of military age, necessary for H.M. Services, in carrying this just war to its successful issue*". Several of the young men from the parish who had been training as Territorials under George Mitchell, enlisted. The local Voluntary Aid Detachment, organized by Dr Skinner and Mrs Mitchell, sent several of its members to help in the war-time hospital at Drumrossie, Insch.

In 1915 the senior pupils at Skene began collecting for the British and Foreign Soldiers Society. They raised £5.11s and the school received a small shield, while the pupils received medals and bibles. Later that year the children received postcards from one soldier in France and one in Gallipoli, thanking them for the parcels of cigarettes they had sent. The same week the children had collected pennies and sent off small parcels of chocolate and cigarettes.

By the first Christmas of the war presents were being sent from America to the forces, but also to British children whose fathers were on military service. Special constables were appointed in December 1914. Subsequently members of the Parish Council and 11 other parishioners got instructions from the Emergency Committee of Aberdeen District regarding routes to be followed in event of an invasion, and steps to be taken to dispose of stock and property. A census was taken of all stock and vehicles. Adam Craigmile remembers that they had three land girls staying at Broadstraik during the war.

As the war continued, the Oldmill Poorhouse (now Woodend Hospital) on the outskirts of Aberdeen was used for military casualties. Skene paupers housed at the poorhouse were returned to the area where accommodation had to be found for them. Funds continued to be raised, and a flag day was held throughout the county in aid of the War Prisoners Bureau. This was held in July 1916 and in December that year a public meeting was held to form a War Savings Association. The parish minister, John McMurtrie, went to France in 1918 to take charge of the Aberdeen Presbytery Hut. Leslie Durno's father, Willie, served in a Welsh Regiment of engineers and received the Military Medal. Leslie's grandfather was farming at Southbank, and when Willie arrived back in Aberdeen from France at one o'clock in the morning he walked all the way to Southbank with his kitbag over his shoulder.

Skene War Memorial

Finally, in December 1918, a public meeting was convened to consider the erection of a memorial to local men killed during the war. It was to be a number of years before anything happened. By 1920 there had been delays because of the shortage of suitable stone. The following year the three remaining members of the Skene Mutual Improvement Society handed over the money in its account as the nucleus of a fund to construct and care for a war memorial. Other money was raised by public subscription. The memorial of Kemnay granite was eventually unveiled by Brigadier-General Hamilton on Sunday 24th April, 1921. It commemorates 32 men of the parish who died in the war, 23 of them serving in the Gordon Highlanders. There is a carved line on the memorial said to be where the name of a soldier was taken off after he subsequently turned up. I have found no one in the area who remembers the soldier's name, but John McMurtrie took a photograph of the memorial as it was being made. By zooming in on the photograph I was able to make out that the soldier's name was T. Livingstone R.H. (Royal Highlanders). As yet, that is all I know about him. A slight mistake was made on one of the other names on the memorial, where G. M. Lowe wrongly has the 'e' at the end. In the book of the memorial he is spelt correctly George Morrison Low, who farmed with his father at Burnside, Skene. The family later farmed at Springhill Farm, Carnie until relatively recently, and are still in Westhill today.

World War II

In World War II, 109 men and 28 women from Skene parish served in the forces and 13 men were killed. The monument to the dead is inside the church. The war affected the lives of those at home in many ways. As youngsters Harold Munro and Bill Troup both remember seeing the bombing of Aberdeen, Harold from Rogiehill, and Bill from Whitestone. Harold being higher up saw it clearly and also remembers a bomber emptying its load on Hill of Keir. The bombs did not explode, so presumably were not charged. Bill remembers the walls of the farmhouse shaking during the bombing of Aberdeen, and the bombers repeatedly turning over the loch, taking their bearings from it.

The late Bunty Milne remembered that Westhill Primary School was a rest centre, stocked with provisions like juice, nappies, etcetera, in case mothers and babies had to be evacuated from Aberdeen. Once the old Free Church or Lochside Church had closed in April 1941 it was taken over by the army, as was the manse. Army huts were erected in its grounds, and it may have been here that Canadian soldiers were based. They built a bridge and rope swings in the woods near the Loch of Skene, presumably for training purposes, but also used by local children to play on.

The Skene War Work Committee in World War II

The records of the Skene War Work Committee were donated to Skene Heritage Society by Dr Ross Munro. Ross's father had been the headmaster of Skene Central School during the war and his mother was secretary of the committee.

The committee began with an open meeting held in the Milne Hall on 12 October, 1939, for ladies of the parish, and a combined association was set up of women's organizations and unattached women. It was to be called the Skene War Work Party. The parish was divided into four sections based on the WRI districts. Office bearers were: president, Mrs Hamilton, Skene House; vice president, Mrs Simpson, Kirkville House; honorary secretary, Mrs Munro, Central Schoolhouse; honorary treasurer, Mrs Imlay, Westhill House. Each sector was also to have a convener: Westhill, Mrs McLeod; Skene Central, Mrs McMurtrie and Miss Allison; Lyne of Skene, Miss Hamilton; Garlogie: Miss Walker.

The second meeting, attended by various organisations, took place at Skene House on 28 October 1939, called by Mrs Hamilton. Those represented were British Legion: Brig. General Hamilton and Mr C. Duncan; Churches: Revs T. Allison, C. Lynch and J. McMurtrie; Girl Guides, Miss Allison; Nursing Association, Mrs Hamilton and Nurse Gall; Schools, Mrs McLeod, Miss Stewart, Miss Walker, Mr Munro and Mr Brownie; Parents' Representative; Scouts: Mr T. Allison; Women's Committee of Lochside Church, Mrs J. Troup; Women's Guild of Old Church, Mrs McMurtrie; WRIs, Mrs Duncan, Mrs Hamilton, Mrs McLeod and Mrs Porter; Dance Committee and Sports Club, Mr Ogg.

By December various fund raising activities had been held, namely, a house to house collection £64.12.1; dances £16.16.2; share of proceedings of British Legion Concert £5.18.0; Donation £1; for a total of £88.6.4. A Christmas parcel of a knitted article, a box of shortbread, chocolate and cigarettes was sent to each serviceman from the parish.

In February 1940 they agreed to amalgamate with the North East Area War Comforts Organisation. Total membership of the Skene War Work Party was now 292, including 40 girls from the Central School, who were to be given wool for knitting on the same basis as other members. At that point, 606 articles had been dispatched.

On Saturday 15 June 1940 a fair was held in the Milne Hall followed by an evening dance from eight o'clock until 11. Sir Robert and Lady Smith of Crowmallie opened the fair, with Elspeth McMurtrie and Muir Junor presenting Lady Smith with a bouquet of flowers, the gift of Brig. General Hamilton. The hall had been decorated on the Thursday evening and thanks were given to Mr Durno for his work in preparing the hall. The total raised by the fair was £1,32.7.10. Subsequently £25 was set aside for sending parcels to servicemen; parcels containing a writing pad, pencil, 50 cigarettes, toothpaste, shaving soap, a handkerchief and six cakes of chocolate.

It was proposed that, at Christmas, postal orders valued at 7/6 be sent to servicemen abroad, and parcels similar to the above be sent to those in this country, with the addition of a plum pudding. Mrs Williamson, Mason Lodge, was asked to supply the goods. A meeting in November 1940 was told that Lyne of Skene and Westhill districts had adopted a prisoner of war and that Central and Garlogie were to consider doing the same. The growing cost of the articles in the parcels led to writing pads and handkerchiefs being left out. The cost would be 7/1 per parcel and eightpence postage.

In April of the following year, 1941, discussion took place as to how best to help with the welfare of troops who were coming to the district. In May Mr Munro had arranged that the Kinellar Players give a performance in the Milne Hall, and Mrs Hamilton proposed a concert with the Dunecht Players and soldiers from the local camp jointly providing the programme.

As well as sending postal orders and parcels to servicemen from Skene, donations were also made to other causes. In 1942 £20 was given to the Red Cross, £14 to Lady Cowdray's Prisoners of War, and £20 to Mrs Churchill's Aid To Russia fund. Mr Brownie proposed that a special function be held for the benefit of the last one, and a whist drive and dance was subsequently held with the amount of the donation increased. The following year donations were again made to the Red Cross and also to the YMCA, Aid to China and Medical Aid to Russia. By 1943 the Committee was sending 200 Players No.3 cigarettes to those serving overseas and 1,000 greetings cards were printed to be sent with gifts and for use on future occasions. Advertisements were also placed in the Press & Journal, Evening Express and People's Journal to find the addresses of servicemen from the parish.

As late as March 1945 the committee was still active, with sums of money being given to various charities. There was also a collection of household goods for Stepney Bombed-out Area. December 1945 seems to have been the last meeting and the agenda indicates that valedictory votes of thanks were made and a press report of the work of the Skene War Workers was prepared. In February 1946 the statement of accounts covering up to 4 January 1946 was lodged with Aberdeen County Council.

The records of the Skene War Work Committee provide a fascinating picture of what those at home, particularly women, were doing to support the troops. Included in the minute book are letters from organizations such as the

Red Cross, the War Comforts Co-ordination Scheme, and Aberdeenshire Prisoners of War Appeal, thanking them for their efforts. There are also two letters from servicemen, one from an A. Davidson, serving in East Africa, who comments on the warm climate in comparison to Scotland. The other was from D. McIntyre who was in India. As well as saying how grateful he is to receive 'Blighty' smokes, he says that he cannot understand why India is described as the "Jewel of the Empire" as there are no jewels where he is. The Register of Quantities even details the number of items each sector of the parish had knitted, as well as the amount of material used.

Elspeth Haston remembers helping her mother, Mary McMurtrie, give out wool in the vestry to the various knitters from the Central Area. They were to knit squares to be made into blankets, and Elspeth says that some knitters could not knit properly and that her mother had to correct the squares. Mrs Hamilton was subsequently awarded the OBE for her services to the war effort. Elspeth also remembers collecting sacks of sphagnum moss for the wounded. This is confirmed by an entry in the school log book, hips also being collected. During Warship Week in 1942 Skene School collected a total of £450.14s. A year later the school subscribed an even more impressive £740.11s towards the County's Warship collection.

The Home Guard

Westhill, Skene, Lyne of Skene and Dunecht all had their Home Guard with Captain Alfred Williamson in overall charge, and Davy Gordon possibly Sergeant. Alf had fought in World War I as a lance-bombardier in the artillery, in charge of trench mortars and also the horses for the gun carriages. He was to be commended for his work after World War II, some of this work being secret, even today. His daughter remembers senior military men coming to the post office, talking to her father and later bringing in locked metal trunks. These were kept in the store through the back for a while, then were taken away, possibly to be hidden elsewhere. A model village of Kirktoun of Skene, made by Alf for training purposes, is at the Alford Heritage Centre. Very few of the men who served in the Home Guard are still around and so it has been difficult to collect much information on their activities. Bill Leslie remembers one of the farm workers at Westhill Mains using all his bullets for shooting rabbits. He could not then go to the meeting that night and so worked for the farmer for nothing to give himself an excuse for missing the meeting. Bill says that a big hullabaloo got up because someone was

Skene Home Guard with Alf Williamson centre of front row

supposed to have landed on the Westhill hill. It was actually a large canister which they took to Wright's Croft to open. Among other things it contained chocolate and all the children were given some.

The Lumberjills and wartime farm work

During the war many of the trees in the woods of Gask, Garlogie and Torshinnoch were cut down to help the war effort, for pit props, for example. Some of this work was done by women under the direction of the Forestry Commission, and a camp was built for them at Garlogie, one of the wooden buildings still surviving as a family home. Women were also mobilized as the Women's Land Army and worked on farms in the parish, as did prisoners of war, brought in daily from camps at Culter and Monymusk. In 1942 the headmaster of Skene School and 15 older boys also did forestry work during the vacation to help the war effort.

War memorial

The war memorial for World War II is a simple and beautifully-designed oak panel. It was designed by T. B. Huxley-Jones who taught sculpture at Gray's School of Art and it is situated inside the church.

Some Skene worthies – and some perhaps not so worthy!

The Wizard Laird

In ancient times the Laird o' Skene
Was kent baith far an' wide
An' stories o' his darin' deeds
Then filled the country wide
Fowk nail'd a horse-shoe on the door
Stuck red thread on the wa'
Hung ran (rowan) tree in the crook an' lum
To scare the Laird awa,
An kankert bairns wha wadna rest
Nor gang to bed at e'en
Were quietit in a minute wi-
See here's the Laird o' Skene

This is part of a very long poem by James Mackay of Cults, printed in 1891. Just over 10 years earlier John Cumming had given Mackay the information for his poem by publishing THE WARLOCK LAIRD O' SKENE, a booklet that ran to three editions, the first selling out in three weeks. Cumming came from Fintry and became a journalist, initially in Aberdeen, then for the

WESTMINSTER GAZETTE. He claimed to be writing down stories that were then current in the country areas to prevent them being forgotten. Even earlier, in 1850, Alexander Gordon had written a poem about the Wizard Laird:

When the winter nichts grow lang and cauld
Strange tales are yet about him tauld
And the haflin or herd, be they e'er so bauld
Grow airgh when they hear o' Skene
The bairns around the fire close creep
And aft to the door and lum-head peep
The big ha' bible at han' they aye keep
To fend aff the Laird o' Skene

Alexander Gordon was born and brought up in Aberdeen, but at the time the poem was published in the ABERDEEN JOURNAL he was living at Ordhead, Cluny. There he no doubt heard tales of the Wizard Laird. The JOURNAL also says that the present laird was fond of recounting tales of the Wizard.

Skene was not the only area in the North-East to have its wizard. His rival came from Tarland and similar stories were also told of the Laird of Gordonston who had his own loch at Spynie.

The superstitions in Mackay's poem relating to red thread and rowen branches were recorded by Mary McMurtrie as surviving into the 20th century at Lyne of Skene. Even today most people will know about the good luck brought by horse shoes (if you hang them the correct way up). In earlier times there were many more superstitions and we have read, in the section on Kinmundy House, how ghost stories were also prevalent.

Tradition has it that Alexander Skene (1663-1724) was the Wizard, and that he encouraged the belief that he was a wizard. We may speculate as to why stories should have arisen about him. Perhaps he did study abroad as the Wizard is said to have done. THE MEMORIALS make no mention of that, nor do they mention the stories of the Wizard. Anyone studying abroad in the early 18th century might well have been viewed with suspicion by superstitious country folk.

Alexander's mother had re-built the old tower of Skene, moving the family back into it and away from the thatched houses they had previously lived in. Alexander began the process of reviving the family fortunes, marrying Giles Adie who brought new lands to the family. This may have led the laird to become more distant from his tenants, a man of business, travelling a lot and leaving the land management to factors, overseers and grieves. As he became a more distant figure, so stories may have grown up about him. On the other hand this may all be speculation, but I think that it is only right to record here some of the stories about the Wizard Laird to help show how our ancestors viewed the world that they lived in.

The stories about the Wizard have been embellished by more recent writers, but those listed here are taken from Cumming's book and Gordon's poem, they being the earliest known recordings. The Wizard Laird is said to have cast no shadow, a trait he shared with a Laird of Straloch. Straloch had studied at Padua and it is there that Skene is also said to have studied, though he studied the black arts, with Auld Nick as his teacher. Skene was said to have been in Padua for seven years and, at the final session, one student announced that fees would have to be paid and that the last out the door would pay for all. There was a rush to the door, Skene stumbled and the Devil caught him. Skene shouted that there was one behind him and the Devil turned round and grabbed Skene's shadow. Hence he never after cast a shadow.

Tales were told of strange goings on at Skene House, noises from the big hall which had no windows, the noises getting louder when the laird appeared; the laird leaving in his coach after midnight but always returning before sunrise. The laird had his own familiars in the shape of a crow, a hawk, a jackdaw and a piet or magpie. They accompanied his carriage, but were also capable of getting up to mischief on their own, the jackdaw in particular tormenting the parish minister by setting fire to his sermons then closing the church ventilators and filling the place up with sulphur.

Several tales of the Wizard Laird concerned his ability to deal with troublemakers by reisting them (freezing them to the spot). One Hogmanay he was returning to Skene House where he was to host a ball. When passing through the woods at Affloch he was stopped by several highway robbers. Calmly the laird told them to sit down and he would give them all his money. He gave each man half-a-crown, but reisted them all to the spot. He then got his coachman to dig up the turf on which the robbers sat and returned with them to Skene House with the turf still attached to them. In that condition he made them dance at the ball to the amusement of everyone, including the piper, Donald Dower from Craigievar. Donald laughed so much he could not play, but the laird made the pipes play themselves. A similar tale places the robbers at Broadiach and on that occasion the Wizard

Laird and his son dug the men out with a "*flauchter spaad*" – a turf cutting spade – and sent for officers of the law to take the men away to be hanged.

Sometimes the laird appeared to be more vindictive – as when his peace was disturbed by dancers at lodgings he had stopped at while on his travels. After trying in vain to sleep, he left the inn, but also left the poor dancers unable to stop dancing, all through the night and the next day, and on into the following day. Eventually the landlord realized that Skene might be involved in what was happening and sent him a message with an apology. In reply the Laird said:

Gang hame, said Skene in yon box bed
Look for a muckle preen
An, when ye draw it frae the wa'
The dancin' will be deen

Needless to say the poor dancers were exhausted by their efforts.

As late as the third edition of Cumming's booklet in 1896 further tales were coming forward that he had not included. One concerned the Wizard Laird and his coachman returning from Aberdeen when the horses shied at a particular point in the road. The laird remarked that he feared some dreadful deed would happen at that spot. Next day, at the very spot, the body of a well-known local man was found, murdered and mutilated. On a more humorous note, the laird was going over the Cairn o' Mount road in the dark when a gust of wind carried off his hat. The coachman set off in search of it and returned a considerable time later with a battered article that the laird refused to recognize as his hat. "*Weel, weel, Laird,*" was the reply "*there's nae wile o' hats here.*" This statement was for many years proverbial in the area.

The Wizard Laird's greatest feat concerned the Loch of Skene and Gordon's poem only deals with this event.

There liv'd in the North, in the days o' yore
A Laird deep skilled in magic lore
In ae nicht's frost, by an oath he swore
He would drive o'er the Loch of Skene

This feat seems to have been prompted by a desire to outdo Skene's rival, the Tarland Wizard. Skene announced his intention in advance and settled on midnight on the last night of the year to carry out the feat, a lovely night with a full moon as it turned out. His favourite coachman, Kilgour, made the coach ready and the Laird's familiars offered support. Kilgour was instructed to head for the Hill of Fare at full gallop and not look behind on pain of being shot by the laird. Kilgour did so, and the coach made off across the loch at full tilt, though the sounds of demons and lashing water were heard behind it. Skene remained calm throughout but, just as the horses and front wheels of the coach alighted on the far bank, Kilgour's curiosity got the better of him and he looked round. There he saw a cloven-footed figure sitting beside the Wizard Laird. The hind wheels broke through the thin ice, two black dogs that were following being plunged into the icy, dark waters.

The carriage, though, made it safely across to waiting warlocks who had gathered to see the event. They proceeded to cheer and a party began in celebration. Even today the marks of his crossing can be seen when the loch freezes over, though others would say that they are simply the line of burns entering the loch! Another version of the story tells that when the eagle at Skene House falls then the Wizard Laird will come back up out of the loch – he having drowned when trying to cross it in his coach.

The ABERDEEN JOURNAL records the story that on his death bed the Wizard Laird heard a noise outside. He was told that a hoodie crow and a pigeon (a piet in Cumming's version) were fighting. The laird told his servant to watch and see who won because on the outcome his own fate depended. The pigeon won after a hard struggle and the crow flew off. On going back inside to inform the laird, the servant found him praying, he had already been told who had won. I suppose that this ending shows that, although the country folk were wary of their Wizard Laird, they nevertheless felt some affection for him and he was granted a happy ending.

The Wizard Laird was buried with his ancestors in Skene Churchyard. The grave later had its railings removed and the vault covered over for safety reasons. But even into the 1920s and 30s local children were told that no grass grew on it because it was the Wizard's grave.

John Smith: horse thief

Jock's Grave was marked on the 1st OS Map of 1865. It was positioned in a low lying field just north of the Gask Wood, about three fields west of Howcroft, and not far from the track which was the old road to Garlogie and Echt. The OS NAME BOOK recorded that by tradition it was the grave of Jock Smith, hanged in Aberdeen for horse stealing around 1760. It also records that when it was dug up around 1852 a wooden coffin was found containing human bones and the remains of a pair of shoes. In fact it is recorded in the BLACK KALENDAR OF ABERDEEN that John Smith was tried for the capital crime of horse-stealing on Saturday, 15 April 1749. He was found guilty, but was not sentenced until the following Tuesday, when he was condemned to be executed on Friday, 2 June.

In the time leading up to his execution John Smith had hoped that his sentence would be commuted to transportation. A few days before his execution he hatched a plan to escape dressed as a women and had managed to get hold of some women's clothes. Unfortunately he was discovered and put in irons. After that it is recorded that he became very penintent and "*seemed thankful for the visits of the ministers*". The ABERDEEN JOURNAL for 6 June 1749 wrote:

> "on the day of his execution he came down to the Laigh Council-house (Town House), dressed in decent grave linen, and from that to the gibbet, where, after the Ministers prayed with him, he prayed very fervently and sung part of the lxxxvi (86th) Psalm, then made a short speech to the spectators, and was turned off. His body was carried to the Gallowhills, and from there to the country to be buried."

Poor Jock Smith, his bones were disturbed on more than one occasion. Prior to 1852, in July 1829 a labourer was casting a ditch for a sunk fence on James Knowles of Kirkville's lands when he dug up a coffin. On investigating he found some vertebrae from the neck, but no head or even any teeth, an arm also appeared as well as a thigh bone, but only one of each and one shoe. Local people did appear to know that someone had been buried in the area and an old man of 82 was found who knew the full story. As a boy his father had dug up a body with one arm and leg near the spot. He had been told then that the man's friends had buried him there but other locals, uneasy about having a criminal buried near them, had informed a medical man from Aberdeen.

The body was to be disinterred for dissection but was found to have been too long in the ground for medical purposes. However, the doctor took away the head and an arm and leg, the rest of the body being re-interred. The old man in 1829 well remembered the dead man's name because it was used as a "*bug-bear*" or bogyman to threaten mischievous children. He still remembered in horror his feelings on being told that if he misbehaved, "*John Smith will tak' ye*'".

There is also a tradition that a coffin was being carried over Taposheetie

SOME SKENE WORTHIES – AND SOME PERHAPS NOT SO WORTHY!

in a snow storm. Not being able to continue, the coffin bearers just buried it at that spot. Mary McMurtrie recorded this story, but did not give the name of the deceased. However, given that Jock's Grave was not far from the Taposheetie track it seems it may indeed have been Jock. Presumably there was some kind of marker when the OS surveyed the area in 1865, but there doesn't seem to be anything to mark the spot now.

Malcolm Gillespie: the Gauger of Skene

Crombie Cottage stood on the Old Skene Road, roughly where Crombie Acres is now. For a time in the early 19th century it was home to Malcolm Gillespie, the infamous Gauger of Skene. Gillespie was a gauger or exciseman at a time when smuggling and illegal distilling were rife in the North-East.

Gillespie was born in Dunblane of respectable parents. He had hoped to serve in the army, but his family declined to buy him a commission and he worked as a recruiting agent for a short time then joined the Excise. He was stationed for six years at Collieston, from 1801, where he had many bruising encounters, including being tied up and left beside a hedge at night in the snow. Then he was at Stonehaven for a further five years. By his own account, he had been very successful at Collieston and Stonehaven, reducing the amount of smuggling to 'limited dimensions' in both places.

In 1812 at his own request he was moved to the Skene Ride, which covered a wild area between the Dee and the Don. Whereas in his previous areas he had dealt mainly with smuggling from the Continent via ships, his main concerns in the Skene Ride were highlanders bringing illicit spirits down to Aberdeen.

His first engagement worthy of note in the Skene area was the interception of a cart load of whisky being moved by four 'notorious delinquents' who fell upon him with bludgeons, mauling him unmercifully. To prevent the possibility of his prize (which turned out to be 80 gallons of whisky) escaping him, he pulled out a loaded pistol and wounded the horse. Some locals heard the shot and came to his assistance, leading to the smugglers being detained. Two of them were found guilty at trial and received sentences of several months' imprisonment.

Gillespie's courage got him into many a scrape. He followed one gang of 10 or 12 smugglers to the Hill of Fare and, with just two assistants, he seized 130 gallons of whisky. On 10 August 1815 he met the same gang at Auchronie with four horses laden with goods. On this occasion Gillespie was armed, but in a desperate struggle he received several severe blows to the body; his horse was nearly killed and one of its eyes was knocked out by a stone. Even when he was armed Gillespie seemed unwilling to use firearms, presumably preferring to take the men prisoner. His gun, if he carried one, was always a last resort.

After a similar escapade near Garlogie he decided to buy a dog, a bull terrier. The first action the dog saw was at Midmar Lodge when Gillespie tackled a gang led by someone called Greig. The dog was trained to attack the horse's nose, preventing the cargo being taken away. The poor dog was eventually killed by a random shot in an engagement near Parkhill, Dyce, on 1 August 1816.

Gillespie employed up to five assistants, but according to Gillespie they did not all possess the strong moral character of their employer. When they intercepted a couple of smuggling carts in the woods at Drum, with a "*strong hardened desperado named Hay*" employed to go along as a protecting bully, a severe engagement ensued, during which one of the excise force was shot in the groin by the accidental discharge of his own pistol. Hay's cheek was nearly severed from his face by a stroke from a sabre wielded by Gillespie himself, and another smuggler got an arm broken, which brought the fight to an end.

He risked his life on numerous occasions suffering several severe beatings, including being sliced in the chin with his own sword, and on another occasion being nearly strangled. In summing up his story, Gillespie said that he had received no fewer than 42 wounds on different parts of his body. By his own account he appeared to be triumphantly successful in his work. Even accepting an element of exaggeration, there was no doubt that he had a determined will and a coarse reckless courage.

Despite this loyal service to the Crown, Gillespie was to meet a very unfortunate end. He had obtained a 38-year lease of 20 acres from Alexander Crombie, the owner of the Leddach Estate. On this land he built a thatched house which he called Crombie Cottage (presumably after his landlord). He also built farm buildings and stabling for his horses. This would have been a substantial property since it housed several assistants as well as servants and his children. By his own account he spent £1,000 on improving the land and the building. He cited the length of the lease and the money he spent on improving the property as one of the reasons he got into debt.

The same year as he was tried (1827) he advertised the cottage for let for the remaining 31 years of the lease. The advertisement describes it as a desirable little farm that would "*answer well as a country residence,*" divided up by good stone dykes. It also says that a considerable sum is payable by the proprietor at the expiry of the lease as compensation for buildings erected by the tenant. So had Gillespie been able to stay for the full length of his lease he would have got back the money he spent on building Crombie Cottage. Unfortunately for him that never happened. THE BLACK KALENDAR OF ABERDEEN (published in 1840) as well as suggesting that his account of his exploits was exaggerated, blamed his extravagance for his financial problems.

Gillespie did have influential supporters, however. When he petitioned the Commissioners of Excise for remuneration he received letters of support from William Gordon, MP for Aberdeenshire; Viscount Arbuthnot; Sir Alexander Keith, Earl Marischal; and the Honourable General Duff. Alexander Smith, the Laird of Blackhills, also supported him and introduced him to the banking houses with which he dealt.

Gillespie was eventually charged with forging bills for payment in the names of local farmers; in the words of the ABERDEEN JOURNAL,

> "wickedly fraudulently, and feloniously forging or procuring to be forged the subscriptions of certain persons as drawers, acceptors, joint acceptors or indorsers of certain bills and notes for the payment of money; as also the fraudulently, wickedly and feloniously using and uttering the same as genuine."

Many of the farmers were from Skene parish and nearby, e.g., one bill was for £38 10s in the name of Joseph Low, Bogfairlie. Also named were John Lawson, Roadside of Lawsondale, Kinmundy; Alexander Troup of Borrowstown near Longcairn; John Troup, Backhill of Counteswells; Patrick Milne, East Cairnie; George Petrie, Gask End; and George Forbes, Auchronie. All the bills were presented for payment to banks to which Gillespie had been introduced by Alexander Smith. Smith's wife was later to say in court that he was 80 years old at this time, his memory was failing and Gillespie had taken advantage of him. One of the forged signatories, Joseph Low of Bogfairlie, could not even read or write. Usually Gillespie got the banks to send statements to him or to a rural post office where he intercepted them. However, Low's one went to Low himself and he got his son to read it. He then passed it to his landlord who contacted the authorities. Gillespie tried to get Low to say he had signed the bill when he was drunk, saying "*it wid save him fae the rope*".

Gillespie's trial was held in Aberdeen on 26th September 1827. His counsel suggested that he wouldn't get a fair trial in the North-East and wanted the trial moved to another part of the country. This was because, as we have already seen, large landowners supported Gillespie, as did distillers and the excise, but he was unpopular with ordinary people who preferred the price and the peat-reek of illegal whisky. This appeal was rejected.

During the trial Gillespie tried to put the blame on his assistant, George Skene Edwards, who was also charged. Gillespie even called an engraver from Edinburgh to testify that the forged signatures were in Edward's handwriting. Two of Gillespie's servants testified that they had seen Edwards forge the signatures, but their testimony was discredited since all the money went to Gillespie, and Edwards was hardly likely to have allowed witnesses to his forgeries. In fact, Edwards did do the actual forging, but it was at Gillespie's command.

The ABERDEEN JOURNAL for 3 October, 1827, reports the case saying that because of Gillespie's exploits and notoriety, the court was crowded to a degree never before witnessed. The paper had no sympathy for Gillespie or his servants and comments *"we had imagined it impossible, from among the people of this country, to have brought together into one dwelling an assemblage of men and women, so totally devoid of morale principle."* It did, however, blame Gillespie for moulding the others to his purpose.

The jury's verdict was due on Saturday, 29 September but one of the jurors, James Davidson of Kinmundy, a near neighbour of Gillespie, had left thinking he had been discharged. The court messenger was sent to Kinmundy to get him and he returned at two o'clock to be severely reprimanded by the court. Another neighbour of Gillespie, James Knowles of Kirkville, was the chancellor or foreman of the jury. Knowles read the verdict finding him guilty of *"forging and uttering"* and he was sentenced to be executed. Edwards was found guilty of forgery. His case was sent to the High Court of Justiciary where he pleaded guilty and was sentenced to banishment for life.

Gillespie had also been charged with insuring Crombie Cottage for £530 with one insurer, the £300 with another, and then getting two of his servants, George Brownie and Alexandrina Campbell, to set fire to it. Gillespie was not tried for this offence because of his death sentence, but the two servants were found guilty and sentenced to seven years transportation.

Gillespie was executed on 16 November. An immense crowd witnessed the execution, conducting themselves with remarkable quietness, according to the BLACK KALENDAR. He died almost immediately and his body was interred at Skene. The Aberdeen Journal reports that before he ascended the scaffold he declared his innocence and in his account of his life and trial he says he repaid the bills before they became due and that *"nobody ever lost a shilling by any of my bill transactions"*. The Journal, in summing up his life, states that he had been distinguished for his activity and prowess in the suppression of smuggling, but had overstepped the bounds of duty, seeking combat for its own sake. It also adds that he was affectionate and kind to his children. To our modern viewpoint it seems harsh in the extreme to execute someone for the crimes committed by Malcolm Gillespie.

Gillespie's unmarked grave is a little to the left of the church door, though originally it seems to have had a simple stone with M.G. on it. There had always been some speculation about Gillespie's grave and whether his body had been taken for dissection. G.M. Fraser was told that James McIntosh, tailor and merchant in the Kirktoun, but also sexton and gravedigger, had been digging a grave next to Gillespie's in 1895. He thought he would have a look at Gillespie's but found only stones along the grave, as if the coffin had been filled with stones. Did Gillespie's body end up at Marischal College?

In 1905 the death was recorded of an old woman of 84, Mary Begg of Letter, who could remember as a girl herding on the common pasturage (barefit and bare-leggit) and watching for Gillespie when the *"brewing pot was in operation"*. Old Miss Eliza Lawson lived in a cottage on the Old Skene Road in Westhill and is still remembered today. An account of Gillespie's trial and burial from the Evening Express of 30 July 1949 records that, then aged 89, she remembered her father telling her that as a youngster he had witnessed Gillespie's execution. His own father, John Lawson, farmer of Lawsondale Farm, had been one of the witnesses at Gillespie's trial, bringing the story down the generations.

John Bruce of the Fornet

Ae Martinmas term I gaed to the fair
To see the braw lasses and snuff the fresh air
I fee'd wi' a mannie to ca' his third pair
They ca' him Jock Bruce o' the Fornet
When I gaed hame to this man Jock Bruce
He lives owre at Skene in a blue-sclated hoose
Sae keen in the fair, but he looket sae douce
When I gaed hame to the Fornet

John Bruce of The Fornet

> Bruce was more than a typical North-East farmer of the time. He was a controversial figure, well known throughout the North-East and beyond, ever willing to air his views and tackle the establishment.

The ballad JOHN BRUCE O' THE FORNET, also sometimes called JOHN BRUCE O' THE CORNER, is not often sung today, though it is known to a few bothy ballad singers.

It is perhaps unusual in actually naming the farmer concerned, but thereafter follows a classic bothy ballad pattern by criticising the conditions of the place e.g. with the horses, "*For they're a' cripple nags at the Fornet*". It then goes through the workforce one by one – gaffer, foreman, baillie, loon, etc., even giving a description of Bruce's daughter:

> *To the kirk ilka Sunday she wears a fite veil*
> *And a yaird o' her goon ahin her does trail*
> *And her hair is tied up like my aul' horses tail*
> *To charm a the lads o' the Fornet*

Fornet is not far from Lyne of Skene and Skene House, and the 1871 Census confirms that John Bruce, then aged 54, did indeed farm South Fornet, a farm of 210 acres employing six labourers and a boy. This was a reasonable sized holding and John Bruce farmed it from 1870-1885 before retiring to live in Aberdeen. Further investigation reveals that Bruce was more than a typical North-East farmer of the time. He was a controversial figure, well known throughout the North-East and beyond, ever willing to air his views and tackle the establishment.

Born in 1816, he was brought up in Oldmeldrum where his father was a baker. He himself also began life as a baker, setting up in business in George Street, Aberdeen. Before that he lived for a few years in London.

In THE HUNGRY FORTIES: LIFE UNDER THE BREAD TAX, edited by Jane Unwin and published in 1904, he contributed a few pages describing the hardship he encountered in the 1830s as a journeyman baker in London.

> "Every night the bakers had to begin work at 10 o'clock at night, and when the dough was made had a mouthful of supper and then lay down on the bare boards, with a sack above us, for an hour until the dough was ready when we commenced and worked making bread and serving customers until seven or eight in the evening."

Worn out by this, John Bruce returned to Aberdeen. Eventually he gave up the bakery work and became a tenant on the farm at Lightnot, near Oldmeldrum, where he farmed 120 acres and employed three labourers and a boy. At the same time he also held the agency of the Town & County Bank at Oldmeldrum. Subsequently he moved to the larger farm of South Fornet in the parish of Skene.

According to his obituary in the ABERDEEN FREE PRESS:
> "he received comparatively little education in his early life, but by study and self-improvement he had come to be an exceedingly well-informed man, familiar with much that is best in literature, and keenly interested in the history of all great reforms."

All his life John Bruce seems to have been involved in radical politics – Chartism, Free Trade and later issues connected with rural affairs. Again in THE HUNGRY FORTIES, written when he was in his 88th year, he rails against the power and privilege of the aristocracy in his early days, when they were allowed free postage on their own and their friends letters and correspondence to the extent that *"their women-folk were sending their lap dogs and fancy birds through the post free, when after a while a new postmaster put an end to it"*. This anti-aristocracy line was echoed in 1887 when Bruce attracted controversy at the Mar Agricultural Association when he was chairman of the show dinner. Letters appeared criticising him for attacking *"in a very wanton and insolent way, absent members."* What happened was that the parish minister proposed a toast to the Proprietors of the District. Bruce replied that as there were no landlords present he would say a few words on their behalf. He began (to laughter):

> "how hath the mighty fallen. Time was, as you can all remember, when the chair at the Mar Agricultural Show Dinner was filled either by a lord, a laird, or a baronet, while today the gap has had to be filled by the poor, distressed individual now before you."

He then went on to criticise the lairds for not doing more to help the tenants in the depressed times on the land. A few had reduced rents but,

"there are not a few landlords who may be seen driving to and from the church on the Sabbath Day, who refuse to grant their suffering tenantry any redress whatever, and trust to landlord-made laws backing up their cruel behests."

It is reported that this was actually one of the most moderate speeches made by Mr Bruce! Nevertheless it was radical for the time, although the Mar Association voted 15-3 to approve Bruce's remarks.

John Bruce was an ardent campaigner and this included speeches, rallies and letter writing. Again his obituary says,

"that he was constantly in demand for meetings and conferences and was one of the leaders of the great rally held in the Music Hall at the formation of the Farmers Alliance."

Prior to taking the farm at Fornet Bruce had campaigned against the game laws, but it was when he moved to Fornet that he really became known for his views, being one of the founders of the Scottish Farmers' Alliance. For several years he was also a member of the Skene School Board and I have already discussed his influence on parish politics. He was also a member of the Skene Liberal Association.

A regular contributor to the ABERDEEN FREE PRESS, this continued even after he retired from farm life and moved to Great Western Road in Aberdeen. As I have already indicated his mind remained active until he was nearly 90, when he wrote of events in his early life. He also described the celebrations that took place in Aberdeen after the passing of the Reform Bill in 1832.

"On the morning of the great procession held in Aberdeen, extending one and a half miles in length, I and two other young men rose at 1 o'clock in the morning and travelled to Aberdeen from Oldmeldrum, and took our places in the procession."

This shows remarkable political awareness and enthusiasm given that he was in his teens. At the time of his diamond wedding anniversary in 1898 the press notice states that,

"Mr Bruce still takes an active interest in politics, and everything that tends to the improvement of the condition of the people."

SOME SKENE WORTHIES – AND SOME PERHAPS NOT SO WORTHY!

In 1900, when aged 84, he addressed a meeting of the Aberdeen Trades Council in the Trade Hall, Belmont Street, on the subject of farm and domestic servants. He criticised the fact that crofters had been driven from the land and a stampede to the town had begun.

> "The country is losing the cream of its population. So long as our industrial and commercial enterprises kept advancing, our political guides gave themselves little or no concern about the depopulation of the country districts."

His obituary in the ABERDEEN JOURNAL ends, *"Mr Bruce was a man of wide sympathies, and if occasionally he was somewhat impetuous in manner, he was warm-hearted and kindly, and up to the end of his life maintained those independent and original characteristics which made him so conspicuous a figure in the public life of the community."*

George Walker, local author, bookseller and baillie in the city of Aberdeen, was a cousin of Bruce, and gives a perhaps more personal and controversial view of the man known throughout the North-East at the time as 'Fornet'. In Walker's hand-written notebooks, held by Aberdeen Central Library, he writes:

> "I suppose no farmer in the country was better known for his quarrelsome temper than he was, in this respect he was his father's child. His penchant for writing letters he derived from my aunt, his mother. My cousin Johnie Bruce has always been a fikey, fidgety and knattery of men and therefore most difficult to deal with both in his business connections and in his family relations. What a blessing to all it is that he can blow off steam by a 'letter to the editor', but for that safety valve he must have exploded"!

This temper is perhaps echoed in the last verse of the ballad:

The hairst bein' dune, and the weather bein' bad
We were a' turned oot wi' a pick and a spad
He tore aff his jacket, the aul nickum gaed mad
Hurrah for John Bruce o' the Fornet

A recorded version of the song by Willie Kemp actually has the last line as – *"and he danced and he raved at the Fornet"*. Evidence of Bruce's temper came in January 1885 when his grieve at Fornet, George Thomson, took him to court over unfair dismissal. Thomson had been hired for the six month from Martinmas 1883 to Whitsunday 1884, but had been dismissed by Bruce and he was trying to recover his fee and other costs amounting to £30. He also alleged slander against Bruce.

337

Bruce alleged that Thomson had been abusive and disobedient when asked to do something. It was further alleged that Thomson had helped himself to his meal allowance without permission and that Bruce charged that this was theft. Thomson's orders to the men were also countermanded by Bruce and Thomson thereby felt he had been made a fool of and lost his temper. Various witnesses testified that Thomson had taunted Bruce by saying that Bruce was a member of the Farmers Alliance and was going about the country advocating improved dwellings for farm workers while his own, "*were not in a very creditable condition*". He was alleged to have called Bruce a "*trotting about bugger or body*."

It seems that both men had a temper and although the sheriff found for Bruce he did hint that Bruce had over-reacted, in particular over the charge of theft of meal since Thomson had taken it in front of the kitchenmaid and another servant. There was undeniably fault on both sides. The sheriff dismissed the charge of unfair dismissal but gave Thomson part of his fee up the time of his dismissal – £5. 1/. Bruce was awarded expenses. Maybe Thomson was the author of the ballad, though in truth there are probably plenty of other candidates who fell out with John Bruce.

There is no doubt that Bruce was a controversial and provocative figure. In 1887 a letter appeared in the press which stated "*Mr John Bruce, Fornet, 'does not labour under the disadvantage of ambiguity of speech.' That is how the* Gazette *puts it when it means to say that Fornet is a garrulous individual who thinks that landlords should be abolished. By the way isn't Fornet a bit of a landlord himself.*"

Walker himself goes on to say that "*He died in December 1905 with no friend or relative to tend him. His wife separated herself from him for a year or two, but rejoined him in his illness and died in his house some years before him. All his numerous children had either left him or were driven out when they got situations or were married. His bad temper seems to me to have been inherited from his father, his gift of facile expression from his mother, my aunt. Almost all the Moir family, but especially the females, had a bit of genius in them.*" In truth his family were well scattered, with four sons in America, one in France, a daughter in New Zealand and the rest of his family in Britain but none in the North East. No doubt Walker had his own family reasons for his views on John Bruce, there is also no doubt that Bruce does seem to have had a temper. Equally he did care about the conditions of working people, especially those on the land.

So there we have Jock Bruce of the Fornet. A fiery, independent, self-opinionated man, perhaps, but also one who cared about social issues and the condition of the rural areas. Like another strong willed farmer in *Sunset Song*, he was not afraid to criticise the lairds and landed aristocracy. He deserves to be remembered and not just in song.

James Elsmie Fowler

As we have already seen, four sons of Andrew Fowler of Brodiach became doctors. James was one of them. He inherited Brodiach from his father and he also became a well know doctor, educated first at the Grammar School then graduating MA from the University of Aberdeen in 1861, and MD, CH in 1865. That same year he bought Ardenville at number 17 Queen Street, Woodside. From there his practice stretched over a huge distance, from Woodside to Nigg, to Dyce and Blackburn. Initially he was a familiar figure travelling about on horseback. Later he changed to a gig and finally a car. He is remembered tying his horse to door handles or lampposts as he visited his patients. His stable was later converted to a garage. He must have been remembered at Brodiach as well since a small coloured drawing of him, done much later, was in the possession of the Alexander family of Brodiach. It now belongs to Bert Rennie, who married one of the Alexanders, and it shows

Sketch of Dr Fowler on his horse at Brodiach

Doctor Fowler on horseback visiting Brodiach. He presented two drinking troughs, one to Bucksburn and one to Kingswellls, so that his horse would never go thirsty.

James Fowler also pulled teeth and became known as 'Myrrh Jim' from his habit of prescribing tincture of myrrh for every dental ailment. He also served as a councillor for Woodside, then a separate burgh, from 1868, becoming chief magistrate from 1871-74. He recalled how in his early years at Woodside the sewage ran in open channels in the streets and the community was hardly ever free of typhoid, and epidemics of smallpox were frequent. He was very good at working with his hands, an organ being one of the things he made. When he left Queen Street the basement of the house was found to be full of splints and pieces of furniture, all beautifully made. He died in 1915 at the age of 76, having four years earlier retired to 73 Fountainhall Road. Thus he had served the community for almost fifty years. A nephew, Andrew Fowler, became an eminent surgeon in Aberdeen, thus continuing this incredible family of doctors from Skene.

James Fowler Abernethy

James Abernethy's stern looking face appears in numerous photographs from the Westhill Congregational Church. He was, though, an example of how a man from a humble background could educate himself and serve his community in many different ways. His father, David, came from Peterculter, and was a stone dyker as well as farming a small croft at Wellcroft, on the Leddach Estate near Elrick. His mother, Mary, came from Newhills. James would later rename the property Wellgrove and this gave its name to Wellgrove Road and Crescent in Westhill. By the age of 34 James was a book agent (on other occasions he described himself as a colporteur which is the same thing). James married relatively late, to one of the Lawsons of Lawsondale farm, and they had a daughter, Edith Eliza, still remembered by many today. While continuing to work his father's croft, James also gave a lifetime of service to his community in both paid and unpaid positions. He was at various times a member, chairman, and then clerk of the School Board, becoming involved in its controversies as we have already seen; he was Inspector of Poor; member of the Parish Council; Chairman of the Aberdeen District licensing court, and was made a Justice of the Peace in 1893. He was also President of the Skene Mutual Improvement Society and Secretary of the Temperance League. In addition, he was a member and office-bearer of the Westhill Congregational Church. He died in July 1926 in his eightieth year, a remarkable man.

John Emslie Skinner

Born in 1866, John Skinner was a farmer's son from Earlsfield in Kennethmont. The story is told that while working as a youngster on the farm he caught his sleeve in the threshing mill and badly wrenched his arm. He followed this up with an attempt at being a circus clown but ended up with the farm horse knocking out four of his teeth. This convinced his father that he would never make a farmer and it was decided he would become a doctor. He graduated in 1895 and spent a year as assistant to Skene man, James Elsmie Fowler at Woodside. From there he bought the Skene practice, renting Leddach House as had his predecessor. He then moved the practice to Westhill House, also rented, where he spent most of his career. Finally he bought Leddach House and moved the practice back there. Doctor D. G. Gordon from Ellon wrote about him that "*I never came across a practice where the people had more faith in their doctor. Everybody knew him from Kingswells to Kinellar and west to Sauchen. He had a wave for everyone he passed in his car. Everybody in the practice knew his bedroom. There was a gravel path outside, and to attract his attention in the night time, the caller threw small pebbles at his window. One black night when so aroused Skinner threw the sash up and asked what was wrong. 'It's the wife, doctor.' 'Whit's wrang with the wife?' 'She's yoky a' ower.' ' Gwa hame an' claw her a' ower,' replied Skinner.*"

An unknown author wrote a lengthy poem about the good doctor. One verse ran:

Ye wid see his aul' gig drawn up at the door
O' fermtoon, cottar or ha'
Fae the tap o' Midmar tae the skirts o' Kintore
For he tended the wints o' them a'

We have an early photograph of Skinner in his car, one of the first three in the parish. The car is an Albion of about 1907, according to Grampian Transport Museum which has a similar car. Mary McMurtrie remembers its large brass gig lamps and Doctor Skinner's warning that one should never exceed 20 miles per hour, anything faster was dangerous driving! Doctor Skinner wore a big, black coat with deep pockets. When you were ill he produced something from that pocket for you. It may not always have done you any good but it did make you feel better. A similar story is told of how a young doctor was temporarily standing in for Skinner. The young doctor was being shown all the bottles of medicine at the surgery. Asking about one particular bottle with no label he was told it was ADT – any damned thing!

Fellow physicians had noticed that John Skinner was growing thinner at each meeting of the Aberdeenshire Panel Committee of which he was chairman. When finally two friends visited him he to enquire about his health, he showed them the cancerous growth that he had discovered six months earlier. Realizing that it was inoperable he had carried on working, dying in January 1937, a week after their visit. He had served Skene for 39 years.

Doctor Skinner's funeral in 1937 was one of the largest seen in Skene for many years. At the service in Skene Parish Church, John McMurtrie spoke of the deep sense of loss felt by the whole community. "He was not only physician, friend and counsellor to many of us individually. He was all that; and many will remember him with gratitude for the ungrudging help – fruits of skill and long experience – rendered in time of need. But he was more than that, and as a community we mourn him today because he was one of the very bonds of our social life – one of those who links us together and make so much of whatever community spirit we have."

Mary McMurtrie

Mary McMurtrie was one of the most remarkable women to come out of the North East – talented in many different ways. Born in Skene in 1902, she was the daughter of the dominie, George Mitchell. In 1920 she went to Gray's School of Art, following her aunt Annie Mitchell who had gone there in 1911. Mary proved to be a very talented artist, so much so that both the Head of School and the Head of Drawing and Painting both sat for her, and her portraits of them survive. However, she was not to pursue a career in art as she married the minister at Skene, John McMurtrie, 23 years her senior. This led to her next career as minister's wife and then mother. She and her husband shared a love of gardening, particularly cultivating and preserving old species, and they developed a nursery at the manse garden. Mary never

SOME SKENE WORTHIES – AND SOME PERHAPS NOT SO WORTHY!

quite gave up art, though, and sketched the local area. This may have helped develop her love of the history of the area, something she also share with her husband, and which she pursued later in life. In some of her sketches Mary recorded buildings and views that were being changed by modern developments, an example being the bowie lum cottages at Skene. Mary also found time to encourage the young orphanage girl, Jessie Kesson, as we have seen already.

The death of John McMurtrie in 1949 meant that Mary had to leave Skene and the manse. She lived in Aberdeen for a number of years, writing the account for Skene Parish in the third STATISTICAL ACCOUNT FOR SCOTLAND. She followed this up writing articles on the Old Skene Road. The information she gathered has proved indispensible for this present work as have Mary's own accounts of her own life-time. We have already seen in her memories of Sundays in Skene at the beginning of the century, that she had a phenomenal memory for detail. This is something I encountered myself when I sent her several large photographs of the staff and students at Gray's School of Art in the early 1920s. Despite being around 100 years old she could put a name to nearly all the faces from 80 years earlier.

In 1960 Mary bought Balbithan House near Kintore. She set about restoring the 16th century property and also created a nursery and garden there. She also began writing about and illustrating plants. One of her first books was Wild Flowers of the Algarve, a place she first visited with her friend and fellow writer and gardener, Nan Patullo. She was also asked to illustrate THE WILD FLOWER GARDEN by Roy Genders. Then in 1982 came her first major work – SCOTTISH WILD FLOWERS – a sumptuous leather bound work produced by Heritage Press at Towie Barclay Castle. Mary continued writing and illustrating right up to her death in November 2003. Since her late 90s she had been Britain's oldest working artist. I saw one of her original paintings for sale in an Aberdeen antique shop a few years ago and it described her as the legendary Mary McMurtrie. I wonder what she would have made of that. Artist, gardener, writer and historian – most of us would be glad to have one of those abilities.

The growth of Westhill and the era of oil

The Westhill Garden Suburb

Mary McMurtrie, writing in the mid-1950s, commented that:

> "...within the span of a generation the way of life has changed greatly: two world wars have shaken the parish out of its rut. In the past it was more self-centred and more self-supporting; families lived on from generation to generation in the same district, often at the same farms, and intermarried to such an extent that a complicated network of kinship grew up. Few people left, and few came into the parish; the latter were for long regarded as strangers. Now, almost overnight, all is different; people come and go more freely, amusements are more abundant and varied, and work has been lightened by modern invention. Young people are tempted forth from home for pleasure and for work. Lonely old folk – and their number is always increasing – whose desire always is to stay on in their own homes, find life difficult even when neighbours are kindly and ready to help. In spite of these changes the country way of life goes on, little altered in its essentials. Now, as in the past, there are those who work on the land and are happy there."

This was written well before the building of Westhill. There is no doubt that the 20th century did bring many changes to Skene Parish, as it did to most rural parishes. The building of Westhill would bring even more significant changes, both good and bad.

It is sometimes said that the town of Westhill came about because of the oil industry that came to Aberdeen in the 1970s. While it may be true that Westhill, as we know it today, was the product of the oil industry, the plan for a garden suburb on the old Westhill Estate pre-dated oil by some years and it was intended from the beginning to be a sizeable town. In 1964 Cuthbert Graham wrote *"it looked until this proposal came along like a bolt from the blue, as if Skene would stay in the purely agricultural country close in distance, yet remote in spirit and character from the growing suburban belt surrounding the city. To anyone who knows the delectable parish on its southward-facing slopes above the lovely Loch of Skene the thought of any changes must at least induce a pang."*

The proposal that seemed to startle the members of the Planning Committee of Aberdeen County Council came from solicitor Ronald Fraser Dean, factor for the estate of Westhill, still belonging to the Farquhar Family in the shape of the Trustees of Mrs Jane Farquhar. It had been submitted in September 1963 but it was not the only proposal for building in Skene parish. Around the same time, according to the unsuccessful Progressive Party candidate in the St Nicholas Ward in Aberdeen, the Town Council was also considering building housing for 2000 people on land they owned at Carnie. Nothing came of this latter proposal akthough it did re-appear in 1981/82 and led to a bitter dispute between the City and the then Gordon District that was only settled by a Scottish Office Inquiry. Dean's proposal did have some support on the County Council and a joint sub-committee visited the site and referred problems with water and drainage back to him. Dean set up a company, Westhill Developments (Aberdeen) Ltd to oversee the development and he had the backing of an un-named private development company. They would take the development forward and Dean had also engaged Professor Tom Findlay Lyon of Strathclyde University to draw up the overall plan. Even as early as 1965 it was planned that Westhill would have 7,000-8,000 people with new schools, shops, a church, public hall and other facilities. The site was of approximately 550 acres and the projected cost £10,000,000, a huge amount at that time. Having won approval from the County Council, Scottish Development Department and the Secretary of State for Scotland, Dean and his backers were ready to buy the Westhill Estate from the Trustees.

Dean's backers, later named as the Commercial Union Assurance Co. Ltd., pulled out in 1965, according to Dean because of *"a wholly unexpected adverse report and valuation."* You have to wonder if they later regretted this move given the eventual success of Westhill. However, Dean turned to a friend for

THE GROWTH OF WESTHILL AND THE ERA OF OIL

Westhill under construction

advice, someone he had had dealings with in the past. This was Sidney Denman, Managing Director of Ashdale Land and Property Company. Denman was enthusiastic about the plan and in 1969 persuaded his board to back it and for Ashdale to become the developers for the whole Westhill project. By this time a small development had already started at Westhill with Dean having sold some land to Persley Development Co. Ltd., at the request of Aberdeen County Council. They therefore built the first house of the new Westhill and what became No. 4 Arnhall Crescent was officially opened on 1st October 1968. It was perhaps fitting that Arnhall Crescent became the first new street in Westhill as it was sited on the line of the old road into Westhill. One of the first householders was Jens Peterson, one of two Danes who came to play for Aberdeen Football Club in the late 1960s.

Right from the start Westhill was to be a well designed community. Professor Lyon was

The first house, No. 4 Arnhall Crescent, was officially opened on 1st October 1968. It was perhaps fitting that Arnhall Crescent became the first new street in Westhill as it was sited on the line of the old road.

associated with Messrs Thomas Cordiner, Cunningham and Partners, architects (later Cunningham Glass) and they would be the planners of the new town. They established an office at Westhill House with W.G. (Liam) Findlay as their project architect. Westhill House had been run as a guest house and Mr and Mrs Alexander, the tenants, agreed to live on rent free and act as caretakers. Ronald Dean and the architects would each have an office in the building. Liam Findlay became a key figure in the development of Westhill and underlined his commitment to the new town by building himself a house in Westhill, half way up the brae beside Wester Kinmundy farmhouse. Rather than have rows of identical houses Westhill was to have smaller clusters of similar styled houses and on a density of six or eight per acre rather than the more normal ten or twelve. Landscaping between the clusters was to be crucial as it was all over Westhill. A park or ornamental garden was created to the south between the town and the A944. This incorporated elements of the Moss of Arnhall, an important plant and wildlife area, once

Aerial view of Westhill

also known as the Moss of Blackhills, where peat had once been cast. The park itself was planned with the assistance of Phillipa Rakusen, Chair of the Northern Horticultural Society, Leeds, and it was named after Sidney Denman.

Development happened fairly quickly once Ashdale finalised the purchase of the Westhill Estate in October 1969. Various builders were involved – Wimpey, Barratt, Kildonan, French etc, as well as Ashdale themselves and Persley. Ashdale used timber frame housing from Guildway Houses and one small local builder successfully tendered for the assembly of these houses. Stewart Milne Construction Ltd. had bought the old Wellgrove Croft, once home to James Abernethy, in 1975 as a base for their operations. It was 15 acres and the cattle shed became a workshop and the neep shed a plant base. The building of Westhill gave them an opportunity to be involved and they built their first ever house in 1977 just across the road, the street being named after the original croft – Wellgrove Crescent. They went on to become a major company, perhaps the first major employer in Westhill, where their headquarters are still located today.

Key dates in the development of Westhill*

1 Sep. 1963	First approach of Aberdeen County Council
1 Feb. 1965	Letter to Ronald Dean from County Clerk intimating approval in principle to development of the whole estate
29 Jul. 1966	First planning permission obtained
1 Oct. 1968	First house opened, built by Persley Development Co. Ltd.
31 Oct. 1969	Ashdale acquired all rights from the Trustees of Mrs Jane Farquhar and Westhill Developments (Aberdeen) Ltd. to purchase Westhill Estate
12 Dec. 1972	Formation of Westhill and District Residents Association
27 Jan. 1973	East-west spine road re-aligned as Old Skene Road and north-south road re-aligned as Westhill Drive
29 Sep. 1973	Original Ashdale Hall officially opened by Mr Denman
1973	Temporary bank and health clinic established at the edge of Denman Park
21 Nov. 1974	Westhill Primary School opened
1975-1977	S.S.H.A. houses built
25 Feb. 1976	Westhill Inn opened by Maitland Mackie

1976-1979	Barratts built their houses
18 Oct. 1976	Golf Course completed. It was designed by Charles Lawrie of Cotton (C.K.) Pennink Lawrie and Partners. Westhill Golf Club was formed on 5th October 1977
Oct. 1977	Crombie Primary school opened
1978-1979	Kildonnan built their houses, first show house opened on 1st December 1977
17 Sep. 1979	Official opening of Denman Gardens
Aug. 1979	Westhill Academy opened
7 Nov. 1981	Dedication of Trinity Church
Oct. 1981	Elrick Primary School opened
Mar. 1983	Library opened in what had been a Council Housing Department rent office. Prior to that the library had been housed in the old Westhill School. A brand new library was built on to in 2011

Taken from a list produced by Ronald Dean

The new church

The continuing growth of Westhill meant that new churches were needed to minister to the varying communities in the town. Initially the Church of Scotland and the Scottish Episcopal Church held joint services twice a month in Westhill Primary School. By 1976 the Congregational Board of the Parish Church decided that a new church was necessary and approached the developers, The Ashdale Land and Development Company. Ashdale offered a site but on the condition that it was interdenominational. Over the next few years discussions took place with the Roman Catholic and Scottish Episcopalian congregations and, in 1978, a questionnaire was sent to every household in Westhill. The result was a yes to a new shared church in the town. A leasing agreement was drawn up between the three churches and work began on the new church in May 1981. Chancel furniture was offered from the former Trinity Church in Aberdeen. This generous offer was accepted and, as a result, it was agreed to name the new church 'Trinity' Church. The service of dedication was held on the 7 November 1981, when Professor Robin Barbour, former Moderator of the General Assembly of the Church of Scotland, preached. Also present in the procession were The Reverend Iain U. Thomson, Minister of Skene Parish Church; The Very Reverend Charles C. McGregor, Administrator of St Mary's Cathedral,

Aberdeen; the Reverend Canon Kenneth D. Gordon, Rector of St Devenick's Church, Bieldside; the Right Reverend Frederick C. Darwent, Bishop of Aberdeen and Orkney; the Reverend Roderick Macdonald, Clerk to the Presbytery of Gordon; the Reverend John Logie, Moderator of the Presbytery of Gordon.

The academy

The organization and running of the new academy at Westhill was to be controversial, and in some ways it still is today. Under its rector, Peter Gibson, it was to be a community school, with facilities and premises shared with the public. Children were to be taught with whole blocks of time allocated to a subject, usually a morning or afternoon. There was to be no corporal punishment, this well before it was banned throughout Scotland, and there was a laissez faire attitude to the wearing of a school uniform. The latter is still controversial among some in the community today. Periodically pupils have been allowed to vote on the issue.

Shops

The first new shop to serve Westhill was built beside the earliest of the houses. It was a VG store and it operated for many years. It is now a nursery. Just opposite was the old Berriedale shop which dated back to the end of the 19th century. From 1959 Berriedale was run by the Kinghorn Family, mainly as a newsagent, with a post office added in 1976. Ashdale developed the main shopping centre in various phases. The first phase with eight shops and offices above was completed in 1980, though the first shop, a florist/greengrocer, had actually opened just before Christmas 1979. What is now the Co-operative was originally a Mace and at the other end the main supermarket has been a Safeway, Norco, Morrisons and now Marks & Spencers.

The VG shop at Westhill

The development of a community idea

From the first proposal Westhill was described variously as taking overspill from Aberdeen, as a satellite town, as a dormitory town. Liam Findlay's view was that *"Westhill would not be an estate of standard-style houses acting purely as a dormitory suburb for Aberdeen. It would, instead, be a self-contained township with as wide a variety of housing designs as possible.*" The architects, developers and landscapers did their bit, then, to make Westhill an attractive place to stay but it would take much more to develop the idea of a community separate from, albeit closely linked to, Aberdeen.

Westhill residents today live in a well-rounded, attractively laid out community, with well established educational facilities, medical facilities, shopping facilities, leisure and social facilities, employment opportunities, and a dual carriage-way into Aberdeen. It was not always like that and, looking back, early residents must feel as though they were pioneers in the way they arrived in a community with none of these. Contrary to Liam Finday and Ronald Dean's dream, Westhill was very much a dormitory suburb of Aberdeen in its early days and was certainly looked on as that by the City.

Early press coverage of the new town highlighted its short-comings. One such from 1973 carried a story about the 9–5 widows, women whose husbands left for work after breakfast and were not seen again until night time. In addition, with the growth of oil, many of their husbands went offshore, adding to the problem. For these women there was literally nowhere to meet other than outside the then two shops. The developers' plans did include the facilities that a new community would need, but there is a real sense in which Westhill residents, along with long serving Regional and District councillors such as Ian Walker, Audrey Findlay and Maitland Livingstone, had to fight for their community.

Crucial to this was the early formation of a Residents Association, something that Ronald Dean supported. The Westhill and District Residents' Association was formed early on, in December 1972, with sixty residents attending the inaugural meeting. They elected David Barringer of Kinmundy Drive as interim chairman and, as early as January the following year, had issued the very first Bulletin. That Bulletin continues today, a much more glossy, professional publication, but fulfilling the same role of informing the population about their community. The Residents' Association has had its ups and downs, even with the growth of the town apathy arose from time to time and, on several occasions, it looked as though the Association might fold. However it continues today, having become the Westhill and Elrick Community Council in 2008, and it has very much been the focus of the community's campaigns for better services, and provides information via its website as well as the Bulletin.

The Gala began in September 1978, organized by various groups under the auspices of the Westhill Community Club, aiming to provide a family day of fun, with a Friday night disco where the Gala Princess was chosen, and a Gala Dance on the Saturday. The following year it moved to June and was subsequently organised by the Round Table and other organizations. Today it is attended by thousands.

I do not really have space to chronicle every battle for improved facilities fought by the residents over the years; that would probably require a separate publication. However, several campaigns were key, I feel, and I would highlight two that were important because they involved widespread action by the whole community.

The campaign for a swimming pool

This began around 1988 and it did win support and backing from Gordon District Council, through the Gordon District Council Leisure Projects Trust There were, though, arguments over the amount of the Trust's budget that was going into this one project. It was hoped that Grampian Regional Council might also make a contribution. Crucial to the campaign, though, was that the community had to raise a significant portion of the money to really show how much it meant to them. One thousand, two hundred people had already signed a petition in favour of the pool and over 300 people turned up at a public meeting in June 1988 to hear that, of the projected cost of £500,000, the community would have to raise between £50,000 and £100,000.

The Westhill & District Swimming Pool Association was formed with Ian Walker as its chairman. One of their first acts was to request a donation of £25 from every one of Westhill's 2,500 households. Thereafter the whole community rallied to the cause and all kinds of fund raising activities were carried out over the next two or three years – fashion shows, netball events, swimathons (in Hazlehead pool), Fun with Flowers evenings, funds from that years Gala, and many more.

By the time work began on the swimming pool in February 1991 the cost of the pool had risen to around £1.7 million. However, the Westhill community, including the surrounding area, had themselves raised £57,000, a huge achievement. The pool was to be Scotland's first pool with a moveable floor, designed in consultation with Hamilton Bland, swimming coach and television commentator. The pool opened to the public on the 22 February, 1993, a dream realized by the councillor and Westhill Primary headmaster,

Ian Walker. Later that year the pool was officially opened by Princess Anne, at the same time she unveiled a plaque at the new Ashdale Hall.

The *Don't Move Westhill* campaign

The same year that the community was celebrating their new pool they were hit by a bombshell from Scottish Secretary, Ian Lang. Under proposals that he brought forward to re-organise Scottish local government, Westhill was to be moved from Gordon District, or rather the proposed new Aberdeenshire unitary authority, and was to become part of the City of Aberdeen. This brought a furious reaction from the community and from politicians in the North East. It also galvanized residents to do something about the proposal and to fight it. The news broke during the month of July 1993, a time when many were away or on holiday, including Councillors Ian Walker and Maitland Livingstone.

The issue provoked tremendous ill feeling with councillors falling out, Aberdeen South Tory MP, Raymond Robertson and city Tory leader, Mike Hastie coming in for particular criticism. City Lord Provost, Jim Wyness, reacted strongly, at a public meeting in Westhill, to what he felt was adverse criticism of the city, despite which he supported Westhill's democratic right to choose where it ended up. There were even accusations that the move was intended to transfer what was thought to be a large of number of Conservative supporting voters into the city for political reasons. If so, the hostility towards the Conservatives would have meant that the plan backfired. One Gordon District councillor appeared to bemoan the money spent, more or less that same year, providing Westhill with the swimming pool, new town hall, and improved sports facilities at Lawsondale, only for the facilities to possibly be lost to the city. Residents of the city also wrote to the press citicising Westhillers who, they said, wanted to work in the city and use its facilities, but were unwilling to pay for them. This, of course, is an issue that has arisen in recent times as well.

The residents of Westhill themselves formed a committee comprising George Morrison, Alan Findlay, Sophie Copland, and Hugh Munro, and they set about organizing a huge petition in favourev of keeping Westhill out of the city. There was a feeling among some that there was too much criticising Aberdeen, rather than giving more positive reasons for staying in a rural authority. This is what antagonized many Aberdonians. Westhill had, by that time, done well out of Gordon District and Grampian Region. They,

THE GROWTH OF WESTHILL AND THE ERA OF OIL

it was argued, were more sensitive to the needs of Westhill as a semi-rural location; it was not simply that Westhillers wanted the lower rates of Aberdeenshire. There were real fears that by joining Aberdeen, the City would grow to engulf the community. Moreover, Westhill had established strong links with surrounding communities in Skene Parish, this being something that the Kirk Session argued.

Eventually MPs representing all the major parties did support the campaign – Malcolm Bruce, George Kynoch, Bob Hughes and Alex Salmond, though I think it is fair to say that it was the Liberals who led the political side of the campaign. The door to door efforts of the Don't Move Westhill campaigners eventually resulted in 98 percent of the population signing the petition, with only 77 refusing. By February the following year the pressure had paid off and the Scottish Standing Committee finally agreed that Westhill would become part of the new Aberdeenshire Council.

These are two examples of the community pulling together for a cause; there are many others I could have highlighted. They were all important in creating the separate identity of Westhill, of making it a community rather than simply a dormitory suburb of Aberdeen. Westhill was a young community together. It has had its ups and downs, some of the latter mirroring the fortunes of the oil and gas industry. However, it developed and it grew, and it has become a mature community together. It is now over 40 years old and very much part of the history of Skene Parish.

APPENDIX

Place-names

I make no claims to be an expert on place-names, or on the Gaelic or Pictish languages from which many of them derive. The problem in trying to identify the original Celtic meanings of places around Aberdeen is that over time they have become Scotticised. It is much easier further west in the mountainous areas of Aberdeenshire to see the Celtic origins of place-names.

This list is compiled from the following sources with some of my own thoughts together with details of early mentions of a place with its variants.

ALEXANDER, William M.   THE PLACE-NAMES OF ABERDEENSHIRE
MACDONALD, James   PLACE-NAMES OF WEST ABERDEENSHIRe
MILNE, James   CELTIC PLACE-NAMES IN ABERDEENSHIRE

Affloch Both Macdonald (*Ach'*) and Milne (*Achadh*) give a derivation using field, but Milne also has place or field. He gives it as wet place or field from *fliuch* – wet, whereas Macdonald has it as field of the loch. Alexander broadly agrees with Macdonald as loch-field.

Arnhall Fermtoun where alders grew, which Milne derives from the prefix *fhearna* with the fh silent.

Auchinclech Listed as Auchincloich in the REGISTER OF THE GREAT SEAL for 1506. Milne has this as the same as Auchincleith i.e. field of concealment (*cleith*). Macdonald has these as two separate names and has Auchinclech as field of stone or stone-field. Alexander agrees with this and this does seem more likely when we consider that the huge *Cloch More* (big stone) stands near it, a name still used for a nearby house. Although the Cloch More is nearer to Concraig, it seems likely that Auchinclech was the original name of the whole area, later split into Concraig and Auchinclech. The OS Name Book in 1864 says that a small clachan or hamlet once stood beside the Cloch More, so maybe this was the original fermtoun of Auchinclech recorded in the Poll Tax Book of 1696. The Dean of Guild documents from 1788 refer to *Cloch More* as a pendicle suggesting that there was some kind of fermtoun or community.

Balmuir Both Milne and Macdonald agree that this is from *baile mor* – big toun, possibly because of its proximity to the manor house (Skene House).

Bervie Milne has this as from *beur* top end, and *chuidh* cattle fold. Thus end of cattle fold. Alexander sees it as a Gaelic stream name – as in Inverbervie. Certainly it does stand near where the Corskie and Bogentory Burns meet.

Birsack Register of the Great Seal has *Birsakismylne* in 1612. In 1665 it appears as *Berlackmiln*. It also appears as *Brissock*. Milne derives it from *Barr* point and *samhach* quiet or pleasant, therefore pleasant point. Less convincingly Macdonald sees it as a diminutive personal name because an early version of it is spelt *Birsakey*. A third variation is given by Alexander who dervices it from *preasach* – a bushy place.

Bluepark It has been suggested that this comes from flax being grown here, but Milne gives Bluefield as meaning the field that gives a lot of milk, from *bliochd* – milk. However, some of the land at Bluepark is described as thin ground in the Skene Estate rentals, suggesting it would not be very productive for cattle.

Bogendinny Macdonald has this as *Bog an t-sionnaich* – fox's bog. Milne prefers Bog of the little hill, from *dunain* – little hill.

Bogentory Both Macdonald and Alexander seem to agree on this one as bog of the little hill or height.

Bothomfauld Macdonald gives this as the fold at the bottom of lower part of the valley. Alexander agrees with this. Milne does not have it in his book but he does have Boddomend which he derives as from *Both* – house (bothy) and *damhan* – oxen. So Bothomfauld could be house in the fold. It is Boddomfawld in the 1696 Poll Tax Book. It does also appear as Boddemford.

Broadshade Macdonald sees this as from *Shed* – a portion e.g. of land.

PLACE-NAMES

Milne agrees on portion or division of land and suggests broad extent of gently sloping land, which would seem to be accurate at any rate.

Broadstraik THE LEDDACH LAND DISPOSITION of 1790 mentions the houses of Straik on the Old Skene Road, so Straik would probably have to stand on its own in terms of meaning. Macdonald has this as *Straik* – a tract or stretch of land. Milne has *Strioch* – stripe, and *Braid* – hill (similar to Macdonald's *braigh*). This would make sense as the ground does rise up from behind where Straik was, up towards the Hill of Keir.

Broadwater Macdonald suggests that this came from the Leuchar Burn spreading out more than it does today, post land drainage.

Brodiach Milne has it as Broad howe – from *Iochd* – howe. Macdonald has it as *Braigh* – brae, and *Dabhach* or *dauch* – a measure of land as in Leddach.

Burrowley Has also been written as *Burrel*-lea and *Burrely*. None of the three authors mention it but James Anderson in his GENERAL VIEW OF AGRICULTURE from 1794 says the following – *"Burrel-fields denotes a waste that has in part been ploughed up into narrow ridges with broad baulkes between so as to be divided into stripes; sometimes the waste being twice the breadth of the ridge. This is very common on the edge of wide moors."* The SCOTS DICTIONARY gives a similar definition.

Carnie/Cairnie Macdonald suggests that this come from *Cairneach* or *Carnach* – place of stones or cairns. Milne has it coming from *Carnach* – place abounding in hills. While the latter might be true of the parish of Cairnie near Huntly, it is not really true of Skene's Carnie, but there are plenty of cairns nearby. As early as the 13th century it was called Cardany and then as Cardeney. Interestingly, Milne has Cardno as seat of judgement with a derivation from *Cathair* – seat and *Dain* – judgement, and then he suggests that the *ai* and *n* have become transposed and the *ai* had become an *o*. This derivation could apply to our Cardany without so much jumping around. Alexander goes back to the old spelling and derives it from *carden* – a wood.

Cloch More Big stone *(Cloch Mhor)*. The huge boulder in a field across the road from Concraig. There was said to have been a clachan here at one time (see Auchinclech). One of the 1788 Dean of Guild documents mentions Clockmore as a pendicle of Auchinclech, suggesting it was a separate holding (see also under Auchinclech).

Concraig Macdonald thinks it might be a corruption of *Ceann Creige* –

Craighead. Milne suggests Hill of small animals with Con as plural of Cu small quadruped, such as rabbit, dog or squirrel. The name is found elsewhere in Scotland, but I have not found any early occurrences in Skene. Alexander sees it as a group of craigs or crags. The earliest mention I have found of it was when part of Auchinclech was broken off to make a separate estate in the 18th century. So it may be that the meaning does not relate to the location here, it was simply given that name when it became an estate.

Craigiedarg Both agree that this is red crag or hill, though how this relates to the area is unclear. It is mentioned in the REGISTER OF THE GREAT SEAL in 1552.

Craigston Macdonald lists the name, but gives no derivation. Milne has a fermtoun named after its owner (Craig) or the fermtoun beside a hill or creag which would seem much more likely given its location.

Elrick Common throughout Aberdeenshire and elsewhere in Scotland. Macdonald quotes another writer who derives it from *iolair*, an eagle, but he says that this would not apply to most of the Aberdeenshire occurrences. Milne has the slope of a rocky hill from *ruigh* – slope near the base of a hill, and *aill* – rock. This would make sense as we have already seen that there are no early occurrences of it as a place name, but that the LEDDACH LAND DISPOSITION of 1790 mentions the Earlick Stone and the Earlick Butts. The 1841 Census mentions Hill of Elrick. So a rocky place at the base of a hill would seem reasonable given the Earlick Stone and the huge dykes around it testify to the rocky nature of the ground.

Fiddie Milne derives it from *chuidan* – a small fold, with the *ch* becoming *ph* equivalent to *f*. Macdonald suggests *feadan* – a small streamlet. The REGISTER OF THE GREAT SEAL for 1598 has Fethnabradach or Feddiebraydiach, which would translate as the Burn of Brodiach which does run nearby. It is also recorded as Feddie and Foddes. Alexander agrees that it comes from *feadan*.

Fornet Fornatht or Fornacht is recorded in the REGISTER OF THE GREAT SEAL for 1506. In 1665 it is Fornet or Fuirdtoun. Quite often it is called The Fornet of Skene. Macdonald quotes another writer as giving bare hill and Alexander says that this is what it means in Ireland. Milne has land in front of a burn from *for* – in front of and *net* – a burn. There is a Forneth near Dunkeld.

PLACE-NAMES

Garlogie Garlogy is recorded in the original disputes between the Skene Family and the Keiths in 1457. Carlogy is recorded in the REGISTER OF THE GREAT SEAL for 1525. Macdonald sees the latter as correct and derives it from *Car logain* – the bend of the little hollow. Alexander thinks this may be correct. Milne has it as *Garbh lagan* – rough howe or hollow.

Gask The bog of Gask is recorded in a charter from David II to Alexander Burnard (Burnett) in 1358. Macdonald derives it from a nook, gusset or hollow, with the latter being applicable to Skene. Milne derives it *rom gasg* – a point or long narrow tail of land, as in Balnagask. Alexander agrees on the tail, but here a tail of higher land projecting over lower ground, which might seem appropriate.

Gullymoss Macdonald gives no meaning for this name. Milne has it meaning hill of dirtiness from *coille* (hill) and *moisaiche* (dirtiness).

Inverord This would be the mouth or infall of the Ord Burn. See also Myrieloup.

Keir From *cathair* a stone fort or round stone circle, similar to *caer* in Wales and *cahir* in Ireland. For some reason Milne prefers *cir* a crest, comb or ridge, but I think the former is generally accepted.

Kinmundy Recorded in a 1554 charter as Hill of Kynmondy. From *ceann* (head) and *monaidh* (hill or moor), therefore head of the hill (Milne) or head of the moor or muirhead/muirend, which Macdonald prefers.

Latch As noted earlier, there was a Latch of Milbuie and a Latch of Carnie. There is agreement that this comes from a mire or bog, a Scots word.

Leddach There is general agreement from Macdonald and Milne, as well as other writers, that this comes from *leth* –half, and *davach* or *dabhoich* – a measure of land. Earliest mention is as Ledache of Skeyn from 1456. Other early versions are Leyddacht, Leddauch, Liddoke and Liddach. Alexander is not convinced and suggests that if it comes from the same word as Lettach then it might derive from *leth-taobh* – half side e.g., of a valley.

Letter All three agree on *leiter* – a hillside. Mentioned in the COURT BOOK OF BARONY in 1627, it is a large fermtoun in the POLL TAX BOOK of 1696.

Leuchar Milne has it from *luachar* – rushes. It is recorded as the water of Locher in the 1358 charter by David II to Alexander Burnard (Burnett).

Lochee Alexander says this is Scotch for loch-eye.

Lyne From *lean* or *loinn* – a meadow or level grassy place. Strangely, though, Macdonald seems to take it literally from a line or straight row of houses, though he gives *lian* – the meadow for the Lyne in the neighbouring parish.

Millbuie This is one of the four lands of Skene referred to in the dispute with the Keith Family in 1456 when it is given as Moylboy. It also appears as Mulboy, Milboy, Milbowie, and Mylnbowie. All three writers agree that it comes from *meall buidhe* – yellow hill.

Myrieloup The farm of Inverord is also called Myrie Loup on a plan of 1832 with the Myrie Loup moss just to the north. The name is also used in the Dean of Guild land document. It does not seem to appear in the first O.S. map, though. It may simply come from *mire* – moss or a bog, with *loup* – jump.

Ord All three writers dervive this from a hill *uird*, with Macdonald further adding that it is a round hill like a hammer or mallet. Alexander also says a round hill.

Rogiehill This is a real mystery.and it has also been written as Rodgerhill and Rogershall. Had there not been early occurrences I might have been tempted to say that the O.S. map makers simply translated the local Rogie into Rodger. However, Rodgerhill appears in the REGISTER OF THE PRIVY COUNCIL for 1636. THE GREAT SEAL for 1653 has Kinrodger. Neither Milne nor Macdonald give a definition for it, but elsewhere Milne has ruigh as the slope of the hill in his definition for Rogerseat and Roger's Well. This would mean that Kinrodger would mean the head of the slope which is ideal for Rogiehill. Alexander suggests that Rogie is simply a form of Roger, if so one would like to know who Roger was.

Sclattie Alexander has this as coming from *sleibhtean* – a moor.

Skene Milne has a simple definition for this – *eas* a burn and *cuithan* a small fold, the *th* being silent. Thus – burn at the small fold. Macdonald equates it with *sgian*, a diminutive of *sgitheach* thorn or hawthorn, variations of this being found elsewhere in Scotland. Alexander says that it has a similar sound in Gaelic to Scone and therefore, in the North-East it would be *skeen*, in Middle Scots *skoon*.

Slack of Larg Milne and Alexander see this as coming from *sloc* – a hollow between two heights, from the same word comes *slochd* and Slug

Road. *Learg* would be hillside or road on a hillside, therefore hollow of the road or path. Macdonald has no definition for it. It also occurs in the 19th century Census returns as Slack of Lurg.

Taposheetie It is a struggle to find anything on Taposheetie. I have even struggled to get people to tell me if it is the name of the road or the hill, they just wave their hand in its direction and say it is Taposheetie. It is not marked on any map that I have seen. The first reference to it I have come across is an entry in Andrew Mathieson's diaires saying that he was coating the Taposheetie Road. Because it is not on the map I suspect it is the road and was named when the road was made. The hill should probably be called Gask Hill. What it means is unknown, the only possible suggestion I have been given is that it refers to the top where you could see the *sheeting* (shooting) of birds on the Loch of Skene.

Terryvale This is an ancient name listed as *Tulivale* in the REGISTER OF THE GREAT SEAL for 1476. It also appears as *Tullivail, Tearavell* and *Terevell*. Milne has quite a convoluted definition whereby it starts as *baile* – town and *tire* – land, i.e. town on the land. He suggests that the meaning became lost and it became *Terry Bhaile,* with bh being pronounced v in Gaelic. This is less than convincing.

Tillybreck This is mentioned as Tullibreloch in 1657 and Macdonald defines it as *tulach broclaich* – knoll of the badgers' den.

Torshinach All three writers agree that it is *torr shionnach* – foxes' hill. It is also marked as the Witches' Hillock on a plan of 1832.

Bibliography

Primary sources and unpublished material

Aberdeenshire Commissioners of Supply:
    Valuation and Assessment Books c.1800
Aberdeenshire Valuation Rolls

Abernethy, James F. Talk on the history of Skene Parish   c.1878
Anderson, James General view of the Agriculture and Rural
    Economy of the County of Aberdeen. Board of Agriculture   1794
Bernard Thorpe & Partners Westhill Garden Suburb:
    sale brochure   1972
Brown, K.M. Records of the Parliament of Scotland to 1707
City of Aberdeen Charters and papers relating to Easter Skene
City of Aberdeen Council Register
City of Aberdeen Description, marches and boundaries of the
    Lands of Easter Skene belonging heritably to the Dean of Guild   c.1790
City of Aberdeen Inventory of charters and papers relating to the
    City of Aberdeen   1851
City of Aberdeen Plan of Hill-Cairnie by William Cruickshank
    for James Knowles   1827
City of Aberdeen Plan of Hill-Cairnie by William Cruickshank
    for James Knowles   1832

City of Aberdeen Plan of Hill-Cairnie by James Forbes Beattie
for the Society of Advocates   1862
City of Aberdeen Sketch of the lands of Easter Cairnie from
a survey by John Innes   1815
Clock and Watch Tax 1797–98 (available through
www.scotlandsplaces.gov.uk)
Dean, Ronald Notes on the history of the creation of
Westhill Garden Suburb
Dunecht Estates Notes of interest on the Parish of Skene
(compiled for Mary McMurtrie by the factor, Mr Lawrie)   c.1950
Edmond, Edna & **Lyall, Roy (senior)** Unpublished notes
on the Lyne of Skene supplied to Mary McMurtrie   c.1971
Farm Horse Tax 1797–98 (available through
www.scotlandsplaces.gov.uk)
Fraser, G.M. Unpublished notebooks
General Register of Sasines
Gordon, James HISTORY OF SCOTS AFFAIRS, 1637-1641 3 vols
[Spalding Club]   1841
Grub, George (ed) ILLUSTRATIONS OF THE TOPOGRAPHY
AND ANTIQUITIES OF THE SHIRES OF ABERDEEN AND BANFF;
four volumes. [Spalding Club]   1869
Henderson, G.D. (ed) George Skene's account of a 1729 journey
to London in MISCELLANY OF THE THIRD SPALDING CLUB   1940
Keith, George Skene GENERAL VIEW OF THE AGRICULTURE OF
ABERDEENSHIRE   1811
Kennedy, William INDEX TO THE COUNCIL REGISTER LIST OF
POLLABLE PERSONS WITHIN THE SHIRE OF ABERDEEN 1696.
[W. Bennett]   1844
McMurtrie, Mary Notes, correspondence and papers collected,
including material for her articles on the Old Skene Road for the SCOTS
MAGAZINE, and DEESIDE FIELD and for the THIRD STATISTICAL ACCOUNT
Mathieson, Andrew Farming diaries 31 vols. 1878-1908 in
Aberdeen University Library Special Collections
Milne Hall Extracts from the minutes   1885-1951
Murray Archaeological Services BROADSHADE RESIDENTIAL
DEVELOPMENT: standing structure survey   2010

BIBLIOGRAPHY

Newspapers ABERDEEN JOURNAL, ABERDEEN FREE PRESS, EVENING EXPRESS, PEOPLE'S JOURNAL
Register of the Great Seal
Register of the Privy Council
Robertson, J. (ed) COLLECTIONS FOR A HISTORY OF THE SHIRES OF ABERDEEN AND BANFF 2 vols. [Spalding Club]   1843
Skene Church Kirk Session Registers
Skene Free Church Kirk Session Registers
Skene Heritage Society Recorded interviews with numerous residents and former residents of Skene Parish
Skene House Papers These comprise a vast collection of estate papers, rentals, correspondence relating to the business affairs of Skene of Skene (including the estates of Careston, Fintry and their commercial activities in London). They subsequently passed to the Earl of Fife and were deposited at Aberdeen University as part of the Duff House/Earl of Fife Paper (MS3175)
Skene House Papers PLAN OF FORNETT 1818 by David Walker (MS3175/RHP/31434)
Skene House Papers GARLOGIE 1826 surveyed by David Walker (MS3175/RHP/31405)
Skene House Papers PLAN OF NETHERTON OF GARLOGIE 1862 (MS3175/ RHP/31098)
Skene House Papers SURVEY PLAN OF SKENE ESTATE 1863 (MS3175/RHP/31036)
Skene Parochial Board Minute books from 1845 onwards and continued as Skene Parish Council
Skene Parochial Board GENERAL REGISTERS OF THE POOR 1845-1870
Skene Reading Society Extracts from eminent authors. (Aberdeen University Library)   c.1834
Skene School Board Minute Books 1873-1919
Skene School Board Log books of Skene, Westhill, Garlogie and Lyne of Skene Schools
Skene Times Printed 'propaganda' sheets under various titles, printed privately   c.1885
Skene Turnpike Road TRUSTEES MINUTE BOOK 1799-1822
Skene War Work Committee Minutes and records
Spalding, John MEMORIALLS OF THE TRUBLES [Spalding Club]   1850

Statistical Accounts for Scotland (1st, 2nd and 3rd)
Stuart, John (ed) SELECTIONS FROM THE RECORDS OF THE PRESBYTERY OF ABERDEEN [Spalding Club]   1846
Taxt Roll of the County of Aberdeen 1554 in
SCOTTISH NOTES AND QUERIES   May 1894
Tayler, A. & H. ABERDEENSHIRE VALUATION ROLL 1667 [Spalding Club]   1933
Tayler, A. & H. THE JACOBITE CESS ROLL FOR THE COUNTY OF ABERDEEN IN 1715 [Spalding Club]   1932
Taylor & Skinner MAPS OF THE ROADS OF NORTH BRITAIN, OR SCOTLAND   1778

Books and pamphlets

Adair, Elizabeth NORTH EAST FOLK [Paul Harris]   1982
Alexander, William NORTHERN RURAL LIFE IN THE 18TH CENTURY [Douglas]   1877
Alexander, W.M. THE PLACE-NAMES OF ABERDEENSHIRE [Spalding Club]   1952
Allan, John R. CROMBIES OF GRANDHOLM AND COTHAL [Central P.]   1960
Bailey, Eileen A. CRANNOG TO CASTLE; A HISTORY OF THE BURNETT FAMILY IN SCOTLAND [Leys Publishing]   2000
Bailey, Eileen A. THE HOLLY AND THE THORN: BURNETT OF LEYS FAMILY AND BRANCHES [Leys Publishing]   2005
Boardman, S. & Ross, A. THE EXERCISE OF POWER IN MEDIEVAL SCOTLAND. [Four Courts]   2003
Buchanan, William GLIMPSES OF OLDEN DAYS IN ABERDEEN [Free Press]   1870
Burnett, George THE FAMILY OF BURNETT OF LEYS [Spalding Club]   1901
Brown, G.F. Echt-Forbes family charters, 1375-1727
Cowan, Ian B. PARISHES OF MEDIEVAL SCOTLAND [Scottish Record Society]   1967
Cumming, John THE WARLOCK LAIRD O' SKENE 3rd ed. [Murray]   1896
Ewing, William ANNALS OF THE FREE CHURCH [T & T Clark]   1914
Fraser, G.M. HISTORICAL WALKS AND NAMES [D. Wyllie]   1927

BIBLIOGRAPHY

In Memoriam An Obituary of Aberdeen and District
Jamieson, Peter Souvenir of the Diamond Jubilee of
  the firm of Peter Jamieson 1850–1910
Jervise, Andrew Epitaphs and Inscriptions in the N.E. of
  Scotland [D.Douglas]   1879
Keith, George S. A General View of the Agriculture of
  Aberdeenshire   1811
Kesson, Jessie The White Bird Passes [P. Harris]   1980
Macdonald, James Place names of West Aberdeenshire
  [Spalding Club]   1899
Mackay, James The Wizard Laird o' Skene and other poems
  [Main]   1891
McMurtrie, Mary Country Garden Flowers
  [Garden Art Press]   2009
Merrill, Adelaide K. The Keith Book
Milne, John Celtic Place-names in Aberdeenshire
  [Aberdeen Daily Journal]   1912
Murray, Isobel Jessie Kesson: writing her life [Canongate]   2000
North East Scotland Museums Service Garlogie Mill
  Power House Museum   c.1995
Oram, Richard Continuity, adaptation and integration:
  the earls and earldom of Mar c.1150 – c.1300 in The Exercise
  of Power in Medieval Scotland, edited by Steve Boardman
  and Alasdair Ross. [Four Courts Press]   2003
Patrick, John The Coming of Turnpikes to Aberdeenshire
  [Centre for Scottish Studies]   c.1981
Paul, William Past and Present of Aberdeenshire [L.Smith]   1881
Proctor's Orphanage Booklet produced at the time of
  the centenary   1992
RCAHMS In the Shadow of Bennachie [rcahms]   2007
Scott, Hew Fasti Eccleiae Scoticanae   1883
Skene, W.F. Memorial of the Family of Skene of Skene   1887
Skene War Memorial Commemorative Notes [W & W Lindsay]   1925
Smith, William M Memoir of the Family of M'Combie
  [Blackwood]   1887
Spiers, Sheila The Kirkyard of Kirkton of Skene [anesfhs]   2001
Taylor, A. & H. The Book of the Duffs [Constable]   1914

Thompson, John H. A Cloud of Witnesses: being the last speeches and testimonies of those who have suffered for the truth in Scotland since 1680. Oliphant, [Anderson & Ferrier] 1714

Thomson, Iain U. (ed) A History of the Parish of Skene [Skene Parish Church] 2001

Articles

Anon. Garden Suburb Grows [Chartered Surveyor Weekly, 25 August] 1983

Archaeology Scotland Discovery Excavation Scotland (numerous reports on archaeological finds in the Skene area)

Braid, K.W. Schools and Schoolmasters in the parishes of Newhills and Skene [Deeside Field 3rd Series No.1] 1974

Gordon, D.G. The Doctors of Deeside [Deeside Field 3rd Series, No.2] 1978

Leopard magazine Various articles on the Skene area have appeared over the years

Miers, Mary Skene House Aberdeenshire [Country Life, May 24] 2001

Pirie, Gordon Railway and Railway Bus operated services to Skene [Skene Heritage Newsletter, No. 8] March 2007

Sim, George Extracts from his Diary [Scottish Notes and Queries] 1929

Skene, A. P. Notes on the origin of the name, family and arms of Skene [Scottish Notes and Queries] June 1890 – July 1891

Sutherland, Joseph Skene – A Duff House in Aberdeenshire [Aberdeen University Review, LIX, no. 207] Spring 2002

SELECTED INDEX

A

Abernethy, James Fowler 77, 120, 123, 124, 138, 165, 175, 188, 190, 191, 192, 193, 198, 199, 201, 340, 349

Affloch 17, 98, 125, 136, 161, 165, 169, 173, 175, 181, 182, 183, 184, 188, 206, 209, 218, 232, 237, 305, 325, 357

Arnhall 44, 47, 87, 283, 292, 296, 347, 348, 357

Auchinclech 6, 36–39, 85–88, 92, 97, 245, 357–359

Auchronie, Hill of 4, 5, 36

B

Berryhill 4, 70, 75, 76, 153

Bervie 1, 5, 15, 40, 98, 125, 204, 205, 206, 209, 212, 235, 305, 358

Birsack 39, 85, 86, 87, 146, 167, 168, 169, 358

Blackhills 37, 39, 44, 46, 48, 50, 51, 57, 70, 82, 97, 106, 115, 116, 117, 118, 121, 146, 168, 170, 171, 210, 212, 292, 331, 349

Bluepark 266, 267, 268, 269, 358

Bogentory Burn 5, 206

Brimmond Hill 11, 142

Broadshade 70, 74, 75, 76, 169, 179, 204, 215, 358, 366

Broadstraik 37, 40, 49, 54, 55, 70, 71, 72, 74, 76, 80, 109, 125, 138, 153, 165, 204, 208, 209, 215, 221, 222, 245, 261, 282, 283, 284, 285, 286, 287, 288, 289, 290, 291, 294, 311, 312, 316, 359

Brodiach 1, 5, 11, 15, 17, 39, 40, 48, 53, 79, 80, 81, 82, 85, 101, 131, 132, 149, 168, 169, 185, 198, 203, 204, 210, 216, 218, 293, 298, 300, 301, 303, 304, 339, 340, 359, 360

Brodiach Burn 1, 5, 15, 168, 204

Bruce, John 174, 185, 188, 189, 190, 191, 192, 193, 194, 198, 199, 333–338

Burnett family 38, 368

Burnett, Jean 95, 224

Burnland 5, 70, 76, 165, 208, 253

C

Carnie 7, 8, 19, 20, 37, 39, 44, 46, 47, 48, 49, 50, 52, 55, 59, 61, 63, 64, 70, 74, 79, 83, 84, 85, 87, 124, 125, 130, 137, 142, 146, 148, 149, 152, 153, 168, 172, 173, 188, 206–209, 221, 245, 267, 276–280, 283, 288, 306, 307, 317, 346, 359, 361

Chisholm, William 266

Civil War 28, 32, 33, 35, 36, 91, 94, 235

Concraig 38, 57, 85, 86, 87, 88, 95, 98, 124, 183, 191, 206, 245, 358, 359

Congregational Church 115–125, 142, 145, 148, 170, 172, 173, 187, 188, 201, 282, 300, 340, 341

consumption dykes 74

Corskie Burn 5, 168

Counteswells 2, 37, 51, 82, 178, 271, 331

Cowdray, Lord 59, 63, 64, 70, 112, 242, 254, 275, 305, 306

Craigiedarg 17, 26, 146, 167, 168, 169, 183, 221, 265, 305, 360

Craigmile, Adam 109, 138, 142, 165, 169, 215, 275, 282, 288, 291, 294, 305, 312, 316

Craigmile, Alexander 76, 222, 288

Cran, William 118, 119, 120, 300

Crombie 32, 51, 58, 61, 70, 71, 72, 75, 76, 124, 148, 149, 174, 179, 186, 209, 210, 211, 284, 285, 286, 329, 330, 331, 332, 350

Cullerlie 1, 174, 280

Culter Burn 5

D

Dean, Ronald 348, 349, 350, 352

Denman, Sidney 347, 349

Drumstone 23, 104–108, 206, 207–209, 256–257

Duff Family 14, 227, 234

Dunecht 1, 2, 3, 63, 69, 70, 76, 84, 127, 134, 135, 136, 159, 162, 169, 174, 179, 180, 183, 208, 216, 218, 219, 220, 226, 269, 288, 305, 306, 307, 319, 320, 366

Dunecht Estate 169, 305

Dunecht Hydro Electric Scheme 3, 307

Dunlop, John 93, 94, 95

Dunlop, Ludovic 92, 95

Durno 112, 159, 178, 253, 260, 297, 316, 318

Durward 16

Dykenook 46, 49, 50, 51, 68, 132, 205, 206, 207, 208, 209, 212, 246, 247

E

East India Company 57, 64, 78

Easter Skene 2, 17, 20, 21, 22, 23, 26, 30, 31, 32, 33, 35, 36, 37, 38, 39, 40, 41, 43, 45, 47, 48, 49, 51, 52, 53, 55, 69, 79, 82, 92, 129, 132, 179, 206, 270, 271, 279, 365

371

SELECTED INDEX

Easterskene 2, 5, 21, 24, 51, 57, 61, 62, 64, 66, 67, 68, 69, 72, 98, 99, 102, 104, 107, 110, 120, 132, 139, 149, 151, 154, 164, 169, 172, 176, 178, 180, 183, 186, 199, 203, 205, 217, 246, 249, 250, 254, 306

Echt 2, 3, 7, 8, 30, 32, 33, 41, 45, 46, 47, 48, 54, 89, 96, 97, 100, 101, 118, 128, 138, 161, 163, 166, 170, 175, 178, 182, 183, 184, 206, 208, 209, 215, 217, 218, 219, 220, 221, 224, 227, 242, 280, 282, 298, 305, 306, 307, 327, 368

Elrick 11, 47, 70, 72, 74, 158, 164, 165, 170, 209, 217, 220, 245, 270, 280, 282, 283, 284, 285, 286, 290, 291, 292, 312, 313, 340, 350, 352, 360

F

Fiddie 49, 57, 79, 149, 168, 178, 179, 215, 275, 298, 360

Fiddy 22, 23, 37, 50, 51, 52, 78, 146, 149, 189

Fife, Earl of 57, 200, 227, 234, 235, 238, 239, 267, 367

Forbes Family 15, 29, 368

Fornet 5, 6, 7, 22, 24, 25, 26, 28, 29, 36, 37, 38, 49, 111, 125, 135, 168, 169, 174, 185, 188, 189, 198, 207, 215, 234, 236, 269, 270, 333, 334, 335, 336, 337, 338, 360

Fowler, Andrew 79, 81, 85, 101, 131, 149, 150, 178, 185, 198, 210, 339, 340

Fowler, James Elsmie 80, 339, 341

Free Church 64, 99, 102, 110, 117, 125–128, 134–136, 149, 151–152, 161, 173, 185, 186–188, 199, 101, 269

Freedom Lands 1, 5, 14, 15, 53

G

Garlogie 1, 2, 7, 22, 26, 30, 36, 37, 39, 40, 41, 44, 45, 46, 48, 50, 53, 54, 55, 69, 97, 98, 118, 125, 126, 128, 135, 136, 137, 138, 140, 142, 143, 144, 146, 148, 150, 151, 152, 159, 163, 165, 167, 168, 169, 174, 179, 186, 191, 192, 199, 200, 207, 208, 209, 221, 237, 240, 245, 256, 270, 271, 272, 273, 274, 275, 276, 277, 305, 307, 318, 319, 321, 327, 330, 361, 367, 369

Garlogie Mill 53, 98, 135, 136, 140, 148, 150, 168, 186, 271, 272, 273, 275, 369

Garlogie Mill School 135–137

Garlogie School 1, 137, 140, 143, 199

Gask 6, 8, 11, 19, 20, 44, 48, 55, 83, 84, 165, 197, 208, 209, 215, 216, 288, 306, 321, 327, 331, 361, 363

gasworks 237, 238

Gibson, William 78, 149

Gillespie, Malcolm 70, 285, 329–333

Guild 2, 26, 38, 40, 41, 43, 44, 45, 46, 47, 48, 51, 52, 53, 55, 67, 68, 79, 83, 85, 86, 106, 110, 112, 128, 129, 132, 148, 186, 206, 207, 211, 247, 248, 249, 271, 283, 284, 310, 318, 358, 359, 362, 365

H

Hadden 186, 272, 273, 274, 305

Hamilton 11, 110, 141, 154, 178, 181, 183, 187, 239, 240, 241, 242, 243, 244, 305, 308, 309, 316, 318, 319, 320, 353

Hatton 61, 83, 84, 168, 263, 264, 265, 276, 306

Hattoun 39, 40

Hogg, James 5, 43, 93, 100, 129, 232

Home Guard 242, 320, 321

I

Innes, Rev. William 126, 173

Ireland, Robert H. 64, 126, 185–186

Irvine 19, 23, 24, 25, 26, 28, 29, 31, 32, 246

J

Jamieson, Peter 72, 73, 74, 282, 368

K

Keir, Hill of 4, 5, 8, 13, 36, 46, 48, 49, 70, 72, 74, 75, 76, 215, 262, 317, 359

Keith 19, 20, 21, 22, 23, 24, 25, 31, 32, 36, 86, 89, 90, 101, 134, 160, 236, 266, 269, 270, 271, 331, 362, 366, 369

Keith, Marshall 101, 134, 266, 269

Kesson, Jessie 1, 157, 158, 248, 253, 254, 344, 369

Kilnhillock 5, 70, 72, 74, 75, 76, 292

Kinellar 2, 31, 48, 89, 163, 319, 341

Kingswells 2, 203, 204, 210, 220, 242, 341

Kinkell 2, 22, 23, 89, 90, 91, 286

Kinmundy 2, 4, 8, 17, 37, 39, 46, 48, 50, 51, 52, 53, 57, 76, 77, 78, 79, 82, 83, 97, 118, 125, 126, 133, 135, 143, 147, 149, 164, 168, 169, 173, 178, 179, 215, 292, 293, 294, 295, 296, 297, 304, 310, 324, 331, 332, 348, 352, 361

Kirktoun 2, 5, 17, 22, 28, 29, 31, 32, 37, 39, 40, 46, 48–52, 55, 58, 63, 64, 67–70, 102, 104, 106, 111, 126, 131-133, 140, 146, 152, 155, 160, 161, 163, 164, 172, 176, 193, 203, 204, 206–208, 210–212, 215, 245,–249, 251, 252–257, 259–263, 265, 267, 269–271, 273, 275, 277–283, 285, 287, 289, 291, 293, 295, 297, 300, 307, 311, 312, 320, 333

Kirktoun Burn 5

372

SELECTED INDEX

Kirkville 13, 51, 57, 58, 59, 60, 61, 62, 63, 64, 65, 70, 79, 83, 84, 102, 104, 111, 120, 122, 124, 125, 126, 134, 136, 140, 147, 148, 149, 153, 155, 157, 172, 173, 186, 187, 188, 207, 208, 212, 217, 246, 248, 249, 251, 252, 254, 276, 280, 306, 318, 328, 332

Knowles 51, 57, 58, 59, 60, 61, 62, 63, 83, 84, 147, 149, 207, 208, 212, 213, 248, 249, 252, 276, 278, 328, 332, 365

L

Lawsondale 78, 122, 123, 161, 163, 294, 331, 333, 340, 354

Leddach 22, 31, 37, 39, 44, 46, 47, 48, 49, 50, 51, 53, 54, 55, 57, 70, 71, 72, 73, 74, 75, 76, 148, 149, 153, 162, 163, 168, 178, 186, 206, 208, 210, 211, 212, 280, 282, 283, 284, 285, 286, 288, 291, 295, 296, 308, 315, 330, 340, 341, 359, 360, 361

Leuchar Burn 3, 5, 20, 59, 270, 307, 359

Leucharbraes 8, 303

Loch of Skene 3, 4, 5, 46, 49, 55, 67, 68, 120, 213, 214, 218, 219, 232, 241, 305, 317, 326, 346, 363

Lochee 40, 204, 362

Lochside 49, 50, 52, 114, 125, 126, 128, 132, 141, 175, 206, 305, 317, 318

Lyne of Skene 2, 5, 6, 23, 29, 44, 45, 101, 102, 104, 110, 125, 128, 133, 134, 136, 138, 139, 144, 152, 163, 165, 167, 173, 182, 188, 194, 200, 206, 207, 208, 210, 223, 237, 243, 245, 262, 263, 265, 266, 267, 268, 269, 270, 288, 299, 307, 309, 318, 319, 320, 324, 334, 365, 367

M

Macintosh, James 104, 106, 161, 164, 176, 196, 198, 251

Mar, Earldom of 16, 17, 89, 369

Marischal, Earl 2, 17, 20, 21, 22, 23, 24, 25, 26, 30, 31, 32, 33, 36, 38, 39, 45, 84, 85, 90, 225, 271, 331

Mason Lodge 8, 9, 10, 48, 53, 70, 72, 125, 134, 135, 136, 162, 163, 173, 174, 175, 199, 207, 215, 220, 221, 245, 253, 276, 278, 279, 280, 281, 282, 289, 311, 319

Mathieson, Andrew 173, 174, 181, 215, 293, 363

McCombie 2, 24, 51, 61, 62, 64, 65, 66, 67, 68, 69, 72, 98, 99, 110, 132, 149, 151, 154, 164, 172, 178, 179, 180, 186, 205, 217, 261, 279, 306

McMurtrie, Mary 3, 73, 77, 80, 81, 82, 103, 112, 120, 131, 134, 142, 157, 203, 204, 205, 239, 240, 247, 248, 253, 257, 258, 262, 267, 270, 277, 280, 284, 286, 288, 298, 307, 311, 312, 320, 324, 329, 342, 344, 345, 366

Millbuie 11, 28, 29, 36, 37, 39, 46, 47, 49, 50, 68, 217, 245, 362

Mills, Corn and Thrashing 26, 39–40, 46, 80, 146, 159, 167–170, 237, 265, 271, 207

Milne Bequest 151, 190, 191

Milne Hall 159, 175, 177, 178, 180, 194, 195, 196, 200, 252, 254, 262, 308, 312, 318, 319, 366

Mission Hall, Lyne of Skene 102–103, 200, 269, 307

Mutual Improvement Society / Association 1, 173-175, 316, 341

N

Newhills 2, 5, 97, 118, 123, 178, 179, 214, 287, 340, 370

O

Oddfellows 176, 177, 180

Ogg 52, 104, 113, 137, 178, 247, 249, 250, 251, 252, 308, 318

Old Skene Road 1, 47, 49, 52, 80, 107, 132, 134, 137, 142, 155, 203, 204, 205, 206, 207, 209, 216, 247, 253, 283, 284, 286, 292, 296, 297, 298, 311, 312, 329, 333, 344, 349, 359, 366

Ord Burn 5, 85, 168, 361

Ord Estate 84–85

Ord, James Basken of 85, 95, 146

Ord, Mill of 5, 49, 168, 169

P

Parochial Board 68, 87, 99, 136, 137, 140, 147, 148, 149, 151, 154, 160, 163, 165, 185, 186, 187, 201, 367

Philip, Rev. William 176, 188, 194–201

Proctor's Orphanage 10, 64, 65, 122, 153, 154–160, 242, 254, 369

R

Rae, George 281, 282, 289

Railway 217–220

Red Star 112, 178, 198, 248, 252

Reform Bill Monument 61, 62–63

Rogiehill 5, 48, 49, 58, 63, 98, 155, 207, 317, 362

373

SELECTED INDEX

S

school board 134, 135, 136, 137, 138, 140, 144, 155, 163, 166, 187, 188, 189, 191, 192, 193, 194, 196, 197, 199, 200, 201, 240, 276, 336, 341, 367

Scott, Sandy 102, 106, 125, 268–269

Shepherd, Captain Thomas 62, 64, 126, 134, 136, 149, 151, 155, 161, 172, 186–188, 217

Skene Choral Society 307, 308, 309

Skene Family 2, 15, 16, 17, 27, 28, 33, 35, 36, 38, 83, 110, 223, 244, 361

Skene Games 68, 74, 178, 180, 291

Skene House 6, 11, 14, 18, 19, 25, 26, 28, 50, 81, 86, 92, 102, 104, 110, 112, 120, 134, 139, 152, 154, 167, 178, 180, 181, 183, 187, 198, 206, 209, 222, 223, 225, 226, 227, 228, 229, 230, 231, 233, 235, 236, 237, 238, 239, 240, 241, 242, 243, 244, 248, 262, 263, 264, 265, 267, 305, 309, 318, 325, 327, 334, 358, 367, 370

Skene mausoleum 231

Skene Reading Society 170, 171, 367

Skene School 50, 51, 81, 107, 132, 134, 137, 138, 141, 180, 188, 190, 194, 205, 207, 210, 260, 261, 267, 276, 309, 320, 321, 336, 367

Skene, Adam of 20

Skene, James 21, 27, 28, 32, 33, 35, 36, 211, 225, 235

Skene, John of 17, 224

Skene, Laird of 15, 22, 24, 28, 32, 36, 38, 43, 53, 92, 95, 98, 146, 160, 168, 225, 226, 241

Skene, Patrick de 16, 17

Skinner, Doctor 76, 121, 162, 222, 275, 282, 295, 341, 342

Slack of Larg 70, 76, 138, 204, 216, 362

Soddie Burn 5

Souterhill 4, 8, 47, 85, 86, 87, 88, 138

Springhill 6, 83, 84, 208, 209, 276, 307, 317

T

temperance 64, 118, 123, 126, 172, 173, 174, 341

Trinity Church 114, 350

W

Watson, Eliza 287–288

Westhill 1, 2, 4, 5, 6, 8, 10, 12, 14, 16, 18, 20, 22, 24, 26, 28, 30, 32, 34, 36, 38, 40, 42, 44, 46, 48, 50, 51–54, 56, 58, 60, 62, 64, 70, 76, 82-83, 102, 109–110, 114–118, 120–125, 133-135, 136–145, 151–153, 161, 163-164, 174, 179, 186, 188, 191–195, 198–200, 201, 204–206, 206–209, 222–223, 245–246, 260–261, 270, 275, 282, 284, 292, 294–305, 308, 310, 311, 317–324, 333–334, 340–341, 345–370

Westhill School 2, 122, 130, 133, 138, 142–144, 191, 193, 195, 275, 350

Whitestone Farm 5, 8, 9, 48, 63, 193, 278

Williamson 76, 83, 87, 107, 121, 124, 125, 126, 173, 174, 179, 187, 253, 259, 269, 279, 280, 282, 292, 293, 294, 319, 320, 321

Wizard Laird 107, 243, 244, 323, 324, 325, 326, 327, 369

Women's Rural 1, 309